T0214264

Communications
in Computer and Information Science　　1334

More information about this series at http://www.springer.com/series/7899

Vanessa Agredo-Delgado · Pablo H. Ruiz ·
Klinge Orlando Villalba-Condori (Eds.)

Human-Computer Interaction

6th Iberomarican Workshop, HCI-Collab 2020
Arequipa, Peru, September 16–18, 2020
Proceedings

 Springer

Editors
Vanessa Agredo-Delgado (iD)
Corporación Universitaria
Comfacauca Unicomfacauca
Popayán, Colombia

Universidad del Cauca
Popayán, Colombia

Klinge Orlando Villalba-Condori (iD)
Universidad Católica de Santa María
Arequipa, Peru

Pablo H. Ruiz (iD)
Corporación Universitaria
Comfacauca Unicomfacauca
Popayán, Colombia

Universidad del Cauca
Popayán, Colombia

ISSN 1865-0929   ISSN 1865-0937 (electronic)
Communications in Computer and Information Science
ISBN 978-3-030-66918-8   ISBN 978-3-030-66919-5 (eBook)
https://doi.org/10.1007/978-3-030-66919-5

This Springer imprint is published by the registered company Springer Nature Switzerland AG
The registered company address is: Gewerbestrasse 11, 6330 Cham, Switzerland

Preface

The Ibero-American Conference on Human-Computer Interaction (HCI), was developed in its 6th version, a conference that throughout these six years has been held in different parts of the world and has been increasingly welcomed and seen increased participation of both papers sent and of people who attend the conferences and different presentations.

Human Computer Interaction has evolved and has taken on greater importance in the world of computing, it is a discipline related to the design, evaluation, development, and study of the phenomena that surround computer systems for human use, its main objective is to make the information exchange efficient: minimizing errors, increasing satisfaction, reducing frustration, and making the interaction between people and technological elements more productive.

This book brings together a set of works related to HCI on specialized topics such as: Emotional interfaces, usability, video games, computational thinking, collaborative systems, IoT, software engineering, ICT in education, augmented and mixed virtual reality for education, gamification, emotional Interfaces, adaptive instruction systems, accessibility, use of video games in education, artificial Intelligence in HCI, among others.

The HCI-COLLAB 2020 call for papers amounted in 128 submissions, of which 34 were accepted. 31 were accepted and are presented in this book. The review was performed by at least three national and international reviewers. In addition, the EasyChair system was used to manage and review the presentations.

We thank the members of our Program Committee for their work and contribution to the success of our conference. To the authors for their presentations, to the organizers, and to Springer who allow us to gather the best papers in this book.

November 2020

Vanessa Agredo-Delgado
Pablo H. Ruiz
Klinge Orlando Villalba-Condori

Organization

Program Committee Members

Agustin Lagunes Dominguez	Universidad Veracruzana, Mexico
Alejandra Beatriz Lliteras	Universidad Nacional de la Plata, Argentina
Alessandra Reyes-Flores	Universidad Veracruzana, Mexico
Alfredo Garcia	Benemérita Universidad Autónoma de Puebla, Mexico
Alfredo Mendoza Gonzalez	Universidad Autónoma de Zacatecas, Mexico
Alicia Mon	Universidad Nacional de La Matanza, Argentina
Antonio Silva Sprock	Universidad Central de Venezuela, Venezuela
Arturo Moquillaza	Pontificia Universidad Católica del Perú, Peru
Arturo Moreno	Universidad Autónoma de Zacatecas, Mexico
Beatriz Beltran	Benemerita Universidad Autónoma de Puebla, Mexico
Blanca Nydia Perez Camacho	Benemérita Universidad Autónoma de Puebla, Mexico
Carina Gonzalez-González	Universidad de La Laguna, Spain
Carlos Domínguez	Tecnológico Nacional de México, Mexico
Carlos Eric Galván Tejada	Instituto Tecnológico y de Estudios Superiores de Monterrey, Mexico
Carlos Lara-Alvarez	Centro de Investigación en Matemáticas, Mexico
Cecilia Camacho	Institución Universitaria Colegio Mayor del Cauca, Colombia
Cesar A. Collazos	Universidad del Cauca, Colombia
Christian Sturm	Hamm-Lippstadt University of Applied Sciences, Germany
Claudia González Calleros	Benemérita Universidad Autónoma de Puebla, Mexico
Cristian Rusu	Pontificia Universidad Católica de Valparaiso, Chile
Cristina Manresa-Yee	University of Balearic Islands, Spain
David Céspedes-Hernández	Benemérita Universidad Autónoma de Puebla, Mexico
Deema Alsekait	Princess Nourah Bint Abdulrahman University, Saudi Arabia
Diego Torres	Universidad Nacional de la Plata, Argentina
Erika Martínez	Benemérita Universidad Autónoma de Puebla, Mexico
Fernando Moreira	Universidad Privada de Tacna, Peru
Francisco Luis Gutiérrez Vela	University of Granada, Spain
Freddy Paz	Pontificia Universidad Católica del Perú, Peru
Gabriel Avila	Institución Universitaria Politécnico Grancolombiano, Colombia

Gabriel Mauricio Ramirez Villegas	Universidad Nacional Abierta y a Distancia, Colombia
Germán Ezequiel Lescano	Universidad Nacional de Santiago del Estero, Argentina
Guillermina Sánchez Román	Benemérita Universidad Autónoma de Puebla, Mexico
Gustavo Eduardo Constain Moreno	Universidad Nacional Abierta y a Distancia, Colombia
Gustavo Rossi	Universidad Nacional de la Plata, Argentina
Hamurabi Gamboa Rosales	Universidad Autónoma de Zacatecas, Argentina
Héctor Cardona Reyes	Centro de Investigación en Matemáticas, Mexico
Huizilopoztli Luna-García	Universidad Autónoma de Zacatecas, Mexico
Ismar Frango Silveira	Universidade Presbiteriana Mackenzie, Brazil
Jaime Muñoz-Arteaga	Universidad Autónoma de Aguascalientes, Mexico
Jeferson Arango Lopez	Universidad de Caldas, Colombia
Jorge I. Galván-Tejada	Universidad Autónoma de Zacatecas, Mexico
José Antonio Pow-Sang	Pontificia Universidad Católica del Perú, Peru
José Guadalupe Arceo Olague	Universidad Autónoma de Zacatecas, Mexico
Jose Maria Celaya Padilla	Universidad Autónoma de Zacatecas, Mexico
Juan Manuel Gonzalez Calleros	Benemerita Universidad Autónoma de Puebla, Mexico
Juan Ruben Delgado Contreras	Tecnologico de Monterrey, Spain
Laura Aballay	Universidad Nacional de San Juan, Argentina
Laura Juliana Cortés	Universidad Militar Nueva Granada, Colombia
Manuel Ortega Cantero	University of Castilla-La Mancha, Spain
Mario Rossainz	Benemérita Universidad Autónoma de Puebla, Mexico
Mayra Nayeli Márquez Specia	Benemérita Universidad Autónoma de Puebla, Mexico
Miguel Redondo	University of Castilla-La Mancha, Spain
Oscar David Robles Sanchez	Universidad Rey Juan Carlos, Spain
Pablo H. Ruiz	Unicomfacauca, Colombia
Pablo Santana Mansilla	Universidad Nacional de Santiago del Estero, Argentina
Pablo Torres-Carrion	Universidad Técnica Particular de Loja, Ecuador
Pascual Gonzalez	University of Castilla-La Mancha, Spain
Patricia Paderewski	University of Granada, Spain
Philippe Palanque	University of Toulouse, France
Raúl Antonio Aguilar Vera	Universidad Autónoma de Yucatán, Mexico
Raul Eduardo Rodriguez Ibañez	Universidad Simón Bolivar, Colombia
Ricardo Mendoza González	Instituto Tecnológico de Aguascalientes, Mexico
Roberto Solis Robles	Universidad Autónoma de Zacatecas, Mexico
Rosa Maria Gil	Universitat de Girona, Spain

Rosanna Costaguta	Universidad Nacional de Santiago del Estero, Argentina
Rubén Edel Navarro	Universidad Veracruzana, Mexico
Sandra Cano	Pontificia Universidad Católica de Valparaíso, Chile
Sergio Zapata	Universidad Nacional de San Juan, Argentina
Silvana Aciar	Universidad Nacional de San Juan, Argentina
Soraia Silva Prietch	Universidade Federal de Mato Grosso, Brazil
Toni Granollers	Universitat de Lleida, Spain
Valeria Farinazzo Martins	Universidade Presbiteriana Mackenzie, Brazil
Vanessa Agredo-Delgado	Corporación Universitaria Comfacauca - Unicomfacauca, Colombia
Víctor López-Jaquero	University of Castilla-La Mancha, Spain
Victor M. R. Penichet	University of Castilla-La Mancha, Spain
Victor Peñeñory	Universidad de San Buenaventura Cali, Colombia
Vitor Jorge	Universidade Federal do Rió Grande do Sul, Brazil
Wilson Javier Sarmiento	Universidad Militar Nueva Granada, Colombia
Yenny Mendez	Universidad Mayor, Chile
Yesenia Nohemi Gonzalez	Instituto Tecnológico de Apizaco, Mexico
Yuliana Puerta	Universidad Tecnológica de Bolívar, Colombia

Academic Committee President

Klinge Orlando Villalba-Condori	Universidad Católica De Santa María, Peru

Program Committee President

César Alberto Collazos	Universidad del Cauca, Colombia

Editorial Committee

Vanessa Agredo-Delgado	Unicomfacauca and Universidad del Cauca, Colombia
Pablo H. Ruiz	Unicomfacauca and Universidad del Cauca, Colombia
Klinge Orlando Villalba-Condori	Universidad Católica De Santa María, Peru

Contents

A Physiotherapist's Matter: Validating a Physical Rehabilitation Exergame
to Enable Safe Evaluation with Patients................................ 1
   Juan Castro, Andrés Serrato, Edwin Gamboa, and María Trujillo

An Architectural Model for Virtual Learning Environments Using
Multicultural Learning Objects 10
   Jaime Muñoz-Arteaga, Alicia Lozano Quiroz,
   and Klinge Villalba Condori

An Experimental Activity to Develop Usability and UX Heuristics 20
   Pedro Reis, César Páris, and Anabela Gomes

Autonomous Driving: Obtaining Direction Commands by Classifying
Images Within a Simulation Platform 30
   Mario Iván Oliva de la Torre, Huizilopoztli Luna-García,
   José M. Celaya-Padilla, Hamurabi Gamboa-Rosales,
   Wilson J. Sarmiento, and Cesar A. Collazos

Breaking the Gap: Collaborative Environment as a Meeting Point
to Provide and Receive Help to Overcome the Digital Gap 42
   David E. Santos Covarrubias, Graciela Karina Galache Meléndez,
   Jorge Alberto Martínez Cerón, Sony Solano Cristóbal,
   and Rocío Abascal-Mena

Challenges in Integrating SCRUM and the User-Centered Design
Framework: A Systematic Review...................................... 52
   Daniela Argumanis, Arturo Moquillaza, and Freddy Paz

Clustering Analysis of Usability in Web Sites of Higher Technological
Institutes of Ecuador 63
   Yeferson Torres-Berru and Pablo Torres-Carrión

Collaborative Learning Group Formation Based on Personality Traits:
An Empirical Study in Initial Programming Courses 73
   Oscar Revelo-Sánchez, César A. Collazos, and Miguel A. Redondo

Communication Preferences of First-Year University Students from Mexico
and Spain... 85
   Eliana Gallardo-Echenique, Luis Marqués-Molías, Oscar Gomez-Cruz,
   and Byron Vaca-Barahona

CovidEmoVis - An Interactive Visual Analytic Tool for Exploring
Emotions from Twitter Data of Covid-19.   94
  Leticia Laura-Ochoa and Franco Tejada-Toledo

Cyber Exposed at Preparatory: Classmates and Teachers Using Social
Networks and Life Satisfaction   107
  Ivan Iraola-Real, Lesly Moreyra-Cáceres, and Luis Collantes-Jarata

Design and Implementation of a Voice-Based Conversational Agent
for the Continuous Training and Learning of Pharmaceutical
Sales Representatives.   117
  Rocío Fernández, Gianfranco Monzón, and Daniel Subauste

Evaluating the Socioenactive Experience with a Tangible Tabletop
Installation: A Case Study   126
  Yusseli Lizeth Méndez Mendoza and M. Cecília C. Baranauskas

Habitar: A Collaborative Tool to Visualize, Distribute, Organize and Share
Domestic Tasks Towards Reducing the Gender Gap in Household Labor. . . .   136
  Axel Alonso García, Alondra Ayala Ramírez, Laura Vázquez Navarrete,
  and Rocío Abascal-Mena

Human Body AR: A Mobile Application for Teaching Anatomy
for Elementary Students Using Augmented Reality   146
  Briseida Sotelo-Castro and Diego Iquira Becerra

Mixed Reality Infotainment Simulator, Work in Progress   155
  F. Cristian Beltrán, Alejandro Aponte, and Wilson J. Sarmiento

Mobile Application to Improve Reading Habits Using Virtual Reality   160
  Estefany Chavez-Helaconde, Cristian Condori-Mamani,
  Israel Pancca-Mamani, Julio Vera-Sancho, Betsy Cisneros-Chavez,
  and Wilber Valdez-Aguilar

Model for Pervasive Social Play Experiences   171
  Ramón Valera Aranguren, Patricia Paderewski Rodriguez,
  Francisco Luis Gutiérrez Vela, and Jeferson Arango-López

Model-Driven Multidisciplinary Production of Virtual Reality
Environments for Elementary School with ADHD.   181
  Héctor Cardona-Reyes, Jaime Muñoz-Arteaga, Lorena Barba-González,
  and Gerardo Ortiz-Aguiñaga

Recommendations and Challenges for Developing English Vocabulary
Learning Games   193
  Diana Toro, Aldemar Rodríguez, Miguel Velasco, Edwin Gamboa,
  and María Trujillo

Reference Framework for Measuring the Level of Technological
Acceptance by the Elderly: A Virtual Assistants Case Study.   203
   Manuel Bolaños, Cesar Collazos, and Francisco Gutiérrez

Relaxing and Familiar, Guidelines to Develop Interactive Applications
for Dementia Patients   213
   Diana Millares, Andrés Serrato, Juan Castro, Nathalia Ceballos,
   Edwin Gamboa, and María Trujillo

Rivit: A Digital Game to Cognitively Train and Entertain Heart
Failure Patients.   223
   David Crespo, Melissa Fuentes, Edwin Gamboa, Kevin Franco,
   Kevin Domínguez, and Maria Trujillo

Smartphones, Suitable Tool for Driver Behavior Recognition.
A Systematic Review   233
   Jovan F. Fernández Joya, Gabriel Ávila Buitrago,
   Huizilopoztli Luna-García, and Wilson J. Samiento

State of the Art of Business Simulation Games Modeling Supported
by Brain-Computer Interfaces.   243
   Cleiton Pons Ferreira and Carina Soledad González González

Tales of Etrya: English Vocabulary Game   253
   Juan José Salazar Salcedo, Diana Katherine Toro Ortiz,
   Edwin Gamboa, and María Trujillo

Towards a Process Definition for the Shared Understanding Construction
in Computer-Supported Collaborative Work   263
   Vanessa Agredo-Delgado, Pablo H. Ruiz, Alicia Mon,
   Cesar A. Collazos, and Habib M. Fardoun

Towards to Usability Guidelines Construction for the Design of Interactive
Mobile Applications for Learning Mathematics.   275
   Carlos Andrés Casas Domínguez, David Oidor Mina,
   Vanessa Agredo-Delgado, Pablo H. Ruiz, and Deema M. AlSekait

Usability Evaluation over Multiplayer Games on Display Wall Systems.   285
   Marc Gonzalez Capdevila, Karine Aparecida Pistili Rodrigues,
   Valéria Farinazzo Martins, and Ismar Frango Silveira

Voluminis: Mobile Application for Learning Mathematics in Geometry
with Augmented Reality and Gamification   295
   Juan Deyby Carlos-Chullo, Marielena Vilca-Quispe,
   and Eveling Castro-Gutierrez

Wireless Haptic Glove for Interpretation and Communication
of Deafblind People.   305
    Lenin R. Villarreal, Bryan J. Castro, and Jefferson A. De la Cruz

Author Index   315

A Physiotherapist's Matter: Validating a Physical Rehabilitation Exergame to Enable Safe Evaluation with Patients

Juan Castro$^{(\boxtimes)}$ ⓘ, Andrés Serrato ⓘ, Edwin Gamboa ⓘ, and María Trujillo ⓘ

Universidad del Valle, Cali, Colombia
{juan.castro.vasquez,andres.serrato,edwin.gamboa,
maria.trujillo}@correounivalle.edu.co

Abstract. Physical Rehabilitation Exergames (PREGs) can be an appropriate tool to motivate patients towards physical rehabilitation treatments. A key problem in the process of developing PREGs is the evaluation of the User Experience (UX) since patients' safety should be guaranteed by a PREG before including patients in an evaluation. The validation defines when a PREG is safe to use in patients or real contexts. The following paper presents validation of a PREG called Baseball targeted at physical rehabilitation of upper limbs. We performed validation tests at a local hospital to assess aspects like therapeutic meaningfulness, personalization, tutorial quality, movement support, therapeutic goal assistance, and user interface navigation. Our findings indicate that these aspects are considered by physiotherapists as relevant to ensure patients safety. Our main contribution is the identification of aspects that can be considered as prerequisites to conduct UX evaluations involving patients when developing PREGs targeted at upper limbs.

Keywords: Physical Rehabilitation Exergames · Validation · Patients' safety · Physiotherapists perspective · User experience prerequisite

1 Introduction

A PREG is an exergame [1] used as part of physical rehabilitation treatments [2, 3] with positive results, being described as pleasant, enjoyable, fun and with great potential in the area of rehabilitation [4–6]. In this context, Playtherapy was developed as a tool to assist physical rehabilitation therapies [7]. Playtherapy goal is to increase patient's motivation to complete their treatments by offering a compelling and personalized experience [7]. Playtherapy is composed of a catalog of 15 mini PREGs, whose prototypes were validated by a group of physical therapists from a local hospital. The Playtherapy PREGs support rehabilitation processes of a trunk, upper limbs, lower limbs, as well as fine movements, such as hand movements. Each mini PREG has the following components (See Fig. 1).

© Springer Nature Switzerland AG 2020
V. Agredo-Delgado et al. (Eds.): HCI-COLLAB 2020, CCIS 1334, pp. 1–9, 2020.
https://doi.org/10.1007/978-3-030-66919-5_1

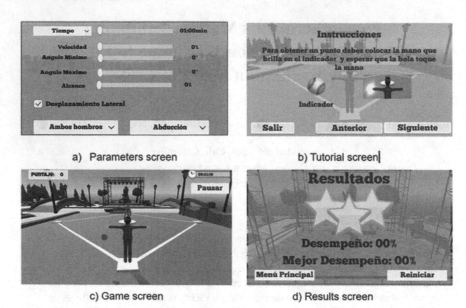

a) Parameters screen   b) Tutorial screen

c) Game screen   d) Results screen

Fig. 1. Playtherapy mini PREGs components (Baseball).

a) Parameter screen: This component allows a physiotherapist to set up the mini PREG before starting a session. The game session to be personalized according to the needs of each patient.

b) Tutorial screen: Includes a set of instructions for patients and physiotherapists. These instructions explain the rules of the game, movements and how to personalize the PREG. Some games tutorials include images, videos, or animations.

c) Game screen: This is the main screen of each PREG. It includes visual and sound elements according to the story of each mini PREG. It offers feedback on each movement executed, indicating whether it achieved the objective expected by the PREG.

d) Results screen: It presents the player's performance. The percentage of success is indicated, the best historical performance and a recognition represented with stars (E.g. The player will get 3 stars when the performance has been excellent).

In this paper, a validation of Baseball mini PREG from a physiotherapist's and developer's perspective is conducted. Baseball is a mini PREG of Playtherapy's catalogue that assists in the recovery flexion and extension of shoulders and elbows. The evaluation was carried out to gather information about the elements of play, mechanics, reactions, and adaptation to patient needs. Since there are several aspects that can be assessed when evaluating a PREG with a therapeutic objective in mind, we have taken in relevant aspects identified for this purpose such as therapeutic meaningfulness, tutorial, personalization/configuration and movement support, as suggested in [6]. Patients are not included in the tests performed in this study for safety reasons. Playtherapy should be fully validated before conducting validations involving patients. The remaining of this paper is organized as follows: in Sect. 2, we outline the details of the conducted study;

then, we present and discuss the obtained results in Sect. 3 and Sect. 4 respectively. Finally, we conclude the paper in Sect. 5.

2 Methods

This study aims to validate a PREG from the physiotherapist's and developer's perspective using Baseball PREG as a case study. According to the results of a previous study [8], we consider the following aspects to evaluate PREGs (Baseball PREG as a case study):

- *Therapeutic meaningfulness:* The components of a patient's treatment should be meaningful to their rehabilitation progress. Some aspects to allow assessing patients' progress using Baseball PREG (according to its therapeutic goal) are a range of motion, functional independence, balance, motor coordination, and flexibility.
- *Configuration/personalization:* Configuration parameters should produce the expected behavior. Also, each movement should be mapped or represented correctly in the mini PREG.
- *Tutorial:* Instructions should be understandable, all the associated movements should be explained and related to a PREG mechanic.
- *Movement support:* It evaluates the meaningful mapping of the movements involved in the PREG. It also gives feedback on the validation of the correctness of the movement executed.
- *User interface navigation:* Evaluates usability principles such as ease of learning, flexibility, consistency, robustness, visibility of system status, user control, and decreased cognitive burden.

2.1 Evaluated Mini PREG

Our mini PREG evaluated is Baseball, that is a mini PREG of Playtherapy catalog that includes flexion and extension movements of shoulders and elbows. Baseball consists of catching some baseballs thrown by a game character. The player must use the hand indicated by the PREG to get points. The Baseball parameters allow a physiotherapist to set up the mini PREG before starting a session. Its importance lies in the fact that it allows the game session to be personalized according to the needs of each patient. The parameters screen has 7 configuration parameters presented in Fig. 2 and described in Table 1. In addition, Baseball mini PREG includes tutorials for patients and physiotherapists. It also includes a pause screen with options to navigate the Playtherapy platform and indicates the patient's performance in the last playing session. The Baseball screens can be seen in Fig. 1.

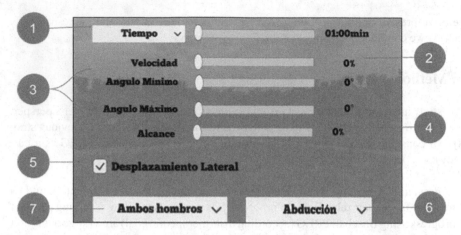

Fig. 2. Baseball configuration parameters screen. Parameters code: 1. Game mode, 2. Object speed, 3. Motion range, 4. Coverage range, 5. Lateral movement, 6. Movements, 7. Involved shoulders.

Table 1. Baseball configuration parameters description.

Id[a]	Name	Options	Description
1	Game mode	Time or Repetitions	Indicates the duration of the mini PREG
2	Object speed	Range 0 to 100 percent	Indicates the speed at which the balls will be thrown to the player position
3	Motion range	Minimum (0°) and maximum (180°) angle range	The balls will be thrown in the range between minimum and maximum angles
4	Coverage range	Range 0 to 100 percent	This parameter causes flexion and extension movements of shoulders and elbows[b]
5	Lateral movement	Selected or not selected	If selected, the player must move from the initial position to catch the ball
6	Movements	Abduction or extension	Indicates the movement that will be used in the game session
7	Involved shoulders	Left, right or both	Indicates which upper extremities will be used in the game session

[a] As presented in Fig. 2. [b] A low value causes elbow flexion and a high value causes shoulder extension.

2.2 Participants

3 PREGs developers and two physiotherapists have been involved in the User Centered Design (UCD) process of mini PREG called Baseball and their characteristics are presented in Table 2.

Table 2. Participants characteristics.

Title	Years of experience	Role	Developed PREGs
Master of Computer Science	3	Project Leader	7
Systems Technology Student 1	1.5	Programmer, Designer	7
Systems Technology Student 2	0.5	Programmer, Designer	3
Physiotherapist 1	3	Tester	7
Physiotherapist 2	2	Tester	7

2.3 Procedure

Data is collected using the Question Asking Protocol [9, 10] (QAP) to identify problems, enhancements and questions related to Baseball's mini PREG. QAP allowed interaction between the physiotherapist and the developer. Also, it allowed us to jointly find improvements, errors, and solutions applicable to Baseball mini PREG and PREGs in general. Participants used the game during 9 sessions (one hour per session).[1] Each session involved 2 physical therapists and at least 2 developers. For each session, physiotherapists use the game under different configuration parameters. In the same way, the evaluators (developers) guide and document the suggestions.

2.4 Analysis

The collected data was transcribed into a spreadsheet and analyzed using the thematic analysis method [11]. We produce a list of statements related to the objective of the study. Then, we assign a code to each statement. After that, the codes are grouped into the relevant evaluation aspects are related to therapeutic meaningfulness, personalization (or configuration), tutorial quality, movement support and therapeutic goal assistance [8] and user interface navigation. Although the subjects of the codes remained the same. Evidence from the analysis is available online[2].

---

[1] Baseball validation sessions https://bit.ly/3bKE3iW.
[2] Baseball validation thematic analysis https://bit.ly/2FuwHE0.

3   Findings

We found 29 statements regarding aspects enhancements, errors, and questions in evaluation of Baseball PREG. These statements are grouped in configuration (11 statements), tutorial (5 statements), therapeutic meaningfulness (3 statements), user interface navigation (6 statements), movement support (4 statements). A summary of the findings is presented in Fig. 3.

Fig. 3. Map of improvements, errors, and questions for Baseball mi PREG, obtained after conducting a thematic content analysis.

3.1   Therapeutic Meaningfulness

The feedback provided by the participants allowed us to identify the following conditions for PREGs to be meaningful to patients from a therapeutic perspective. First, the technology used must be free of any interference inside or outside the device. In one of the sessions, for example, the microphone of the sensor presented sound interference that affected the patient concentration. Second, according to the participants the play area should be controlled by the technological tools used (e.g. virtual platform, motion sensors) according to the automatic calculation of the patient's size. Lastly, the use of the correct sound signals is essential to differentiate between a movement executed correctly or incorrectly.

3.2   Tutorial

The participants mentioned that not all parameters are very cleared. Therefore, it should be considered a strategy to make it easy for physiotherapists to understand the parameters.

For instance, including a section in tutorials for physiotherapists. Also, the differentiation between each parameter and its explication makes it easier to understand. In this aspect, all possible clarifications for the effective use of the platform and strategies for giving instructions such as video tutorials and/or voice instructions should be considered. The participants mentioned that this allows easy incorporation of a new physiotherapist, in the same way, that helps the patient's understanding of the therapeutic meaningfulness of the PREG.

3.3 Configuration

The participants mentioned that for Baseball PREG there should be a default configuration. For them, the parameterization must be presented in a logical and uniform order to ensure the integrity of the configuration and the functional dependency of the parameters (e.g. maximum angle range depends on minimum angle range). In the same way, related parameters should be grouped into sections, (e.g. selection of shoulders in the category articulations). Moreover, not allowing configurations that interrupt the patient's experience while playing or those that do not make sense. (e.g. minimum angle same maximum angle or angles same 0).

3.4 Movement Support

The participants mentioned that Baseball PREG presents a comfortable movement, although in some cases when the player goes outside of the sensor capturing range, the avatar appears out of the base, causing the movement to become difficult. For this purpose, we propose to establish a physical delimited playing area in which the player can move, within the range of the sensor. On the other hand, the player must be told when the hand is in the correct position before the point is made to help clarity of movement.

3.5 User Interface Navigation

In particular, the easy navigation of the platform should facilitate the work of the physiotherapists. This is high relevance since physiotherapists usually have a plan to be carried out during therapy sessions, hence, they cannot lose time learning to use a PREG. Therefore, different ways to directly access important points of the application should be considered (e.g. tutorials, main menu, login menu). The PREG must include control options like confirmation dialogs, keyboard shortcuts and icons or buttons in strategic locations.

4 Discussion

This study aims to show relevant aspects that must be considered when developing a PREG using an UCD iterative process. The aspects involved to carry out this study are related to movement support, configuration/personalization capability, tutorial quality (i.e., user guidance), therapeutic meaningfulness [8] and user interface navigation. Based on the findings, we identified a set of issues, enhancements, and questions to improve the Player Experience in Baseball PREG.

According to our findings, when developing PREGS targeted at arm movements, it is important to provide the greatest comfort in terms of movement, i.e., designing attractive mechanics with comfortable movements that assist motion recovery. That is, the PREG must allow the player a form of correction or calibration when correctly positioned in both their physical and virtual environment.

The participants agree that the play area should be controlled by the virtual platform according to the player size, as well as not allowing or reduce distractions related to technology (like signal interferences). Neglecting both aspects in the development process may slow therapy or reduce meaningfulness in patients' rehabilitation progress. Our findings confirmed some recommendation presented in other works. As claimed in [1], input devices, such as Kinect motion sensor in Baseball PREG, should enable a meaningful mapping of player movements. Kinect motion sensor was previously evaluated considering aspects such as usability and motivation. Using Fugl-Meyer Assessment of Motor Recovery after Stroke scale [12] in [13]. In addition, monitoring the correctness of movement is essential in a PREG [8]. The PREG should automatically, immediately, realistically, and specifically alert patients about the correctness of movements [13]. Feedback should be understandable to the physiotherapists and patients, as it is important in a PREG implementation for the correction or monitoring of the movement performed. Participants suggested a sound and/or visual feedback.

Furthermore, generating feedback corresponding to the quality of the movement is important since therapeutic meaningfulness depends on patients feeling of progress. On the other hand, it is important to include aspects that facilitate the understanding of the relevant aspects to be considered by the physiotherapist when conducting a session, adding tools such as instructions or video tutorials. In the same way, PREGs should offer a logical standard for the parameterization of the game, as well as not allowing any type of wrong configuration within it. Thereby, avoiding diminishing the time that physiotherapists have during a therapy session, which could be short due to a high number of patients. Considering the above-mentioned aspects and having continuous participation of physiotherapy experts in the validation process of a PREG may allow assuring safety of patients. Then, they can be included in the validation process.

4.1 Limitations and Future Work

The main limitation of this study is that the patient's perspective is not included. Nevertheless, as mentioned, all the identified recommendations should be addressed before patients can be included in the validation process. Additionally, PREG Baseball does not have a very extensive movement catalog. Therefore, some of our findings are limited to PREGs targeted at upper limb movements. Thus, future work should be conducted regarding PREGs targeted at other joints (e.g. lower limbs and hip). Similarly, future work should include statistical information to overcome the qualitative approach of this study.

5   Conclusion

This paper presented a study to identify aspects to consider during the UCD of PREGs associated with arm movements, taking the therapist's perspective as a user, as well as showing aspects that include other PREGS in a general way. We found that the mechanics of PREG should be centered on motion recovery in order to be meaningful for physiotherapists and patients. In general, we confirmed that the configuration of PREGs should offer a logical way of presenting the information, ensuring understanding and ease of use for physiotherapists. Our findings can be used as guidelines for the development of PREGs targeted at upper limbs.

References

1. Gamboa, E., Trujillo, M.: Characterising physical rehabilitation exergames for player experience evaluation purposes. In: pHealth, vol. 261, pp. 55–61 (2019). https://www.ncbi.nlm.nih.gov/pubmed/31156091
2. Mader, S., Natkin, S., Levieux, G.: How to analyse therapeutic games: the player/ game/ therapy model. In: Herrlich, M., Malaka, R., Masuch, M. (eds.) ICEC 2012. LNCS, vol. 7522, pp. 193–206. Springer, Heidelberg (2012). https://doi.org/10.1007/978-3-642-33542-6_17
3. Mueller, F., et al.: Designing sports: a framework for exertion games. In: Proceedings of the SIGCHI Conference on Human Factors in Computing Systems, pp. 2651–2660 (2011). https://doi.org/10.1145/1978942.1979330
4. Flynn, S., Lange, B.: Games for rehabilitation: the voice of the players. In: Proceedings of the 8th International Conference on Disability, Virtual Reality & Associated Technologies, pp. 185–194 (2010)
5. Lohse, K., Shirzad, N., Verster, A., Hodges, N., Van der Loos, H.M.: Video games and rehabilitation: using design principles to enhance engagement in physical therapy. J. Neurolog. Phys. Ther. 37(4), 166–175 (2013). https://doi.org/10.1097/NPT.0000000000000017
6. Shelton, P., Scott, R.: Gaming for health. J. mHealth 2(4), 42–44 (2015). http://www.thejournalofmhealth.com/issues
7. Gamboa, E., Ruiz, C., Trujillo, M.: Improving patient motivation towards physical rehabilitation treatments with Playtherapy exergame. In: pHealth, pp. 140–147 (2018)
8. Gamboa, E., Trujillo, M.: Identifying aspects, methods and instruments to evaluate player experience in physical rehabilitation exergames. In: Proceedings of the 5thWorkshop on ICTs for improving Patients Rehabilitation Research Techniques, pp. 136–139 (2019). https://doi.org/10.1145/3364138.3364166
9. Trulock, V.: Question asking protocol. http://hci.ilikecake.ie/evaluation/questionasking.htm
10. Kato, T.: What "question-asking protocols" can say about the user interface. Int. J. Man Mach. Stud. 25(6), 659–673 (1986)
11. Burnard, P., Gill, P., Stewart, K., Treasure, E., Chadwick, B.: Analysing and presenting qualitative data. Br. Dent. J. 204(8), 429–432 (2008). https://doi.org/10.1038/sj.bdj.2008.292
12. Langhorne, P., Coupar, F., Pollock, A.: Motor recovery after stroke: a systematic review. Lancet Neurol. 8(8), 741–754 (2009). https://doi.org/10.1016/S1474-4422(09)70150-4
13. Pirovano, M.: The design of exergaming systems for autonomous rehabilitation. Ph.D. thesis, Italy (2015)

An Architectural Model for Virtual Learning Environments Using Multicultural Learning Objects

Jaime Muñoz-Arteaga[1]([✉]) [iD], Alicia Lozano Quiroz[1] [iD],
and Klinge Villalba Condori[2] [iD]

[1] Universidad Autónoma de Aguascalientes, Av. Universidad #940. C.P.,
20131 Aguascalientes, Mexico
jaime.munoz@edu.uaa.mx, alloqui9@gmail.com
[2] Universidad Católica de Santa María, Arequipa, Peru
kvillalba@ucsm.edu.pe

Abstract. Learning objects are considered as educational resources that can be employed in technology support learning. They are a digital piece of knowledge to put together in order to form online courses. Considering cultural aspects is possible to reuse them in different context for a large diversity of community of users. Nevertheless, current virtual learning environment give a few supports for manage course in terms of multicultural learning objects. This work purposes an architectural model for virtual learning environment taken into account multiples sources of multicultural learning objects in an effective manner. The proposed model is applied throughout a case study showing the design of a multicultural learning object related to one significative tradition in Mexico.

Keywords: Arch model · Multicultural learning objects · Interaction patterns

1 Introduction

Nowadays a large number of universities are producing their courses in terms of learning objects and saving these objects in their own repositories, these repositories in general support several local queries with different criteria thanks to the information in the metadata. Such repositories have the goal of opening access to a wide variety of materials to anyone around the globe. A large diversity of learning environments allows users access the repositories to design and develop academic content in online courses.

Learning objects are considered as educational resources that can be employed in technology support learning. They are a digital piece of knowledge to put together in order to form courses online. A traditional learning object is composed of four main components such as: theoretical knowledge, evaluation, related subjects and practical knowledge [1, 2].

Whenever as teacher you create an academic content, the teacher put a bit of yourself into the content. This part is often a representation of your own culture and even if you

V. Agredo-Delgado et al. (Eds.): HCI-COLLAB 2020, CCIS 1334, pp. 10–19, 2020.
https://doi.org/10.1007/978-3-030-66919-5_2

deliver that content in your classroom where you are intimately familiar with your students, there are parts of that content that are difficult for all of your students to understand that have nothing to do with the educational content [3].

However, previous issues have been less pronounced than what occurs now when several mentors create content in different part of world. Internet allows us to find, create easily different good quality of academic contents and deliver them to a large number of societies. A learning object can be created in different locations and in different languages need to be re-built or localized in order to satisfy the requirements of each location.

Monocultural perspectives hamper learning in a number of ways. Students are not exposed to or do not engage with different forms of knowledge or realities. Students are not encouraged to learn about or engage with a diverse group of people. As a consequence, there is no conception of alternative ways of thinking and acting, hindering imagination and criticism, with the potential to promote arrogance, insensitivity, providing a fertile ground for prejudice. Multiculturalism puts forward the existence of multiple (multi) cultures as opposed to one (mono) particular culture within an educational system and society at large. As a countermovement to the established educational system, it attacks a constructed reality that is often referred to as ethnocentrism or monocultural. This is essentially to change the conceptualization of culture, moving from unitary to pluralistic perspectives [3, 4].

Today, educational content can be easily distributed worldwide via the internet. While this is easy to do, it is apparent that in all of these materials there is both intentional educational content and unintentional cultural content. We prefer to say here that culture is in whatever you create. A traditional learning object can be enrichment through the clear identification of cultural aspects such traditions, best practices and customs. For simplicity, a multicultural learning object is presented in the Fig. 1.

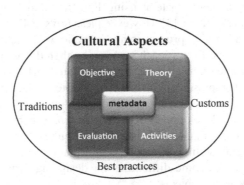

Fig. 1. Elements of a Multicultural Learning Object (MLO).

It is possible consider several cultural aspects (such as traditions, customs and best practices) in every component (evaluation, related topic, theoretical and practical knowledge) of a traditional learning object. Then, a Multicultural Learning Object (MLO) can be defined as a learning object that can be used for different cultures and the learners can better understand in their own educational terms. On the other hand, in the literature of e-learning and human computer interaction (HCI) several works have proposed the foundation the multicultural education: Hofstede [4] and Banks [5] a have considered the multicultural education as an emerging paradigm, Oshlyansky et al. [6] have pré-cised the difference between cultural aspects from usability aspects for the graphical user interfaces at analysis stage, Milheim discusses the influence of cultural difference in online learning and provides ways courses can be more inclusive [3].

Unfortunately, current virtual learning environments offer a few supports for manage course in terms of multicultural learning objects. This work purposes an architectural model for learning environment taken into account multiples sources of multicultural learning objects in an effective manner. For this goal, next section specifies an outline of problem; section three presents the proposal in terms of a conceptual model. Finally, section four shows an architectural design for a virtual learning environment as a case study, in order to prove the current proposal.

2 Problem Outline

A multicultural learning object always pursue the idea of reusable interactive compo-nents, it is necessary a good quality of graphical user interfaces for different contexts, so a MLO can be delivered for an initial population but also to as many groups with another culture. Nowadays, there are Virtual Learning Environments (VLE) that with the goal to facilitate education through computer-based system. A VLE is a social space where multiple actors (also called users) produce, share, etc.... information. It is pos-sible to see the social space as an organizational unit where each user has a job (the total collection of tasks, duties, and responsibilities assigned to one or more users) and a hierarchical position inside the social space. Between the principal users are: trainers, learners, domain experts, managers. Learners play a dynamic role during the learning process as they can actively participate by using the different tools available in the VLE, forums, chats, questionnaires, etc. [3]. However, these tools lack of features to facilitate the trainer to describe a learning process in a systematic way, a learning process which includes a set of steps to be follow, each step can be then decomposed into tasks, for each task a multicultural learning object can be associated. What is more, once defined such learning process its representation should be adapted to learner's preferences and available resources for such displaying. Creating such content efficiently present sev-eral challenges including: development of content in a reasonable amount of time and following a structured method, consider usability guidelines, follow standards, support multiplatform, and several facilities to represent information, context adaptation, among others. This work identifies some difficulties for designing virtual environment that support multicultural learning objects:

- It is necessary different abstraction levels to deal with the complexity for developing virtual learning environment using multicultural content [5].
- A course with multicultural learning objects requires a large number of graphical resources then it is necessary to mechanisms for an easy maintenance and easy to use.
- Multicultural learning objects need to be portable and reusable across multiple platforms including mobile devices and portable game consoles.

- It is necessary identify some new criteria to evaluate the quality of virtual learning environment using multicultural learning objects [7]

Unfortunately, these design issues are generally left to solve only during the software development. Next sections describe some alternatives solutions to the aforementioned problems.

3 Architectural Model

We propose an architectural model composed of five layers for virtual learning environments where the courses can support multicultural learning objects. The proposed architectural model allows different abstraction levels to separate concerns between the technological issues from conceptual design. Every MLO requires a large number of graphical resources to display in an interactive manner the academic contents. In addition, it is quite difficult to develop the external aspect of a VLE without being immediately stuck into the inherent relation with the internal aspects of VLE. Taking into account the external aspect during the development of an interactive VLE, it is necessary to work with the code of the graphical user interface as well also the code concerning to internal function of a VLE. This architectural model proposed here is adapted of Arch model [8] coming from the area of human computer interaction, next figure shows the proposed model as follow (Fig. 2):

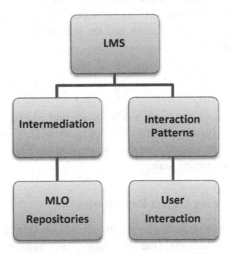

Fig. 2. Architectural model for virtual learning environments (inspired of Arch model [8]).

Multicultural Learning Object Repositories regroup a set of distributed repositories of multicultural learning objects.
Intermediation layer contains the protocols to manage and communicate heterogeneous repositories independent of any data base protocol or operating system.

Learning Management Systems (LMS). This layer represents a plethora of platforms that can help to manage academic contents in term of online courses, in particular open source platforms such as: Moodle [9], Claroline [10], TalentLMS [11] etc. With these platforms a teacher can easily create, maintain and extend management functions for online courses.

The interaction patterns layer offers a series of solutions in terms of better practices to graphical design for the structure of courses online composed in term of multicultural learning objects. In the literature of HCI exists a large number of interaction patterns [12] that can make easy the design of online courses.

User Interaction layer. This layer represents the software of multiplatform graphical user interface where the multicultural learning objects can be displayed and used in an 'interactive and easy manner by a large diversity of devices such as laps, pc's, tablets and smart phones.

Once the multicultural learning objects have been produced, they can be saved in one of the repositories. The group of repositories requires to be managed by online services offered by the intermediation layer, example of these online services are download, upload, order, search, delete multicultural learning objects etc. These services can be implemented using the web service technology in order to warrant the interoperability into repositories. Then, the teachers can develop their courses in terms of multicultural learning objects coming from different repositories; every teacher can choice and selects the multicultural learning objects using their proper LMS without worry of any operating system or data base. The interactive patterns layer offers a set of best practices to help the teacher in the instructional design with a large number of interactive patterns. Finally, the interaction layer assures the visualization and the interaction of multicultural learning objects in different platforms.

4 Case Study

México is recognized as a country with a rich culture and a large diversity of traditions, one of the main traditions is the celebration day of the dead [13]. Main characteristics of every layers of virtual learning environment are presented in this case study according the architectural model proposed here.

4.1 Multicultural Learning Object Repositories

The Multicultural learning objects can be produced and saved throughout different repositories of universities from Mexico. Thanks to the collaboration of some research groups in learning objects, it was possible to connect the repositories of Universidad Veracruzana, Cenidet and, Universidad Autónoma de Aguascalientes (see Fig. 3). These repositories have registered several multicultural learning objects specifying the day of the dead, these objects were regrouped in different categories of Mexico's region as follow:

North of México Region. Halloween is a tradition usually celebrated in México in particular in the border states with the United States of America. Some typical Halloween

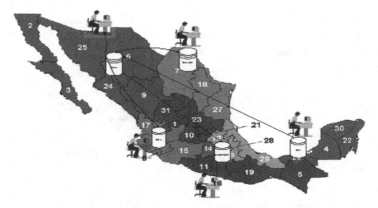

Fig. 3. Distributed repositories with multicultural learning object in México

activities include costumes and attending costume parties, ghost tours, and watching horror films, bonfires, haunted attractions telling ghost stories or other frightening tales.

Center of México Region. Most México guidebooks make special mention of day of the dead tradtitions celebrated in the center of Mexico, in particular in the Janitzio Island, familes celebrate the day of dead with dishes, music and night candlelight vigils in the cemeteries.

South of México Region. Some altars with some pictures, dishes and meals appreciated in life by the dead, These altars in honnor to dead of familie with several dishes and flowers are installed in the houses at south of Mexico.

Center-Occident of México Region. The people of region centre occident remember this day with Mexican revolution style with several representations of skeleton. One of the skeleton is the Catrina representig a woman who was member the high society. Also the mexican revolution skeletons are considedered to wear by the people during the day of dead in Center-Occident of Mexico.

Península of Yucatán Region. The people of Peninsula of Yucatan celebrate the day of dead with traditions of Maya culture incorporating certain pre-hispanic customs into christian practices.

4.2 Intermediation

The different repositories of this case study can access the multicultural learning objects using the protocol SQI (Simple Query Interface) defined by CEN [14]. SQI provides a detailed description of the functionalities that each repository must meet in order to be compatible with the others, and describes the names of the methods that must be implemented along with parameters received and returned during the search process. In particular search service has designed and implemented in order to get MLO with different criteria [15] (Fig. 4).

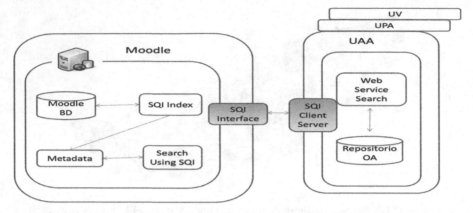

Fig. 4. Service search of multicultural learning object from distributed repositories

The previous figure describes the connection for several learning object repositories from Moodle [9]. A client can directly ask a federated search engine, which in turn forwards the query to a number of repositories and returns the answer to the client. Multicultural learning objects in the repositories are usually described by metadata under a standard such as SCORM [16], IMS [17], UDL [18]. Therefore, accessing multicultural learning objects can take advantage of queries upon metadata for selecting the objects that are most suited to the needs of learners or teachers. In addition, many learning objects include textual material that can be indexed, and such indexes can also be used to filter the objects by matching them against user-provided keywords.

Here, there are other advantages to use the SQI protocol [14]:

1. To be more robust in its operation due to the collapse of one or more of its components (repositories) does not interrupt the operation of all.
2. Allow each participating institution or unit carrying out the administration of its resources locally, in their own repository.
3. Supporting the persistence of information through the replication of resources in several independent systems.

4.3 Learning Management System (LMS)

The open source platform Moodle [9] has been proposed to use in this case study, we have extended some functionalities in a such way the teachers can create, show and maintain their online course in terms of multicultural learning objects.

4.4 Interaction Patterns

Interaction patterns give solutions to design the user interface for online courses [19]. Next Fig. 5. describes the navigation interactive patterns used to structure every multicultural learning object of this case study.

According the community site pattern the content is showed in the right side of windows in function of item menus associated to the main components (theory, put in

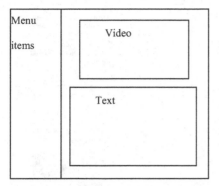

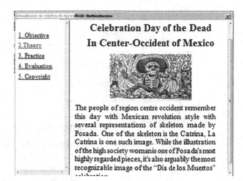

Fig. 5. Frame for community site pattern interaction patterns.

Fig. 6. Instantiation of navigation interaction pattern.

practices, evaluation and related topics) of every multicultural learning object (see Fig. 5 and 6). Note, the specified solution of interaction patterns can be applied independently of any graphical toolkit or any learning management system.

4.5 User Interaction

In this case study a teacher can use the platform Moodle to create the course about the celebration day of the dead in Mexico; this platform was extended to have access to different repositories distributed in different universities of Mexico. The teacher can use the web service search of platform Moodle in order to looking for some multicultural learning objects. As answer, it is displayed several multicultural learning objects describing some cultural traditions and activities of the day of the dead from different regions of Mexico. Next, the teacher defines the general structure of course selecting the general interaction template from the catalogue of interaction patterns of current approach.

According the interaction layer of architectural model proposed in the Fig. 7, when a student in México is going to require a multicultural learning object, the student can be motivated notably to study the content of the day of the dead of region where this learner is living. This VLE also gives support for users that are interested of different forms of celebration of these traditions in México, the user can use the research service to get several multicultural learning objects about the celebration day of the dead in the different regions of México (see Fig. 7), as follow:

1. North of México region
2. Center of México region
3. South of México region
4. Center-Occident of México region
5. Península of Yucatán region

The student can access and display the content of multicultural learning objects from different user interfaces of mobile devices such as tablets, laps and, smart phones.

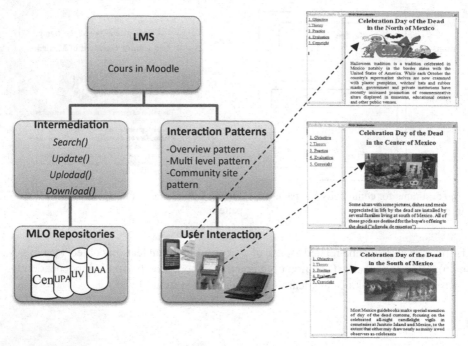

Fig. 7. Architectural Model for a virtual learning environment with a multicultural learning object titled Celebrating day of the dead in México.

5 Conclusions

This work purposes an architectural model for virtual learning environment taken into account multiples sources of multicultural learning objects in an effective manner. Current work helps to give a general specification of virtual learning environments with online courses, where learning objects take into account multicultural aspects such as traditions, customs and best practices of a society. The architectural model proposed here can be used as a reference model for designers to specify virtual learning environment independently of any graphical toolkits or any operating system.

Current work has proposed a way to better take advantage of a set of existing learning object repositories through traditional content management systems. Access to said repositories is under the use of standards such as the SCORM and IMS standards for metadata. These standards contribute to the reuse and portability of learning objects to be used in academic content management systems such as Moodle that facilitate the administration of courses in various areas of knowledge.

As future work, several topics are possible such as the adaptability, evaluation and massive production of online course with multicultural learning objects.

Acknowledgements. This work was developed thanks to PRODEP support to UAA research team (Reference UAA-CA-48). The authors gratefully appreciate the collaboration with software engineering researchers from Universities of UV, CENIDET, UPA and UAA.

References

1. Wiley, D.A.: Connecting learning objects to instructional design theory: a definition, a metaphor, and a taxonomy, pp. 1–35. Wiley (2000)
2. Muñoz-Arteaga, J. Alvarez, F., Chan, M.E.: Tecnología de objetos de Aprendizaje. Editorial Universidad Autónoma de Aguascalientes y UdG Virtual (2007)
3. Milheim, K.: Cultural inclusivity in online learning. In: Wright, R.D. (ed.) Student-Teacher Interaction in Online Learning Environments, pp. 76–88. IGI Global (2008) https://doi.org/10.4018/978-1-4666-6461-6.ch004
4. Hofstede, G.: Culture's Consequences, Comparing Values, Behaviors, Institutions, and Organizations. Across Nations. Sage Publications, Thousand Oaks (2003). https://doi.org/10.1509/jmkg.67.2.151.18611
5. Banks, J., Banks, C.: Multicultural Education: Issues and Perspectives. Wiley, Hoboken (2019)
6. Oshlyansky, L., Thimbleby, H., Cairns, P.: Breaking affordance: culture as context. In: Third Nordic ACM Conference on Human-Computer Interaction, pp 81–84 (2004). https://doi.org/10.1145/1028014.1028025
7. Castro, L., López, G., Gamboa, R., Muñoz-Arteaga, J, Contreras J., Curlango C., Villa, R.: Norma Mexicana. volumen 1. marco teórico de la interoperabilidad entre entornos para objetos de aprendizaje. Editorial Universidad Autónoma de Baja California (2014)
8. Gram, C., Cockton, G. (eds.): Design principles for interactive software. Chapman et Hall, London (1995)
9. Moodle. http://moodle.org/
10. Claroline. http://www.claroline.net/
11. Talentlms. https://www.talentlms.com/
12. Tidwell, J., Brewer, Ch., Valencia, A.: Designing Interfaces: Patterns for Effective Interaction Design, 3rd edn. Editorial Oreilly (2020)
13. Campos, A., Cardaillac, L.: México de mis amores: Una guía cultural de la A a la Z. Editorial Oceano (2009). ISBN 978-1-449-37970-4
14. CEN ("Comité Européen de Normalisation"): A Simple Query Interface Specification for Learning Repositories (2005). http://www.prolearn-project.org/. Accessed 1 May 2020
15. Muñoz-Arteaga, J., Ochoa, X., Calvillo, E., Vincent, G.: Integration of REDOUAA to the Latin American Federation of repositories of learning objects. In: LACLO 2007 (Conference Latin American of Objects of Learning), Chile (2007)
16. IMS- Interoperability Standards | IMS Global. https://imsglobal.org
17. UDL - Universal Design for Learning. http://udlguidelines.cast.org/
18. SCORM-Sharable Content Object Reference Model. https://scorm.com/
19. Warburton, S., Mor, Y., Kohls, C., Köppe, C., Bergin, J.: Assessment driven course design: a pattern validation workshop. Presented at 8th Biennial Conference of EARLI SIG 1: Assessment & Evaluation, Munich, Germany (2016)

An Experimental Activity to Develop Usability and UX Heuristics

Pedro Reis[1] , César Páris[1(✉)] , and Anabela Gomes[1,2(✉)]

[1] Coimbra Polytechnic – ISEC, Coimbra, Portugal
pmreis27@gmail.com, {cparis,anabela}@isec.pt
[2] Coimbra Polytechnic – ISEC and Centre for Informatics and Systems
of the University of Coimbra (CISUC), Coimbra, Portugal

Abstract. The heuristic evaluation is one of the most used inspection methods to assess the usability of interactive systems and interfaces. It can be performed using generic heuristics, such as Nielsen's heuristics, or domain-specific heuristics, that can detect relevant domain related usability issues. In the mobile scope, more and more applications are starting to emerge with particular characteristics. This paper intends to analyse specific heuristics to evaluate mobile applications that interact with external equipment. The inexistence of such domain-specific heuristics led us to create an experimental activity in order to propose a more suitable list of heuristics, following the methodology proposed by Quiñones et al. to develop usability and UX heuristics for a specific domain. Therefore, this paper contains the output of the application of the first two phases of this methodology, giving particular emphasis to the "experimental phase" analysing and discussing data from different experiments in order to obtain additional information about the chosen domain.

Keywords: Heuristic evaluation · Human computer interaction · Mobile applications · Usability · User experience

1 Introduction

Usability and User Experience (UX) are two concepts extremely important to have in mind when developing interactive systems. There are many ways to achieve a better product in terms of usability and UX. However, the Heuristic Evaluation is one that stands out. It is a usability inspection method that involves a set of experts who evaluate the software interface and assess its compliance with the heuristics - a set of pre-defined principles and guidelines. When performed, this inspection results in a list of potential usability issues that the interface might have.

In this work, we are particularly focused in evaluating mobile applications that interact with external equipment allowing its users to make purchases on vending machines. After researching on heuristics for this kind of application, no specific sets of heuristics were found so we thought to propose, validate and refine a new list of heuristics to perform heuristic evaluations suitable for these new types of interactions. For this,

© Springer Nature Switzerland AG 2020
V. Agredo-Delgado et al. (Eds.): HCI-COLLAB 2020, CCIS 1334, pp. 20–29, 2020.
https://doi.org/10.1007/978-3-030-66919-5_3

after a comprehensive reading on methods used by several authors [1], the methodology proposed by D. Quinõnes et al. [2] was selected, analysed and implemented. This paper reports the accomplishment of the first two phases of this methodology focusing specially in the second stage where experiments are encouraged to be performed. The paper is organized as follows. Section 2 presents the context and related work review. Section 3 describes the specific domain of the mobile applications used in the investigation. Section 4 explains the methodology proposed by D. Quiñones et al. to develop usability and UX heuristics for a specific domain, the outputs of each phase and describes the experimental activity, their results and analysis. Section 5 concludes the paper and states future work.

2 Context

The vending market used to be outdated technology wise, but recently, many companies started to develop tailored solutions for this area. One of the companies that has invested some efforts in making software and hardware solutions for vending machines in Portugal is Luope, a software company based in Coimbra. One of their most promising projects is a mobile application for Android and iOS called BuyOn that allows its users to make purchases on selected vending machines.

Since the application is recent and is currently branching out to more users, a lot of feedback has been received by them. This feedback has allowed the team to understand that the application has potential and has really interesting features, but perhaps it has some usability and UX flaws.

It was then decided that we needed to execute a more profound analysis of the application in terms of usability and user experience, find as many problems as possible and apply the most suitable methodologies in order to achieve a set of improvements. This could make the users/target audience have a more satisfying experience. We then proceeded to research on formal methodologies to develop usability and UX heuristics and that's when we found D. Quiñones et al. work, which was considered extremely appropriate and a great source to start this investigation.

3 Applications Domain

Before diving into the chosen methodology, we needed to define the specific domain where BuyOn would fit in. Therefore, we analysed the interaction inherent to it, which is detailed in another document [3]. However, the most important aspect that we have realized is that, most of the mobile applications only require an interaction between a user and a device (either a smartphone or a tablet), but for this particular case, the interaction involves a third element – the vending machine. Consequently, the interaction is no longer so linear. This means that, besides taking into account the interaction between the user and the device, it is also necessary to keep in mind the interaction with this third element which we've called "external equipment". The general domain was then defined as "mobile applications that interact with external equipment".

Additionally, we decided to select two more mobile applications that interact with external equipment to be used in the methodology: MEO Go and MB WAY. The first one is a mobile application that allows their clients to check all the programs broadcasted in the last 7 days (from their catalog) and select one of them to be streamed to a MEO box so that they can watch in on their TVs. MB WAY consists of an application that allows the user to access a physical ATM machine through their smartphone/tablet.

The analysis on the main features for each application, which focuses on the interaction each one has with the external equipment, is reported in another document [3].

4 Methodology

As previously stated, the chosen methodology proposed by D. Quiñones et al. is divided into eight steps: (1) Exploratory stage: to perform a literature review; (2) Experimental stage: to analyse data from experiments; (3) Descriptive stage: to select and prioritize information; (4) Correlation stage: to match the features of the specific domain with the selected usability and UX attributes and heuristics (5) Selection stage: to keep, adapt and/or discard heuristics; (6) Specification stage: to formally specify the new set of heuristics; (7) Validation stage: to validate the set of heuristics through several experiments; (8) Refinement stage: to refine and improve the new set of heuristics.

This paper consists of the outputs of the first two out of eight phases of the selected methodology. More specifically, the first phase, also addressed as the exploratory stage, consisted of a literature review to collect relevant information about a specific domain. In the second phase, or the "experimental stage", it is necessary to analyse the data obtained in different experiments to collect additional information that has not been identified in the previous stage. This phase can provide the researcher with a list of additional specific features of the application, some detected usability problems and problems with existing heuristics. The description of the way we implemented the two first stages of the methodology are described next.

4.1 Exploratory Stage

Firstly, a thorough investigation on the chosen used cases was done in order to collect some functionalities that could help to define key requirements for mobile applications that interact with external equipment. The research performed for this stage, helped to define the following general requirements: (1) The applications within this domain serve as a bridge between the user and the external equipment (interaction between 3 elements); (2) The applications allow its users to control a device by distance that previously only worked when the user physically interacted with it; (3) The applications can be used, for example, in the context of the SmartHomes, SmartVending, among others; (4) The applications allow users to have a greater and more centralized control of their equipment enabling the interaction with equipment at a fair distance.

Moreover, the key functionalities for the applications within the domain are the following: (1) Showing the nearest equipment to the user or most used ones; (2) Selecting external equipment to interact with; Sending commands/actions to the equipment; (3) Controlling what is happening with the equipment in real time.

Additionally, some sets of heuristics were selected to go through analysis in the second stage of the methodology. The chosen sets were Jakob Nielsen's 10 usability heuristics [4], some heuristics proposed by R. Miranda in her master thesis [5] and, some of the ones proposed by Gómez et al. [6]. The criterium for this selection is explained and detailed in another document [3].

Also, as intended for the methodology, we have selected 8 usability and 5 UX attributes that must be covered by the new set of heuristics. The usability attributes were "learnability", "efficiency", "memorability", "errors" and "satisfaction" based on Nielsen's work [7] and "user needs", "design" and "feedback" based on the work by Alturki and Gay [8]. For the UX attributes, after some review on this topic, the chosen attributes were "useful", "usable", "accessible", "credible" and "valuable", based on Peter Morville work [9].

4.2 Experimental Stage

For this stage, and as previously stated, a research on usability experiments made for the chosen domain should be performed. Therefore, after an exhaustive research on usability studies about heuristics for mobile applications that interact with external equipment, no relevant study could be found that would benefit our investigation. Although the methodology proposes a set of experiments that can be performed in this phase (Heuristic Evaluation, Usability Test, Interview and Survey), we decided to create a whole new experiment designed specifically for this phase which consisted of an integration of some activities. The new experiment, called "Discussion with Specialists", was then defined by the authors of this paper having in mind the available resources and the final outputs of this stage which was a list of additional features of the chosen applications, a list of usability problems detected for each one of them and, finally, a list of problems/limitations of the previously chosen sets of heuristics. Additionally, the feedback provided would then be carefully analysed to create a preliminary list of heuristics for the specific domain. It consists in a collection of ideas, opinions and reactions in relation to the chosen application by a small group of specialists that are set to perform some tasks in order to get important feedback about the applications that serve as a case study for the experiment.

The activities of this experiment are divided in three parts: A – Discussing the application; B – Questionnaire regarding usability and UX attributes; C – Questionnaire about usability and UX problems.

Experiment: Protocol. The first part of the experiment "A – Discussing the application" took place in three sessions (1 activity per application), in the headquarters of the company Luope. We have selected 5 participants with background in designing user interfaces (UI), user experience (UX), developing mobile and/or web software (frontend). They were previously notified of the experiment and received a document describing what the activities would consist of. During the sessions, the moderator (the main author of this paper) explained the purpose of the application to be evaluated and its key functionalities. After this brief explanation, each participant had some time to explore the application under analysis on both smartphones and tablets running either Android or iOS. With this, the participants were encouraged to discuss their general opinion about the application, if they thought that it offered a good user experience, if they had any problems accomplishing any task, their difficulties, and so on. This provided feedback for the first part of the activity "A - Discussing the application".

Then, the second part "B - Questionnaire regarding usability and UX attributes" was given to analyse their attributes. The usability attributes were B1 – Learnability, B2 – Efficiency, B3 – Memorability, B4 – Errors, B5 – Satisfaction, B6 – User needs, B7 – Design and B8 – Feedback. The UX attributes were B9 – Useful, B10 – Usable, B11 – Accessible, B12 – Credible and B13 – Valuable. It consisted of a set of 13 questions (one per attribute) to rate the chosen attributes on a scale of 1 to 5 (1 being strongly disagree and 5 totally agree). The questions (such as "Are the error messages clear, well written and do they help the user to overcome the possible error?", related to the usability attribute "Errors") were based on the SUMI - Software Usability Measurement Inventory [10]. This inventory is a rigorously tested and proven method of measuring software quality that, although extremely useful for general usability evaluations, wasn't the most adequate to measure some of the selected attributes such as the "user needs" and "feedback".

Afterwards, the third part "C – Questionnaire about usability and UX problems" was handled. This questionnaire consisted of 62 questions regarding various types of usability and UX problems that the applications could have. Most of them were related to the sets of heuristics chosen, while others were introduced in order to understand whether the existing heuristics would be sufficient to evaluate the used cases and their specific domain. The questions were a mix of Yes or No answers (e.g. "When a dialog is shown, can the user dismiss it by clicking outside?"), and opinion answers, also based on the SUMI questionnaire and identical to the survey reported in the previous part (part B), with questions like "Does the application have a well thought out, appealing and clean interface/design?".

Upon reaching the end of the experiment, and having feedback on all the chosen applications, the analysis of the results, discussion of the limitations of the previously chosen heuristics and elaboration of the preliminary list of heuristics was carried out. This stage originated a lot of important information for the following stages of the methodology and allowed the moderator and the experts to create and validate the new list of heuristics.

Experiment: Results Analysis. The experiment provided a lot of important feedback about each one of the applications in terms of usability and UX flaws. The first part, consisting of the participants opinions on the applications discussed provided the feedback stated in Table 1.

Then, part B, consisted of the questionnaire regarding the chosen usability and UX attributes, pointed out that all the applications have some problems related to such attributes. The BuyOn application had problems that could be related to the following attributes: B1 – Learnability, B4 – Errors, B10 – Usable and B11 – Accessible. MEO Go had problems with B4 – Errors, B10 – Usable and B11 – Accessible. MB WAY had problems mapped to the B1 – Learnability, B3 – Memorability, B7 – Design and B10 – Usable attributes.

Finally, part C, consisted of a questionnaire on usability and UX problems, also helped to find many usability and UX problems as the questions were about possible problems related to each one of the previously chosen heuristics (from the three sets)

Table 1. Feedback from the first part of the activity (A - Discussing the application).

Application	Feedback
BuyOn	It has a very appealing design but the accessibility is low; it is not very intuitive and a little hard to use; there is no indication of required fields; there are views with different buttons that do the same thing (e.g. login and register button both redirect the user to the login view); there is no feedback when the user clicks on button or list items (no "ripple effect"); some buttons appear to be deactivated when in fact they are not, such as the social login ones; there is no apparent difference from tapping on a product or a value to send to the machine; the feedback when the app is connecting to the machine is really poor and sometimes the user doesn't know what is happening (especially when the app is connecting to the server) and finally, there are no tutorials nor a FAQ view
MEO Go	It is considered to have low accessibility and has a huge problem according to the specialists: it only works when the device is horizontally oriented (landscape mode), that can be uncomfortable for the user when using it on a smartphone. Also, the bottom bar is considered confusing; the dialogs can't be dismissed when clicked outside; the user can't easily figure out that the app is connected to the TV box (external equipment) and there is no feedback that the chosen program has started being broadcast
MB WAY	The interface/design is not considered to be appealing, the bottom bar is too small and some of the labels used are not very intuitive, such as the tab "Activity" which should be renamed to "Cards". In terms of security, the option to logout from the account cannot be found. Another flaw in the application was the dialogs that, when shown, did not let the users know what was happening since the view appeared blank

and about other aspects relevant to the specific domain that seemed not to be covered by none of them. Quantitatively, 27 usability and UX problems were found in BuyOn, 15 problems in MEO Go and 14 in MB WAY. As can be seen in Table 2, most of these problems could be mapped to the Nielsen's heuristics and others to those chosen specific heuristics for mobile systems, however some problems didn't have any adequate heuristic to be mapped to. Therefore, the final list of heuristics should be refined to cover all of these.

After this analysis, the last stage of the experiment was performed: "Analysing the results, discussing the limitations of the heuristics chosen in the exploratory stage of the methodology and elaborating a preliminary list of heuristics that covers all usability and UX problems encountered". Therefore, the participants discussed some changes to be made in the chosen heuristics based on the results of all experiments, in order to obtain a more adequate list to evaluate mobile applications that interact with external equipment. The analysis and obtained list are reported in the next section.

Experiment: Results Discussion. With all the feedback, and after carefully analysing all the results, we were able to verify limitations in the sets of heuristics and propose a more suitable list to evaluate mobile applications that interact with external equipment. The first part (A – Discussing the application) allowed us to verify that BuyOn is

Table 2. Usability and UX problems found in the applications mapped to the chosen heuristics.

Heuristic	BuyOn	MEO Go	MB WAY
N1 – Visibility of system status[a]	3 problems	1 problem	2 problems
N2 – Match between system and the real world[a]	2 problems	0 problems	1 problem
N3 – User control and freedom[a]	0 problems	1 problem	1 problem
N4 – Consistency and standards[a]	1 problem	0 problems	1 problem
N5 – Error prevention[a]	1 problem	0 problems	0 problems
N6 – Recognition rather than recall[a]	0 problems	0 problems	0 problems
N7 – Flexibility and efficiency of use[a]	2 problem	5 problems	1 problem
N8 – Aesthetic and minimalist design[a]	0 problems	0 problems	0 problems
N9 – Help users recognize, diagnose, and recover from errors[a]	3 problems	0 problems	0 problems
N10 – Help and documentation[a]	3 problems	1 problem	1 problem
MH1 – Pleasurable and respectful interaction with the user[b]	4 problems	2 problem	5 problems
MH2 – Privacy[b]	1 problem	0 problems	1 problem
MH3 – Interruptions[b]	0 problems	0 problems	0 problems
MH4 – Waiting times[b]	3 problems	0 problems	0 problems
MH5 – Focus[b]	0 problems	0 problems	0 problems
MH6 – Don't lie to the user[b]	1 problem	1 problem	0 problems
MH7 – Deal properly with the screen orientation[b]	0 problems	2 problems	0 problems
No suitable heuristic	3 problems	2 problems	1 problem

[a]N – Nielsen's Heuristic, [b]MH – Mobile Heuristic.

hard to use, does not have a great error prevention, sometimes misleads the user with non-existent links, does not have sufficient documentation/ways of guiding the user to perform tasks and has some problems regarding the feedback it provides when connecting with the vending machines. The MEO Go application only works in landscape mode (horizontally), is difficult to use on smartphones and also has some issues regarding the feedback when the application is connecting to the external equipment. Finally, MB WAY is hard to use and has security problems regarding the logout button (which could not be found).

This feedback allowed us to verify a set of topics correlated to the problems identified within the applications such as: A1 – "Hard to use"; A2 – "Errors not being well treated"; A3 – "Misleading links (non-existent)"; A4 – "Lack of documentation/tutorials"; A5 – "Poor feedback when the application and the external equipment are communicating"; A6 – "Orientation of the device"; A7 – "Type of device (smartphone/tablet)"; A8 – "Security".

Regarding the questionnaire about usability and UX attributes (part B), there were the following problems identified with the previously defined usability attributes: B1 – "Learnability", B2 – "Memorability", B4 – "Errors" and B5 – "Design" and with the UX attributes B6 – "Usable" and B7 – "Accessible".

Finally, the results obtained from part C of the activity, and as previously stated, helped us to find 27 usability problems in the BuyOn application, 15 problems in MEO Go and 14 in MB WAY. Of this total, 18 problems were possible to map to Nielsen's heuristics and 19 to the mobile specific heuristics, however there were 4 problems that could not be mapped to any chosen heuristic, namely: C1 – "There are features with little interest for the user"; C2 – "Dialogs requesting the user to give permission (e.g. location, push notifications, etc.) are not shown only when needed"; C3 – "When the device is communicating with the external equipment, there is no constant information/feedback on what is happening"; C4 – "When the device is communicating with the external equipment, the messages of what is happening are not clear".

With all the results of the experiments on the application, it is necessary to analyse them, discuss the limitations of the sets of heuristics and elaborate the preliminary list of heuristics which is the final output of this experiment. After carefully analysing the previously chosen sets of heuristics we have concluded that all of the Nielsen's heuristics revealed to be extremely important to evaluate the chosen domain, covering many usability aspects, so this set of heuristics should be part of the final list. However, for the domain-specific heuristics that have been selected, there are a few changes to be made as stated next.

The heuristics "MH2: Pleasurable and respectful interaction with the user", "MH4: Interruptions", "MH5: Waiting times", "MH6: Focus" and "MH7: Don't lie to the user" should be kept as they are relevant for both mobile applications in general as for the specific domain of selected applications. Therefore, we have considered that the existence of these heuristics might help to identify more usability and UX problems.

The heuristic "MH3: Privacy" should be maintained but, as seen with the problem C2 – "Dialogs requesting the user to give permission (e.g. location, push notifications, etc.) are not shown only when needed", it should be noted that if an application asks for all the needed permission at once, it can cause some discomfort to the users and make them feel "invaded" and/or insecure with it. The best way to overcome this problem is to ask the user for permission only when necessary (for example, only ask for location permission when the user enters a view that has a map). Although there is no heuristic related to security problems, an extremely important aspect to which users tend to give more and more importance today, there is one about privacy. As these two concepts complement each other, it was decided that the "MH3: Privacy" heuristic should be changed to "Privacy and Security". Additionally, this would cover the aspect A8 – "Security" from the first stage of the experiment.

Regarding problem C1 – "There are features with little interest for the user", it was decided that it is a problem that can be covered by the heuristic "MH6: Focus" since it refers to the possibility of the user losing interest with the application therefore the focus to achieve/complete tasks is also lost. However, it seems important that the description of this heuristic refers to the fact that there should be no features that are not useful to the user.

For "MH8: Deal properly with the screen orientation", our suggestion is that it must be changed in order to include other important and interconnected aspects in the development of mobile applications. Part A of the experiment pointed out some aspects regarding the orientation of the device and the type of device (tablet/smartphone). Therefore, the operating system (for example Android or iOS) is an aspect to consider, since there are specific guidelines and different components specifically used in each of these systems. The type of device the application runs on (a smartphone or a tablet), which might be relevant due to the screen size of each device and the way it is used, is another aspect to consider. This heuristic should then be changed to "Deal properly with the operating system, device type and screen orientation".

Then, topic A5 – "Poor feedback when the application and the external equipment are communicating", problems C3 – "When the device is communicating with the external equipment, there is no constant information/feedback on what is happening" and C4 – "When the device is communicating with the external equipment, the messages of what is happening are not clear" reveal another major problem. It is the importance of a constant, clear and transparent communication between the two devices, something that is not foreseen/covered by any heuristic. In other words, during all the time that the application, server and external equipment are in communication, the user must clearly know what is happening both in the application and in the equipment. It is a very important feature to be considered as it will be able to prevent errors from various situations. Therefore, a new heuristic must be created in order to cover this peculiarity of the domain of mobile applications that interact with external equipment: "Constant, transparent and complementary communication with the external equipment".

Finally, the list of heuristics proposed after the activity "Discussion with specialists" and the analysis of the obtained results is the following: PHSD1[1]: Visibility of system status (Formerly N1); PHSD2: Match between system and the real world (Formerly N2); PHSD3: User control and freedom (Formerly N3); PHSD4: Consistency and standards (Formerly N4); PHSD5: Error prevention (Formerly N5); PHSD6: Recognition rather than recall (Formerly N6); PHSD7: Flexibility and efficiency of use (Formerly N7); PHSD8: Aesthetic and minimalist design (Formerly N8); PHSD9: Help users recognize, diagnose and recover from errors (Formerly N9); PHSD10: Help and documentation (Formerly N10); PHSD11: Pleasant and respectful interaction with the user (Formerly MH2); PHSD12: Privacy and Security (Formerly MH3, changed); PHSD13: Interruptions (Formerly MH4); PHSD14: Waiting times (Formerly MH5); PHSD15: Focus (Formerly MH6); PHSD16: Don't lie to the user (Formerly MH7); PHSD17: Deal properly with the operating system, device type and screen orientation (Formerly MH8, changed); PHSD18: Constant, transparent and complementary communication with the external equipment (new).

5 Conclusions and Future Work

In conclusion, we consider that heuristic evaluations can be extremely helpful in finding usability and UX flaws that interactive systems might have. One of the most commonly

---

[1] PHSD - Proposed Heuristic for Specific Domain.

used and well-known lists of heuristics is the one proposed by Nielsen, although many domain specific heuristics are being developed in order to have more suitable heuristics to find usability problems regarding certain characteristics that these systems have. This option has proven to be extremely profitable, and, in order to achieve these lists, some methodologies have been proposed. Since there was no list of heuristics specifically designed to evaluate the particular case of mobile applications that interact with external equipment, the methodology proposed by D. Quiñones et al. was carefully analysed and its "exploratory" and "experimental" stages were implemented in order to propose our own list. We've also proposed a new experiment as part of the "experimental stage", which consisted of a discussion of the selected applications, filling out a questionnaire about usability and UX attributes and a questionnaire about usability and UX problems of the chosen applications. In addition, after performing all these tasks, the limitations of the selected heuristics list in the exploratory stage of the methodology were discussed. The experiment provided a lot of important feedback on the selected applications and enabled us to propose a list of 18 more suitable heuristics to evaluate mobile applications that interact with external equipment. As future work, the implementation of the other stages of the applied methodology is intended to be executed in order to validate and refine, if necessary, the final list of heuristics for this specific domain.

References

1. Quiñones, D., Rusu, C.: How to develop usability heuristics: a systematic literature review. Comput. Stand. Interfaces **53**, 89–122 (2017). https://doi.org/10.1016/j.csi.2017.03.009
2. Quiñones, D., Rusu, C.: Applying a methodology to develop user eXperience heuristics. Comput. Stand. Interfaces. **66** (2019). https://doi.org/10.1016/j.csi.2019.04.004
3. Reis, P., Páris, C., Gomes, A.: Heuristics for mobile applications that interact with external equipment. In: EdMedia + Innovate Learning, pp. 501–506. Association for the Advancement of Computing in Education (AACE), Waynesville, NC, Coimbra, Portugal (2020)
4. Nielsen, J.: Enhancing the explanatory power of usability heuristics. In: Conference on Human Factors in Computing Systems - Proceedings (1994). https://doi.org/10.1145/259963.260333
5. Miranda, R.M.: Analysis of the usability of mobile device applications based upon heuristics (2014). https://doi.org/10.1017/CBO9781107415324.004
6. Gómez, R.Y., Caballero, D.C., Sevillano, J.L.: Heuristic evaluation on mobile interfaces: a new checklist. Sci. World J. **2014** (2014). https://doi.org/10.1155/2014/434326
7. Nielsen, J.: Usability 101: introduction to usability. All Usability (2012)
8. Alturki, R., Gay, V.: Usability attributes for mobile applications: a systematic review. In: Jan, M.A., Khan, F., Alam, M. (eds.) Recent Trends and Advances in Wireless and IoT-enabled Networks. EICC, pp. 53–62. Springer, Cham (2019). https://doi.org/10.1007/978-3-319-999 66-1_5
9. Morville, P.: User experience honeycomb. Semant. Stud. (2004). http://semanticstudios.com/user_experience_design/. Accessed 31 July 2020
10. Kirakowski, J., Corbett, M.: SUMI: the software usability measurement inventory. Br. J. Educ. Technol. **24**, 210–212 (1993). https://doi.org/10.1111/j.1467-8535.1993.tb00076.x

Autonomous Driving: Obtaining Direction Commands by Classifying Images Within a Simulation Platform

Mario Iván Oliva de la Torre[1]([✉]) [iD], Huizilopoztli Luna-García[1] [iD],
José M. Celaya-Padilla[2] [iD], Hamurabi Gamboa-Rosales[1] [iD], Wilson J. Sarmiento[3] [iD],
and Cesar A. Collazos[4] [iD]

[1] Centro de Investigación e Innovación Automotriz de México (CIIAM), Universidad
Autónoma de Zacatecas, Jardín Juárez 147, Centro, 98000 Zacatecas, Zac., Mexico
marioivan.delatorre.94@gmail.com, {hlugar,hamurabigr}@uaz.edu.mx
[2] CONACYT, Universidad Autónoma de Zacatecas, Jardín Juárez 147, Centro,
98000 Zacatecas, Zac., Mexico
jose.celaya@uaz.edu.mx
[3] Grupo de Investigación en Multimedia – GIM – Universidad Militar Nueva
Granada, Bogotá D.C., Colombia
wilson.sarmiento@unimilitar.edu.co
[4] Grupo de Investigación y Desarrollo en Ingeniería de Software (IDIS), Universidad del Cauca,
Calle 5 N° 4-70, Popayán, Colombia
ccollazo@unicauca.edu.co

Abstract. The Mexican Robotics Tournament "Torneo Mexicano de Robotica
(MRT)" holds an international tournament of autonomous driving with open
source/hardware vehicles with a scale of 1:10, said vehicles must complete several by their self, using several machine learning algorithms. With the purpose of
improving the results in the autonomous car contest a novel driving simulation
platform was developed. For this, the Udacity driving simulator which is built in
Unity software was used. First, a virtual track was elaborated according to the
measures established by the MRT specifications, then, a 1:1 replica of the MRT-
vehicle was used to simulate the collection of 420 images, then, in order to validate
the proposal, a neural network was developed to classify the images captured by
the virtual camera placed in the vehicle of the simulation platform. These images
were classified into three categories according to the actions of the vehicle must
perform (turn left, right and move forward). The results were satisfactory, obtaining 79% of accuracy and a recall value of 0.93, offering a standalone platform for
the training of the vehicle.

Keywords: Autonomous driving · Simulation · Supervised learning · Neural
networks

1 Introduction

The Mexican Robotics Tournament (MRT) is a robotics competition that takes place
year after year in Mexico, and brings together students, professors and researchers. Its

© Springer Nature Switzerland AG 2020
V. Agredo-Delgado et al. (Eds.): HCI-COLLAB 2020, CCIS 1334, pp. 30–41, 2020.
https://doi.org/10.1007/978-3-030-66919-5_4

main objective is to promote research and development of robotics in the country with the purpose of achieving integral development at an international level. For this, different categories of competition are included where the participating teams put their knowledge and skills in robotics to the test.

In 2019, for the second time in the history of the MRT, the category of scale autonomous cars was opened, where different challenges or autonomous driving missions are proposed to be executed by an AutoModelCar. AutoModelCar vehicles are unmanned 1:10 scale automobiles whose objective is to promote the development of algorithms for perception, planning and autonomous driving in controlled environments [1]. The autonomous driving tests are performed on a rolling surface made with a black plastic material whose dimensions are 8 meters high and 12 meters wide. An example of a circuit is shown in Fig. 1, with specifications for lane widths, external and internal radii of the curves.

Currently, there is no single one simulation platform that has an environment with the necessary measures to perform driving tests through integration with different learning algorithms for autonomous driving. Most of the simulation platforms have been equipped with environments inspired by the urban landscape, as is the case with Carla [2], or racing circuits, such as TORCS [3].

For this reason, in order to obtain better results in the autonomous driving category of the MRT, it is intended to develop a simulation environment using the specifications by the MRT. For this, some elements and source code of the simulation platform developed

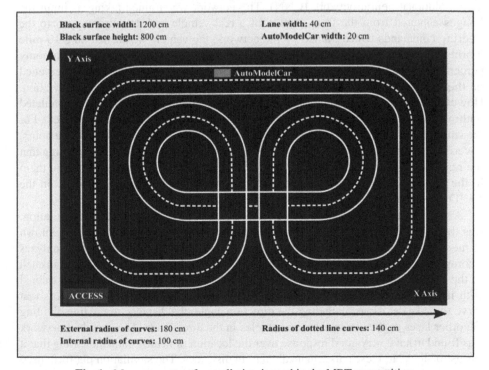

Fig. 1. Measurements of a small circuit used in the MRT competition.

by Udacity will be taken as a basis. Said platform has been built in Unity, and consists of a vehicle with three embedded cameras to capture images (one on the left, one on the right, and one on the front), however, only the front camera is used to simulate the characteristics of the AutoModelCar. Once the images were obtained, it is necessary to classify them into three different categories according to the basic actions that the vehicle is capable of carrying out (turn left or right, and continue moving forward), for this, a deep neural network was implemented and trained, which is described in Sect. 4.

2 Related Works

One of the oldest researches works in the area of autonomous driving was developed in 1989 at Carnegie Mellon University, where an autonomous driving test vehicle called Navlab was used. The development consisted in the implementation of a shallow neural network called ALVINN (Autonomous Land Vehicle in a Neural Network), which works as a classification model that takes as input small images of 30 pixels wide and 32 pixels high (all them captured by the vehicle's camera), while the output is divided into 45 different categories, each one of them is associated with an angle of the vehicle's steering. The vehicle was able to drive accurately over 400 meters at a speed of a half meter per second [4]. Despite being a very simple job, it showed that supervised learning methods such as neural networks are useful when classifying images taken from the road and performing an action according to that classification.

More recently, in 2016, NVIDIA developed an autonomous driving system using a convolutional neural network (CNN). The network was trained taking as input the images captured from the front camera of a real vehicle and directly mapped to the steering commands. Once trained by the network, the vehicle was tested on a 10-mile journey in Monmouth County, in the state of New Jersey, achieving a 98% autonomy percentage, which was calculated based on the number of times that a user intervened on the steering wheel to reposition the vehicle within the lane in case of a deviation. However, before evaluating the vehicle on the road, the neural network was evaluated within a simulation platform using the same images captured in the real environment. For the simulation, a circuit from the same county was developed and tested for three hours, covering a 100-mile route and achieving 90% autonomy [5]. It is worth mentioning that the result obtained in the simulation tests was very important before performing them in the real circuit. Figure 2 shows a block diagram where the testing process on the NVIDIA simulation platform is briefly described.

Another example of training using real photographs to later be tested in simulation, was the work developed at Princeton University in 2015 [6]. Here the paradigm known as mediated perception was adopted. Under this approach, the neural network analyzes a complete image to make a decision based on the distance to the vehicles ahead in each of the lanes of the road. The neural network, which was called ConvNet, was trained with images from the KITTI dataset [7], while the output provides 13 indicators that serve to make decisions, including the direction angle, the distance to the line dividing the other lanes or the distance to the vehicles in the three lanes. The ConvNet network was found to have very good response over the location of nearby cars, indicating that it learns to "look" at these cars when calculating distances. The simulation platform used in this work was TORCS.

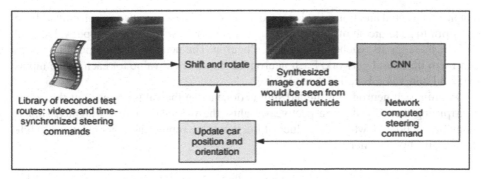

Fig. 2. Block diagram illustrating the NVIDIA simulation testing process.

In 2017, Valeo, a company that offers systems and equipment for the reduction of CO_2 emissions based in Paris, proposed a framework that in addition to including CNN also incorporates Recurrent Neural Networks (RNN) and Deep Q Networks (DQN). The framework was tested using the TORCS simulation environment [8]. The proposed framework consists of a series of tasks divided into three categories:

1. **Recognition:** Identifying components of the surrounding environment using Convolutional Neural Networks.
2. **Prediction:** It consists of building internal models capable of predicting the future states of the environment. Recurrent neural networks are used in this step.
3. **Planning:** An efficient model that incorporates recognition and prediction will be generated to plan the future sequence of actions that will allow the vehicle to be driven successfully. This step uses Reinforcement Learning and Deep Q Networks.

The results showed successful lane keeping functionality, while at the same time limiting speed when any vehicle is in front. As can be seen, the framework was fully developed on a simulation platform and neural networks were used in each of the steps.

As mentioned in the previous section, there is currently no simulation platform that incorporates a track with the characteristics described by the MRT, therefore, if the results are to be improved, the development of a virtual environment with these characteristics is vitally important.

3 Materials and Methods

In order to have an approach to the development of an autonomous driving algorithm, an artificial neural network was implemented to classify images obtained by the virtual camera of a vehicle within a driving simulation environment. The Udacity simulation platform, which is open source, was used as a basis for the creation of the track with the measures described by the MRT. This driving platform has been developed in Unity and provides the necessary components for capturing images by simulating three front cameras, of which only the central one was used.

Artificial neural network. Artificial neural networks are a model inspired by the function of the human brain. It is conformed by a set of nodes known as artificial neurons that are connected and transmit signals to each other. These signals are transmitted from the input to generate an output value. The networks receive a series of input values and each of these inputs reaches a node called neuron. The neurons are grouped into layers that form the neural network. Each neuron has a numerical value for each of the inputs received, this value is called "weight" [9].

Within each neuron, a weighted sum is done using the values of each of the inputs multiplying them by their respective weights, the formula for this weighted sum is described in Eq. (1), where the values of the inputs are represented by the letter x, while the weights by the letter w.

$$\sigma = w_1 x_1 + w_2 x_2 + w_3 x_3 + \ldots + w_n x_n \tag{1}$$

Once the weighted sum has been calculated, the resulting value is sent as a parameter to a mathematical function known as the activation function, which normalizes the value of the weighted for placing it in a range between 1 and 0, or between -1 and 1, depending on the function used [10]. For this particular case, the sigmoid function was used, because the output value is between 1 and 0, which is ideal for obtaining classification values. The sigmoid function is described in Eq. (2). In Fig. 3, a graphical representation of a neuron is shown where the input values are described with letters x, and the output value of the neuron with the letter y.

$$f(\sigma) = 1 / (1 + e^{-\sigma}) \tag{2}$$

The process is repeated in each neuron of the network. As mentioned above, neurons are grouped in different layers. The initial layer is called the input layer and the final layer is known as the output layer. The layers located between the input layer and the output layer are called hidden layers. The output values calculated in the all of the neurons of a layer conform a set of input values for each of the neurons in the next layer. Figure 4 shows a graphical representation of a neural network, where each neuron is represented by a circular node, and each vertical grouping of neurons represents a layer. The fit of the weights is done using the backpropagation algorithm, optimizing the mean square error function.

Confusion Matrix. For the network evaluation in the testing phase, a confusion matrix was used, which is a table with different combinations of classified and actual values. It works as a performance measurement for machine learning classification problem where output can be two or more classes. The confusion matrix contrasts the elements that were labeled in a category by the classification model (the network), with those elements that actually belong to the category. It is useful for measuring Accuracy, Precision, Recall and Specificity [11], measures thar are described below along with their respective formulas in the Eqs. (3), (4), (5) and (6):

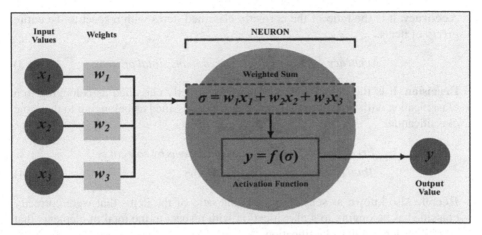

Fig. 3. Graphical representation of a neuron.

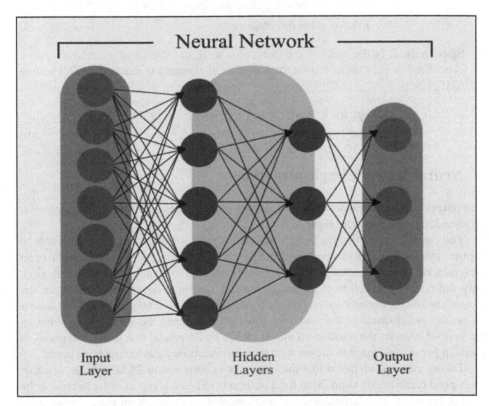

Fig. 4. Graphical representation of an Artificial Neural Network

1. **Accuracy.** It is the ratio of the correctly classified items with respect to the entire group of items.

$$Accuracy = Correctly\ classified\ items/Total\ of\ items \qquad (3)$$

2. **Precision.** It is the ratio of items that were correctly classified as belonging to a classification with respect to all items that were classified as belonging to the same classification.

$$Precision = Correctly\ classified\ items\ by\ category/$$
$$Total\ of\ classified\ items\ by\ category \qquad (4)$$

3. **Recall.** Also known as sensibility, it is the ratio of the items that were correctly classified as belonging to a classification with respect to the total of elements that actually belong to that classification.

$$Recall = Correctly\ classified\ items\ by\ category/$$
$$Total\ of\ items\ by\ category \qquad (5)$$

4. **Specificity.** It is the ratio of the items that were not classified as belonging to a classification with respect to the total number of elements that actually don't belong to it [12].

$$Specificity = Items\ classified\ correctly\ out\ of\ category/$$
$$Total\ of\ items\ actually\ out\ of\ category \qquad (6)$$

4 Neural Network Implementation

The purpose of the neural network is to classify input images into three different classes: go ahead, turn left, and turn right.

The central camera that the vehicle has within the simulation environment is able to capture images of 320 pixels wide and 160 pixels high. Figure 5 shows an example of an image captured by the central vehicle camera. However, for the network implementation, only the pixels of a section of the image are taken as input data for the first layer, the area of interest for classification is only a section comprised of 80 pixels high, because it shows the visualization of the road, therefore, when cropping the initial image to obtain the area of interest, the result is an image of 320 by 80 pixels, that is, 25,600 pixels in total. In Fig. 6, the image is shown with the aforementioned cut having been made.

Taking into consideration that the images are composed of 25,600 pixels, and that each pixel corresponds to an input for a neuron in the first layer, in order to reduce the load of the input, an interpolation was implemented by means of an extraction of rows and columns in order to further reduce the number of pixels. In the end, only the rows and columns that were multiples of 5 were taken. So, the input images were reduce to a size of 64 by 16 pixels (1024 pixels in total), as shown in the example in Fig. 7.

Based on previous experiences, a neural network architecture with two hidden layers was selected, containing 3 and 5 neurons respectively. The input layer consists of 1024

Fig. 5. Image captured with the vehicle's central camera.

Fig. 6. Cropped image containing the area of interest.

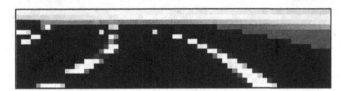

Fig. 7. Rows and columns extracted from the cropped image.

neurons that correspond to each pixel of the image, while the output layer consists of three neurons, which each correspond to the classification of the image (turn left, keep moving forward and turn right).

In color images, each pixel contains three numerical values (red, green and blue), therefore, once the image is reduced, it is also necessary to convert it to grayscale, so it would be only one numerical value per pixel, and it would be the input for each of the neurons in the first layer.

The final output of the network is a set of three different numerical values located in the range between 0 and 1, each of these values is associated with one of the classifications. The image will be classified according to the output that has the greatest value, if the straight value is greater than the other two, then the image is classified as an indicator to continue advancing without needing to turn to either side.

The diagram in Fig. 8 shows the entire classification process performed by the neural network.

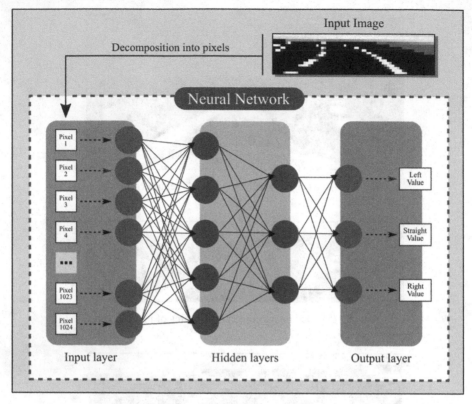

Fig. 8. Neural network implementation

5　Network Evaluation

For image capturing, a 4-lap tour was performed within the simulation environment. From the images obtained, 420 images were used for the training process, 140 from each category, while in the testing process, 60 images from each category, that is 180. Of those 180, 79% of them were classified correctly, that is, 143 images out of 180 were classified as what they really are. That is a good percentage of accuracy for a classification model and is an indication that the neural network is working correctly. Figure 9, 10 and 11 show three examples of images from each category and each one of them has a green arrow according to the classification made by the network.

Once the images were classified, the confusion matrix was elaborated, which is shown in Fig. 12. It shows in color blue the amounts of images classified correctly according to each category, while those classified incorrectly are displayed in cyan. For example, in the first column of the first row, a value of 56 is shown in color blue, which indicates that 56 images out of 60 were correctly classified as indicators of turning to the left, while the third column of the same row shows a value of 1 in color cyan color, because one image was incorrectly classified as indicative of turning to the right when in fact the image indicates a turning to the left. The bottom green line indicates the total number of images that were classified in each category.

Also, the precision, recall and specificity values for each category were calculated using formulas (4), (5) and (6) respectively, all of them described in Sect. 3, while the

Fig. 9. Image classified as a turn left command indicator.

Fig. 10. Image classified as a move forward command indicator.

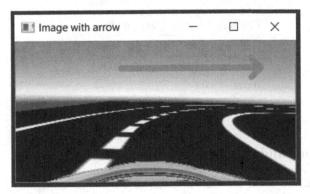

Fig. 11. Image classified as a turn right command indicator.

accuracy of the all the classification model was calculated using formula (3). Table 1 shows the precision, sensitivity and recall values calculated for each category.

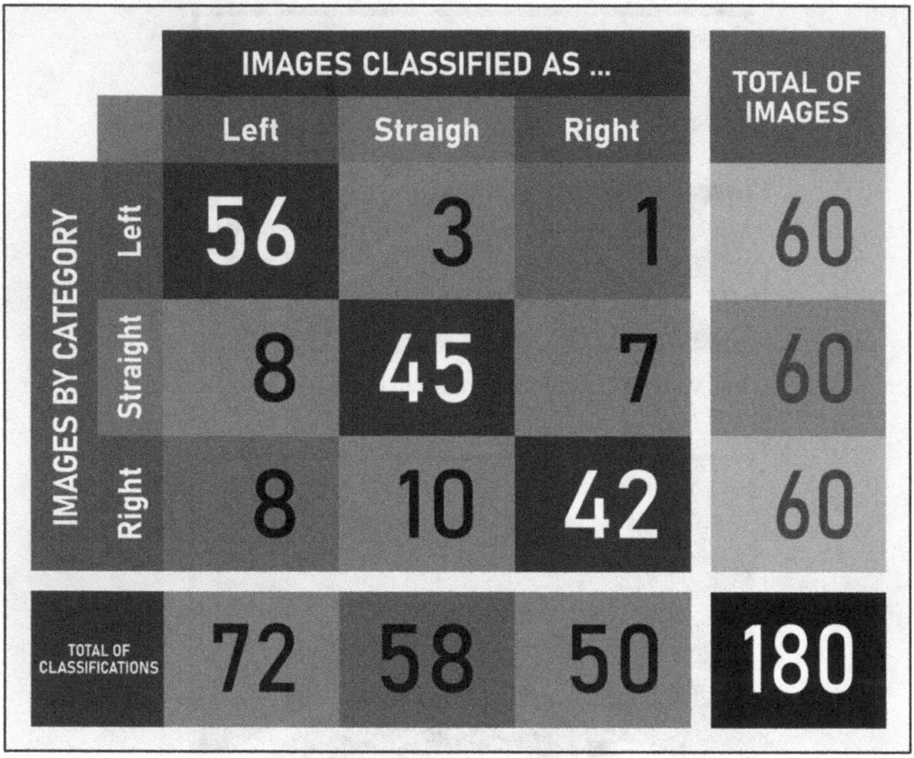

Fig. 12. Confusion matrix.

Table 1. Precision, recall and specificity values calculated for each category.

Category	Precision	Recall	Specificity
Left	0.77	0.93	0.8
Straight	0.77	0.75	0.8
Right	0.84	0.7	0.77

6 Conclusions and Future Works

The proposed development was able to generate the images needed by the algorithms of the autonomous vehicle AutoModelCar, said images were then used by the proposed neuronal network to train and test the performance of the simulator. The obtained performance was satisfactory and indicates that the training data can be done using small amount of data. The accuracy value of 79% and the precision values, whose are around 80%, indicate that almost only 2 images out of 10 are incorrectly classified, which may not generate major problems when driving because the vehicle would quickly rejoin the road in case of deviation. Also, the Udacity platform provides a way to get better results in TMR, in contrast to other platforms that are not flexible when integrating new circuits. In addition, that flexibility opens the door for new research work in autonomous driving.

Once a simple classification model has been tested on the simulation platform, it is intended to make a connection under a Client-Server architecture with the vehicle's interface in order to manipulate its actions. By having the possibility of accessing the vehicle's commands from an external application, it will be possible to implement more machine learning algorithms in the autonomous driving area. For example, reinforcement learning algorithms and convolutional neural networks.

References

1. Negrete, M., Morales, A., Sossa, H., Castelán, M., Morales, M.: Reglamento del Torneo Mexicano de Robótica 2019. Rulebook presented at the Mexican Robotics Tournament 2019 - Categoría: AutoModelCar, CDMX, México (2019). https://www.femexrobotica.org/tmr2019/wp-content/uploads/2019/03/AutoModelCarRulebook.pdf
2. Dosovitskiy, A., Ros, G., Codevilla, F., Lopez, A. Koltun, V.: CARLA: an open urban driving simulator. In: Proceedings of the 1st Annual Conference on Robot Learning, in PMLR, vol. 78, pp. 1–16 (2017). http://proceedings.mlr.press/v78/dosovitskiy17a/dosovitskiy17a.pdf
3. Wymann, B., Espi´e, E., Guionneau, C., Dimitrakakis, C., Coulom, R., Sumner, A.: TORCS, the open racing car simulator, v1.3.5 (2013). http://www.torcs.org
4. Pomerleau, D.: Alvinn, an autonomous land vehicle in a neural network. Technical report, Carnegie Mellon University, Computer Science Department (1989). https://papers.nips.cc/paper/95-alvinn-an-autonomous-land-vehicle-in-a-neural-network.pdf
5. Bojarski, M., et al.: End to end learning for self-driving cars. Cornell University (2016). https://arxiv.org/pdf/1604.07316.pdf
6. Chen, C., Seff, A., Kornhauser, A., Xiao, J.: DeepDriving: learning affordance for direct perception in autonomous driving. In: 2015 IEEE International Conference on Computer Vision (ICCV), pp. 2722–2730 (2015). https://doi.org/10.1109/iccv.2015.312
7. Geiger, A., Lenz, P., Stiller, C., Urtasun, R.: Vision meets robotics: the kitti dataset. Int. J. Robot. Res. (2013). http://www.cvlibs.net/datasets/kitti/
8. Sallab, A., Abdou, M., Perot, E., Yogamani, S.: Deep reinforcement learning framework for autonomous driving. Electron. Imaging **2017**(19), 70–76 (2017). https://doi.org/10.2352/issn. 2470-1173.2017.19.avm-023
9. Qué son las redes neuronales y sus funciones. (2019). https://www.atriainnovation.com/que-son-las-redes-neuronales-y-sus-funciones/. Accessed 10 June 2020
10. 7 Types of Activation Functions in Neural Networks: How to Choose? (2020). MissingLink.Ai. https://missinglink.ai/guides/neural-network-concepts/7-types-neural-network-activation-functions-right/
11. Narkhede, S.: Understanding confusion matrix. Towards Data Science (2019). https://towardsdatascience.com/understanding-confusion-matrix-a9ad42dcfd62
12. Ghoneim, S.: Accuracy, recall, precision, f-score & specificity, which to optimize on? Towards data science (2019). https://towardsdatascience.com/accuracy-recall-precision-f-score-specificity-which-to-optimize-on-867d3f11124

Breaking the Gap: Collaborative Environment as a Meeting Point to Provide and Receive Help to Overcome the Digital Gap

David E. Santos Covarrubias[1]([⊠]) [iD], Graciela Karina Galache Meléndez[1] [iD],
Jorge Alberto Martínez Cerón[1] [iD], Sony Solano Cristóbal[1] [iD],
and Rocío Abascal-Mena[2] [iD]

[1] Master in Design, Information and Communication (MADIC), Universidad Autónoma
Metropolitana, Unidad Cuajimalpa Avenida Vasco de Quiroga 4871, Colonia Santa
Fe Cuajimalpa, Del. Cuajimalpa de Morelos, Distrito Federal, C.P. 05300 Mexico City, Mexico
surikatofic@hotmail.com, karina.galache@gmail.com,
neuroalbertounam@gmail.com, scs.pedagogia@gmail.com
[2] Department of Information Technologies, Universidad Autónoma Metropolitana, Unidad
Cuajimalpa Avenida Vasco de Quiroga 4871, Colonia Santa Fe Cuajimalpa, Del. Cuajimalpa
de Morelos, Distrito Federal, C.P. 05300 Mexico City, Mexico
mabascal@cua.uam.mx

Abstract. As a result of the COVID-19 the teaching staff has been required to use
technological tools that allow them to follow their activities under confinement.
Teachers have highlighted the problem of the digital gap, updating and inequality
that they suffer in Mexico as one of the historical problems to be addressed in this
sector. This paper presents a platform designed to work as a meeting point between
teachers with the digital gap and people willing to help them. The process was
based on the User Centered Design approach in order to find a relevant solution.

Keywords: User centered design · Digital gap · Teacher · Education · Usability ·
COVID-19

1 Introduction

The global context is going through one of the most devastating historical events of
this century. From the outbreak of the SARS-CoV-2 virus and the COVID-19 disease
in Mexico, as in other countries around the world, the state of alert and confinement
was declared. This has affected most of the social and productive sectors of the population. The pandemic isn't yet over and, without a doubt, there will be repercussions in
practically all the areas of daily life.

Due to official regulations, the formal education sector had the urgent need to solve
and formulate emerging and improvised strategies for the implementation of education
from home using the available Information and Communication Technologies (ICT).
In this entrustment, the collaboration of the entire school community has been deci-
sive because, in addition to covering specific tasks to the school environment, teachers,

V. Agredo-Delgado et al. (Eds.): HCI-COLLAB 2020, CCIS 1334, pp. 42–51, 2020.
https://doi.org/10.1007/978-3-030-66919-5_5

students and parents have had to face daily life in an environment of uncertainty and affected mental health. Now, classroom practices move to digital and private spaces, and that is strongly questioned for the needed and rapid adaptation to new technological dynamics.

In this sense, breaking the digital divide in teachers is one of the most difficult tasks to be filled. The uncertainty in the use of technological tools, the constant updating of them, together with the little time available to learn them, prevents the adequate and pertinent educational domain to allow teaching and learning experiences. According to Sanchez [1] the types of problems range from logistical, technological, pedagogical and socio-affective ones that affect circumstances related to emotional, affective and health aspects that impact teachers, such as feelings of sadness, frustration, anxiety, fatigue, among others.

The objective of this project is to present a digital environment that serves as a meeting point and accompaniment space for teachers. This space aspires to support in overcoming the digital divide, connecting people who need help to solve specific doubts with people willing to help, who are easy and familiar with the diversity of technological tools. In addition, it will store different possibilities of presenting meaningful information for the solution of doubts such as tutorials and articles generated by the same community.

The rest of the paper is divided into four parts. The first presents the general concept of the digital divide, as well as the current situation in Mexico regarding teachers who suffer from it; it also shows the state of the art of similar proposals. The second part explains the methodology followed by the teamwork to design a digital environment that serves as a meeting point for people to be able to offer and receive help; on the other hand, the functions, operation and a test of its parts are exposed. The third part shows the final prototype as a result. Finally, the last part reveals the conclusions reached in the design process and the further work.

2   Conceptual Theoretical Framework

The *"knowledge divide"* is a concept that historically had hinted at a separation between people and knowledge mainly due to economics and geographic factors. Nowadays, is important to emphasize the relevance that technology has over information access and therefore to knowledge [2]. The separation of knowledge is closely linked to digital skills, as they say: *"Now, the conception of digital fracture values the necessities of digital knowledge and skills, not only access. To this effective access, it is adequate to add the capacity to manage big amounts of information to convert into knowledge. All of this, in many cases, is directly linked to a generational issue"* [2].

On the other hand, other authors such as George Sciadas [3] mention that exists a gap between ICT. This involves many variables that regularly are not considered as income, education, age and geographic area. In the last decades, it has been used the term "digital divide" to refer to the "knowledge divide" that exists in the digital information area. This reflects the inequality that existed in information access, and today has been coined by everyone and reflects a social phenomenon that emerges with the growth of the digitization of information.

We are in an era in which it has become essential to know how the technology works to move freely across the information. However, not all people possess the ability to face this reality. In a world where digital information predominates, a new type of literacy becomes relevant to these people, as Selfe indicates: *"Today the definition of literacy has expanded from traditional notions of reading and writing to include the ability to learn comprehended, and interact with technology in a meaningful way"* [4].

2.1   Digital Gap in Mexico

The sectors that face the digital divide are diverse and involve multiple factors. However, one of the sectors where the problem is most evident is in education. This affects different actors such as students, teachers and parents. Evangeline Pianfetti [5] emphasize the importance that the teachers have when facing digital divide, not only to do their job but also to empower students with digital skills and knowledge *"Teachers need to be digitally literate so that they can empower students with the skills and knowledge that they can need to be successful in a workplace dominated by technology"*.

Especially in Mexico, the transition to the digital world has not been an easy task for teachers, because of the economic and social reality that currently exists. On the other hand, the gap can also occur due to generational gaps or simply disinterestedness in technologies.

In the face of the COVID-19 pandemic, many teachers in digital gap situations were forced to use technologies to teach from home. As is evident, many of them have failed to adapt to these new concepts. In the following research, we give the task of approaching a group of teachers with a certain level of digital gap to understand their behaviors and motivations when facing technologies to teach from a distance. And then, we present a Human-Centered Design approach, composed of several steps, that we have followed in order to propose a solution that seeks to reduce, even partially, the gap.

2.2   State of the Art

In the state of the art, we can find different ways of approaching the problem of the digital gap. There are programs that seek to train and instruct people with a digital gap in the use of computers and devices, suPEOch as the Vasconcelos digital literacy program[1] in Veracruz, to bring technologies closer to vulnerable communities. Despite considering not only the material resource but also technological training, these attempts have a local scope.

Also, there are projects that seek to take advantage of ICTs to reduce the gap with a broader scope, such as the app "Mint". These have the problem that not all people can access this form of digitization, so they focus on attacking the gap for lack of knowledge. Focusing in this last example, as the BUAP site posted in its page, this app is an application created by the students of the BUAP Faculty of Computer Science, in collaboration with students from Mexico City, to support primary education teachers, to help reduce the digital gap in schools [6]. With this application, teachers will share with their students the interactive classes they have created.

Unlike the existing projects, the one exposed in this document proposes to generate a community of accompaniment and collaborative support, accessible to teachers with

---

[1] *Vasconcelos digital literacy program*: https://www.sev.gob.mx/programa-vasconcelos/.

digital gap. The objective is to build a multidirectional platform that democratizes the knowledge of technology for educational purposes and in accordance with an open repository with *on purpose* information. The above, within a space that values and respects the knowledge of the community itself and serves as a meeting point to connect with people willing to provide help in real time and optimize search times and problem solving, from a focus of flexible and lifelong learning.

3 Development Process

The project was started from the focus of inclusion in the Human-Computer Interaction, an interdisciplinary area that carries out a recursive process of design, analysis, implementation and evaluation aimed at generating usable and easy to manipulate products, which allows the end-user to focus and perform a task in the best way. To do this, User-Centered Design (UCD) was a key perspective for the design of the interactive system prototype, where experience and satisfaction are the foundation in the process.

The stages to follow were: the definition of the problem through remote interviews, construction of people or archetypes of the main users, the establishment of points of view and inspiration board, construction and testing the prototype, evaluation and final prototype.

3.1 Definition of the Problem

Observations, interviews and evidence collection were carried out remotely to three groups of possible users who are part of the school community affected by forced confinement and the digital gap: students, parents and teachers. Each group was made up of members of different ages, economic situations, and locations within Mexico City and the Metropolitan Area. After these observations, the work team decided to focus on teachers as potential users, because they integrated several of the problems found in the three groups and are main actors in teaching and learning, being the point of support between parents and students.

The group of teachers shared that, as parents, they are forced to divide their time and space to solve family, work and school stuff for their own children. However, the worrying thing for they were the excessive time and effort they invested in learning to use technologies to communicate with their superiors, peers, parents and students. In addition, the educational institutions which they belong, didn't send them clear instructions about how they should carry out the transition of the different activities to the virtual environment, so the process has been arduous, demanding and based on trial and error. Teachers may be updated in their respective areas of knowledge, but many times they are disconnected from the digital world that they could use to share their teachings. Not being able to carry out their work makes them feel frustrated, guilty and inefficient, therefore they would like to have support and accompaniment to efficiently manage conflicts, uncertainty and resolve doubts for the appropriation of digital media. The digital gap in this group, and the conditions to carry out its work, become an urgent problem to solve, with specific characteristics that led to the next stages of the project.

3.2 Personas

As Alan Cooper [7] indicates, a *persona* is a prototypical representation of asset of users with similar motivations and behaviors. It represents an archetype modeled from the investigation of real users and synthesized in a user prototype.

In order to attend the different motivations and needs of potential users that were discovered throughout the research, the *persona* methodology was used. From an in-depth investigation and analysis of the different profiles, three *personas* were created that characterize the main profiles of teachers with a digital gap.

- The first one, named *Juan*, represents teachers with a digital gap because of a relative lack of interest in technology. This type of teacher prefers *face-to-face* contact to teach; however, the pandemic forced him to get closer to the technological tools. It's frustrating to him that technology is becoming increasingly important to everyday and professional life.
- The second one, named *Marisol*, is the representation of the teacher who presents a digital gap due to a limited economic situation and poor access to digital resources. Despite wanting to update herself, she doesn't have the time or the resources to do it, so she has lagged behind in the use of technology to teach in the best way.
- The third one, named *Federico*, is the prototype of a teacher who suffers from the digital gap due to advanced age. Despite being an experienced teacher, he is not a frequent user of digital technology, so he has faced various complications to teach his subjects in a *non-face-to-face* mode. Despite trying, he cannot adapt to digital systems, so he constantly requires counseling.

Once the personas were defined, each member of the work team made a storyboard with the main need observed. This visualization was carried out individually and in isolation to identify the patterns of understanding the motivations and needs when compared.

3.3 Viewpoint and Inspiration Board

The *storyboards* were shared and compared within the work team and each of the represented needs was analyzed. The main observations were:

1. The teacher seeks help with close people, but many times he doesn't find someone available and he doesn't know how to solve the problems by himself, so he feels alone and unmotivated;
2. Teachers are curious and willing to learn technologies but they don't know where to look and find timely support to answer their questions.

Once the analysis of the perspectives observed by each member was carried out, it was agreed that the general point of view for this project would be "Overcoming the digital gap is based on an environment of comprehensive support". In addition to *storyboards*, important support in the process of this research was the creation of an inspiration board, that helped to concentrate on existing ideas of possible solutions and to know the state of the art (see Fig. 1). The search for resources was made through the web that concentrates applications, services, artifacts and products on the market.

Fig. 1. Inspiration board with related work.

3.4 Pretotype

Alberto Savoia proposes this stage for "make sure you are building the right it before you build *it* right" [8]. The work team decided to use the "false door" technique, which is to offer a product or service that doesn't yet exist to users, in order to easily identify the level of interest before prototyping. The implementation consisted in publishing on Facebook pages and groups dedicated to teachers, these included a poster with the invitation to become part of a community that helps other teachers to overcome the digital gap in the days of COVID-19 and a *call to action* to enter in a landing page with project descriptions. This sought to measure two different levels of interaction: the first with impressions on Facebook and the second with income and interaction with the site.

The scope of the technique was high; however, more interaction was expected from people, which led to the conclusion that the announcement was presented in a reserved manner because it didn't present more false information that caught the attention of potential users. However, at this stage, a new user appeared who wasn't initially contemplated: the ordinary citizen with technological skills who wants to collaborate supporting teachers for altruism. This showed that there is a genuine interest in people to want to help.

From these findings, the work team began to outline the elements of the prototype design, respecting the original idea of addressing teachers with a digital gap, but also considering users willing to help. What was initially interpreted as a low response, became an area of opportunity to strengthen the idea of simplicity in access, interface and use of an effective tool.

3.5 Wireframe

To develop the wireframe, the work team focused on the need to have a support and accompaniment environment that serves as a meeting point between people who want to give or receive help to overcome the digital gap. Therefore, to start, two main categories of users were carried out: one for those who receive help and the other for those who have the possibility of giving it. The Fig. 2. shows the main screen for the two types of users "I need help" and "I want to help".

In the research, it was discovered that one of the tools that people with a little approach to digital technology use minimally was WhatsApp, so the prototype was thought of with references to its structures and dynamics. Above all, ease of use was considered, based on simple dynamics, intuitive forms and familiar metaphors. In addition to the possibility of connecting teachers with other people to receive help in real-time, an alternative way of solving doubts was planned, based on content that does not involve direct connection with another user. This is because, according to the results of the interviews, some teachers feel more comfortable solving their questions directly with content but aren't sure where to look. In this situation, the possibility of storing and having a repository of specialized articles and videos was integrated into the prototype so that the teacher requesting help has the possibility of choosing what suits him or her best, according to his needs and disposition. Because the prototype focused primarily on teachers with a digital gap, the "resolve a question" section was fully developed, while the "I want to help" section was partially constructed. At the end of the wireframe construction, the first version was evaluated and faults and possible improvements in the interaction were identified.

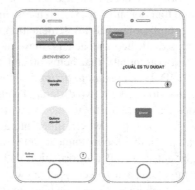

Fig. 2. Firsts screens for the wireframe.

3.6 Evaluation

At this stage, the instructions were designed for testing six voluntary users, in a remotely way, all of them teachers of universities, to carry out three tasks and, based on the observation of their interaction with the first version of the prototype, the necessary adjustments were made. For the above, the ten heuristic proposals of Jakob Nielsen [9] were reviewed as minimum aspects that a digital prototype should have. The main screens used in the evaluation are shown in Fig. 3.

In order or importance, the main problems that the six users showed were: confusion in completing a task, returning to a specific section, having to evaluate an advisor, exploring all the possibilities of the interface, distinguishing between the different information resources, having the opportunity to rectify their decisions during registration and that some iconographic elements weren't entirely clear.

Fig. 3. Main screens used in the evaluation.

On the screen to contact advisors and receive help, teachers did not know if the users were people looking for information or others with questions. Furthermore, there was a confusion between the videos and the posts due to the absence of graphic identifiers. Another one of the doubts, on the part of the users, was the location of the help button, which was located in the three points on the upper right side. This was resolved by changing the points to the question mark.

The above showed the need to reinforce heuristics such as: showing the status of the system at all times, using familiar metaphors and language, preventing errors, providing control and freedom, making it possible to recognize, diagnose and recover from errors, have an esthetic and minimalist design, having help at all times, consistency, control and freedom in the system. All these needs are materialized in the final prototype stage.

4   Final Prototype

After detecting the interaction problems in the wireframe, the final prototype was developed, taking as reference the ten heuristic proposals of Jakob Nielsen, correcting the errors and refining the graphic identity. Assessments were also made during refinement to ensure interaction was adequate. It should be noted in the final observations, the users who interacted with the latest version had a better experience of use and understanding thanks to the modification in the language and reinforcement of the graphic composition.

The Fig. 4 shows the latest version of the prototype which was remotely evaluated with six new volunteer teachers. In this test, it was found that new users were using the prototype more fluently, due to errors being corrected.

On the other hand, aspects that were initially considered key to the prototype were recovered, such as reinforcing the idea of having different communication channels, the possibility of gamification dynamics, offering security and support in the formation of the collaborative network built from the healthy interaction of the different user profiles.

5   Conclusions

In this work, we presented a significant approach to the attention of the digital gap in Mexico from the DCU methodological approach. At different moments of the research,

Fig. 4. Final prototype, usability errors were corrected and a graphic image is consistent with what users needed.

new problems and users emerged to be considered within the framework of the IHC, which reveals a broad interdisciplinary field of action from an inclusive and participatory social approach.

Designing systems and prototypes for people in contexts of uncertainty opens the possibility for innovation and to rethink the ways of integrating digital collaboration networks that provide support and accompaniment in overcoming problems such as the digital gap in teachers. On the other hand, implementing the methodology in confined conditions demonstrates that it's possible to carry out interdisciplinary research using ICT, so the construction of proposals of this type allows the fundamental principles of DCU and IHC to be recovered at the service of educational, training and upgrade.

The project aroused genuine interest in the teachers and other people involved, showing that the proposed solution addresses the correct motivations and needs. This openness on the users leads us to believe that the project has sufficient relevance and significance to continue developing in the future. It's necessary to resolve some issues in direct evaluations with the user, impossible in this study because of the confinement, such as the platform usability by people with a high level of digital gap or its relevance in marginalized sectors. It's also necessary to prototype the section of the site dedicated to users who can provide help.

The research findings give indications of some issues to develop regarding the creation of a community for the possible use of the tool. It is extremely important to delve into engagement strategies and attract new users, as well as social interaction dynamics and gamification techniques that motivate them to constantly use the platform. Finally, it is important to consider aspects of technological operation, programming and database that were not possible to implement at the time of this investigation, for example: automatic search, content classification, message processing, types of system users, privacy and data protection.

References

1. Sánchez, M., et al.: Retos educativos durante la pandemia de COVID-19: una encuesta a profesores de la UNAM. Rev. Digit. Univ. **21**(3), 9 (2020). https://doi.org/10.22201/codeic.16076079e.2020.v21n3.a12
2. Empresa Actual: Alfabetización digital, la solución a la brecha digital (2020). https://www.empresaactual.com/alfabetizacion-digital-solucion-fractura-digital/
3. Sciadas, G.: The digital divide in canada. science, innovation and electronic information division. Statistics Canada, Ottawa (2002). https://www150.statcan.gc.ca/n1/en/pub/56f0009x/56f0009x2002001-eng.pdf?st=STYLpg_q
4. Selfe, C.L.: Technology and Literacy in the Twenty-First Century. Illinois University Press, Carbondale Southern (2000)
5. Pianfetti, S.E.: Focus on research: teachers and technology: digital literacy through professional development. Lang. Arts **78**(3) (2001). https://www.jstor.org/stable/41483145. https://doi.org/10.2307/41483145
6. Benemérita Univerisdad Autónoma de Puebla (BUAP). Estudiantes de la FCC diseñan app para reducir la brecha digital en las escuelas (2016). https://www.buap.mx/content/estudiantes-de-la-fcc-dise%C3%B1an-app-para-reducir-la-brecha-digital-en-las-escuelas
7. Cooper, A.: About Face 3 The Essentials of the Interaction Design. Wiley, Indianapolis (2007)
8. Savoia, A.: Pretotype it: make sure you are building the right it before you build it right, 69p. (2012). https://www.pretotyping.org/uploads/1/4/0/9/14099067/pretotype_it_2nd_pretotype_edition-2.pdf
9. Nielsen, J.: 10 usability heuristics for user interface design. Nielsen Norman Group (1994). https://www.nngroup.com/articles/ten-usability-heuristics/

Challenges in Integrating SCRUM and the User-Centered Design Framework: A Systematic Review

Daniela Argumanis(✉) 📧, Arturo Moquillaza📧, and Freddy Paz📧

Pontificia Universidad Católica del Perú, Lima 32, San Miguel, Peru
{daniela.argumanis,amoquillaza,fpaz}@pucp.pe

Abstract. This paper presents the results of a systematic review conducted in order to identify the challenges integrating user-centered design and Scrum, as well as the techniques and methodologies that would allow the Scrum Team to overcome these challenges. A total of 416 studies where identified, out of which only 29 studies where selected for this review. According to the analysis, most challenges are related to the insufficient importance assigned to Usability and the User Experience in general, insufficient communication between designers and developers, insufficient resources assigned to Scrum for upfront activities, and clients trying to represent final users without being aware of their real needs. Additionally, 30 techniques and methodologies have been identified as possible solutions to these challenges, which should be further analyzed to determine whether they should be adapted and incorporated into the Scrum framework.

Keywords: Systematic review · Agile methodologies · User-centered design · Usability · User Experience

1 Introduction

In recent years, agile methodologies have become the most popular approach for software development. However, they give focus to the functional requirements of the project, and do not describe explicitly the techniques and methodologies that should be applied to guarantee a good user experience (UX) for the final product. Therefore, software development is given the highest priority during every phase of the project life cycle, while time and resources assigned to interface design are limited. Frequently, this situation generates a final product with a poor user experience, and even if it meets the functional requirements established by the client, it may have a high risk of failure in the market.

Taking into account the popularity of agile methodologies, it is necessary to find a way for an agile project to incorporate good Usability and User Experience in its design and evaluation processes. For this matter, professionals from different organizations develop their own techniques for integrating Agile frameworks and User Experience design frameworks. However, they must face challenges such as the insufficient importance assigned to Usability and UX, insufficient communication between designers and

© Springer Nature Switzerland AG 2020
V. Agredo-Delgado et al. (Eds.): HCI-COLLAB 2020, CCIS 1334, pp. 52–62, 2020.
https://doi.org/10.1007/978-3-030-66919-5_6

developers, insufficient resources assigned for upfront activities and clients trying to represent final users without being aware of their real needs.

The aim of this study is to examine case studies that were lately described in the literature in order to identify the challenges integrating Scrum (most popular agile framework) and User Centered Design (design framework focused on satisfying user needs), and methodologies and techniques to overcome these challenges.

2 Main Concepts

2.1 Scrum

Scrum is one of the most popular agile frameworks, given that 70 percent of agile projects are based on Scrum [1]. It is adaptable, interactive, fast, flexible, effective and designed to offer considerable value in a quick way throughout the project. Teams are multi-functional, and work cycles (sprints), are short and concentrated.

2.2 User-Centered Design

User-Centered Design (UCD) is an iterative design process focused on user research, user interface design and usability evaluation to provide useful and usable software [2]. The purpose of this framework is to create an optimal product based on the user needs, rather than forcing users to adapt to the features of a product [3].

3 Methods and Materials

The systematic literature review was developed using the methodology proposed by Kitchenham [4]. Two research questions were defined to focus the systematic review of the state of the art, which were established using the "PICOC" criteria (Population, Intervention, Comparison, Outcomes, and Context). In addition, a search string was defined to retrieve papers published from the last five years.

3.1 Definition of the Research Questions

The purpose of the systematic review was to evidence challenges to the integration of the user-centered design framework and Scrum, as well as the methodologies and techniques proposed to overcome these challenges. The information search was structured using a PICOC table, which defines the Population, Intervention, Comparison, Output and Context criteria related to the systematic review. However, given that this review does not consider the comparison of the frameworks to be evaluated (Scrum and UCD), the comparison criteria was not used. The concepts are detailed in Table 1.

Based on the concepts established on the Table 1, the following research questions were specified:

RQ1: What challenges do agile teams face when they integrate Scrum and UCD?
RQ2: What methodologies, methods and techniques are reported in the literature that consider the incorporation of UCD in a project developed following Scrum?

Table 1. General concepts defined using the PICOC criteria

Criterion	Description
Population	Agile software development
Intervention	User-centered design
Outcomes	Basic guidelines for the inclusion of UCD in agile development
Context	Academia

3.2 Database Selection

The following databases were selected for systematic review because they are the most relevant in the field of Computing and Software Engineering: (1) IEEEXplore, (2) ACM Digital Library, (3) Scopus, and (4) Thesis Repository of the *Pontifical Catholic University of Peru* (http://tesis.pucp.edu.pe/repositorio/).

3.3 Development of the Search String

For the elaboration of the search strings, key terms were stablished for each criterion, considering abbreviations, synonyms, and similar terms. Afterward, the terms were joined using the logical operators "OR" and "AND":

- **C1:** "agile" OR "lean"
- **C2:** "UCD" OR "UX" OR "user-centered" OR "user centre" OR "user centered design" OR "user experience"
- **C3:** "developer" OR "developers" OR "programmer" OR "programmers" OR "programming team" OR "development team"
- **C4:** "software development" OR "software construction" OR "software project" OR "software projects" OR "software process" OR "software processes" OR "software engineering"

The resulting search string was as follows:

C1 **AND** C2 **AND** C3 **AND** C4

3.4 Inclusion and Exclusion Criteria

In order to identify relevant papers, inclusion and exclusion criteria were established. The following exclusion criteria were considered: (1) Studies in languages other than English and Spanish, (2) Studies related to hardware usability instead of software usability, (3) Descriptions of workshops, meetings or talks where the topics discussed are not detailed, (4) Studies focusing on a defined context, (5) Studies based on defined software tools (e.g. DevOps or NoSQL), and (6) Teaching based studies.

Relevant publications include the following topics: (1) Strategies for the integration of usability in agile methodologies, (2) Communication and cooperation between designers and developers, (3) Practical models of usability in agile methodologies, (4) Lean UX, and (5) Challenges in the integration of usability in agile methodologies.

3.5 Search and Selection Process

The databases considered for the systematic review retrieved a total of 416 papers. Based on the previously defined exclusion criteria, 387 non-relevant papers were discarded, and the remaining 29 papers were selected as significant for the research. The summary of the search results is shown in Table 2 and the selected studies are listed in Table 3.

Table 2. Summary of search results

Database name	Search results	Duplicated papers	Relevant papers
IEEExplore	11	–	7
ACM digital library	27	1	12
Scopus	376	10	8
Thesis PUCP	2	0	2
Total	**416**	**11**	**29**

4 Data Analysis and Results

In order to determine the most significant challenges when integrating Scrum and UCD, we identified the number of times each challenge was reported in relevant papers. We labeled each challenge with a code for future reference in the discussion on Sect. 4.1. All results are summarized in Table 4.

4.1 Challenges Integrating Scrum and UCD

The results of the systematic review show that the three most significant challenges integrating Scrum and UCD are the insufficient importance assigned to usability and user needs (D1), the insufficient time assigned for upfront activities in Scrum (D2), and the communication problems between designers and developers (D3).

First, the insufficient importance assigned to usability in a software project has as consequence that clients are not willing to spend time and resources for usability (D8), given that UCD techniques are heavy and expensive (D11). Therefore, clients do not prioritize UCD activities (D9), rejecting usability tests (D7) and representing users without being aware of their real needs (D5).

On the other hand, given that Scrum does not assign enough time for upfront activities, it is difficult to complete the documentation required by UCD activities (D4), which is necessary to preserve a coherent UI structure as design activities are not easily modularized (D14). Also, it is difficult to estimate usability activities in order to distribute them evenly along the Scrum Sprints (D18).

Finally, the poor communication between designers and developers is caused not only because of their different ways of working (D6), but also because of problems

Table 3. Complete list of selected studies

Study ID	Author(s)	Year
A01 [5]	K. Kuusinen	2015
A02 [6]	M. Seyam, S. McCrickard	2015
A03 [7]	M. Seyam	2015
A04 [8]	L. Alperowitz, A. M. Weintraud, S. C. Kofler, B. Bruegge	2017
A05 [3]	O. Almughram, S. Alyahya	2017
A06 [9]	S. M. Butt, A. Onn, M. M. Butt, N. T. Inam, S. M. Butt	2014
A07 [10]	S. Kikitamara, A. A. Noviyanti	2018
A08 [11]	B. Losada	2018
A09 [12]	M. Lundström, J. Åberg, J. Blomkvist	2015
A10 [13]	L. A. Liikkanen, H. Kilpiö, L. Svan, M. Hiltunen	2014
A11 [14]	E. Manwaring, J. N. Carter, K. Maynard	2017
A12 [2]	D. Teka, Y. Dittrich, M. Kifle	2018
A13 [15]	G. Novakova Nedeltcheva, E. Shoikova	2017
A14 [16]	T. Øvad, N. Bornoe, L. Bo Larsen, J. Stage	2015
A15 [17]	A. Friedman, I. Flaounas	2018
A16 [18]	D. Salah, R. F. Paige, P. Cairns	2014
A17 [19]	P. McInerney	2017
A18 [20]	C. Felker, R. Slamova, J. Davis	2012
A19 [21]	S. Krusche, B. Bruegge	2014
A20 [22]	D. A. Magües, J. W. Castro, S. T. Acuña	2016
A21 [23]	C. Zapata	2015
A22 [24]	A. Jones, V. Thoma, G. Newell	2016
A23 [25]	S. Bordin, A. De Angeli	2016
A24 [26]	S. Bordin, A. De Angeli	2017
A25 [27]	D. Salah, R. Paige, P. Cairns	2014
A26 [28]	M. del Carmen Aguilar, C. Zapata	2017
A27 [29]	M. del Carmen Aguilar	2015
A28 [30]	D. Victoria	2016
A29 [31]	L.A. Rojas, J.A. Macias	2015

in their team structure. Because of the lack of UCD specialists in the industry (D13), designers are usually distributed between different projects at the same time (D12), and they tend to leave the projects before its release (D17). Besides, developers often refuse to participate in design activities (D16), making it difficult for the designers to be aware of every technical restriction of the project during the design (D19). In consequence, the design usually must be modified in later stages of the project, and the designers may have already left the team.

Likewise, we identified the methodologies and techniques that could overcome the challenges, and the number of times they were reported in relevant papers. We labeled each methodology and technique with a code for future reference in the discussion on Sect. 4.2. All results are summarized in Table 5 and Table 6.

4.2 Methodologies and Techniques for Integrating Scrum and UCD

The most significant methodologies for integrating Scrum and UCD, according to the results of the systematic review, are design in parallel to sprints, design within sprints,

Table 4. Papers that report each challenge (RQ1)

Code	Challenge	Papers that report the challenge	Quantity
D1	Lack of importance assigned to usability and user needs	A01, A02, A03, A08, A09, A17, A22, A23, A24, A29	10
D2	Scrum does not assign time for upfront activities	A02, A03, A08, A16, A17, A18, A21, A24	8
D3	Communication between designers and developers	A01, A08, A09, A16, A22, A24, A27	7
D4	Conflicts in documentation quantity between Scrum and UCD	A01. A08, A09, A16, A22, A24, A27	6
D5	Clients represent users without knowing their real needs	A06, A12, A17, A22, A24, A29	6
D6	Designers and developers have different ways of working	A01, A08, A21, A22	4
D7	Clients reject usability tests	A16, A17, A22, A24	4
D8	Lack of resources assigned to usability	A16, A17, A22, A24	4
D9	Difficulty prioritizing UCD activities	A08, A09, A16	3
D10	Developers do not cooperate with designers from the beginning of the project	A01, A21	2
D11	UCD techniques are heavy and expensive	A12, A23	2
D12	Designers are distributed between different projects	A16, A24	2
D13	Lack of UCD specialists in the industry	A23, A24	2
D14	Difficulty in modularization of design activities	A16, A25	2
D15	Users might not have well defined needs	A12	1
D16	Developers do not want to participate in the design process	A14	1
D17	Designers leave the project before the release	A09	1
D18	Difficulty estimating usability activities	A18	1
D19	Designers are not aware of the technical restrictions of the project	A21	1
D20	Difficulty lining up design sprints and development sprints	A22	1

(*continued*)

Table 4. (*continued*)

Code	Challenge	Papers that report the challenge	Quantity
D21	Difference of duration of the iterations between Scrum and UCD	A27	1

Table 5. Papers that report each methodology (RQ2)

Code	Methodology	Papers that report the challenge	Quantity
M1	Design in parallel to sprints	A05, A07, A16, A24, A29	5
M2	Lean UX	A07, A10, A11, A14	4
M3	Design within sprint	A07	1
M4	Design thinking	A13	1

Lean UX and Design Thinking. In addition, 26 techniques for integrating Scrum and UCD were reported within the results.

The first methodology reported is design in parallel to sprints (M1), where designers could support the developers in the implementation of a sprint, while designing the interface for the next sprint. However, this could imply conflicts in communication, given that the development project would be divided in two teams. Therefore, the literature proposes a methodology where the design is included within the sprints (M3), which would guarantee an effective communication, but would require team cooperation from the beginning of the project. On the other hand, Lean UX (M2) focuses on minimizing risk of wasted resources by the release of fast prototypes (minimum viable product) to be tested by users. Finally, Design Thinking (M4) is focused on user centered innovation to generate, test and refine ideas, with the purpose of solving client problems.

Additionally, based on the results of the systematic review, the following UCD techniques were considered the most significant: (1) Low fidelity prototypes (T1): Low cost prototypes (discount usability) and fast feedback, (2) Personas (T2): Creation of hypothetical individuals to include in user stories, (3) Sprint 0 (T3): Sprint before the sprint 1, to understand user needs and start with the design process, and (4) Pair designing (T4): A designer and a developer working on the same computer, in order to guarantee product quality.

Table 6. Papers that report each technique (RQ2)

Code	Technique	Papers that report the challenge	Quantity
T1	Paper prototyping	A06, A08, A09, A12, A18, A19, A20, A22, A23, A25, A26, A27, A28, A29	14
T2	*Personas*	A08, A10, A12, A20, A22, A23, A26, A27, A29	9
T3	Sprint 0	A05, A08, A09, A16, A17, A24, A28	7
T4	Pair designing	A02, A03, A12, A21, A22	5
T5	Heuristic evaluation	A06, A12, A28, A29	4
T6	Usability conducted by developers	A14, A16, A17	3
T7	Card sorting	A06, A12, A29	3
T8	Contextual inquiry	A18, A20, A29	3
T9	Scenarios	A26, A27, A29	3
T10	Upfront design (large scale)	A06, A08	2
T11	Thinking aloud	A12, A23	2
T12	Software development conducted by designers	A09, A18	2
T13	Surveys	A28, A29	2
T14	Expert evaluation	A23, A29	2
T15	Cognitive walkthrough	A06, A29	2
T16	Design in panorams	A06	1
T17	Brainstorming	A08	1
T18	Ethnography	A08	1
T19	Performance acceptance tests	A12	1
T20	High level business metrics	A15	1
T21	UI Spikes	A17	1
T22	Storyboarding	A06	1
T23	Planning poker	A23	1
T24	Filming of facial expressions of users	A26	1
T25	Audio recording with comments	A26	1
T26	Continuous prototyping	A04	1

5   Conclusions and Future Works

The results of the systematic review prove that, even though nowadays there are not formal guides for integrating Scrum and UCD, there is a need to incorporate usability into agile methodologies.

Throughout the investigation, we identified several papers reporting challenges in the integration between Scrum and UCD. Between these challenges, the most significant were the low importance assigned to usability and user needs, the lack of time assigned for upfront activities in Scrum, and the poor communication between designers and developers. On the other hand, different methodologies were reported for integrating Scrum and UCD: Design in parallel to sprints, design within sprints, Lean UX and Design Thinking. Also, the results show that techniques such as low fidelity prototypes, Personas and Sprint 0 could be adapted for a Scrum-UCD framework.

In conclusion, there is interest on the integration of Scrum and UCD, and the creation of an explicit framework that integrates both approaches would be useful for the development of usable software products. However, in order to achieve this objective, it is necessary to evaluate, select and adapt the methodologies and techniques reported in this investigation, integrate them into the new Scrum-UCD framework, and evaluate and improve this framework by using it in real development projects.

Acknowledgement. This study is highly supported by the *Pontifical Catholic University of Peru* "HCI, Design, User Experience, Accessibility & Innovation Technologies" Research Group.

References

1. CollabNet: 12th Annual State of Agile Report. Technical report, CollabNet VersionOne, Brisbane, CA, USA (2018)
2. Teka, D., Dittrich, Y., Kifle, M.: Adapting lightweight user-centered design with the Scrum-based development process. In: 2018 IEEE/ACM Symposium on Software Engineering in Africa (SEiA), pp. 35–42, May 2018. https://doi.org/10.1145/3195528.3195530
3. Almughram, O., Alyahya, S.: Coordination support for integrating user centered design in distributed agile projects. In: 2017 IEEE 15th International Conference on Software Engineering Research, Management and Applications (SERA), pp. 229–238, June 2017. https://doi.org/10.1109/SERA.2017.7965732
4. Kitchenham, B., Charters, S.: Guidelines for performing systematic literature reviews in software engineering. Technical report EBSE 2007-001, Keele University and Durham University (2007)
5. Kuusinen, K.: Overcoming challenges in agile user experience work: cross-case analysis of two large software organizations. In: 2015 41st Euromicro Conference on Software Engineering and Advanced Applications, pp. 454–458, August 2015. https://doi.org/10.1109/SEAA.2015.38
6. Seyam, M., McCrickard, S.: Collaborating on mobile app design through pair programming: a practice-oriented approach overview and expert review. In: 2015 International Conference on Collaboration Technologies and Systems (CTS), pp. 124–131, June 2015. https://doi.org/10.1109/CTS.2015.7210412
7. Seyam, M.: Enhancing usability through agility: pair programming for a practice-oriented integration approach. In: 2015 International Conference on Collaboration Technologies and Systems (CTS), pp. 460–463, June 2015. https://doi.org/10.1109/CTS.2015.7210467
8. Alperowitz, L., Weintraud, A.M., Kofler, S.C., Bruegge, B.: Continuous prototyping. In: 2017 IEEE/ACM 3rd International Workshop on Rapid Continuous Software Engineering (RCoSE), pp. 36–42, May 2017. https://doi.org/10.1109/RCoSE.2017.7

9. Butt, S.M., Onn, A., Butt, M.M., Inam, N.T., Butt, S.M.: Incorporation of usability evaluation methods in agile software model. In: 17th IEEE International Multi Topic Conference 2014, pp. 193–199, December 2014. https://doi.org/10.1109/INMIC.2014.7097336
10. Kikitamara, S., Noviyanti, A.A.: A conceptual model of user experience in Scrum practice. In: 2018 10th International Conference on Information Technology and Electrical Engineering (ICITEE), pp. 581–586, July 2018. https://doi.org/10.1109/ICITEED.2018.8534905
11. Losada, B.N.: Flexible requirement development through user objectives in an agile-UCD hybrid approach. In: Proceedings of the XIX International Conference on Human Computer Interaction, Interacción 2018. ACM, New York (2018). https://doi.org/10.1145/3233824.323 3865
12. Lundström, M., Åberg, J., Blomkvist, J.: Perceptions of software developers' empathy with designers. In: Proceedings of the 2015 British HCI Conference, British HCI 2015, pp. 239–246. ACM, New York (2015). https://doi.org/10.1145/2783446.2783563
13. Liikkanen, L.A., Kilpiö, H., Svan, L., Hiltunen, M.: Lean UX: the next generation of user-centered agile development? In: Proceedings of the 8th Nordic Conference on Human-Computer Interaction: Fun, Fast, Foundational, NordiCHI 2014, pp. 1095–1100. ACM, New York (2014). https://doi.org/10.1145/2639189.2670285
14. Manwaring, E., Carter, J.N., Maynard, K.: Redesigning educational dashboards for shifting user contexts. In: Proceedings of the 35th ACM International Conference on the Design of Communication, SIGDOC 2017. ACM, New York (2017). https://doi.org/10.1145/3121113. 3121210
15. Nedeltcheva, G.N., Shoikova, E.: Coupling design thinking, user experience design and agile: Towards cooperation framework. In: Proceedings of the International Conference on Big Data and Internet of Thing, BDIOT 2017, pp. 225–229. ACM, New York (2017). https://doi.org/ 10.1145/3175684.3175711
16. Øvad, T., Bornoe, N., Larsen, L.B., Stage, J.: Teaching software developers to perform UX tasks. In: Proceedings of the Annual Meeting of the Australian Special Interest Group for Computer Human Interaction, OzCHI 2015, pp. 397–406. ACM, New York (2015). https:// doi.org/10.1145/2838739.2838764
17. Friedman, A., Flaounas, I.: The right metric for the right stakeholder: a case study of improving product usability. In: Proceedings of the 30th Australian Conference on Computer-Human Interaction, OzCHI 2018, pp. 602–606. ACM, New York (2018). https://doi.org/10.1145/329 2147.3292224
18. Salah, D., Paige, R.F., Cairns, P.: A systematic literature review for agile development processes and user centred design integration. In: Proceedings of the 18th International Conference on Evaluation and Assessment in Software Engineering, EASE 2014. ACM, New York (2014). https://doi.org/10.1145/2601248.2601276
19. McInerney, P.: UX in agile projects: Taking stock after 12 years. Interactions **24**(2), 58–61 (2017)
20. Felker, C., Slamova, R., Davis, J.: Integrating UX with Scrum in an undergraduate software development project. In: Proceedings of the 43rd ACM Technical Symposium on Computer Science Education, SIGCSE 2012, pp. 301–306. ACM, New York (2012). https://doi.org/10. 1145/2157136.2157226
21. Krusche, S., Bruegge, B.: User feedback in mobile development. In: Proceedings of the 2nd International Workshop on Mobile Development Lifecycle, MobileDeLi 2014, pp. 25–26. ACM, New York (2014). https://doi.org/10.1145/2688412.2688420
22. Magües, D., Castro, J., Acuña, S.: Requirements engineering related usability techniques adopted in agile development processes, vol. 2016-January, pp. 537–542 (2016). https://doi. org/10.18293/SEKE2016-057

23. Zapata, C.: Integration of usability and agile methodologies: a systematic review. In: Marcus, A. (ed.) DUXU 2015. LNCS, vol. 9186, pp. 368–378. Springer, Cham (2015). https://doi.org/10.1007/978-3-319-20886-2_35
24. Jones, A., Thoma, V., Newell, G.: Collaboration constraints for designers and developers in an agile environment. In: Proceedings of the 30th International BCS Human Computer Interaction Conference: Fusion! HCI 2016. BCS Learning Development Ltd., Swindon, GBR (2016). https://doi.org/10.14236/ewic/HCI2016.37
25. Bordin, S., De Angeli, A.: Focal points for a more user-centred agile development. In: Sharp, H., Hall, T. (eds.) XP 2016. LNBIP, vol. 251, pp. 3–15. Springer, Cham (2016). https://doi.org/10.1007/978-3-319-33515-5_1
26. Bordin, S., De Angeli, A.: Inoculating an agile company with user-centred design: an empirical study. In: Baumeister, H., Lichter, H., Riebisch, M. (eds.) XP 2017. LNBIP, vol. 283, pp. 235–242. Springer, Cham (2017). https://doi.org/10.1007/978-3-319-57633-6_15
27. Salah, D., Paige, R., Cairns, P.: A practitioner perspective on integrating agile and user centred design, pp. 100–109 (2014). https://doi.org/10.14236/ewic/hci2014.11
28. Merino, E., Zapata, C., Aguilar, MdC: UCD and agile methodology in the development of a cultural heritage platform. In: Marcus, A., Wang, W. (eds.) DUXU 2017. LNCS, vol. 10288, pp. 614–632. Springer, Cham (2017). https://doi.org/10.1007/978-3-319-58634-2_45
29. Aguilar, M.D.C.: Integración del diseño centrado en el usuario con metodologías ágiles en el desarrollo de un catálogo de plantas. Un estudio de investigación – acción (2015). http://tesis.pucp.edu.pe/repositorio/handle/20.500.12404/6364
30. Victoria, D.: Caso de estudio: desarrollo de una aplicación móvil para android para la medición del nivel de ruido integrando metodologías ágiles y técnicas de usabilidad (2016). http://tesis.pucp.edu.pe/repositorio/handle/20.500.12404/6683
31. Rojas, L.A., Macías, J.A.: An agile information-architecture-driven approach for the development of user-centered interactive software. In: Proceedings of the 16th International Conference on Human Computer Interaction (Interacción 2015) (2015). https://doi.org/10.1145/2829875.2829919

Clustering Analysis of Usability in Web Sites of Higher Technological Institutes of Ecuador

Yeferson Torres-Berru[1](✉) ⓘ and Pablo Torres-Carrión[2](✉) ⓘ

[1] Instituto Superior Tecnológico Loja, Av. Granada y Turunuma, 1101608 Loja, Ecuador
ymtorres@tecnologicoloja.edu.ec
[2] Universidad Técnica Particular de Loja, San Cayetano Alto S/N, 1101608 Loja, Ecuador
pvtorres@utpl.edu.ec

Abstract. Techniques for evaluating usability continue to be innovated. This document shares the application of a heuristic-based framework for measuring web usability - SIRIUS, complemented by two machine learning techniques for clustering: a) Hierarchical, with the Ward.2 method and Euclidean; and b) K-means clustering. For data processing, CRISP-DM has been proposed as a general method. Since our objective is to evaluate the usability characteristics of the websites of the Technical and Technological Institutes of Ecuador, data has been obtained from the web portals of 83 Institutes (34 public and 49 private). As a result, three clusters have been obtained, which encompass the 10 aspects of the framework, and which allow us to identify the levels of usability of technological institutes. As a result, 18 institutes have been categorized into the group of websites with above-average usability (cluster1), 32 institutes with below-average usability (cluster2), and the remainder with an acceptable degree of usability. The method used and proposed has made it possible to have a general usability map of the web portals of the technical and technological institutes of a country, as input for decision-making.

Keywords: Clustering · Heuristics · SIRIUS · Usability · Unsupervised learning

1 Introduction

The Higher Education System of Ecuador, to date there are 59 accredited universities, of which three only offer postgraduate degrees, and 83 Technical and Technological Institutes, being 34 public and 49 private[1]. Each institution has a public web domain, from which academic and management resources are administered. After having carried out a Systematic Literature Review, no studies on the usability of all institutional websites have been found. In [1] n analysis is made of 24 websites of universities belonging to CEDIA, using the Prometheus tool from SIRIUS and Kmeans, obtaining as relevant data that 50% are at an adequate level, but fail to highlight in which aspects they present problems. In [2] the websites based on the ISO 9241-151 standard in 59 universities are analyzed, classifying them by the category obtained in the evaluation by CACES (A,

---

[1] https://www.educacionsuperior.gob.ec/ Sitio Web de la Secretaría de Educación Superior, Ciencia, Tecnología e Innovación del Ecuador.

© Springer Nature Switzerland AG 2020
V. Agredo-Delgado et al. (Eds.): HCI-COLLAB 2020, CCIS 1334, pp. 63–72, 2020.
https://doi.org/10.1007/978-3-030-66919-5_7

B, C), also detecting problems in content design, general design and especially in the search criteria. In [3] the study at the University of Riobamba is singled out, determining that the main problems are the use of Search Engine and Interacting with Links and Download Information. This research complements the previous ones, completing the entire Ecuadorian higher education system. The proposed objectives are of interest to higher education authorities, knowing the usability of their web spaces, which are the point of contact with the community.

To assess usability on the web, there are many methods and techniques, which, Perurena [4] very accurately details. Granollers [5] proposes the use of heuristics, as a technique to evaluate usability in user interfaces; Storm [6] uses time Series Analysis of Selected Episode Graphs; In [7] they make use of the ISO/IEC 9126 quality model standard, applying techniques such as observation guide, satisfaction questionnaire and attractive interface questionnaire to evaluate each metric. In [8] card sorting method is applied to construct the shape of the site focused on user shared cognition. In [9] the use of the eye tracking tool is exposed, as an input for the analysis of user behavior when interacting with the web. Artificial intelligence has also been applied to enhance data collection and perform sustained analysis in machine learning algorithms; Thus, Zainab [10] applies clustering techniques as an input to categorize data obtained from the web, which are then analyzed from a standard system usability scale. To improve the automation of software evaluation (including usability), Stouky [11] proposes the use of machine learning techniques and big data. Chamba [1] applies data mining techniques to collect data from 24 Universities Web portals, as input for the subsequent application of usability techniques. In this work, Chamba's proposal [1] is followed to collect data from 83 institutional websites.

In this research, it is proposed to work with the User-Oriented Web Usability Assessment System based on the determination of Cryptic Tasks (SIRIUS by its Spanish acronym), developed by Torrente [12] as part of his work on PhD research; It is composed of 10 aspects, divided into 83 variables (criteria) that cover the various areas of functionality of a web-based solution. Torrente exposes it in [13] like as a heuristic-based framework for measuring web usability adapted to the type of website. Sai Aparna [14] adapts it as SIRIUS-DWUEP (Web Usability Evaluation Process), operationalizing this empirical validation technique in the WebML method. Muñoz-Egido [15] applies it to analyze eighteen academic library web portals, obtaining as a result that the average usability of the websites of the analyzed university libraries is 72.30 out of 100 with a standard deviation of 5.57. In [1] his technique is used in 24 Universities Web portals, obtaining three clusters that relate the 10 aspects of SIRIUS. In this research, SIRIUS is applied, and techniques based on clustering that have allowed us to categorize the web portals of the 63 institutes of higher education since the fulfillment of each of the aspects of this technique.

2   Materials y Methods

As a general method of automatic learning, the CRISP-DM method is proposed [16], adapted to the singular requirements of the study. This method is composed of six iterative stages: business understanding, data understanding, data preparation, modeling, evaluation and deployment.

2.1 Business Understanding

The usability evaluation of 83 public (34 eq = 40%) and private (49 EQ = 60%) institutes websites was performed following the Sirius framework: A heuristic-based framework for measuring web usability adapted to the type of website [13]. Sirius has 83 evaluation criteria grouped into ten aspects, which are detailed in Table 1. The data for the analysis was obtained through a project carried out at the "Instituto Tecnológico Loja", and is available on the web[2], in open access format.

2.2 Data Understanding

2.3 Data Modeling

Two clustering techniques are used for data modeling:

a) **Hierarchical**, with the Ward.2 method and euclidean distance between two points p and q, which is defined as the length of the segment that joins both points. Hierarchical combined with descriptive stadia [17], o determine the suitable number of centers for Kmeans. Once the dendrogram is created, the extent to which its structure reflects the original distances between observations is evaluated, using the correlation coefficient between the cophenetic distances of the dendrogram (node height) and the original distance matrix.

b) **K-means** clustering [18] to group the observations in K different clusters (centers), based on the evaluations previously carried out, it was determined that the value of K = 3, with 100 iterations to guarantee the process.

The computational analysis was carried out with the R Studio[3] software, using the packages: *clValid* to validate the ideal clustering algorithm; *factoextra* for Multivariate Analysis); and, *cluster* and *stats* for Clustering Analysis; In addition to the official sites, these packages can be downloaded from the project website[4]. To find the similarity, the Euclidean distance is used, making a hierarchical classification where the groups are merged (or subdivided) successively, following a priority or hierarchy, decreasing the homogeneity as they become wider. Therefore, for the evaluation of clustering, the coefficient of correlation is considered, which allows finding the distance between the clusters.

---

[2] https://bit.ly/UsabilityInstitutes.

[3] https://rstudio.com/.

[4] https://torresyeferson.github.io/UsabilityInstitutes/.

Table 1. Sirius aspects and criteria's

Aspect	Criteria
General Aspects (GA)	*10 variables*: goals of the site are concrete and well defined, contents and services are precise and complete, general structure of the site is user-oriented, general look & feel is aligned to the goals of the website, general design of the website is recognizable, general design of the website is coherent, user's language is used, other languages are supported, translation of the page is complete and correct, website is updated regularly
Identity and Information (II)	*7 variables*: identity or logo is significant, identifiable and visible, identity of the website is present in every page, slogan or tagline is suited to the goal of the site, information about the website or company is provided, contact mechanisms are provided, information about privacy of personal data and copyright of web contents is provided, information about authorship, sources, creation and revision dates of articles, news and reports is provided
Structure and Navigation (SN)	*14 variables*: welcome screen is avoided, structure and navigation are adequate, element organization is consistent with conventions, number of elements and terms per element is controlled in navigation menus, depth and breadth are balanced in the case of hierarchical structrure, links are easily recognized as such, link depiction indicates its state, redundant links are avoided, broken links are avoided, self-links to the current page are avoided, image links indicate the content to be accessed, a link to the beginning of the page is always present, elements hinting where the user is and how to undo the navigation exist
Labelling	*6 variables*: labels are significant, labelling system is precise and consistent, page titles are planned and correct, home page url is correct, clear, and easy to remember, inner page urls are clear, inner page urls are permanent
Layout of the page	*10 variables*: higher visual hierarchy areas of the page are used for relevant content, information overload is avoided, clean interface with no visual noise, white areas between information objects are provided for visual rest, visual space on the page is used correctly, visual hierarchy is correctly used to express "part of" relationships between page elements, page length is under control, print version of the page is correct, page text can be read easily, zblinking/moving text is avoided
Comprehen-sibility and ease of interaction	*7 variables*: concise and clear language is used, language is user friendly, each paragraph expresses an idea, interface controls are used consistently, visible metaphors are recognizable and comprehensible by any user, coherent or alphabetic order indrop-down menus, available options in a user-input field can be selected instead of written
Control and feedback	*10 variables*: user controls the whole interface, user is informed about what is happening, user is informed about what has happened, validation systems are in place to avoid errors before the user sends information, clear and non-alarmist information, and recovery actions are provided to the user when an error has occurred, response time is under control, website windows cancelling or superimposing over browser windows are avoided, proliferation of windows is avoided, user downloading of additional plugins is avoided, in task with several steps, user is informed of the current step and the number of steps remaining to complete the task
Multimedia elements	*6 variables*: images are well-cropped, images are comprehensible, images have the correct resolution, some added value is provided by using images or animations, cyclical animations are avoided, some added value is provided by using sound

(continued)

Table 1. (*continued*)

Aspect	Criteria
Search	*8 variables*: if necessary is accessible in every page, easily recognizable, easily accessible, text box width is enough, simple and clear search system, advanced search is provided, search results are comprehensible for the user, user is assisted in case of empty results for a given query
Help	*5 variables*: help link is located in a visible and standard place, easy access to and return from the help system, context help is offered for complex tasks, faq query selection and redaction is correct, faq answers are correct
10 aspects	*83 variables (criterias)*

3   Results

In Fig. 1 we observe the grouping of the institutes applying the Hierarchical method and obtaining 3 groups with a correlation coefficient of 0.9526396.

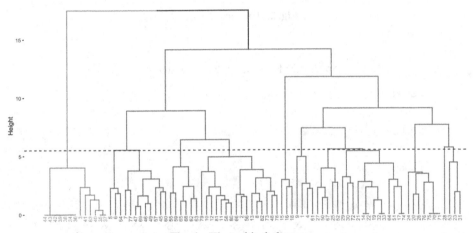

Fig. 1. Hierarchical cluster

The clustering analysis allowed to identify 3 groups of institutes (Fig. 2) with 18, 32 and 33 institutions respectively. Regarding the classification by financing of the institutions, we find that Cluster 1 is made up of 17 private and one public institute, Cluster 2 of 17 private and 15 public, and cluster 3 of 25 private and 8 public.

In Fig. 3 the values of the cluster with respect to the 10 aspects of SIRIUS are shown. Cluster1 predominates in 2 aspects (search and help); Cluster 2 predominates in 4 aspects (General aspects, layout, control and multimedia); and cluster3 predominates in 4 aspects (identity and information, structure and navigation, labeling and comprehensibility).

Table 2 details the distribution of the 3 general clusters and the clustering of the 83 criteria among the 10 aspects evaluated by SIRIUS, classifying the institutes between public and private. These significance values allow us to observe that 73.49% of the institutes evaluated obtained a high evaluation in Labeling, besides that only 25.50%

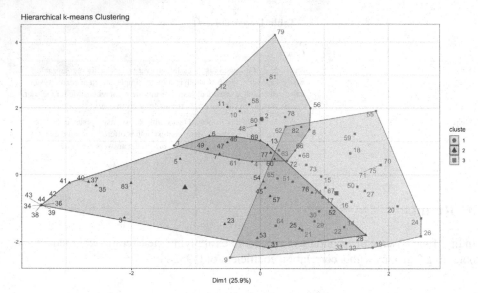

Fig. 2. Kmeans cluster

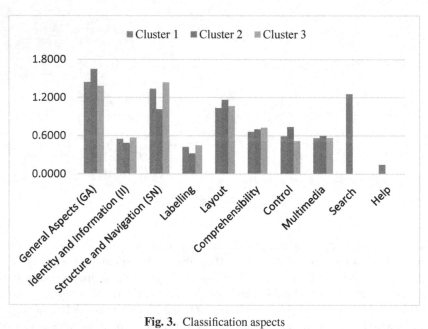

Fig. 3. Classification aspects

obtained a high evaluation in Control, we also highlight that 88% of institutes do not have a search incorporated in the website, finally we observed that only 19% of institutes show user help on site.

Table 2. Cluster Sirius Aspects

GA	II	SN	Labelling	Layout	Comprehensibility	Control	Multimedia	Search	Help
CLUSTER 1 (Usability Average 80.04 min_value = 66 max_value = 84)									
1.4417	0.5497	1.3404	0.4256	1.0369	0.6622	0.5911	0.5651	1.2561	0.1467
n = 34	n = 30	n = 45	n = 43	n = 46	n = 15	n = 33	n = 43	n = 10	n = 13
priv = 24	priv = 20	priv = 35	priv = 36	priv = 30	priv = 13	priv = 21	priv = 32	priv = 2	priv = 9
pub = 9	pub = 10	pub = 10	pub = 7	pub = 16	pub = 12	pub = 12	pub = 11	pub = 8	pub = 4
CLUSTER 2 (Usability Average 64.71 min_value = 54 max_value = 72)									
1.6491	0.4863	1.0170	0.3233	1.1652	0.7030	0.7397	0.5990	0.00	0.0000
n = 43	n = 16	n = 17	n = 22	n = 23	n = 41	n = 22	n = 1		n = 67
priv = 9	priv = 8	priv = 8	priv = 6	priv = 18	priv = 32	priv = 12	priv = 0		priv = 47
pub 15	pub = 8	pub = 9	pub = 16	pub = 5	pub = 9	pub = 10	pub = 1		pub = 20
CLUSTER 3 (Usability Average 71.25 min_value = 71 max_value = 82)									
1.3825	0.5713	1.4419	0.4503	1.0670	0.7283	0.5199	0.5657	0.000	0.0017
n = 6	n = 37	n = 21	n = 18	n = 14	n = 17	n = 28	n = 39		n = 3
priv = 6	priv = 31	priv = 16	priv = 17	priv = 11	priv = 14	priv = 26	priv = 27		priv = 3
pub = 0	pub = 36	pub = 5	pub = 1	pub = 3	pub = 3	pub = 2	pub = 12		pub = 0

Finally, to better understand the usability margins of the three clusters, a graph with measures of central tendency and a usability center line are detailed in Fig. 4. It is observed that the percentage of usability of the institutes belonging to the cluster1 is above the average; however, the institutes belonging to cluster2 and cluster3 are below the average, with better results for the last group.

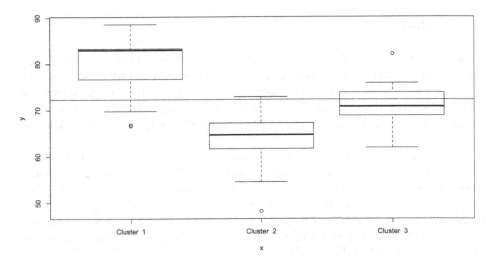

Fig. 4. BoxPlot cluster – usability percent

4 Discussion

Being our objective to evaluate the usability characteristics of the institutes' websites, we have identified 3 types of institutes and the most significant aspects are search and help, the search aspect presents similarity with problems previously found in university websites [1, 3]. As indicated by research [19, 20] the user must be able to retrieve information easily, therefore, it is important to provide adequate search systems, because the websites of educational institutions allow the presentation of academic offerings, news and achievements in teaching, research and networking. In this area, the importance of the understanding of a website is highlighted [21, 22], as shown in this research, most Ecuadorian institute sites present information, but care must be taken to ensure that this is done through appropriate web interfaces that speed up understanding.

The analysis based on heuristics used in this research, and adaptable to the type of website, can be adapted to the information and usability needs of educational institutions; this presents a similarity to the work [2], However, research such as [3] use the ISO 9241-151 standard, which evaluates all types of sites with the same metrics; furthermore, these studies are based on the categorization of type A, B, C universities etc. and the present study, classifies according to the analysis performed by the artificial intelligence technique used, based on the 81 parameters and 10 aspects evaluated with SIRIUS.

Of the aspects found with SIRIUS, the one corresponding to Help is shown as a weakness in most institutes, so it presents an opportunity to decongest the traditional communication channels and provide the user with a better web experience in educational sites [23], being this an aspect to improve, implementing sections of frequent questions, tutorials, chatbots etc.

5 Conclusions

Group 1 is characterized by high values in Search and Help and low values in Understandability and Multimedia elements, Group 2 is characterized by high values in Page Layout, Control and Feedback, low values in Tagging and null values in Search and Help; on the other hand Group 3 presents high values in Site Identity, Structure and Navigation, Tagging, Understandability, Multimedia elements, low values in Help and null values in Search.

Evaluating the aspects and criteria of usability of 83 technological institutes of Ecuador we can conclude that Cluster 1 composed by 18 institutes is a group that to improve its usability must improve its understandability and multimedia elements, Cluster 2 composed by 32 institutes is a group whose scores must improve in most aspects except in Page Layout and Control and Feedback, on the other hand Cluster 3 composed by 33 institutes is a group whose values are high in 6 of the 10 but must improve in help and implement search in the web site.

Acknowledgement. We thank the students of the Interface Design Subject of the Instituto Superior Tecnológico Loja Extension Vilcabamba for the support in the data collection.

References

1. Chamba-Eras, L., Jacome-Galarza, L., Guaman-Quinche, R., Coronel-Romero, E., Labanda-Jaramillo, M.: Analysis of usability of universities web portals using the Prometheus tool - SIRIUS. In: 2017 4th International Conference on eDemocracy eGovernment, ICEDEG 2017, pp. 195–199 (2017). https://doi.org/10.1109/ICEDEG.2017.7962533
2. Pincay-Ponce, J., Caicedo-Ávila, V., Herrera-Tapia, J., Delgado-Muentes, W., Delgado-Franco, P.: Usabilidad en sitios web oficiales de las universidades del Ecuador. Rev. Ibérica Sist. Tecnol. Inform. (2020)
3. Rosas-Chavez, P., Mora-Fernandez, J., Suarez, C.: Comparative analysis of usability of the public universities' web sites of Riobamba City in Ecuador. In: Ahram, T., Falcão, C. (eds.) AHFE 2019. AISC, vol. 972, pp. 742–752. Springer, Cham (2020). https://doi.org/10.1007/978-3-030-19135-1_73
4. Perurena Cancio, L., Moráguez Bergues, M.: Usability of Web sites, methods and evaluation techniques. Rev. Cuba. Inf. Cien. Salud. **24**, 176–194 (2013)
5. Granollers, T.: Usability evaluation with heuristics. New proposal from integrating two trusted sources. In: Marcus, A., Wang, W. (eds.) DUXU 2018. LNCS, vol. 10918, pp. 396–405. Springer, Cham (2018). https://doi.org/10.1007/978-3-319-91797-9_28
6. Storm, K., Kraemer, E., Aurrecoeche, C., Heiges, M., Pennington, C., Kissinger, J.C.: Web site evolution: usability evaluation using time series analysis of selected episode graphs (2009). https://doi.org/10.1109/WSE.2009.5630633
7. Salazar-Grandes, M.C., et al.: Usability evaluation mechanism with standard ISO/IEC 9126. Case study: Tourism portals (2017)
8. Shieh, J.-C., Lin, H.-W.: The study of web findability based on its breadth and depth. J. Educ. Media Libr. Sci. **50**, 255–288 (2013). https://doi.org/10.6120/JoEMLS.2012.502/0484.RS.CM
9. Menges, R., Kramer, S., Hill, S., Nisslmueller, M., Kumar, C., Staab, S.: A visualization tool for eye tracking data analysis in the web (2020). https://doi.org/10.1145/3379156.3391831
10. Zainab, S.S.E., Mehmood, Q., Zehra, D., Dietrich, R.-S., Hasnain, A.: PrEVIEw: clustering and visualising pubmed using visual interface (2016)
11. Stouky, A., Jaoujane, B., Daoudi, R., Chaoui, H.: Improving software automation testing using jenkins, and machine learning under big data. In: Jung, J.J., Kim, P., Choi, K.N. (eds.) BDTA 2017. LNICSSITE, vol. 248, pp. 87–96. Springer, Cham (2018). https://doi.org/10.1007/978-3-319-98752-1_10
12. Suárez Torrente, M.D.C.: Sirius: sistema de evaluación de la usabilidad web orientado al usuario y basado en la determinación de tareas críticas (2011)
13. Torrente, M.C.S., Prieto, A.B.M., Gutiérrez, D.A., De Sagastegui, M.E.A.: Sirius: a heuristic-based framework for measuring web usability adapted to the type of website. J. Syst. Softw. **86**, 649–663 (2013). https://doi.org/10.1016/j.jss.2012.10.049
14. Sai Aparna, S., Baseer, K.K.: SIRIUS-DWUEP: a heuristic-based framework for measuring and evaluating web usability in model-driven web development (2015). https://doi.org/10.1007/978-3-319-13728-5_34
15. Muñoz-Egido, D., Osti, M.V: Evaluation of usability of Spanish academic library web portals using a cognitive-emotional heuristic model. Rev. Esp. Doc. Cient. **40** (2017). https://doi.org/10.3989/redc.2017.1.1379
16. Wirth, R., Hipp, J.: CRISP-DM: towards a standard process model for data mining. In: Proceedings of the 4th International Conference on the Practical Applications of Knowledge Discovery and Data Mining, pp. 29–39. Springer, London (2000)
17. Hotelling, H.: A generalized T test and measure of multivariate dispersion. In: Second Berkeley Symposium on Mathematical Statistics and Probability, pp. 23–41 (1951)

18. Macqueen, J.: Some methods for classification and analysis of multivariate observations (1967)
19. Martín Fernández, F.J., Iazza, G., Hassan, Y.: Diseño web centrado en el usuario: usabilidad y arquitectura de la información - hipertext - (UPF), pp. 1–15 (2014)
20. Folmer, E., Bosch, J.: Architecting for usability: a survey. J. Syst. Softw. **70**, 61–78 (2004). https://doi.org/10.1016/S0164-1212(02)00159-0
21. Yusof, U.K., Khaw, L.K., Ch'ng, H.Y., Neow, B.J.: Balancing between usability and aesthetics of Web design. In: Proceedings 2010 International Symposium on Information Technology - Visual Informatics, ITSim 2010 (2010). https://doi.org/10.1109/ITSIM.2010.5561310
22. Sindhuja, P.N., Dastidar, S.: Impact of the factors influencing website usability on user satisfaction. IUP J. Manag. Res. **8**, 54–66 (2009)
23. Calisir, F., Bayraktaroğlu, A.E., Gumussoy, C.A., Topcu, Y.I., Mutlu, T.: The relative importance of usability and functionality factors for online auction and shopping web sites. Online Inf. Rev. **34**, 420–439 (2010). https://doi.org/10.1108/14684521011037025

Collaborative Learning Group Formation Based on Personality Traits: An Empirical Study in Initial Programming Courses

Oscar Revelo-Sánchez[1]([✉]) [iD], César A. Collazos[2] [iD], and Miguel A. Redondo[3] [iD]

[1] University of Nariño, San Juan de Pasto, Colombia
orevelo@udenar.edu.co
[2] University of Cauca, Popayán, Colombia
ccollazo@unicauca.edu.co
[3] University of Castilla-La Mancha, Ciudad Real, Spain
Miguel.Redondo@uclm.es

Abstract. Considering that the group formation is one of the key processes when developing activities in collaborative learning scenarios, the aim of this paper is to propose a technique based on an approach of genetic algorithms to achieve homogeneous groups, considering the students' personality traits as grouping criteria. The main feature of this technique is that it allows the consideration of as many traits of the student as desired, converting the grouping problem in one of multi-objective optimization, given the combinatorial explosion that can occur depending on the number of students and of groups. For its validation, an experiment was designed with 132 first semesters engineering students, quantifying their personality traits through the "Big Five Inventory", forming work groups and developing a collaborative activity in initial Programming courses. The experiment made it possible to compare the results obtained by the students applying the proposed approach to those obtained through other group formation strategies. It was demonstrated through the experiment that the homogeneous groups generated by the proposed technique produced better academic results compared to the formation techniques traditionally used by the teachers, when developing a collaborative activity.

Keywords: Collaborative learning · Genetic algorithms · Group formation · Personality traits

1 Introduction

Outside of academia, groups constitute a basic social structure. They are formed and reformed in different ways for various purposes: people meet in social situations, coordinate to perform work-related tasks, or constitute commissions because of common interests. Although, in academic fields, groups are also formed easily and for very diverse purposes, the group creation in the classroom can be a complicated and unnatural process. However, for collaborative learning to be successful, it is important to make effective groups [1].

© Springer Nature Switzerland AG 2020
V. Agredo-Delgado et al. (Eds.): HCI-COLLAB 2020, CCIS 1334, pp. 73–84, 2020.
https://doi.org/10.1007/978-3-030-66919-5_8

This paper presents the results of the research process carried out to structure a homogeneous group formation technique in collaborative learning scenarios, formation based on personality traits. For this, the "Big Five Inventory" is used as an instrument for measuring the traits of the participants' personality, a standardized inventory or questionnaire based on the psychological model of the Big Five [2]. On the other hand, given that the group formation is a combinatorial problem that involves multiple characteristics, the heuristic search offered by evolutionary algorithms was used as an optimization technique.

The proposed technique was validated with four different groups belonging to the Academic Programs of the Faculty of Engineering of the University of Nariño Camus Pasto, Systems Engineering and Electronic Engineering, for the initial Programming course in the academic period B-2019. Two of these groups were managed as experimental groups and the other two as control groups. Finally, a comparative analysis of the results of the proposed evaluative activities was carried out, applying statistical tests, for purposes of a basic initial measurement of the level of learning achieved by the students participating in the experiment. This allowed to show a positive incidence of the treatment given to the experimental groups compared to the control groups, that is, academic performance benefits.

The paper is organized as follows: initially the proposed solution is presented in detail in Sect. 2; Sect. 3 subsequently describes the empirical process developed; Sect. 4 presents the results of the proposed experiment. Finally, Sect. 5 presents a set of conclusions.

2 Proposed Technique

The technique is explained below in three parts: the first describes in general the methodological proposal, the second presents the instrument proposed for the measurement of personality traits, followed by a description of how the formation of working groups as such is carried out, through the application of genetic algorithms.

2.1 Methodological Proposal

The group formation in collaborative learning scenarios based on personality traits is presented as a sequential process comprising three stages that are described in the following sections. The boxes at the top are the inputs required in each stage, and the boxes at the bottom describe the outputs at each stage. Figure 1 schematically summarizes this process.

It is clarified that, as such, the proposed group formation technique would only go up to the second stage. Stage three, related to the collaborative activity or activities to be developed, is incorporated into the process solely for the purpose of validating the technique. This stage would be relative to the academic space in which it will be implemented.

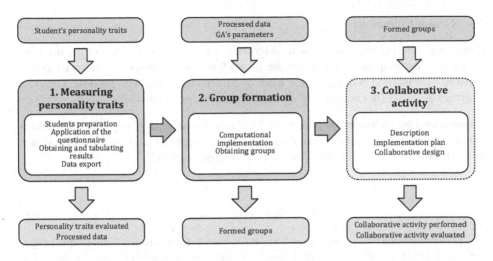

Fig. 1. Methodological scheme.

2.2 Measurement of Personality Traits

A Spanish adaptation of the BFI (Big Five Inventory) by John et al. is used as an instrument to measure the personality traits of students [3]. The aim of using this instrument is to have a scientifically accepted way to quantify the personality traits of an individual, which, as will be seen later, is the input required by the grouping algorithm. At no time is it intended to issue any type of concept or psychological diagnosis of the study participants, as this is outside the scope of this. The adaptation of the BFI into Spanish by Oliver P. John and Verónica Benet-Martínez [4] is used, with the corresponding consent for investigative purposes.

Once the BFI has been applied to each of the n students to be grouped, the results obtained must be stored as shown in Table 1. Each row corresponds to a student, the first two columns being their identifier and his name, and the remaining five measures each of the personality dimensions considered by the "Big Five" model: extraversion, agreeableness, conscientiousness, neuroticism and openness.

Table 1. BFI results matrix.

Id	Student	E	A	C	N	O
1	Student 1	3,0000	2,4444	2,2222	2,6250	3,4000
2	Student 2	2,5000	3,3333	3,1111	3,1250	4,1000
⋮	⋮	⋮	⋮	⋮	⋮	⋮
n	Student n	3,1424	3,4383	3,4753	2,6944	3,5750

2.3   Group Formation

Considering the principles of Genetic Algorithms, as well as the nature of the problem of interest, the proposed method for the group formation is described in detail in this section. This method is based on the work of Moreno et al. [5], who propose a method to group elements (not necessarily students) in a homogeneous way.

Representation of Students. Since the idea is to consider not only one, but several characteristics of the students, each student n can be represented by means of a vector in the following way, where M is the number of characteristics:

$$E_n = \{C_1, C_2, \ldots, C_M\} \tag{1}$$

These characteristics could have a different nature, for example, demographic (age, sex, etc.), psychological (*personality traits*, abilities, etc.), academic (grades, pre-tests, self-assessment, etc.), and cognitive (learning styles, types of intelligence, etc.), among others. This representation requires that every characteristic m ($1 \leq m \leq M$) be quantified by a numerical value in a predefined range, which does not mean that they can be considered categorical attributes. In these cases, a prior numerical discretization process would be required. For example, if an attribute takes values "high", "medium" and "low", these could be changed from 1, 2 and 3, respectively.

The total number of students can be represented by an $M \times N$ matrix, where N is the number of students, as shown in Table 2.

Table 2.   Representation of a total set of students.

Id	C_1	C_2	...	C_m
1	70	0.50	...	25
2	20	0.83	...	−10
⋮	⋮	⋮		⋮
N	45	1.22	...	13

Once the data are organized in this way, they may need to be scaled to a common range, so that there are no disturbances in the calculation and that they are easily comparable. A simple way to achieve this is for all the data to be in the range 0–1, applying statistical normalization based on the unit [6], using the following expression:

$$X' = \frac{X - X_{min}}{X_{max} - X_{min}} \tag{2}$$

Representation of Individuals. In the case of grouping, an individual corresponds to a specific collection of G groups, each with up to N/G students, with N being the total number of students. In most studies that use genetic algorithms, the data structure used is a vector where each position corresponds to a gene in the solution. In the proposed model it is proposed to use a matrix, where the number of rows corresponds to the desired number of groups G and the number of columns corresponds to the maximum size of each group N/G. In this way, each gene that makes up the chromosome contains the identifier of an element, and its position within the matrix defines the group to which it would belong. This representation, in addition to its clarity, facilitates the use of the genetic crossover operator proposed below.

In the group formation problem, as well as in other combinatorial problems, a chromosome cannot have repeated genes [5], which means that an individual (feasible solution) is one in which each element is in a single position of the chromosome. For example, if you have a total of 20 students and you want to form 4 groups, each one would contain exactly 5 students. In this case a possible individual, if the students are numbered consecutively, could be like the one presented in Table 3.

Table 3. Representation of an individual.

1	2	3	4	5
6	7	8	9	10
11	12	13	14	15
16	17	18	19	20

Fitness Measure. Since the objective of this method is to obtain homogeneous groups with respect to all the students, it is necessary to define a measure of this homogeneity. One possible way to do this is described below. First, the average of each characteristic of the totality of students (TM) is calculated:

$$TM = \{\overline{C_1}, \overline{C_2}, \ldots, \overline{C_M}\} \tag{3}$$

Then for each group g ($1 \leq g \leq G$) of each individual, the average of each characteristic is calculated. Since each individual i is represented as a matrix X^i, these averages (IM) can be represented as follows:

$$IM_g^i = \left\{\overline{X_{g,1}^i}, \overline{X_{g,2}^i}, \ldots, \overline{X_{g,M}^i}\right\} \tag{4}$$

Subsequently, the sum of the squared differences between the M characteristics for each group g of individual i and the average of each characteristic in all the elements is calculated, as follows:

$$D^i = \sum_{g=1}^{G}\left[\left(\overline{C_1} - \overline{X_{g,1}^i}\right)^2 + \left(\overline{C_2} - \overline{X_{g,2}^i}\right)^2 + \ldots + \left(\overline{C_M} - \overline{X_{g,M}^i}\right)^2\right] \tag{5}$$

The lower this value (with a minimum of 0), the more similar each of the groups will be on average with respect to the total number of students. Therefore, the objective function of the problem could be expressed as follows:

$$\min Z = \sum_{g=1}^{G} \left[\left(\overline{C_1} - \overline{X_{g,1}^i} \right)^2 + \left(\overline{C_2} - \overline{X_{g,2}^i} \right)^2 + \ldots + \left(\overline{C_M} - \overline{X_{g,M}^i} \right)^2 \right] \qquad (6)$$

To clarify this metric and apply the concepts presented so far, the following example is considered where there are 6 students with the 5 dimensions of the "Big Five" model valued, as shown in Table 4.

Table 4. Sample students.

Id	Student	E	A	C	N	O
1	Student 1	3,1424	3,4383	3,4753	2,6944	3,5750
2	Student 2	4,0000	3,0000	3,7778	3,1250	4,4000
3	Student 3	2,5000	3,3333	3,1111	3,1250	4,1000
4	Student 4	3,7500	4,1111	3,8889	1,7500	3,8000
5	Student 5	3,1250	3,2222	3,3333	2,2500	3,9000
6	Student 6	3,3750	2,7778	3,5556	2,2500	3,7000

After scaling these values according to the procedure described at the end of the Section "*Representation of students*", Table 5 is obtained.

Table 5. Scaled values.

Id	Student	E	A	C	N	O
1	Student 1	0,4282	0,4954	0,4683	0,6869	0,0000
2	Student 2	1,0000	0,1667	0,8572	1,0000	1,0000
3	Student 3	0,0000	0,4166	0,0000	1,0000	0,6364
4	Student 4	0,8333	1,0000	1,0000	0,0000	0,2727
5	Student 5	0,4167	0,3333	0,2857	0,3636	0,3939
6	Student 6	0,5833	0,0000	0,5715	0,3636	0,1515

Now we want to form two groups, each with three students. Two possible individuals are shown in Table 6.

By applying (3), we obtain:

$$TM = \{0.5436, 0.4020, 0.5304, 0.5690, 0.4091\}$$

Table 6. Example individuals.

Individual 1			Individual 2		
1	2	3	1	3	5
4	5	6	2	4	6

When calculating IM_g^i according to (4) from Tables 5 and 6, we obtain:

$$IM_g^1 = \begin{Bmatrix} 0.4761 \ 0.3596 \ 0.4418 \ 0.8956 \ 0.5455 \\ 0.6111 \ 0.4444 \ 0.6191 \ 0.2424 \ 0.2727 \end{Bmatrix}$$

$$IM_g^2 = \begin{Bmatrix} 0.2816 \ 0.4151 \ 0.2513 \ 0.6835 \ 0.3434 \\ 0.8056 \ 0.3889 \ 0.8095 \ 0.4545 \ 0.4747 \end{Bmatrix}$$

Finally, calculating the aptitude measures applying (5), $D^1 = 0.2790$ and $D^2 = 0.3282$ are obtained. It can be observed that the grouping represented by Individual 1 is more inter-homogeneous than Individual 2, that is, with this distribution, Individual 1's group reflect the total set of students with greater precision when looking for all dimensions together.

Initial Population and Evolution. In the example represented in Table 6, a trivial group formation is shown: assign each student in order to a group according to the identifier they have. The first N/G students (in this case 3) belong to Group 1, the next N/G to Group 2 and so on. Although this conformation is valid, the idea of the initial population is to generate k individuals randomly, using the matrix representation described in the Section *"Representation of individuals"* and fulfilling the restriction that each element must be in one and only one of the positions in the array.

Once the initial population is obtained, and in accordance with the general scheme of a genetic algorithm, the evolution process is carried out in which it is passed from one generation to another using the genetic selection operators (roulette for minimization [7]), crossover (C1 operator [8]), and mutation (by exchange [9]), until a desired fitness measure is obtained or until a total of h generations is reached.

3 Method

The empirical process was developed under an experimental design based on four Solomon groups [10], as shown in Table 7.

The validation of the proposed group formation technique was carried out with four different groups belonging to the Academic Programs of the Faculty of Engineering of the University of Nariño Pasto Campus, Systems Engineering and Electronic Engineering, for the initial Programming course in the period academic B-2019. Table 8 shows the experimental design applied in each course:

Groups G_1 and G_2 correspond to the experimental groups of each program and G_3 and G_4 were the control groups respectively, in addition X was the experimental treatment that

Table 7. Experimental design.

	Pre-test	Experimental stimulus	Post-test
RG_1 (Experimental group)	O_1	X	O_2
RG_2 (Experimental group)	–	X	O_3
RG_3 (Control group)	O_4	–	O_5
RG_4 (Control group)	–	–	O_6

Table 8. Experimental design by program.

Program	Course	Experimental design			
Systems Engineering	Programming I	RG_1	O_1	X	O_2
		RG_3	O_4	–	O_5
Electronic Engineering	Programming Foundations	RG_2	–	X	O_3
		RG_4	–	–	O_6

consisted of forming the required groups applying the proposed technique and carrying out an activity collaborative learning process during the work sessions scheduled for the control structures theme. In turn, O_1 and O_4 were the pre-tests applied at the beginning of the experiment to the groups of the Systems Engineering Program; O_2, O_3, O_5 and O_6, were the post-tests applied at the end of the experiment for both the experimental and control groups. The pre-test and the post-test were the same questionnaire with exercises related to the subject of control structures.

The first experimental group G_1 was made up of 43 students from the Programming I - Group 1 course of the first semester of Systems Engineering, to whom a pre-test (O_1), the experimental treatment X and finally a post-test (O_2). The control group G_3 was made up of 36 students from the Programming course I - Group 2, from the same semester and academic period, to whom a pre-test (O_4) was also applied, and the experimental treatment was not applied.

The second experimental group G_2 was made up of 32 students from the Programming Foundations course - Group 1 of the first semester of Electronic Engineering, to whom the experimental treatment X and finally a post-test (O_3) were applied. The control group G_4 was made up of 21 students from the Programming Foundations course I - Group 2, from the same semester and academic period, to whom the experimental treatment was not applied.

4   Results

In this section, the results obtained in the development of the research are presented in detail, starting with a description of how a class session would be carried out applying the proposed technique, then the results of the application of the instrument for the measurement of personality traits in students, and ends with the results obtained in the development of the experiment.

4.1 Class Session

Before presenting the results obtained in the research process, it is convenient to show at an example level how a class session would be carried out in which you want to form groups with the proposed technique. A class session is taken as an example to support the theme of "Control Structures (conditionals and cycles)" in an initial Programming course. To do this, the teacher, considering the methodological scheme presented in Fig. 1, performs the steps indicated in the activity diagram shown in Fig. 2.

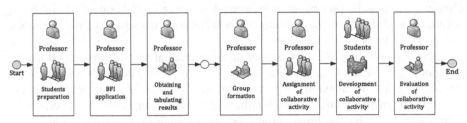

Fig. 2. Activity diagram class "Control Structures".

It is important to clarify that the first three activities, corresponding to the measurement of the personality traits of the students, are carried out once in the academic period (for the particular case, once a semester), since the group, generally, remains stable throughout the period, and the results can be used as many times as desired for the formation of new working groups, in terms of members or quantity.

4.2 BFI Results

As mentioned in Sect. 3, groups G_1 and G_2 are the groups to which the experimental treatment was applied, initially requiring the application of the instrument for measuring personality traits described above. The BFI results should be organized as shown in Table 1, taking into account that the students who do not fill out the instrument (if any) should be assigned as values to each of the dimensions considered, the mean of the total group in each of them. Tables like these were supplied to the genetic algorithm, the processing results of which are presented below.

4.3 Group Formation

Once acceptable parameters have been established for the configuration of the genetic algorithm, we proceed to form groups of four students for the two experimental groups (G_1 and G_2), using a test application, preparing the corresponding plain text files with the results of the BFI in each of the groups. Given that the total number of students in G_1 is not a multiple of four, it was necessary to supplement the missing student with a "dummy", to which the mean of all the students in each of the dimensions considered was assigned as scores. That means that one of the 11 groups was made up of three students. The group formation was obtained in 100 generations, with a population size of 2500 individuals, with a survival of 40%, and with a mutation probability of 0.01, which yielded an adaptation of 0.4525 in a time of 44.72 s.

4.4 Experiment Results

Finally, the most important analysis was carried out on the final results of the experiment, which consisted of contrasting the measurements of the experimental groups versus those of the control groups, seeking to verify in a basic way if there is an improvement in the learning process by applying the proposed technique with respect to the group formation techniques traditionally used by teachers, when developing a collaborative activity. Next, a parallel is made between the experimental and control groups for each of the courses involved in the study.

Figure 3 shows the positive impact of the experimental treatment proposed for the Programming I course of the Systems Engineering Program. The results show that, on average, the grades obtained in the post-test by the experimental group are higher than those obtained by the control group. Similarly, the positive impact of the experimental treatment proposed for the Programming Foundations course of the Electronic Engineering Program is shown. The results show that on average the grades obtained in the post-test by the experimental group are higher than those obtained by the control group.

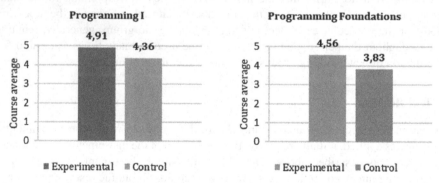

Fig. 3. Experimental groups versus Control groups.

Finally, and in order to provide some conclusion regarding the goodness of the proposed group formation technique, an analysis was carried out using the t-Student test, used for the comparison of two independent samples, given that the grades achieved by the students follow a normal distribution; seeking to determine a possible statistical difference between the grades obtained by the experimental groups versus the control groups, that is, a basic difference in the level of learning achieved by the students in the specific subject.

The results of the application of the t-Student test are shown in Table 9, which were obtained using the Microsoft Excel™ Data Analysis tool, with a significance level of

95% and considering the following hypotheses: H_0: the means are the same, H_1: the means are different.

Table 9. t-Student tests.

	G_1	G_3	G_2	G_4
Mean	4,9116	4,3639	4,5625	3,8314
Variance	0,0839	1,9327	0,9637	0,5767
Observations	43	36	32	21
Mean hypothetical difference	0		0	
Degrees of freedom	77		51	
t statistical	2,5220		2,8890	
P(T ≤ t) two tails	**0,0137**		**0,0057**	
t critical value (two tails)	1,9913		2,0076	

When comparing the experimental group G_1 with the control group G_3 of the Programming I course, a P value of 0.0137 was obtained; as this value is less than 0.05, the null hypothesis is rejected in favor of the alternative hypothesis, with a significance level of 95%, that is, the means are different, with a difference of 0.5477 in favor of G_1. When comparing the experimental group G_2 with the control group G_4 of the Programming Foundations course, a P value of 0.0057 was obtained; as this value is less than 0.05, the null hypothesis is rejected in favor of the alternative hypothesis, with a significance level of 95%, that is, the means are different, with a difference of 0.7311 in favor of G_1.

The previous statistical analysis demonstrates the positive impact of the treatment presented in this research in the experimental groups compared to the control groups, establishing that forming homogeneous groups for collaborative learning scenarios considering the personality traits of the students, benefits their academic performance.

5 Conclusions

From the results obtained, both from the methodological implementation of the proposed group formation technique and from the controlled experiment described above, the following conclusions can be stated:

- The measurement of personality traits through the "Big Five Inventory - BFI" turned out to be a practical and easy process at the time of its computational implementation, which greatly facilitated the collection of the data required by the optimization algorithm. It is clarified that, for the purposes of the study, only the purely quantitative process was considered, qualitative aspects related to the personality of the participating students were not considered.
- Considering that the problem of obtaining homogeneous (equitable) groups from a group of students where not only one but several of their personal characteristics are

taken into account, is difficult to solve by analytical or exhaustive search methods due to the combinatorial explosion which may occur depending on the number of students and groups, a heuristic search method such as genetic algorithms is a good candidate to solve it.

- With the results obtained through various tests, the usefulness of the method could be verified, since it manages to obtain quite homogeneous groups (considering the proposed aptitude measure) for multiple characteristics, even when the number of possible combinations is high, without implying high computation time.
- It was demonstrated through the experiment that the homogeneous groups generated with the proposed technique produced better academic results compared to the formation techniques traditionally used by teachers, when developing a collaborative activity.
- The grades obtained in three of the four courses are above the quantitative scale of 4.0/5.0, which shows that there is an important appropriation of the specific subject by the students, at the end of the collaborative support activity.
- In the field of programming teaching, it is necessary to involve didactic aspects that place the student as a central and active element of the learning process, instilling in them the need for self-learning in a collaborative environment that improves the attitudes and skills study and work group.

References

1. Barkley, E.F., Major, C.H., Cross, K.P.: Collaborative Learning Techniques: A Handbook for College Faculty. Jossey-Bass, San Francisco (2014)
2. Soto, C.J., Kronauer, A., Liang, J.K.: Five-Factor Model of Personality the Encyclopedia of Adulthood and Aging, pp. 1–5. Wiley, Hoboken (2015). https://doi.org/10.1002/978111852 1373.wbeaa014
3. Rammstedt, B., John, O.P.: Measuring personality in one minute or less: a 10-item short version of the Big Five Inventory in English and German. J. Res. Pers. **41**, 203–212 (2007). https://doi.org/10.1016/j.jrp.2006.02.001
4. Benet-Martínez, V., John, O.P.: Los Cinco Grandes across cultures and ethnic groups: multitrait-multimethod analyses of the Big Five in Spanish and English. J. Pers. Soc. Psychol. **75**, 729–750 (1998). https://doi.org/10.1037/0022-3514.75.3.729
5. Moreno, J., Rivera, J.C., Ceballos, Y.F.: Agrupamiento Homogéneo de Elementos con Múltiples Atributos Mediante Algoritmos Genéticos. DYNA **78**, 246–254 (2011)
6. Dodge, Y.: The Oxford Dictionary of Statistical Terms. Oxford University Press, New York (2006)
7. Weise, T.: Global Optimization Algorithm: Theory and Application, Self-Published (2009)
8. Reza Hejazi, S., Saghafian, S.: Flowshop-scheduling problems with makespan criterion: a review. Int. J. Prod. Res. **43**, 2895–2929 (2005). https://doi.org/10.1080/0020754050056417
9. Araujo, L., Cervigón, C.: Algoritmos evolutivos: Un enfoque práctico, Alfaomega Grupo Editor, Ciudad de México (2009)
10. Hernández Sampieri, R., Fernández Collado, C., Baptista Lucio, P.: Metodología de la investigación, McGraw-Hill Education (2014)

Communication Preferences of First-Year University Students from Mexico and Spain

Eliana Gallardo-Echenique[1](✉) ⓘ, Luis Marqués-Molías[2] ⓘ, Oscar Gomez-Cruz[3] ⓘ, and Byron Vaca-Barahona[4] ⓘ

[1] Universidad Peruana de Ciencias Aplicadas, Prolongación Primavera 2390, Lima 15023, Peru
eliana.gallardo@upc.pe
[2] Universidad Rovira i Virgili., Ctra. de Valls, s/n, 43007 Tarragona, Spain
luis.marques@urv.cat
[3] Universidad Autónoma de Chiapas. Blvd., Belisario Domínguez Km. 1081, s/n, Tuxtla Gutiérrez, Chiapas, Mexico
oscar.gomez@unach.mx
[4] Escuela Superior Politécnica de Chimborazo, Panamericana Sur Km. 1 1/2, Riobamba 060155, Ecuador
bvacab@espoch.edu.ec

Abstract. The aim of this study is to analyze how Mexican and Spanish university students communicate with peers and professors when they have an academic or administrative question. The methodology is quantitative and descriptive; it follows a comparative case study design that has been carried out over time, emphasizing two different contexts that share a common goal. In both universities, there are some differences in the way that first-year university students communicate with each other. When students have academic or administrative doubts, they rarely contact their professors or the university administrative structure as a means of solving them. Communication is a fundamental topic to work to improve the way how faculty communicate with students. Students are less willing to appropriate social networks as a formal learning tool, preferring it as a form of course-related communication or using it for non-academic purposes.

Keywords: Digital communication · E-mail · Social networks · Higher education

1 Introduction

In many developed countries, the environment where young people grow up before they reach university is saturated with digital technologies such as social networks, the Internet, email, digital media, and the Web. 2.0, as well as digital and cloud platforms, among others [1]. Studies suggest that their use is restricted, limited, and specific to technologies that focus primarily on the basic functions of the cell phone and the Internet. These functions include sending email, searching for information, or watching videos. Evidence suggests that very few students use all of the advanced capabilities and affordances of smartphones, for example [1, 2]. In terms of their communication habits, students use few

© Springer Nature Switzerland AG 2020
V. Agredo-Delgado et al. (Eds.): HCI-COLLAB 2020, CCIS 1334, pp. 85–93, 2020.
https://doi.org/10.1007/978-3-030-66919-5_9

technologies for rapid communication, such as a cell phone for voice calls or text messaging. They also use social networking sites such as Facebook and instant messaging apps [2]. Most universities in developed countries have successfully introduced various digital technologies into the teaching profession [3] and in the research process [4]. For example, digital technologies can be objects, tools and research spaces simultaneously (i.e. research on costs, content and users of online social networks) [4]. However, in many developing countries, access to digital technologies is much more limited [5, 6]. For example, 96% of 15-year-old students in countries belonging to the Organization for Economic Cooperation and Development (OECD) reported that they had a computer at home [6, 7]; meanwhile, in developing countries, these figures are much lower and limited access is often the first problem faced by students.

1.1 Research Context

The state of Chiapas, one of the locations where this research was conducted, is located in the southwestern region of Mexico. It is a multicultural state [8] that does not have educational services adapted to the linguistic and cultural needs of indigenous communities, scattered rural populations and migrant groups [9]. Higher education presents massive challenges such as high levels of illiteracy or dropout rates in dispersed rural areas, where indigenous or migrant populations are prevalent, resulting from the gap that separates the country's entities and regions in terms of coverage, quality and equity [10]. Chiapas is one of the four regions lagging behind in this area, with a coverage rate of only 21%, and ranks second to last at the national level [10]. This study was conducted at the Autonomous University of Chiapas (UNACH for its initials in Spanish) which is the main institution for higher education in the Mexican state of Chiapas [11]. It serves more than 22,301 students in 16 faculties, offering 71 undergraduate programs, including eight non-conventional (distance learning) and 55 graduate programs [12].

This study was also carried out in the Faculty of Educational Sciences and Psychology at the University Rovira i Virgili (URV) in Tarragona, Spain. The URV is a public university that is ranked among the 600 best universities in the world by the Times Higher Education (THE) and the Shanghai ranking (ARWU). It consists of 12 departments and schools with more than 1,700 professors and researchers, offering quality degrees to 11,448 undergraduate students, 2,791 in master's programs and 1,197 doctoral students, who attend courses in various fields of knowledge: sciences, health sciences, social and legal sciences, engineering and architecture, arts and humanities, all adapted to the European Higher Education Area [13]. It is a system with multiple campuses, located in the cities of Tarragona, Reus, Vila-Seca, Tortosa and El Vendrell [14].

2 Introduction

The research aim is to analyze how students in two public universities in Mexico and Spain communicate when they have an academic or administrative question.

The proposed methodology is quantitative and descriptive, with a comparative case study design, that has been carried out over time [15], emphasizing the comparison between two different contexts (Mexico and Spain) that share a common focus or goal.

The instrument used to collect information was the "Student Communication and Study Habits" questionnaire, developed in Canada by Bullen, Morgan, Belfer and Qayyum [16]. The questionnaire was translated into Spanish by experts from the UOC [17] who validated it to that context. This version consists of 78 Likert-type items (from "never" to "always"; "strongly disagree" to "strongly agree") divided into four sections: (a) Sect. 1 contains demographic information; (b) Sect. 2 addresses who students turn to for help; (c) Sect. 3 addresses how and where students communicate with their peers and professors; and, (d) the last section addresses study and communication habits with peers and professors. To apply a tool developed in a new country, culture, and/or language to another [18] it must be validated to be linguistically and culturally equivalent to the original [19]. The Spanish version was adapted to the Mexican context through the expert judgment technique [20].

To determine the study sample, first-year students from UNACH's Faculty of Humanities were invited, comprising a total of 190 students distributed as follows: Undergraduate degrees in Pedagogy (102), Communication (67), Hispanic-American Language and Literature (10), Philosophy and Library Science (7) and Information Management (4). Their ages ranged from 19 to 45 years, where 63.2% were women and 36.8% men. This sample is part of a total population of 1,493 students distributed in the same number of academic programs. In the case of Spain, 204 first-year students in the degrees of Pedagogy (17), Social Education (22), Early Education (86) and Primary Education (79) answered the questionnaire. Their ages ranged from 18 to 54, where 86.8% were women and 13.2% were men.

3   Results and Discussion

In this section, we present the data obtained in relation to the student's actions when he or she has an academic or administrative question, along with the resources and frequency with which he or she uses them to communicate with classmates and professors.

In a first analysis, it can be seen that, in both countries, students rarely talk to their professors when they have a doubt about the content of a subject (Table 1). For example, Mexico yields 51.1%, while for Spain it is similar with 46.1%. It is assumed (although more studies are needed) that, due to their income and their adaptation to the environment, this phenomenon is more prevalent in both countries. This seems to be in line with previous studies [1, 21, 22] that point out that current communication between professors and their students is rare, and largely limited to formal, structured situations such as classroom lectures. Moreover, it is evident that the majority of these interactions occur face-to-face, with their peers, in both contexts. One aspect that is noteworthy is the scarce contact that students establish with their tutors/academic coordinators, a situation that is repeated in the case of student assistance services available at the university. It is worth noting that, when it comes to answering their questions through the Internet, most do so frequently, although it is remarkable that the number of Mexican students who always use the Internet to solve their academic questions is almost double, when compared to the Spanish case. A similar trend is observed when they say that they try to solve their doubts autonomously.

With regard to administrative issues (Table 2), a similar situation occurs, where students from both countries prefer their classmates rather than professors in order to

Table 1. What the student does when in doubt about the content of a subject.

Students	Never		Rarely		Often		Always	
	Sp.	Mx.	Sp.	Mx.	Sp.	Mx.	Sp.	Mx.
I contact my professor	5.9%	0.0%	46.1%	51.1%	32.4%	28.4%	7.8%	20.5%
I contact a classmate	0%	2.6%	1%	22.1%	26.5%	38.9%	64.2%	36.3%
I contact a tutor, coordinator, etc.	56.9%	43.7%	24.5%	44.2%	8.8%	9.5%	1%	2.6%
I contact other students who are not in the course	30.4%	36.8%	34.3%	41.1%	19.6%	17.9%	6.4%	4.2%
I contact someone else	17.6%	27.4%	38.7%	40.0%	19.1%	24.7%	15.2%	7.9%
I head to a university support center	77.5%	65.8%	8.8%	27.9%	3.9%	5.3%	0.5%	1.1%
I search the Internet	1.5%	4.7%	29.4%	22.1%	43.1%	40.0%	17.6%	33.2%
I contact a co-worker	52.5%	46.8%	11.8%	23.2%	13.7%	20.5%	12.7%	9.5%
I try to solve it myself	1%	6.3%	14.7%	25.8%	45.1%	45.8%	29.9%	22.1%

address this type of problem. This could be explained by the fact that many students feel comfortable discussing these issues with their peers, since they are sharing a common experience and purpose throughout the academic program by means of common tasks, deadlines, and administrative requirements [23]. In a study conducted in Canada, classmates were also the first choice for students when asked about what to do when they have a question about the content of a subject or an administrative issue. This suggests that classmates are very important resources for students [23]. It is relevant to note the differences in the use of administrative staff to solve these problems. Mexican students seem to use these services much less than Spanish students: 64.9% (N/PV) versus 31.9% (N/PV). It is not clear why, but this is of interest when addressing future qualitative research on the subject in order to shed light upon possible explanations. There is also a difference in the use of the university's institutional website. On the one hand, 62.3% of Spanish students say they use the information provided by the website "often" or "always" to resolve their administrative doubts, compared to 35.5% of Mexican students who claim this same frequency of use.

Below are the results obtained in terms of the use of technologies by students while carrying out activities at the university and in relation to communication with their peers and professors (Tables 3 and 4).

In both countries, there is a clear preference (Table 3) for the use of personal email rather than the institutional account, followed by fairly frequent use of instant messaging and social networks. In this sense, the increased use of Facebook by Spanish students compared to their Mexican counterparts to communicate with their peers is noteworthy, which is in line with studies that indicate that this social network seems to be a good tool for communication and social interaction [24].

Table 2. What the student does when he or she has an administrative question.

Students	Never		Rarely		Often		Always	
	Sp.	Mx.	Sp.	Mx.	Sp.	Mx.	Sp.	Mx.
I contact my professor	33.8%	11.2%	33.8%	42.0%	25.5%	33.5%	5.4%	13.3%
I contact my classmates	0.5%	9.1%	13.2%	31.7%	42.6%	37.6%	41.2%	21.5%
I contact other representatives	35.3%	15.0%	32.4%	32.1%	21.%	34.2%	8.3%	18.7%
I contact other students who are not in the course	34.3%	30.9%	35.8%	47.9%	21.6%	16.0%	5.9%	5.3%
I contact the person in charge of the academic aspects of the degree	44.6%	41.7%	28.9%	42.8%	15.7%	11.2%	8.3%	4.3%
I contact the staff at the office	12.3%	37.8%	19.6%	27.1%	26.5%	21.3%	39.2%	13.8%
I search the UNACH website	7.4%	26.3%	28.4%	38.2%	40.7%	26.3%	21.6%	9.1%
I try to solve it myself	13.7%	56.5%	33.8%	25.3%	31.4%	13.4%	18.6%	4.8%

Table 3. Frequency of use of the following resources by the student to communicate with peers.

Students	Never		Rarely		Often		Always	
	Sp.	Mx.	Sp.	Mx.	Sp.	Mx.	Sp.	Mx.
Email UNACH	25%	43.7%	34.3%	43.2%	20.6%	8.9%	10.8%	4.2%
Personal email	1.5%	10.0%	13.2%	39.5%	27.9%	30.5%	48%	20.0%
Instant Messaging	14.7%	31.2%	15.7%	28.6%	25.5%	21.2%	34.3%	19.0%
Mobile text message	7.8%	10.5%	21.1%	31.1%	31.9%	26.3%	29.9%	32.1%
Facebook/MySpace	2.9%	7.9%	4.4%	26.8%	11.8%	31.1%	70.6%	34.2%
Videoconference systems	70.1%	58.0%	13.7%	30.3%	5.9%	8.5%	1%	3.2%
I speak on the phone	7.8%	9.0%	27.5%	22.8%	30.9%	24.5%	69%	36.5%
I speak in person	0%	3.2%	3.4%	8.6%	20.1%	23.5%	65.7%	64.7%
Moodle Resources	38.2%	36.5%	32.3%	39.7%	14%	18.0%	5.6%	5.8%

In relation to the use of resources relative to their professors, email stands out as the main tool used by students, but with significant differences between the two countries. While in Spain the institutional email is the most prevalent, in Mexico, personal email is preferred. In line with Qayyum [23], students prefer to contact faculty via email, especially when seeking help with subject content. Email (personal and institutional) is one of the most widely used digital resources in society as a means of interaction

Table 4. What the student does when in doubt about the content of a subject.

Students	Never		Rarely		Often		Always	
	Sp.	Mx.	Sp.	Mx.	Sp.	Mx.	Sp.	Mx.
Email UNACH	1%	50.3%	12.7%	36.0%	30.4%	11.1%	52.9%	2.6%
Personal email	66.2%	10.6%	15.7%	42.6%	9.8%	32.4%	4.9%	14.4%
Instant Messaging	91.7%	47.6%	2.9%	27.3%	1.5%	19.8%	1.5%	5.3%
Mobile text message	92.2%	38.1%	2%	29.6%	1.5%	22.8%	2%	9.5%
Facebook/MySpace	86.8%	49.2%	6.9%	28.0%	0.5%	11.6%	2.5%	11.1%
Videoconference systems	93.6%	75.9%	3.9%	19.3%	0%	4.3%	0%	0.5%
I speak on the phone	87.7%	49.2%	5.9%	23.8%	2%	18.0%	1.5%	9.0%
I speak in person	5.4%	6.5%	12.7%	14.1%	33.8%	21.1%	45.1%	58.4%
Moodle Resources	33.3%	53.2%	27%	33.0%	26%	10.1%	10.3%	3.7%

to establish connections between people [25]. In this sense, students use email with professors who demand a great deal of formal and structured situations such as classroom classes [26], or where it was desirable to maintain a certain distance [27]. The very limited use of instant messaging and the telephone in both countries is noteworthy. This may be justified because students consider that speaking to professors in person is one of the main sources of academic information, rather than through an online communication tool or program.

In both contexts, a very low usage level is observed. The potential disadvantages of video conferencing include the difficulty of maintaining student interest, the lack of training and guidance for professors and/or students [28] given that it is a technology that requires certain types of criteria and knowledge that could be quite complex and difficult to achieve [29]. The goal is to raise awareness about the usage level of virtual training tools (e.g. discussion forum, wiki), which is low in both countries in terms of communication with professors. Unlike social networks, Moodle (the system used by both universities), tends to be very focused and lacks the personal touch offered by platforms such as Facebook, which actively encourages the construction of online communities, extending learning beyond the boundaries of the classroom [30]. Likewise, students in both countries are not using the resources offered by their institutions; therefore, it is necessary to clarify this scenario with a longitudinal study, in order to determine if this behavior occurs in other semesters, and with this, to determine the reinforcement of institutional measures to ensure that the student feels a sense of belonging to the institution from the very first moment.

4   Conclusions

In both countries, when students have administrative doubts or academic questions, they rarely turn to their professor or the administrative staff. They prefer to seek out their peers first to try to resolve it, which indicates that there seems to be more trust in the relationship with their fellow students than with their professors. In relation to communication between students–administrative staff, there is a clear trend towards a lack of communication with university support centers, which may indicate a lack of intervention towards better university integration by the institutions. This seems to indicate, from our point of view, that the first-year student does not yet make preferential use of the resources available at the university and seeks solutions from those who are in the same situation first. These issues would merit further work to identify the reasons.

Communication is a fundamental aspect of the work with first-year students in order to significantly improve the way in which they relate to the aforementioned actors, an aspect that can help in different dimensions of university management, such as avoiding dropout rates and withdrawal in the first years of training. Although much of the communication between students and their professors is asynchronous, the results show that email and instant messaging are the means most used by students to communicate, regardless of context, probably because it provides a sense of immediacy. Also, it is concluded that the use of resources available from the university is low and uneven in both contexts. This needs to be analyzed in depth, since it represents a very high financial cost for universities. However, in the case of Spanish students, it is the primary means of communication with professors, an aspect that seems to indicate that in a more structured and efficient context in which professors encourage such use, the more "official" environments are used.

The fact that only small differences are observed in the use of technologies and in the ways in which students communicate with their professors in two such different contexts, both in its methodological and socio-educational development parameters, suggests the potential for transferring policies for the improvement of academic activities between the two universities with some ease. It could be said that the existing differences do not seem to be in the area of communication or interaction between students and professors but may have to do with educational planning or administrative organization.

In light of recent technological developments and the realities of young people's access to social networks, it appears that students are less likely to appropriate social networks as a formal learning tool, preferring them as a subject-related means of communication or for socializing. In this sense, studies carried out with university students in Catalonia (Spain) [31] demonstrated that students do not seem to have a clear perception of how productive social networks can be for learning, an aspect that should be added to their reluctance in terms of their possible educational use, since they consider that there should be a separation between the personal and academic spheres. These aspects have emerged in some way in this work so they could be future lines of study to further explore.

References

1. Gallardo-Echenique, E., Bullen, M., Marqués-Molías, L.: Student communication and study habits of first-year university students in the digital era. Can. J. Learn. Technol. **42**, 1–21 (2016). https://doi.org/10.21432/T2D047
2. Thompson, P.: The digital natives as learners: technology use patterns and approaches to learning. Comput. Educ. **65**, 12–33 (2013). https://doi.org/10.1016/j.compedu.2012.12.022

3. Greenhow, C., Robelia, B., Hughes, J.E.: Learning, teaching, and scholarship in a digital age. Web 2.0 and classroom research: what path should we take now? Educ. Res. **38**, 246–259 (2009). https://doi.org/10.3102/0013189X09336671
4. Tsatsou, P.: Digital technologies in the research process: lessons from the digital research community in the UK. Comput. Hum. Behav. **61**, 597–608 (2016). https://doi.org/10.1016/j.chb.2016.03.053
5. Libaque-Saenz, C.F.: Strategies for bridging the internet digital divide in Peru: a benchmarking of South Korea and Chile. In: CONF-IRM 2016 Proceedings (2016)
6. Organización para la Cooperación y el Desarrollo Económicos (OCDE): Students, Computers and Learning: Making the Connection. PISA. OECD Publishing, Paris, France (2015). https://doi.org/10.1787/9789264239555-en
7. Organización para la Cooperación y el Desarrollo Económicos (OCDE): Panorama de la educación 2017: Indicadores de la OCDE. Fundación Santillana; OCDE & Ministerio de Educación, Cultura y Deporte, Madrid, España (2017). https://doi.org/10.1787/eag-2017-es
8. Universidad Autónoma de Chiapas: Plan de Desarrollo Institucional 2030. UNACH, Chiapas (2019)
9. Núñez Medina, G., Jiménez Acevedo, H.M.: Evaluación de Indicadores. Secretaría de Educación - Fondo de Aportaciones para la Nómina Educativa y Gasto Operativo FONE 2015. Consejo de Investigación y Evaluación de la Política Social del Estado (CIEPSE), Tuxtla Gutiérrez Chiapas, Mexico (2016)
10. Universidad Autónoma de Chiapas: Programa Institucional de Trayectorias Escolares. UNACH, Chiapas (2017)
11. Secretaría de Educación Pública México: Programa @prende 2.0: Programa de Inclusión Digital 2016 – 2017. SEP, Ciudad de México, México (2016)
12. Instituto Nacional de Estadística y Geografía (INEGI): Tecnologías de la información y comunicaciones: TIC's en hogares. https://www.inegi.org.mx/temas/ticshogares/
13. Universitat Rovira i Virgili (URV): La URV en cifras. https://www.urv.cat/es/universidad/conocer/presentacion/cifras/
14. Universitat Rovira i Virgili (URV): Universitat Rovira i Virgili. http://www.urv.cat/
15. Goodrick, D.: Síntesis metodológicas. Sinopsis de la evaluación de impacto N° 9. Estudios de caso comparativos. Cent. Investig. UNICEF. 13 (2014)
16. Bullen, M., Morgan, T., Belfer, K., Qayyum, A.A.: The digital learner at BCIT and implications for an e-strategy. In: Paper presented at 2008 Research Workshop of the European Distance Education Network (EDEN), Researching and Promoting Access to Education and Training: The Role of Distance Education and e-Learning in Technology-Enhanced Environments, Paris (2008)
17. Romero, M., Guitert, M., Sangrà, A., Bullen, M.: Do UOC students fit in the Net generation profile? An approach to their habits in ICT use. Int. Rev. Res. Open Distance Learn. **14**, 158–181 (2013)
18. Muñiz, J., Elosua, P., Hambleton, R.K.: Directrices para la traducción y adaptación de los tests: Segunda edición. Psicothema **25**, 151–157 (2013). https://doi.org/10.7334/psicothema2013.24
19. Kuzmanić, M.: Validity in qualitative research: Interview and the appearance of truth through dialogue. Horiz. Psychol. **18**, 39–50 (2009)
20. Gallardo-Echenique, E., Marqués Molias, L., Gomez Cruz, O.D., De Lira Cruz, R.: Cross-cultural adaptation and validation of the "Student communication & study habits" questionnaire to the Mexican context. In: Proceedings - 14th Latin American Conference on Learning Technologies, LACLO 2019. pp. 104–109. IEEE, San Jose Del Cabo, Mexico (2019). https://doi.org/10.1109/LACLO49268.2019.00027
21. Bullen, M., Morgan, T., Qayyum, A.: Digital Learners in Higher Education: Generation is Not the Issue. Can. J. Learn. Technol. **37**, 1–24 (2011)

22. Garcia, I., Escofet Roig, A., Gros, B.: Students' attitudes towards ICT learning uses: a comparison betweeen digital learners in blended and virtual universities [Special issue]. Eur. J. Open, Distance E-Learning – EURODL. 51–66 (2012)
23. Qayyum, A.: Student help-seeking attitudes and behaviors in a digital era. Int. J. Educ. Technol. High. Educ. 15(1), 1–16 (2018). https://doi.org/10.1186/s41239-018-0100-7
24. Gallardo Echenique, E., Marqués Molías, L., Bullen, M.: Students in higher education: Social and academic uses of digital technology. Int. J. Educ. Technol. High. Educ. 12(1), 25–37 (2015). https://doi.org/10.7238/rusc.v12i1.2078
25. Chan, M.: Mobile-mediated multimodal communications, relationship quality and subjective well-being: an analysis of smartphone use from a life course perspective. Comput. Hum. Behav. 87, 254–262 (2018). https://doi.org/10.1016/j.chb.2018.05.027
26. Li, L., Finley, J., Pitts, J., Guo, R.: Which is a better choice for student-faculty interaction: synchronous or asynchronous communication? J. Technol. Res. 2, 1–12 (2010)
27. Bullen, M., Morgan, T., Belfer, K., Qayyum, A.A.: The Net generation in higher education: Rhetoric and reality. Int. J. Excell. E-Learn. 2, 1–13 (2009)
28. Candarli, D., Yuksel, H.G.: Students' perceptions of video-conferencing in the classrooms in higher education. Proc. Soc. Behav. Sci. 47, 357–361 (2012). https://doi.org/10.1016/j.sbspro.2012.06.663
29. Hedestig, U., Kaptelinin, V.: Re-contextualization of teaching and learning in videoconference-based environments. In: Stahl, G. (ed.) Proceedings of the Conference on Computer Support for Collaborative Learning Foundations for a CSCL Community - CSCL 2002. pp. 179–188. International Society of the Learning Sciences, Boulder, CO, USA (2002). https://doi.org/10.3115/1658616.1658642
30. Petrovic, N., Jeremic, V., Cirovic, M., Radojicic, Z., Milenkovic, N.: Facebook vs. Moodle: what do students really think? In: Morris, L. and Tsolakidis, C. (eds.) International Conference on Information Communication Technologies in Education - ICICTE 2013 Proceedings, pp. 413–421. UNESCO, Crete, Greece (2013)
31. González-Martinez, J., Ruiz, A.: #ActitudesMaestros: Las actitudes de los futuros maestros hacia el uso educativo de las redes sociales. Educ. Siglo XXI 31, 287–312 (2013)

CovidEmoVis - An Interactive Visual Analytic Tool for Exploring Emotions from Twitter Data of Covid-19

Leticia Laura-Ochoa[(⊠)] [iD] and Franco Tejada-Toledo [iD]

Universidad Nacional de San Agustín de Arequipa, Arequipa, Peru
{llaurao,ftejadat}@unsa.edu.pe

Abstract. Due to the Covid-19 pandemic, nowadays people comment a lot in Twitter expressing emotions around this. It can be very difficult to analyze and obtain information from big amounts of unstructured data, the objective of this work is the processing of high volumes of these tweets and to get a temporal visual exploration analysis of emotions through an interactive visual analytic tool from Twitter Data of Covid-19. This useful tool could help to the specialists in Psychology to know more about the emotional profile of users and the tweets posted daywise. Further it helps to see the important words of the tweets through word cloud and a two-dimensional plane graph to see the word of each tweet with its VAD (valence, arousal and dominance) scores and emotions. First we preprocessed the data to delete the stopwords, then we used a RNN (Recurrent Neural Network) to get an emotion related to the tweet, then we calculate VAD scores and fill missing emotions, this data can be visualized across this tool on a timeline interactively.

Keywords: COVID-19 · Emotion analysis · Visual analytics · Social media text

1 Introduction

Nowadays millions of people use social media, generating a lot of information according a specific topic, this information as posts or comments reveal one's emotional situation [1]. The huge information volumes from social medias sources and has created great interest in sentiment analysis to obtain the emotional responses of users. If we can visualize users' emotions then we could help to the specialists in a topic to better understand the essential trends in events [2].

Sentiment analysis is one of the most important text mining tasks and has been generally used to analyze, for example, social media data for many applications, including marketing and customer service [3]. In addition, effective analysis of data to obtain valuable information enables analysts to design successful strategies and make good decisions [4].

With the rapid evolution and daily use of social media, large volumes of multifaceted public opinion information on entities and events are increasingly available to users on

© Springer Nature Switzerland AG 2020
V. Agredo-Delgado et al. (Eds.): HCI-COLLAB 2020, CCIS 1334, pp. 94–106, 2020.
https://doi.org/10.1007/978-3-030-66919-5_10

the Web. Understanding the changes in these data over time is important for psychologists as they can assist in research and trends.

The papers in the categories of space & time and graph still mostly focus on visual mappings and user interactions. One possible reason is that the data used by space & time and graph is usually structured data. Textual information can be found almost everywhere in newspapers, books, social media sites, and so on. With the advance of technologies, an immense amount of text data is being produced, collected, and saved each day. However, effective analysis of the text data is challenging for two reasons. First, the text data is often free, unstructured text corpora, the data is inherently ambiguous due to natural language ambiguity. Second, the volume of the text data is usually huge, this doesn't help to the analysts to read the entire text corpora [4].

It is not possible visualize big amounts of unstructured data in a specific space & time, the scalability and complexity of the data have big challenges for effective analysis to do temporal visual exploration of emotions, which requires advanced computational techniques and algorithms to do the data processing and to treat this kind of data in an interactive tool for the visualization, furthermore it needs the appropriate hardware resources with high performance to do the processing.

Every country is taking preventive measurements to fight against the COVID-19 pandemic. "Social Distancing" or "Stay at home" became the most widely used directive all over the world. Social distancing is forcing people to stay at home. As a result, this is impacting the public event, business, educations, and almost every other activity of the human life. People are losing their jobs, and getting infected from corona and therefore, stress is rising at the personal and at the community levels. Studies of behavioral economics show that emotions (Joy, Anger, Worry, Disgust, Fear, etc.) can profoundly affect individual behavior and decision-making [5].

The objective of this work is the processing of high volumes of information and a temporal visual exploration analysis of emotions from Twitter data related to the COVID-19 pandemic, presenting eight emotions suggested by Plutchik [6] that are made up of four pairs of primary emotions (anger-fear, anticipation-surprise, joy-sadness and trust-disgust). We also characterize all the detected emotions or moods by the continuous dimensional model with three measurements (VAD): valence (degree of positiveness), arousal (degree of excitement), and dominance (degree of aggressiveness). To calculate the emotional category of a word and the VAD scores, we combine two dictionaries most used for emotion detection: NRC-VAD-Lexicon and NRC-Emotion-Lexicon taken from the work NRC Word-Emotion Association lexicon [7].

First of all, we do the pre-processing of the data, leaving stopwords and COVID related words to clean the data, then through text mining algorithms, a RNN (Recurrent Neural Network) and Dictionaries: Lexicon and VAD, we transform complex multidimensional results of emotion analysis into an emotional visual profile.

2 Motivation

This work aims to develop a visual text analysis tool applied to the Covid-19 pandemic from Twitter data, to show the most predominant emotions in a timeline to help the specialist for exploring multidimensional emotion analysis. The questions that our visual analysis project tries to answer are:

Q1: What are the predominant emotions in percentages for a given date?
Q2: On which day was the lowest level of emotion e?
Q3: Which emotion had the lowest level (value) on day d?
Q4: In which range of dates did emotion e1 and emotion e2 have the same pattern of behavior?
Q5: Which emotion changed the most during the event (comparing values of first and last days)?
Q6: On which day did the users express the highest level of emotions?
Q7: What was the trend of the emotions after one specific event?
Q8: What are the most used words of tweets in a specific date?

To construct all these questions we based on the defined tasks in the study [2].

3 Related Works

We reviewed some existing visual text mining tools for emotional analysis.

PEARL [1] is a visual timeline-based analytical tool that allows users to interactively discover and find a person's emotional style derived from that person's social media text. This work offers three unique contributions. First, it supports multidimensional emotion analysis of social media text to automatically detect a person's expressed emotions at different times and summarize those emotions to reveal the person's emotional style. Second, it effectively visualizes complex, multi-dimensional emotion analysis results to create an individual's visual emotional profile, helping users to explore and interpret one's emotional style. Third, it supports visual interactions that allow users to interactively explore and validate emotion analysis results. The disadvantages about this work are it assumes that it can process a person's all social media text at once, also PEARL uses a lexicon-based approach to identify emotional cues (unigrams) and derive basic emotions. While such approach is very portable and fast, it ignores many important linguistic features when inferring emotions, e.g., handling negations (e.g., "I'm not happy").

Xu et al. [8] studied the competition between topics through the dissemination of information on social networks, as well as the impact of opinion leaders on competition. They developed a system with three views: a timeline visualization with a ThemeRiver integration and Storyline visualization to visualize the competition, radial Word Cloud visualizations to summarize the relevant tweets, and a detailed view to list all the relevant tweets. The system was used to illustrate the competition between six main themes, such as the economy, elections and well-being, during the 2012 presidential elections on Twitter. This work found that different groups of opinion leaders, such as the media and grassroots communities, played different roles in the competition.

TextFlow [9] integrates topic mining techniques into interactive visualizations to visually analyze the evolution of topics over time. Use some text mining algorithms to model trends in topic evolution, detect critical events, and find keyword correlations. Three visual views including a topic flow view, a timeline view, and a word cloud are used to interactively visualize mining results and gain insight into bulk text data.

EmoTwitter [10] introduce the concept of enduring feelings based on psychological descriptions of feelings as enduring emotional dispositions that have formed over time.

Taking tweets written over a period of time as input to the analysis, taking a lexicon-based approach, the system identifies Plutchik's eight categories of emotions and displays them over the period of time the tweets were written. Lasting like and dislike feeling patterns are calculated over the time period using the flow of emotion categories, however it doesn't do a deeper linguistic analysis to better understand the expressed emotions. The main contribution of this work is based on the ability to extract intrinsic emotional knowledge through the Twitter social network and provide a detailed visualization of that knowledge.

Whisper [11], one of the first works of visual analysis to represent and analyze the process of spreading temporal spatial information around the world, which includes a visual sunflower metaphor, which describes how tweets on a topic spread from the hometown region to users around the world. Users can perceive temporal trends, that is, the evolution of the topic in the spatial context of said diffusion process.

Yu and Wang [12] collected real-time tweets from U.S. soccer fans during five 2014 FIFA World Cup games. They used a simple line chart to show the emotional changes during a game, where each of the eight basic Plutchik emotions is mapped to a different color, and the total number of tweets is shown on a different scale. This work revealed that sports fans use Twitter for emotional purposes and that the big data approach to analyze sports fans' sentiment showed results generally consistent with the predictions of the disposition theory when the fanship was clear and showed good predictive validity.

4 Proposal

For this work, a dataset of tweets related to the Covid-19 was used, it was necessary to perform a preprocessing to clean frequent words such as Covid, coronavirus, etc., which we will obtain the "processed text", here we begin to use the "Emotion Engine" which uses internally Deep Learning to find the probabilities of Plutchik's eight basic emotions regarding a tweet text, as well as the predominant emotion, then the calculation of the VAD scores is performed using two dictionaries: NRC-VAD-Lexicon and NRC-Emotion-Lexicon, at the end of this process we found some tweets without emotion classification because they do not exist in the NRC-Emotion-Lexicon dictionary, to correct these missing values we used the implementation [13], which instead of preprocessing tweets into tokens, they treat the whole tweet as a sequence of characters and pass characters one by one into the RNN. The task of the RNN is hence to combine characters into a suitable representation and predict emotions. Finally, we got a csv of tweets classified with the corresponding VAD values and Plutchik's emotions (see Fig. 1).

The users of the tool can interact with the generated visualization to perform an exploratory analysis, the visualizer displays the following: Time Series organized by emotions which follows Plutchik's color scheme.

- Word Cloud of a set of tweets of a specific date.
- List of Tweets for a specific date, for each tweet we can see a two-dimensional plane graph with VAD values.

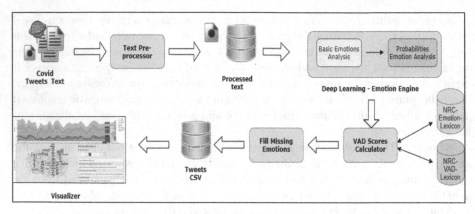

Fig. 1. Pipeline of CovidEmoVis

4.1 Data Description

We used a dataset from a work on COVID-19 tweets in the USA [5], we used the data collected from March 5 to April 9, 2020. We chose that dataset because it was available and the biggest Twitter dataset are in English. Table 1 shows the description of the attributes of the data set.

Table 1. Attributes description.

Attributes	Description
tweet_id	Tweet identifier
created_at	Date of tweet creation
loc	Locality, state of USA
text	Tweet message
user_id	User ID
verified	Verified or not verified

There are 36 CSV files, with a total of 3722519 tweets and a size of approximately 485 MB on the hard drive.

4.2 Implementation

For this work we followed the steps described in the algorithm of the Table 2, which is implemented in Python, we started getting the dataset of Tweets related to the Covid-19 pandemic. First of all, it is necessary a pre-processing of the tweets to erase the stopwords then we use the character based Recurrent Neural Network from [13] to obtain the probabilities of the eight Plutchik's emotions [14] and classify the main emotion for each analyzed tweet. After this, for each word of a tweet we verify if that

Table 2. Algorithm CovidEmosVis

Algorithm 1: Process_Emotions_Tweets

Input: *TWEETS_DS* = {tweet₁, tweet₂, tweetₙ} => dataset

N_TWEETS => max number of tweets

Output: *TWEETS_DS_PROCESSED*

1: **for** i = 1 .. *N_TWEETS*

2:   delete_stopwords(*TWEETS_DS*[i])

3: **update** *TWEETS_DS*

3: *PREDICTIONS* = Predict_classes(*TWEETS_DS*)   [13]

4: *PROBABILITIES* = Predict_probabilities(*TWEETS_DS*)   [13]

5: **for** i = 1 .. N_TWEETS

6: TWEETS_DS_PROCESSED[i].Tweet = TWEETS_DS[i].Tweet

7: TWEETS_DS_PROCESSED[i].Emotion = PREDICTIONS[i]

8: TWEETS_DS_PROCESSED[i].Kind_of_emotion = PROBABILITIES[i]

9: **for** i = 1 .. N_TWEETS

10:   TWEET = TWEETS_DS_PROCESSED[i]

11: **for** word = 1 .. length(TWEET)

12: **if exists** word in ('NRC-VAD-Lexicon')

13:    VAD_WORD = Obtain_VAD(word, 'NRC-VAD-Lexicon')

14:   **if** exists word in ('NRC-Emotion-Lexicon')

15:     EMOTION_WORD = Obtain_Emotion(word, 'NRC-Emotion-Lexicon')

16:    **else**

17:   *PREDICTIONS* = Predict_classes(word)   [13]

18:   *PROBABILITIES* = Predict_probabilities(word)   [13]

19:    **update** *EMOTION_WORD*

20: **update** *TWEETS_DS_PROCESSED* with *VAD_WORD* and *EMOTION_WORD*

21: **for** i = 1 .. N_TWEETS

22:   *TWEET = TWEETS_DS_PROCESSED*[i]

23: **for each** emotion in *TWEET*

24:   Obtain_Average_VAD(emotion)

25: **update** *TWEET*

26: **update** *TWEETS_DS_PROCESSED*

27: **RETURN** *TWEETS_DS_PROCESSED*

---

word is present in the dictionary NRC-VAD-Lexicon to obtain the VAD values (valence, arousal, dominance), then we search for the same word in the second dictionary NRC-Emotion-Lexicon to obtain the emotion associated to the word, otherwise if the word is absent in the second dictionary we decided to use again RNN to solve this problem. Finally, we obtain the average VAD values of each emotion per tweet.

Due to the fact that we worked with huge volumes of data, we decided to use Google Colab to agilize the processing of each csv file in the step of searching for each word of a tweet in the dictionaries: NRC-VAD-Lexicon and NRC-Emotion-Lexicon and obtain the values: valence, arousal, dominance and emotions so we used the native library *multiprocessing* of Python to reduce the time of processing.

For the visualization module we based on the Pearl Visual Analytic Tool [1], using D3 JavaScript toolkit [15], the module of visualization contains three sections: a stack graph to analyze the emotion profile over time, a word cloud for a specific date and the list of tweets of that date due to the huge quantity we use an automatic pagination to order the list, when we select a tweet it shows a plane graph for each word component of the tweet with its VAD values and emotion related.

5   Results

The testing was performed on the computer with the following features: CPU 1.80 GHZ Intel Core i7, Ram 8 GB running on Windows 10. The size of the processed tweets become 2.5 GB aprox on the hard drive. We had limitations while loading the complete processed information, following we show a sample of all the dataset to analyze the emotions and interact with CovidEmoVis. To test the functionality of CovidEmoVis let us answer the proposed questions of the work's motivation.

Q1: What are the predominant emotions in percentages for a given date?
In the Fig. 2, we can see the functionality of this tool to allow to select a state and show its emotional profile on a timeline derived from its tweets from 05 March to 09 Apr, the colors refer to the eight categories of emotions of Plutchik as seen in the legend. For this case, we selected the emotional profile for Texas on April 5, for the predominant emotions are: joy 54.49%, trust 54.43% and surprise 34.63%. We assume it is due to the Public Safety Department of Texas began checkpoints at Louisiana border on April 5 [16].

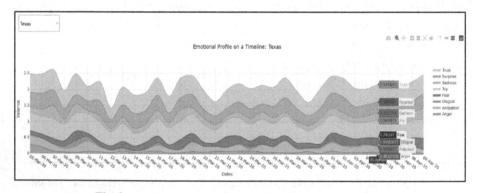

Fig. 2. Analyzing the Emotional profile for Texas on April 5

Q2: On which day was the lowest level of emotion e?

In the Fig. 3, we can see the emotional profile for New York in fear emotion, we can see this on March 10. We assume it is due to that only 36 coronavirus cases were confirmed in New York City [17] so the people continued with their normal life.

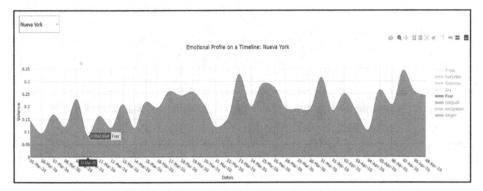

Fig. 3. Analyzing the Emotional profile for New York in Fear Emotion

Q3: Which emotion had the lowest level (value) on day d?

In the Fig. 4, we can see the emotional profile for California, we can see on March 10 the lowest level for Anger with 0.0187. We assume it is due to on that day the government announced education online [18] will begin to minimizing infections.

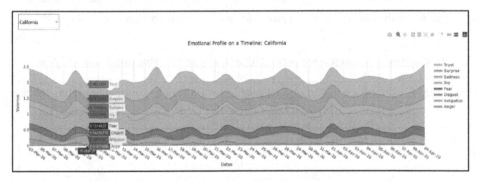

Fig. 4. Analyzing the Emotional profile for California on March 10

Q4: In which range of dates did emotion e1 and emotion e2 have the same pattern of behavior?

In the Fig. 5 and Fig. 6, we can see the emotional profile for Washington and we can observe the same pattern for fear and sadness, in Fig. 5 for the range from March 05 to Apr 09 and Fig. 6 for the range from March 20 to March 30.

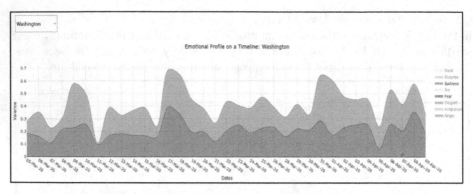

Fig. 5. Analyzing the Emotional profile for Washington from March 05 to Apr 09

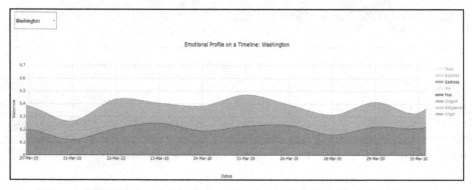

Fig. 6. Analyzing the Emotional profile for Washington from March 20 to March 30

Q5: Which emotion changed the most during the event (comparing values of first and last days)?
In the Fig. 7, we can see the emotional profile for Florida in surprise emotion, we can

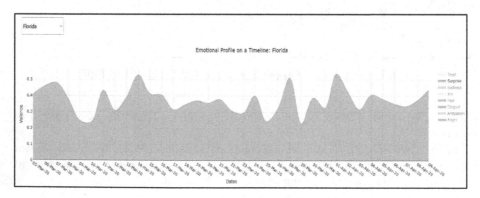

Fig. 7. Analyzing the Emotional profile for Florida.

see how has changed this emotion over time for example on March 09 the lowest value and April 01 the highest value.

Q6: On which day did the users express the highest level of emotions?
In the Fig. 8, we can see the emotional profile for New York, we can observe on March 09 the highest value of emotions. We assume it is due to that Wall Street stocks fell again on Monday amid fears of the coronavirus spreading globally and Confusion reigns in Italy, where the first business day of a mandated lockdown took place in the northern portion of the country [19].

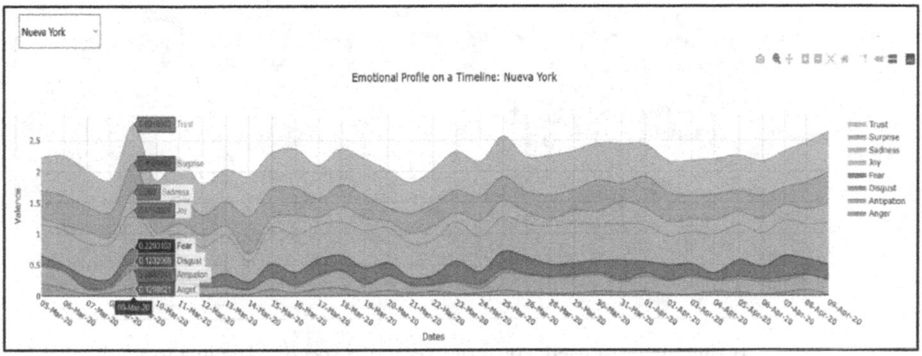

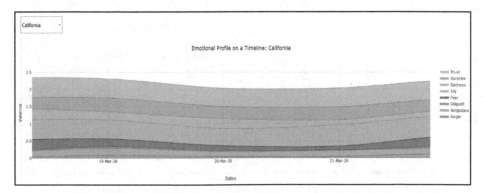

Fig. 8. Analyzing the Emotional profile for New York.

Q7: What was the trend of the emotions after one specific event?
In the Fig. 9, we can see the emotional profile for California from March 19 to March 21, on March 19 the government announced mandatory and indefinite quarantine [20]. We assume it is due to since March 19 the level of fear and sadness was lower and the level of anticipation was higher.

Fig. 9. Analyzing the Emotional profile for California.

Q8: What are the most used words of tweets in a specific date?
In the Fig. 10, we can see the emotional profile for Texas, on April 05 we can observe the most used words: quarantine, stay, probate, think. CoviEmoVis allows to explore the emotions of a specified date, showing a pop-up Word Cloud window and a view of its related tweets, which can be browsed through the implemented pagination.

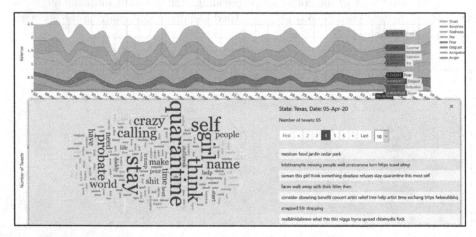

Fig. 10. Analyzing the most used words of tweets in a specific date in a word cloud

From the tweets view, we can select one and show its respective two-dimensional plane graph with its words and VAD values, as well as the emotion. We can move by dragging with the mouse and in the lower right part of its tweets view from which we can select and display the words with their VAD values and emotion related (see Fig. 11).

Fig. 11. Exploring words and their VAD values from tweets with pagination

6 Conclusions and Future Works

In this work presented CovidEmoVis as a tool that allows specialists in Psychology to do the analysis and interaction of the Tweets Data to know more about the emotional profile of users and the tweets posted daywise, it represents a useful tool because it helps to see the important words of the tweets through word cloud and a two-dimensional plane graph which helps to see every word of each tweet with its VAD scores and emotions. In this work we used a part of a dataset of Tweets about Covid-19 from 05-mar to 09-apr, we preprocessed them to delete some stop words, then using a RNN we got an emotion related to the tweet, obtaining VAD scores and fill missing emotions, finally this data can be visualized through this tool.

An extension of this work could be the analysis in real time of tweets, so that we can get an updated dataset with the emotion profiles. We could use some outstanding topics from some hashtag and analyze the emotions. All this implementation is based on Tweets in English, the lexicon dictionaries too, it will be interesting apply this work for another countries like Peru retrieving tweets per regions, it would help us to see how their emotions change for some given event in a period of time. Also we hope to work in huge volumes of information in the visualization so it is necessary think about granularity of the data to reduce the data and to load a consistent sample.

Acknowledgement. We want to thank to the Universidad Nacional de San Agustín de Arequipa with contract IBA 0021-2017-UNSA for supporting the research project "Smart city: Diseño de un Modelo conceptual para integración de sistemas sectoriales en ámbitos inteligentes: Medio Ambiente, Seguridad, Sanidad, Salud, Movilidad, Educación, Economía y Gobierno".

References

1. Zhao, J., Gou, L., Wang, F., Zhou, M.: PEARL: an interactive visual analytic tool for understanding personal emotion style derived from social media. In: IEEE Conference on Visual Analytics Science and Technology (VAST) (2014). https://doi.org/10.1109/vast.2014.7042496
2. Sheidin, J., Lanir, J., Kuflik, T.: A comparative evaluation of techniques for time series visualizations of emotions. In: Proceedings of the 13th Biannual Conference of the Italian SIGCHI Chapter: Designing the next interaction, pp. 1–9 (2019). https://doi.org/10.1145/3351995.3352054
3. Cao, N., Cui, W.: Visualizing sentiments and emotions. In: Introduction to Text Visualization, pp. 103–114. Atlantis Press, Paris (2016). https://www.springerprofessional.de/en/introduction-to-text-visualization/10959336
4. Sun, G.D., Wu, Y.C., Liang, R.H., Liu, S.X.: A survey of visual analytics techniques and applications: state-of-the-art research and future challenges. J. Comput. Sci. Technol. **28**(5), 852–867 (2013). https://doi.org/10.1007/s11390-013-1383-8
5. Kabir, M., Madria, S.: CoronaVis A Real-time COVID-19 Tweets Analyzer. arXiv preprint arXiv:2004.13932 (2020). https://www.researchgate.net/publication/341040078_CoronaVis_A_Real-time_COVID-19_Tweets_Analyzer
6. Plutchik, R.: The nature of emotions. Am. Sci. **89**(4), 344 (2001) https://pdfs.semanticscholar.org/4008/2a9d05ca89d3dcd28fe5528fc79bdddb8f94.pdf

7. Mohammad, S.M., Turneym P.H.: NRC Emotion Lexicon, National Research Council, Canada, vol. 2 (2013). http://www.saifmohammad.com/WebDocs/NRCemotionlexicon.pdf
8. Xu, P., et al.: Visual analysis of topic competition on social media. IEEE Trans. Visual. Comput. Graph. **19**(12), 2012–2021 (2013). https://doi.org/10.1109/TVCG.2013.221
9. Cui, W., Liu, S., Tan, L., et al.: TextFlow: towards better understanding of evolving topics in text. IEEE Trans. Visual. Comput. Graph. **17**(12), 2412–2421 (2011). https://doi.org/10.1109/TVCG.2011.239
10. Munezero, M., Montero, C.S., Mozgovoy, M., Sutinen, E.: EmoTwitter – a fine-grained visualization system for identifying enduring sentiments in tweets. In: Gelbukh, A. (ed.) CICLing 2015. LNCS, vol. 9042, pp. 78–91. Springer, Cham (2015). https://doi.org/10.1007/978-3-319-18117-2_6
11. Cao, N., Lin, Y.R., Sun, X., Lazer, D., Liu, S., Qu, H.: Whisper: tracing the spatiotemporal process of information diffusion in real time. IEEE Trans. Visual. Comput. Graph. **18**(12), 2649–2658 (2012). https://doi.org/10.1109/TVCG.2012.291
12. Yu, Y., Wang, X.: World Cup 2014 in the twitter world: a big data analysis of sentiments in U.S. sports fans' tweets. Comput. Hum. Behav. **48**, 392–400 (2015). https://doi.org/10.1016/j.chb.2015.01.075
13. Colneriĉ, N., Demsar, J.: Emotion recognition on twitter: comparative study and training a unison model. IEEE Trans. Affect. Comput. (2018). https://doi.org/10.1109/taffc.2018.2807817
14. Mehrabian, A.: Basic Dimensions for a General Psychological Theory. Oelgeschlager, Gunn & Hain Inc. (1980). https://www.amazon.com/-/es/Albert-Mehrabian/dp/0899460046
15. Bostock, M., Ogievetsky, V., Heer J.: D3 data-driven documents. IEEE Trans. Visual. Comput. Graph. **17**(12), 2301–2309 (2011). https://doi.org/10.1109/tvcg.2011.185
16. News page. https://www.kiiitv.com/article/news/texas-department-of-public-safety-to-begin-covid-19-checkpoints/503-1dc797c0-a217-4eed-bf90-e66145a2e4d3. Accessed 10 Sept 2020
17. Spectrum News NY1. https://www.ny1.com/nyc/all-boroughs/news/2020/03/10/corona virus-case-numbers-in-nyc-update. Accessed 10 Sept 2020
18. EdSource: Highlighting Strategies for Student Success. https://edsource.org/2020/col leges-in-california-and-across-the-country-move-to-online-instruction-in-response-to-cor onavirus/625099. Accessed 10 Sept 2020
19. SILive page. https://www.silive.com/coronavirus/2020/03/coronavirus-developments-on-march-9-ny-most-impacted-state.html. Accessed 10 Sept 2020
20. Washington Post. https://www.washingtonpost.com/world/2020/03/19/coronavirus-latest-news/. Accessed 10 Sept 2020

Cyber Exposed at Preparatory: Classmates and Teachers Using Social Networks and Life Satisfaction

Ivan Iraola-Real[1]($\boxtimes$) (iD), Lesly Moreyra-Cáceres[2]($\boxtimes$) (iD),
and Luis Collantes-Jarata[3]($\boxtimes$) (iD)

[1] Universidad de Ciencias y Humanidades, Lima 15314, Peru
iiraola@uch.edu.pe
[2] Universidad Nacional Mayor de San Marcos, Lima 15081, Peru
lesly.moreyra@unmsm.edu.pe
[3] Universidad Tecnológica del Perú, Lima 15046, Peru
collantes.acj@gmail.com

Abstract. The present study aims to identify the predictive relationships between the exhibition in the social networks by classmates and teachers, and the life satisfaction in Peruvian adolescents. The sample was of 93 university students (65 men (69.9%) and 31 women (30.1%) between 16 to 19 years old ($M = 17.09$, $S = .30$), of the participants 62 (66.7%) were capital city, 16 (17.2%) were of province, and 3 (3.2%) students were of other country. One concludes that the analysis of multiple lineal regressions the cyber exhibited by classmates predicts positively the cyber exhibited by teachers ($\beta = .53$), and predicts positively the cyber exhibited by myself ($\beta = -28$). Then, cyber exhibited by teachers predicts positively the cyber exhibited by parents ($\beta = .47$). Finally, cyber exhibited by myself predicts positively the cyber exhibited by parents ($\beta = .30$), and predicts positively the life satisfaction ($\beta = -.30$).

Keywords: Social networks · Life satisfaction · Adolescents

1 Introduction

It is common to hear that technologies and specifically social networks have gained great popularity becoming part of people's lives [1], and especially in the lives of adolescents. From the creation of the first virtual servers such as CompuServe Information Services (CIS) in the 60's of the last century and the first virtual messaging services to the appearance of Facebook [2], or mobile phone applications such as WhatsApp (which has emerged in the last decade becoming one of the most popular social networks) [3], it has been possible to observe quantitative and qualitative improvements in virtual services. This growth in overcrowding and in the use of social networks are facts that cannot be denied, and with them, speculation has also gradually arisen about all its benefits and damages [1]. For example, among its benefits are studies that expose the creation of family groups for better communication, educational experiences of social

© Springer Nature Switzerland AG 2020
V. Agredo-Delgado et al. (Eds.): HCI-COLLAB 2020, CCIS 1334, pp. 107–116, 2020.
https://doi.org/10.1007/978-3-030-66919-5_11

networks in basic education [4], and even benefits of the use of social networks in life satisfaction of adolescents (only if accompanied by adequate levels of self-esteem) [5], using them to learn various topics, to feel satisfied with their social identity, to seek communication, entertainment, empathy and social support among adolescents from female sex, increasing personal [6] and collective self-esteem [7]. But, on the contrary, there are also studies that report the disadvantages of the use of social networks, such as, for example, in the reduction of self-esteem [1], in dysfunctions in family communication, in the reduction of social circles increasing loneliness [8] more in (male adolescents) who even resort to social networks as a way to balance their lack of security of being able to speak personally to someone [7] favouring depression [8]. And, of course, some negative uses by some adolescents who practice cyberbullying [1, 9] and, as is normal, the parents' repeated fear regarding the way in which their children expose their lives on social networks (such as Facebook) which could be used in a harmful way by someone unknown [10].

In this last aspect it is important to pay special attention. It is normal for a person to try to expose their life on social networks, and if it were an adult, the freedom to do so is approached with more ease. But what would happen if the person who exposes her life on social networks is a child or a teenager? Parents' concerns about the dangers to which they would be exposed are reiterated [7]. The concern remains evident even though the child is an adolescent older than 16 years (that is, he is not an early adolescent) [10]. This type of teenager in many countries is considered a free person to decide. For example, in the case of Peru (the country to which the sample of this study corresponds) according to Law No. 27337 of the Civil Code of Children and Adolescents (in Spanish: Código Civil del Niño y del Adolescente), he is considered a person free to make decisions that may involve seeking employment, to be part of a union of workers with rights to labour claims and even to get married (with the authorization of a judge) because they are in full use of their powers to authorize the aforementioned [11]. These reasons being enough to be considered a free person to decide what to publish or not on social networks; mainly on Facebook or WhatsApp.

But another question arises in this context. What to do if someone else publishes information about a teenager? And what to do if it is someone from the adolescent's educational environment and does it without their consent? This would motivate us to think about new effects of the use of social networks in the school climate, and at the same time, effects on the person who is the subject of these publications. To reflect on this problem, you can start from the principle that being a friend or not, posting something of another person on Facebook is unethical, especially if this person is tagged (identified) and in the worst case if they are photographs of shameful events [12]. This also happens on WhatsApp, which is one of the social networks most visited by young people and where unfortunately ethical desecration practices such as harassment, intimidation and cyberbullying are observed [13]. These studies allow us to reflect on some negative consequences of the inappropriate use of social networks, however, one cannot be too quick to assume that they are entirely negative, because there are studies that associate them with life satisfaction [14] or psychological well-being that people achieve [15].

And taking up the previous questions; if the person who posts on the networks is the teacher and the classmates, what would be the effects on the satisfaction with life or psychological well-being of the young people? For these reasons, the need to study how the exposure of personal life on social networks (on the part of teachers and classmates) influences life satisfaction in university students from Lima - Peru is evident. This study is motivated by the knowledge that some social networks such as Facebook and WhatsApp are widely used by young people [1, 13]. So also, by means of the following hypotheses it is intended that:

- (1) the exhibition in the social networks of the adolescents (cyber exhibited by teachers) positively predicts the life satisfaction [14], then,
- (2) the exhibition in the social networks of the adolescents (cyber exhibited by classmates) positively predicts the life satisfaction [14] (Fig. 1).

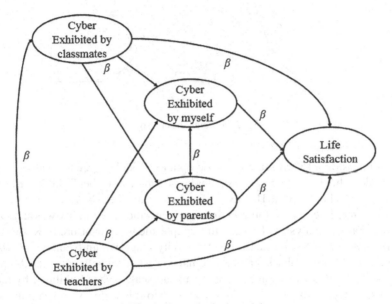

Fig. 1. Hypothetical model

2 Methodology

2.1 Participants

The sample was of 93 university students (65 men (69.9%) and 31 women (30.1%) between 16 to 19 years old (M = 17.09, SD = .30), of the participants 62 (66.7%) were capital city, 16 (17.2%) were of province, and 3 (3.2%) students were of other country (Fig. 2).

2.2 Measures

Cyber Exhibited in Social Networks Scale (SCESN) [5]. This scale evaluates the evaluate exhibition in social networks such as Facebook, WhatsApp, etc. It is made up of 16 items

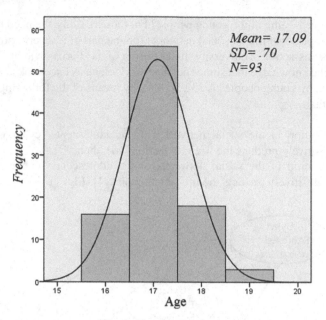

Fig. 2. Frequencies (age).

with five-dimensional Likert scale response options (Totally agree to totally disagree). The sub-scale Cyber Exhibited by classmates has 4, sub-scale Cyber Exhibited by teacher has 4, sub-scale Cyber Exhibited by myself has 4 items and the sub-scale Cyber Exhibited by the parents has 4 items (see Table 1). In the present study the validity was analyzed by Exploratory Factor Analysis (EFA) and the sample adequacy measure of Kaiser Meyer and Olkin (KMO) was .83 and the Bartlett Sphericity Test was significant ($\chi^2 = 702.083$, $gl = 120$, $p < .001$). Cronbach's alpha internal consistency coefficient was .80 to sub-scale Cyber Exhibited by classmates, of .83 to sub-scale Cyber Exhibited by teacher, .73 to sub-scale Cyber Exhibited by myself, and .76 to sub-scale Cyber Exhibited by the parents; thus, demonstrating adequate levels of reliability [16].

Life Satisfaction Scale (SWLS) [15]. The present scale assesses the life satisfaction levels. It has 5 items with seven-dimensional Likert scale response options (Completely in accordance to completely in disagreement). In this study, we obtained adequate evidence of validity ($KMO = .77$) and the Bartlett Sphericity Test was significant ($x^2 = 187,659$, $gl = 10$, $p < .001$). Cronbach's alpha internal consistency coefficient was .79.

Table 1. Items and sub-scales

Dimensions and Items	Item total	Cronbach if item is removed
Sub-scale Cyber Exhibited by classmates		
3. My friends and classmates like to post on their Facebook what I do	.48	.88
7. My friends and classmates like to post what happens to me in their WhatsApp status	.60	.88
11. My friends and classmates find it pleasant to post videos in which I am present	.62	.87
15. My classmates at school like to post emojis, photos or phrases of what my classmates and I do or feel	.59	.88
Sub-scale Cyber Exhibited by teacher		
4. I think my teachers like to post on their Facebook what students do	.55	.88
8. My teacher finds it nice to post what students do on his WhatsApp statuses	.56	.88
12. My teachers really like to publish school or classroom videos that I am in	.66	.87
16. My teachers like to post emojis, photos or phrases of everything that my classmates and I do or feel	.59	.88
Sub-Scale Cyber exhibited by myself		
1. I like to post my photos on Facebook	.31	.87
5. I really enjoy posting what I do in my WhatsApp status	.44	.88
9. I feel satisfying to publish videos that I star in on the internet	.52	.88
13. I like to publish with emojis, photos or phrases what I feel and what I do	.48	.88
Sub-scale Cyber Exhibited by the parents		
2. My parents really enjoy posting what I do on Facebook	.36	.88
6. Dad and mom really enjoy posting what happens to me on their WhatsApp status	.63	.87
10. My parents really like to post family videos in which I am	.54	.88
14. My parents enjoy publishing with emojis, photos or phrases everything I do or how I feel	.66	.87

Note: According Aiken the ideal value of correlation item total is of .30 to more [17]. In addition, it is observed that by eliminating any item the scale continues with adequate levels of reliability [16].

3 Results

After analyzing the validity and reliability of the scales one proceeded to analyze the results as the following order.

3.1 Relations Between Variables

The relations analysis between variables was done by means of Pearson's r and to evaluate the interrelation coefficients the Cohen's criteria were used for social sciences (*light, r = .10 − .23; moderated, r = .24 − .36; strong, r = .37 to more*) [18]. This way in Table 2 it is observed the variable exhibition of the adolescents in the social networks on behalf of its partners (cyber exhibited by the classmates) is related in a positive way, strongly and significant with the exhibition in the social networks of the life of the adolescent on the part of the teachers (cyber exhibited by the teacher) ($r = .53, p < .001$). This allows to observe that when the adolescents are exhibited in the social media by its classes partners, it influences that the teachers also are predisposed to exhibit the life of its students with publications in Facebook and WhatsApp.

Then in the Table 2 it is observed that the variable exhibition of the adolescents in the social networks on the part of its classes partners (cyber exhibited by the classmates) is related in a positive way, strongly and significant with its own exhibition of its life in the social networks (cyber exhibited by myself) ($r = .41, p < .001$). Another positive, strong and significant relation with the exhibition of its life in the social networks on behalf of the parents (cyber exhibited by parents) ($r = .45, p < .001$). This find allows to observe when the adolescents are exhibited by means of publications in social networks by its partners this it influences straight with the exhibition that they and its parents do of its lives.

Also it is observed in the Table 2 that the variable exhibition of the adolescents in the social networks on the part of the teachers (cyber exhibited by the teacher) is related in a positive way, moderate and significant with its own exhibition of its life in the social networks (cyber exhibited by myself) ($r = .30, p < .01$). Another positive, strong and significant relation with the exhibition of its life in the social networks on the part of the parents (cyber exhibited by parents) ($r = .62, p < .001$). This find allows to observe that when the adolescents are exhibited by means of publications in social networks by its teachers it is related straight to the exhibition that they and its parents do of its lives in social Facebook and WhatsApp.

Finally, in the analysis of bivaried relations (inter scale), it is possible to observe in the Table 2 that the variable exhibition of the adolescents in the social networks on behalf of its partners (cyber exhibited by the classmates) is related in a positive way, light and significant with the life satisfaction ($r = .20, p < .05$). And, the variable exhibition of the proper life of the adolescents in the social networks (cyber exhibited by myself) is related in a positive way, moderate and significant with the life satisfaction ($r = .33, p < .01$). This indicates that when the adolescents are exhibited in the social networks by its partners and for themselves, they feel major satisfaction with its lives.

Table 2. Means, Cronbach's Alpha, correlations between variables

Variables		Mean	α	1	2	3	4	5
1	Cyber Exhibited by the classmates	2.81	(.80)	–	.53***	.41***	.49***	.20*
2	Cyber Exhibited by the teachers	2.42	(.83)		–	.30**	.62***	.05
3	Cyber Exhibited by myself	2.64	(.73)			–	.42***	.33**
4	Cyber Exhibited by the parents	2.20	(.76)				–	.01
5	Life Satisfaction	4.60	(.79)					–

Note. * $p < .05$, ** $p < .01$, *** $p < .001$ (bilateral). Alpha Cronbach (α) it is shown in brackets.

3.2 Linear Regressions

On having identified significant relations, a multiple linear regression analysis was realized to estimate the predictive value between the studied variables [19]. This way, in the Fig. 3 observes that the variable exhibition of the adolescents in the social networks on the part of its partners (cyber exhibited by the classmates) predicts in a positive way and significant to the exhibition in the social networks of the life of the adolescent for himself (cyber exhibited by myself) ($\beta = .28$, $p < .01$). Turned out that it allows to anticipate that the adolescents will exhibit its lives in social networks if what they happens is published (in Facebook and WhatsApp) by its classes partners.

And also, the variable exhibition of the adolescents in the social networks on the part of its teachers (cyber exhibited by the teachers) predicts in a positive way and significant to the exhibition of the adolescents on behalf of its parents (cyber exhibited by the parents) ($\beta = .47$, $p < .001$). This find demonstrates that when the life of an adolescent is published in social networks on the part of its teachers this allows to anticipate that the parents also will publish it.

Finally, one was realized in the multiple linear regression analysis in which the variables cyber exhibited by myself and cyber exhibited by parents they registered like entry variables, or the variable life satisfaction as variable of exit like that in the Fig. 3 observes that only the variable exhibition of the adolescents in the social networks (cyber exhibited by myself) predicts in a positive way and significant to the variable life satisfaction ($\beta = .30$, $p < .01$). Find that he confirms the proper exhibition of the personal life of the adolescents anticipates its vital satisfaction.

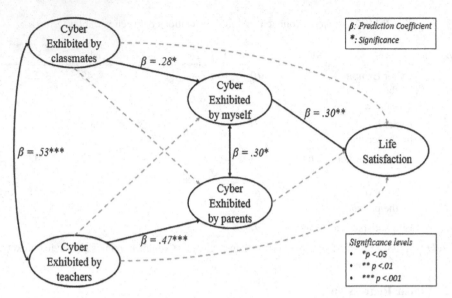

Fig. 3. Hypothetical model confirmed (multiple lineal regression).

4 Discussion

This research aimed to identify the predictive relationship between exposure of personal life on social networks (on the part of teachers and classmates) and its influence on life satisfaction in university students from Lima - Peru. This sample was considered because adolescents and young people use Facebook and WhatsApp the most; being part of their lives [1, 13].

At the level of predictive analysis, it was possible to show that the exposure of adolescents' lives by their classmates predicts that the same students are more likely to publish their lives on Facebook and WhatsApp. Then the exhibition that teachers make of their students predicts future publications by parents. This result could be of concern because according to the studies by Light and McGrath it is not entirely ethical to post other people's lives on Facebook due to the consequences that may arise [12]; as, for example: adolescents could be exposed to negative experiences such as cyberbullying. This could be evidenced in the studies by Moreno and Kolb, who identified that, although there is a tendency among adolescents to constantly publish social networks, this could present some benefits and even some risks for their mental health [9]. And in the Siphamandla studies with a sample of 60 young people it was confirmed that the frequency of the social networks use was constant and that this could lead to cyberbullying, which is harmful to the victims, they could be more prone to the consumption of drugs, alcohol, low self-esteem, depression, suicidal ideas, and educational difficulties such as dropout or low academic performance [13]. In addition, since it is a sample of Peruvian adolescents, it is necessary to consider that according to the Civil Code of Children and Adolescents (in Spanish: Código Civil del Niño y del Adolescente) greater care must be taken when exposing information about minors. Although this regulation explains that those over 16 years of age are considered people who have the mental capacity to decide on their actions; this in some way contemplates that they continue to be vulnerable to various types of risks [11].

Finally, what was found in the present research confirms once again that when a person exposes their own life on social networks, they have high levels of satisfaction with life. This result confirms the studies of Zou, Ingram and Higgins who, when studying a sample of 573 people from different cultural groups (American, Asian, Hispanic American, etc.) identified that the social networks use favored their psychological well-being and their life satisfaction level [14]. Result that should continue in consideration of the possible benefits and disadvantages that the exhibition in social networks implies [10, 13]. For example, they can be analyzed in the research by Burga, Fernández-Meza, Llanca-Bravo, Tafur-Muñoz, Vera-Bances and Díaz-Velez in a sample of 596 Peruvian high school and university students with an average age of 15 to 23 years, in which it is evidenced that more than 60% had high life satisfaction levels and the risk of acquiring an addiction to Facebook is 7%. Furthermore, it is revealed that students who scored very high on the life satisfaction scale have a lower risk of addiction to Facebook compared to students who have a score below average, who have a higher risk of addiction [20]. Also, in the studies of Jan, Anwwer and Ahmad who studied a sample of 150 students (between the age of 18 and 25), they managed to identify that among young people the use of social networks was more and more frequent and that the use an average of one hour on Facebook per day was associated with a significant decrease in self-esteem [1]. Thus, it is due to these empirical evidences that it is essential to consider the importance of other mediating variables such as self-esteem as a precondition for life satisfaction in adolescents [5]. For example, in the studies by Diener and Diener, specifically with a sample of 13,118 university students from 31 countries, it was possible to identify that self-esteem is related to satisfaction with life [15]; being one reason why the mediation of self-esteem should be considered as an essential element to feel life satisfaction when publishing on social networks [5].

5   Conclusions and Future Works

It is concluded that the social networks use by adolescents predisposes them to publish their lives on social networks more frequently among themselves. And that the unethical practices on the part of teachers to publish the lives of students on social networks, encourages an inappropriate practice in parents, who also end up publishing the lives of their children on social networks. This allows us to reflect on the need to be able to carry out studies to identify the reasons why teachers and parents publish the lives of their children on social networks; due to possible negative consequences. On the other hand, although it is concluded that the publication of personal life on social networks is related to life satisfaction of adolescents, caution should be exercised and not fall into the hasty idea that using social networks generates greater satisfaction psychological, without considering mediating variables such as self-esteem. Finally, it is necessary to reflect on the results because from the educational field it is necessary to take the issue of social networks very carefully, and continue guiding both students, teachers and parents on the ethical aspects and the possible negative consequences of exposure of students' lives on social media.

References

1. Jan, M., Anwwer, S., Ahmad, N.: Impact of social media on self-esteem. Eur. Sci. J. **13**(23), 329–341 (2017). https://doi.org/10.19044/esj.2017.v13n23p329
2. McIntyre, M.: The evolution of social media from 1969 to 2013: a change in competition and a trend toward complementary, niche sites. J. Soc. Med. Soc. **3**(2), 5–25 (2014)
3. Bouhnik, D., Deshen, M.: Whatsapp goes to school: mobile instante messaging between teacher and student. J. Inf. Technol. Educ.: Res. **3**, 217–231 (2014). https://doi.org/10.28945/2051
4. Awada, G.: Effect of whatsapp on critique writing proficiency and perceptions toward learning. Cogent Educ. **3**, 1–25 (2016). https://doi.org/10.1080/2331186x.2016.1264173
5. Iraola-Real, I., Moreyra-Cáceres, L., Cáceres-Buleje, V., Collantes-Jarata, A., Iraola-Real, E., Iraola-Real, M.: Cyber exposed: the social networks and the life satisfaction. In: III IEEE World Engineering Education Conference – EDUNINE (2019). https://doi.org/10.1109/edunine.2019.8875756
6. Shaw, L., Gant, L.: In defense of the internet: the relationship between internet comunication and depressionl loneliness, self-esteem an perceived social support. Cyber Psychol. Behav. **5**(2), 157–172 (2002). https://doi.org/10.1089/109493102753770552
7. Barker, V.: Older adolescents' motivations for social network site use: the influence of gender, group identity, and collective self-esteem. Cyber Psychol. Behav. **12**(2), 209–213 (2009). https://doi.org/10.1089/cpb.2008.0228
8. Kraut, R., Patterson, M., Lundmark, V., Kiesler, S., Mukophadhyay, T., Scherlis, W.: Internet paradox: a social technology that reduces social involvement ando psychologicas well-being. Am. Psychol. **53**(9), 1017–1031 (1998). https://doi.org/10.1037//0003-066x.53.9.1017
9. Moreno, M., Kolb, J.: Social networking sites and adolescent health. Pediatr. Clin. North Am. **59**(3), 601–612 (2012). https://doi.org/10.1016/j.pcl.2012.03.023
10. Lewis, K., Kaufman, J., Christakis, N.: The taste for privacy: an analysis of college student privacy settings in an online social network. J. Comput.-Mediated Commun. **14**(23), 79–100 (2008). https://doi.org/10.1111/j.1083-6101.2008.01432.x
11. Congreso de la República del Perú, Ley Nro 27337 - Código Civil del Niño y del Adolescente. https://www.mimp.gob.pe/files/direcciones/dga/nuevo-codigo-ninos-adolescentes.pdf
12. Light, B., McGrath, K.: Ethics and social networking sites: a disclosive analysis of facebook. Inf. Technol. People. **23**(4), 290–311 (2010). https://doi.org/10.1108/09593841011087770
13. Siphamandla, L.: Cyberbullying a desecration of information ethics: perceptions of post-hihg school youth in a rural community. J. Inf. Commun. Ethics Soc. **14**(4), 313–322 (2016). https://doi.org/10.1108/jices-04-2016-0009
14. Zou, X., Ingram, P., Higgins, E.T.: Social networks and life satisfaction: the interplay of network density and regulatory focus. Motiv. Emot. **39**(5), 693–713 (2015). https://doi.org/10.1007/s11031-015-9490-1
15. Diener, E., Diener, M.: Cross-cultural correlates of life satisfaction and self-esteem. J. Pers. Soc. Psychol. **68**(4), 653–663 (1995). https://doi.org/10.1037//0022-3514.68.4.653
16. Field, A.: Discovering Statistics Using SPSS, 3era edn. Sage Publications, Lóndres (2009)
17. Aiken, R.: Psychological Testing and Assessment, 11th edn. Allyn & Bacon, Boston (2002)
18. Cohen, J.: A power primer. Psychol. Bull. **112**, 155–159 (1992). https://doi.org/10.1037/0033-2909.112.1.155
19. Bingham, N., Fry, J.: Regression: Linear models in statistics. Springer, New York (2010)
20. Burga-Cueva, J., Fernández-Meza, M., Llanca-Bravo, L., Tafur-Muñoz, D., Vera-Bances, P., Díaz-Vélez, C.: Nivel de satisfacción con la vida personal y riesgo de adicción a Facebook en estudiantes de instituciones educativas en una región del Perú. Revista Hispanoamericana De Ciencias De La Salud **1**(2), 87–93 (2015). http://www.uhsalud.com/index.php/revhispano/article/view/55

Design and Implementation of a Voice-Based Conversational Agent for the Continuous Training and Learning of Pharmaceutical Sales Representatives

Rocío Fernández$^{(\boxtimes)}$ (iD), Gianfranco Monzón$^{(\boxtimes)}$ (iD), and Daniel Subauste$^{(\boxtimes)}$ (iD)

Universidad Peruana de Ciencias Aplicadas, Lima 15023, Peru
{u201510797,u201510540}@upc.edu.pe, daniel.subauste@upc.pe

Abstract. The increasing popularity and enhanced capabilities of intelligent personal assistants, such as Google Assistant, Siri, and Alexa, have allowed them to disrupt in numerous fields, some of which are: customer service, banking, and tourism. Notwithstanding, the application of intelligent personal assistants for training and learning of professional workers has been limited and not well researched. The current paper will explore a solution for these purposes applied to pharmaceutical sales representatives by using a voice-based conversational agent. The pharmaceutical sales representatives will be able to ask the agent about the properties of the medicaments and to take frequent exams about the information available to verify their knowledge. The agent is implemented in Dialogflow and is available to all devices compatible with Google Assistant.

Keywords: Intelligent personal assistants · Conversational agents · Pharmaceutical sales representative · Dialogflow · Google Assistant

1 Introduction

Given the recent improvements in natural language processing and speech recognition technology [1], intelligent personal assistants like Alexa, Google Assistant, and Siri, have attained a high level of popularity and usage. One of the critical points for their adoption is their availability in different platforms and hardware, including smartphones, speakers, vehicles, and televisions [2]. Another key point for their success is verbal communication. Since people communicate with the intelligent personal assistant by talking and issuing voice commands, it creates an interactive, enjoyable, and intimate relationship between the person and the assistant [3, 4]. Combined with both the portability of smartphones and verbal communication, intelligent personal assistants can be used virtually anywhere at any time.

Traditionally, intelligent personal assistants have been used for home tasks, for example, controlling thermostats, lights, alarms, and locks; personal duties, including setting timers, creating calendar entries, making phone calls, and sending and reading text messages and emails; and informational queries like climate, directions, time and exchange

© Springer Nature Switzerland AG 2020
V. Agredo-Delgado et al. (Eds.): HCI-COLLAB 2020, CCIS 1334, pp. 117–125, 2020.
https://doi.org/10.1007/978-3-030-66919-5_12

rates [2, 5]. Nonetheless, the application of intelligent personal assistants for training and learning of professional workers has been limited and not well researched.

As a step towards exploring this application, the present paper presents a voice-based conversational agent for the continuous training and learning of pharmaceutical sales representatives. Even though they receive group training sessions about their company's products, these pieces of training are not enough since they need to learn the information of many different medicaments, and each person has a distinct learning rate [6].

The solution will allow these professionals to ask a voice-based agent about the properties of the medicaments and to take periodic exams about the information available to verify their knowledge, similar to what they do after each training session [6].

The voice-based agent was implemented with Dialogflow and is available to all devices compatible with Google Assistant. The solution was evaluated with a group of pharmaceutical sales representatives from a transnational pharmaceutical laboratory for one week. During the evaluation, the researchers collected data from the interactions between the users and the agent and performed follow-up interviews to obtain feedback and opinions from the participants.

The rest of this paper is organized as follows. Section 2 describes related work with voice-based conversational agents in work environments and oriented for professional workers, and in education and learning. In Sect. 3, the authors present the design and implementation of the agent. Section 4 describes the experimentation and results. Finally, Sect. 5 presents the conclusion of the research and future works.

2 Related Work

The current section presents the literature related to the application of voice-based conversational agents in working and educational environments.

2.1 Work Environments and Professional Workers

The application of voice-based conversational agents in work environments and for professional workers has been scarcely researched; however, there have been some explorations in these fields.

Damacharla et al. [7] developed a training module integrated with voice assistant Amazon Alexa and the Amazon Echo smart speaker for emergency care providers. Through both the voice assistant and the smart speaker, emergency care providers can receive feedback in real-time as they perform the required actions for a specific procedure and indicate the assistant what they are doing. With the input from the emergency care provider, the assistant checks if they are performing the correct actions for the procedure and notifies them in case the actions deviate from the standard procedure or do not match the timing specified in the procedure.

Similarly, with the use of Amazon Alexa and Amazon Echo, Austerjost et al. [8] developed a custom skill for the voice assistant to help laboratory operators control laboratory instruments via voice interaction. With this skill, the voice assistant can recognize the commands from the operators and the names of the instruments. Later, the assistant manipulates the laboratory instruments and performs the required measurements and readings from the instruments.

In a different domain, Kleinert et al. [9] proposed the use of assistant-based speech recognition to support air traffic controllers with their workload in air traffic control rooms. Typically, air traffic controllers employ paper flight strips. These strips contain commands related to speed, direction, and flight attitude, and the air traffic controllers give these strips to a pilot during a flight. However, as air traffic control centers are modernized, new digital systems are introduced. These new systems require air traffic controllers to enter the strips manually and hence, increase their workload. With the help of the voice assistant, air traffic controllers issue voice commands from the strips, and then the assistant saves these commands in the system.

In the interest of helping workers in their workplace about reflection, self-consciousness, and awareness, Kocielnik et al. [10] developed a custom skill for Amazon Alexa to allow workers to register their daily activities, goals, and achievements. By using a voice registration device named Amazon Dash Wand, workers also answer reflective questions asked by the voice assistant at the end of the day about their tasks, planning, and organization, short-term and long-term activities and goals, motivation, and satisfaction at work.

2.2 Education and Learning

Similar to the previous subsection, the application of voice-based conversational in education and learning is limited, but there are some antecedents.

For instance, Dizon [11] applied voice assistant Amazon Alexa to help students acquire a second language (L2), particularly, English as a second language. The popular skilled named Earplay was used, which involves the user in a story by interacting with the characters and deciding the unfolding of the events, and a list of commands that the users must say out loud for the assistant to recognize them. The interactions showed that the voice assistant played an essential role in the context of second language acquisition, helped students to improve their pronunciation and speaking, and represented an extraordinary opportunity to enhance language learning.

Within the context of Learning Management Systems (LMS), Kita et al. [12] prototyped a custom skill for Google Assistant to interact with the Moodle platform. Using the skill, students can take a quiz by answering multiple-choice questions, take simulated lessons (e.g., disaster management in earthquakes), and receive notifications about grades, forums, and assignments. Then, all the interactions between the student and Google Assistant are uploaded to the Moodle platform, including answers and grades.

3 Design and Implementation

The voice-based conversational agent was developed using the Dialogflow platform. Since pharmaceutical sales representatives need to ask the agents questions about the properties of the medicaments, multiple entities were created, each one representing a particular property of the medicament. Similarly, as the users have to take periodic exams about the information of the medicaments, we generated entities that model the concepts of exams and answers.

For the properties of the medicaments, we declared the following entities: adverse effects (see Fig. 1), cautions, composition, contraindications, dose, excipients, indication, interactions, presentation, and use cases. In the case of exams, we defined two entities: exams and answers. Additionally, for each entity defined, at least two synonyms were added to allow the agent to properly recognized the required entities by the users.

When the user asks the conversational agent about a specific property of a medicament, the agent invokes the appropriate intent. For example, the composition intent presents all the active and inactive ingredients of a given medicament in a table card. In contrast, the indication intent only presents the information in plain text. Figure 2 shows the composition and indication intents.

Concerning the exams, the flow starts when the user requests the conversational agent to take an evaluation. The agent informs the user that the evaluation is about to begin and asks the first question. Each exam is composed of ten questions and graded from 0 to 20 points. Each question is a multiple-choice question, and for each question, the agent presents three options. Also, at the bottom of the screen, the agent shows three chips that represent an answer for the current question. One thing we noticed was the lack of support to break sentences into new lines from Dialogflow, so it was needed to show the answers in the same line. At this point, the user can answer the question in three different ways. First, the user can select one of three chips from the bottom of the screen. Second, the user can tell the agent the answer by saying one of the following phrases:

- "Option A" or "The first one"
- "Option B" or "The second one"
- "Option C" or "The third one"

The third way the user can answer the question is by saying the complete or approximate response. Then, the agent compares the response with the answers through the Sørensen-Dice coefficient. If the rating of the best match computed by the coefficient is lower than the minimum threshold, which was defined as 0.35, the agent reports that it could not understand the answer and prompts the user to give a new answer.

When the user finishes the exam, the agent presents the final grade for the exam and a table with three columns: questions, answers given by the user, and the correct solutions. For the last column, when the user answers the question correctly, the cell indicates that the answer was correct, but when it was incorrect, the cell shows the solution for the given question. It was also noticed that the table did not space equally the columns, and therefore, the table did not properly wrap the cells of the last column. Figure 2 and Fig. 3 show the composition and indications intents, and the evaluations and answers intents, respectively.

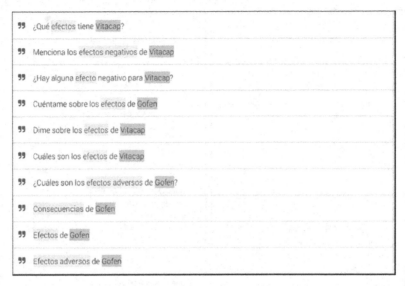

Fig. 1. Intent for adverse effects.

Fig. 2. Composition and indications intents.

Fig. 3. Evaluations and answers intents.

4   Experimentation and Results

The proposed solution was evaluated with a team of eight pharmaceutical sales representatives from a transnational pharmaceutical laboratory for one week. The characteristics
of the group are described in the following lines:

- 50% of the participants are between 31 and 40 years old and the other 50%, between
  41 and 50 years old.
- 25% are female, and the rest are male.
- All the participants have used a voice assistant before, and 75% have used Google
  Assistant in the past.
- All the participants had Android phones.

Since the solution was deployed on Actions on Google, the official app store for
the Google Assistant, the pharmaceutical sales representatives were able to use our
conversational agent from their mobile devices.

By leveraging the analytics embedded in Dialogflow and Actions on Google, we
found that the average time per user with the agent was 11 min and 20 s, the average
daily sessions per user were 2.3 sessions, and the average user messages per session
were 9.9 messages.

Once the evaluation was finished, the pharmaceutical sales representatives completed an end-of-study survey. In this survey, they answered 5 questions about the conversational agent on a 5-point Likert scale. The questions were related to the characteristics of the conversational agent: tone, rhythm, and voice intensity, recognition of the names of the medicaments, recognition of the properties of the medicaments, information about the medicines, and the overall experience. Figure 4 shows the results of the survey.

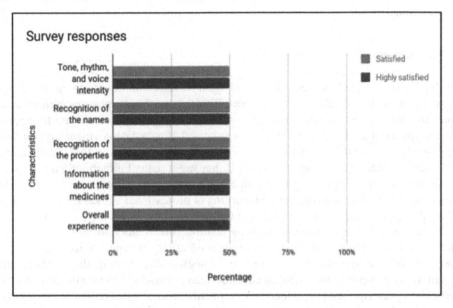

Fig. 4. Survey responses about the conversational agent.

From the survey, we obtained the following results:

- 50% were satisfied with the tone, rhythm, and voice intensity f our agent, and the other 50% were highly satisfied.
- 50% were satisfied with the recognition of the name of the medicaments, and the rest were highly satisfied.
- 50% were satisfied with the recognition of the properties of the medicaments while the rest were highly satisfied.
- 50% were satisfied with the information about the medicines, and the other 50% were highly satisfied.
- In general terms and the overall experience, 50% were satisfied with our conversational agent while the other 50% were highly satisfied with it.

We also asked the pharmaceutical sales representatives if they would use our agent daily in their phones, and 50% answered that they would use it, but the other 50% said that they did not know and were unsure about it.

After gathering and presenting all the results, it is noticeable that the answers are always divided equally. We realized that the participants older than 40 years old indicated that they were satisfied with the conversational agent, while the younger participants responded that they were highly satisfied with the agent. We believe that these results are correlated with the fact that older participants are not very familiar with new technologies and prefer them to have less intrusion in their lives. On the contrary, younger participants are more open to embrace and try new technologies.

Given that our sample is relatively small and not well diverse in the age distribution, further studies are required to explore and dive deeper into the results of the conversational agent.

5 Conclusions

We introduced a voice-based conversational agent for the continuous training and learning of pharmaceutical sales representatives. Through our agent, pharmaceutical sales representatives can learn more about the properties of the medicaments and take periodic exams about the medicines. Our one-week validation and deployment suggest that our primary users find our conversational agent a new and innovative tool to help them with their learning and can benefit from it if they use it daily. Furthermore, our project demonstrates that it is possible to use intelligent personal assistants, such as Google Assistant, to help with the training and learning of professional workers; however, it is required to personalize the experience and the conversation for each type of worker.

Moreover, it is the responsibility of the pharmaceutical laboratories to continue to find and push new ways to enhance the training and learning of their pharmaceutical sales representatives through the usage of new technologies, since high-quality medicament information and a continuous medical education can positively influence the behavior of medication prescriptions [13]. Nonetheless, pharmaceutical sales representatives have to perceive these new technologies as useful and easy to use in order to increment their adoption and success [14]. We believe that our conversational agent represents a significant advance towards this goal.

In future works, we plan to add more medicaments properties and polar questions, also known as yes-no questions. Likewise, we plan to add support for more intelligent personal assistants, mainly Amazon Alexa and Siri, and to improve the text formatting and the responses from the conversational agent. Additionally, we plan to carry out new studies where we include a more diverse and larger sample to validate the characteristics and functioning of the conversational agent thoroughly.

References

1. Sarikaya, R.: The technology behind personal digital assistants: an overview of the system architecture and key components. IEEE Signal Process. Mag. **34**(1), 67–81 (2017). https://doi.org/10.1109/MSP.2016.2617341
2. Tulshan, A.S., Dhage, S.N.: Survey on virtual assistant: google assistant, Siri, Cortana, Alexa. In: Thampi, S.M., Marques, O., Krishnan, S., Li, K.-C., Ciuonzo, D., Kolekar, M.H. (eds.) SIRS 2018. CCIS, vol. 968, pp. 190–201. Springer, Singapore (2019). https://doi.org/10.1007/978-981-13-5758-9_17

3. Han, S., Yang, H.: Understanding adoption of intelligent personal assistants: a parasocial relationship perspective. Ind. Manag. Data Syst. **118**(3), 618–636 (2018). https://doi.org/10.1108/IMDS-05-2017-0214

4. Guzman, A.L.: Voices in and of the machine: source orientation toward mobile virtual assistants. Comput. Hum. Behav. **90**, 343–350 (2019). https://doi.org/10.1016/J.CHB.2018.08.009

5. Hoy, M.B.: Alexa, Siri, Cortana, and more: an introduction to voice assistants. Med. Ref. Serv. Q. **37**(1), 81–88 (2018). https://doi.org/10.1080/02763869.2018.1404391

6. Mintzes, B., et al.: Understanding and Responding to Pharmaceutical Promotion. 1st edn. World Health Organization/Health Action International (2010)

7. Damacharla, P., et al.: Effects of voice-based synthetic assistant on performance of emergency care provider in training. Int. J. Artif. Intell. Educ. **29**(1), 122–143 (2018). https://doi.org/10.1007/s40593-018-0166-3

8. Austerjost, J., et al.: Introducing a virtual assistant to the lab: a voice user interface for the intuitive control of laboratory instruments. SLAS Technol. Trans. Life Sci. Innov. **23**(5), 476–482 (2018). https://doi.org/10.1177/2472630318788040

9. Kleinert, M., et al.: Adaptation of assistant based speech recognition to new domains and its acceptance by air traffic controllers. In: Karwowski, W., Ahram, T. (eds.) IHSI 2019. AISC, vol. 903, pp. 820–826. Springer, Cham (2019). https://doi.org/10.1007/978-3-030-11051-2_125

10. Kocielnik, R., Avrahami, D., Marlow, J., Lu, D., Hsieh, G.: Designing for workplace reflection: a chat and voice-based conversational agent. In: Proceedings of the 2018 on Designing Interactive Systems Conference 2018 - DIS 2018, pp. 881–894 (2018). https://doi.org/10.1145/3196709.3196784

11. Dizon, G.: Using intelligent personal assistants for second language learning: a case study of Alexa. TESOL J. **8**(4), 811–830 (2017). https://doi.org/10.1002/tesj.353

12. Kita, T., Nagaoka, C., Hiraoka, N., Suzuki, K., Dougiamas, M.: A discussion on effective implementation and prototyping of voice user interfaces for learning activities on moodle. In: Proceedings of the 10th International Conference on Computer Supported Education, pp. 398–404 (2018)

13. Rizwan, R., Vveinhardt, J., Streimikiene, D., Awais, M.: Mediating and marketing factors influence the prescription behavior of physicians: an empirical investigation. AMFITEATRU Econ. J. **18**(41), 153–167 (2016). Accessed 29 May 2019. https://econpapers.repec.org/article/aesamfeco/v_3a41_3ay_3a2016_3ai_3a18_3ap_3a153.htm

14. Kwak, E.-S., Chang, H.: Medical representatives' intention to use information technology in pharmaceutical marketing. Healthc. Inform. Res. **22**(4), 342–350 (2016). https://doi.org/10.4258/hir.2016.22.4.342

Evaluating the Socioenactive Experience with a Tangible Tabletop Installation: A Case Study

Yusseli Lizeth Méndez Mendoza[1]([⊠]) ⓘ and M. Cecília C. Baranauskas[1,2] ⓘ

[1] Institute of Computing, University of Campinas, Campinas, SP, Brazil
yusseli.mendoza@students.ic.unicamp.br, cecilia@ic.unicamp.br
[2] Nucleus of Informatics Applied to Education, University of Campinas, Campinas, SP, Brazil

Abstract. A multitude of methods for evaluating the interaction and experience exists, but there is a lack of discussion on methods that evaluate the experience in enactive and socioenactive scenarios. In this work, we investigate whether current evaluation methods are sufficient to evaluate the socioenactive experience that emerges of the coupling of three main elements (physical, digital, and social) as part of those scenarios. We conducted a case study to evaluate the experience resulting from the interaction with TangiTime, a tangible tabletop installation, using the AttrakDiff questionnaire as an evaluation method for the socioenactive experience. Based on findings from this case study, we provide insights on other design aspects to be covered in the evaluation of socioenactive scenarios.

Keywords: Evaluation method · Experience · Tangible user interfaces

1 Introduction

The recent technological evolution has brought new possibilities of making real Mark Weiser's vision of ubiquitous computing [1] and new challenges for the HCI community to design and evaluate computational systems. In this way, researchers are considering phenomenological approaches based on Varela et al. [2] to understand the nature of the human experience when interacting with technology and the environment. In the HCI field, Kaipainen et al. [3] proposed the concept of an *enactive system* based on the more recent discourse of the embodied mind. An enactive system is constituted by dynamically coupled human and technological processes in which the technology is part of a two-way feedback system and the role of the interface becomes implicit. The scenario presented by Kaipainen et al. [3] is limited to an individual human-technology coupling and the social element in its design is left undiscussed. The project which hosts this work seeks to clarify the tripartite coupling of physical, digital, and social elements for the design of computational systems in a concept named *Socioenactive* [4].

Tangible technologies like tangible tabletops [5] can enable learning experience closer to how we live and interact with our physical environment using tangible objects as elements of interaction. Currently, there is a lack of discussion on methods that

V. Agredo-Delgado et al. (Eds.): HCI-COLLAB 2020, CCIS 1334, pp. 126–135, 2020.
https://doi.org/10.1007/978-3-030-66919-5_13

evaluate the experience in enactive and socioenative scenarios with artefacts based on enactive and tangible approaches. The situation mentioned added to the complexity of these new scenarios brought the need to revisit traditional methods to evaluate the experience. Using the AttrakDiff [6] instrument as an evaluation method, we conducted a case study to evaluate the experience of interacting with TangiTime [7], a tangible tabletop installation. By presenting and discussing the results of this study and raising new research questions, we provide insights on design considerations to evaluate the *socioenactive experience* in a socioenactive scenario.

The paper is organized as follows: Sect. 2 introduces the socioenactive experience concept and provides information about evaluation methods applied with tangible tabletops. Section 3 describes the case study and results. Section 4 provides a discussion about the evaluated aspect of the experience, and the last section concludes with new research questions on design considerations involved in a socioenactive scenario.

2 Background and Literature Review

2.1 The Socioenactive Experience

The new scenarios created with today's ubiquitous technologies brought up design considerations towards integrating physical artefacts and digital processes. The project which hosts this work [4] argues for the consideration of three main elements as part of those scenarios: a physical, a digital, and a social as illustrated in Fig. 1. This tripartite coupling is being studied in a developing concept named *socioenactive*. As so, efforts are being made for the development of the concept in different scenarios of interaction. As discussed in [7], a *socioenactive experience* emerges from the coupling of the three elements (physical, digital, and social). For a better understanding of the tripartite coupling, we describe the scenario constructed with a tangible tabletop installation named TangiTime.

In the scenario constructed with TangiTime, physical objects have to be placed on the tabletop display to start interacting with the installation. For instance, when the software system detects a physical object, it projects a digital avatar on the tabletop display that moves according to the position and angle of the physical object. Besides, physical

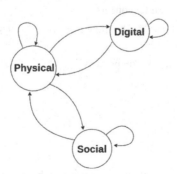

Fig. 1. Digital, physical and social elements of a socioenactive scenario.

objects can be provided with physical effects like movement, lights, or sounds. The effects on the physical objects along with their digital avatars characterize an example of physical and digital coupling. Whereas, an instance of physical and social coupling is given when the actions of one person impact the sequence of actions of another person saying something or acting.

2.2 Tangible Tabletops and Evaluation Methods

Tangible tabletops are a genre of TUI artefacts in which physical objects are the elements of interaction. The physical objects can be manipulated on the tabletop display [5] and also outside of it [7] to interact with the installations. Indeed, tangible tabletops offer a set of functional features, and provide experiences of perceiving and acting in the scenarios that they constitute. To understand what is evaluated at tangible tabletop installations and what evaluation methods are used with it, we conducted an exploratory literature review for works that present tangible tabletops installations and their evaluation process. As a result, we explored 9 works but only 7 of them evaluated the interaction, experience, or learning concepts. Some works only presented the description and implementation of their installation. Thus, we identified different evaluation methods such as interviews, questionnaires, observations, and audio/video recordings, and subjects of evaluation as illustrated in Table 1.

Table 1. Summary of the exploratory literature review.

Tangible tabletop	Subject of evaluation	Evaluation method
Reefs on the Edge [8] (2014)	Interaction process, experience	Ethnographic observation, one-on-one interviews
Mapping Place [9] (2015)	Interaction process, learning concept	Interview questions, talk aloud, video analysis
Plankton Population [10] (2015)	Interaction process, experience	Talk aloud, video analysis
Morita et al. [11] (2017)	Learning concept	Questionnaire
BacPack [12] (2017)	Interaction process, experience, learning concept	Questionnaire, video analysis
Raffaele et al. [13] (2018)	Usability, learning concept	Usability questionnaire, open-ended assessment
TangiTime [7] (2019)	Interaction process	Video analysis

3   A Case Study

Our goal for this case study was to investigate how much an instrument to evaluate the user experience as the AttrakDiff questionnaire is adequate for evaluating the socioenactive experience. Thus, we conducted a case study to evaluate the experience of interacting with TangiTime [7], a tangible tabletop installation, using the AttrakDiff questionnaire as a method for evaluating the socioenactive experience. We selected this instrument because it is one of the most influential and widely used to evaluate the user experience in interactive scenarios [14].

3.1 Context and Participants

The study took place in the Nucleus of Informatics Applied to Education (NIED) of the University of Campinas (UNICAMP) and lasted approximately two hours. Seven members (N = 7) of the InterHAD (Human-Digital Artifact Interaction) group participated in the study: one professor and six graduate students. Additionally, members of the NIED, who were in the institution when the study was conducted, also participated by observing and interacting with the installation.

3.2 Method and Materials

TangiTime. TangiTime is a tangible tabletop installation for experiencing the concept of 'deep time', the time of geological processes, designed and developed by Mendoza and Baranauskas [7]. To approach the deep time concept, TangiTime randomly projects images of geological eras on its surface, and use five components of geological eras as tangible objects (a volcano, a meteorite, a dragonfly, a Triceratops and a Tyrannosaurus rex) to interact with the installation. The installation was developed as a low-cost tangible tabletop capable of detecting on its surface the five physical objects with special visual markers. Besides, three of the physical objects were enhanced with ubiquitous technology to enable a two-way feedback system and interaction outside the tabletop display.

TangiTime allowed users two ways of object manipulation: a) Just placing and moving tangible objects on the tabletop display, and b) Manipulating objects outside the tabletop display and continuing to receive feedback on the physical object itself. Users receive three types of feedback according to the physical object manipulated: digital responses on the tabletop display as digital simulations, physical responses in the object itself using controllers and actuators embedded into the objects, and sounds. For instance, when the system detects a physical dinosaur, it projects a digital avatar on the tabletop display that moves according to the position and angle of the physical object. Besides, the physical dinosaurs are provided with physical effects like the lighting of their eyes and the sounds of their roars. Figure 2 illustrates an example of a socioenactive scenario with TangiTime.

AttrakDiff. The AttrakDiff questionnaire was developed by [6] to measure the perceived pragmatic and hedonic qualities, and the attractiveness of interactive products. While pragmatic qualities refer to functional aspects, hedonic qualities refer to the product attributes to evoke pleasure. The AttrakDiff questionnaire is an instrument of measurement in the format of semantic differentials. The answer options consist of 28 opposite adjectives (e.g., "complicated - simple", "conservative - innovative", "ugly - attractive") presented as seven-point scales with values ranging from −3 to +3 and a

Fig. 2. Example of a socioenactive scenario with TangiTime illustrated by a randomly projected image and one of its representative tangible objects.

neutral value in the middle. Each of the mean values of a group of items creates a value for pragmatic quality (PQ), hedonic quality (HQ) and attractiveness (ATT). For the case study, we applied an adapted version of the AttrakDiff questionnaire, as proposed and experimented by [15]. The adapted questionnaire is composed of 20 opposite adjectives which were translated to Brazilian Portuguese.

3.3 Procedure

The study was composed of three phases: 1) introduction, 2) exploration, and 3) evaluation, described as follows:

Introduction. We started the study by introducing the concept of *deep time*. To this, we projected a video about the evolution of life on the tabletop display of the installation, and raised related motivational questions. The original video was created by undergraduate students in their final group project in a Human-Computer Interaction (HCI) course, and we made an adaptation, reducing the time of the video. Next, we raised motivational questions, such as: *What first appeared, insects or dinosaurs? Has there always been life on the planet? Do you know what the ozone layer is? Has it always existed?* For example, one participant said that life appeared when a meteorite fell on Earth and brought with it some bacteria that started life on the planet.

Exploration. For this phase, the participants were distributed around the tabletop and we presented the installation to them, describing what each tangible object represented. Then, the participants had to observe the characteristics of the projected geological era and determine what object(s) belong to that era according to feedback generated by the system. The participants were free to interact with the installation, however, a researcher acted as facilitator and was responsible for encouraging them to take some of the five tangible objects distributed around the tabletop display and interact with the installation.

Evaluation. For this phase, we invited the participants to answer a printed version of the adapted AttrakDiff questionnaire, anonymously, to understand how people perceive and value the installation. After collecting the answers, we transferred the data with the participant's responses to an online tool to proceed with the analysis of the answers. The online tool [16] uses the original model of 28 opposite adjectives, so the data of the word-pairs removed in the adapted questionnaire were entered with value zero (0) in order to not interfere in the results. This online tool allows us to see result diagrams such as the distribution of response patterns, the portfolio of results, and the diagram of average values.

3.4 Results

The participant's responses to the questionnaire were analyzed based on the obtained result diagrams of the online tool as follows:

Portfolio of Results. This diagram illustrates the medium value of pragmatic and hedonic quality and the confidence interval of results. Figure 3 shows that according to participant consensus, the hedonic quality is higher than the pragmatic quality, extending from the self-oriented area to the desired area. The medium value is located into the "self-oriented" quadrant suggesting that the result points out that hedonic attributes of the installation were highlighted during the case study. In terms of pragmatic quality, the experience was evaluated positively (0,80) with a confidence value of 0,42. Regarding hedonic quality, the results show a positive value of 1,62 with a confidence interval of 0,33.

Diagram of Average Values. This diagram illustrates the average values of the AttrakDiff dimensions for the evaluated product: Pragmatic quality (PQ), Hedonic Quality - Identity (HQ-I), Hedonic Quality - Simulation (HQ-S) and Attractiveness (ATT). In Fig. 3, the PQ value indicates the degree of success in achieving the objectives and obtained a score of 0.80. The HQ-I value indicated that there was a good identification of the user with the installation with a score of 1.43. The HQ-S value, which measures whether the experience is original, interesting and stimulating, obtained a score of 1.82. Finally, the ATT value indicates how attractive the product was to the participant and obtained a score of 2.02, the highest among the categories.

The Description of Word-Pairs. The description of word-pairs diagram illustrates the distribution of response patterns for each word-pair of the AttrakDiff dimensions. In Fig. 4, most of the blue squares are located significantly to the right side of the diagram. These results suggest that all participants considered the experience with TangiTime as creative, attractive and good. Only the Pragmatic Quality (PQ) in the word-pair "unpredictable – predictable" was positioned to the left side with a value between −1 and 0. We argue that functionalities such as the random projection of geological eras, incorporated into the conceptual model of TangiTime may explain this "not predictable" behavior.

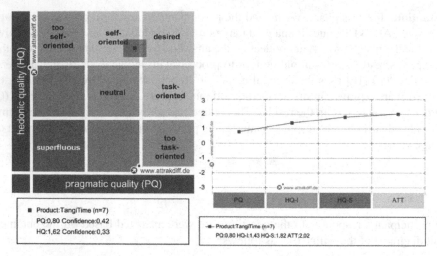

Fig. 3. Portfolio of results (left) and diagram of average values (right).

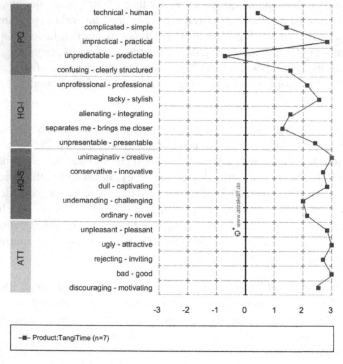

Fig. 4. The description of word-pairs.

4 Discussion

We conducted a case study to explore whether the AttrakDiff questionnaire is sufficient to evaluate the experience with an artifact in a socioenactive scenario. The AttrakDiff questionnaire uses a model that evaluates functional aspects of an artefact grouped in pragmatic attributes (e.g., it is simple/complicated, predictable/not predictable). The instrument captured the designer's intention to add an unpredictable factor as soon as participants interacted TangiTime. The questionnaire also evaluated whether the installation was perceived as hedonic providing stimulation and identification. In the TangiTime case, the stimulation was provided by creative, innovative, captivating, and novel functionalities that it incorporates. The identification attributes are related to social aspects (e.g., it separates me/brings me closer). However, the questionnaire does not consider how the actions of one participant can influence the sequences of actions of other participants, as part of the social aspects in a socioenactive scenario.

We consider that the AttrakDiff questionnaire evaluated important aspects of the experience related to emotional aspects such as satisfaction or pleasure. Satisfaction is linked to the success in using an artefact to achieve particular desirable behavioral goals (e.g., manipulate the TangiTime objects onto or outside the tabletop display). Pleasure is linked to using an artefact in a particular situation and encountering something desirable but unexpected (e.g., place the dragonfly on the tabletop display and it moves its physical wings). Nevertheless, we consider necessary to have attributes for a socioenactive experience related to concepts such as embodiment, coupling, sense-making and autonomy. For instance, the embodiment concept considers the physical body involvement in interaction and is materialized in TangiTime through the interactions with physical objects enacting out knowledge by manipulating them. The coupling can be characterized by considering ubiquity between physical and digital elements. In TangiTime, a physical object and its avatar is an example of physical and digital coupling. The Sense-making concept is illustrated in TangiTime when people interacting with the installation perceive the effects of their actions on the environment and its effects. The autonomy concept is illustrated in TangiTime when it allows people to be autonomous in exploring, grasping, and manipulating the physical objects to interact with the installation, without a predefined sequence of actions.

5 Conclusions

In this work, we conducted a case study to investigate whether the AttrakDiff questionnaire as an evaluation method is sufficient to evaluate the socioenactive experience resulting from interacting with an artefact in a socioenactive scenario. We reported the results of evaluating the experience of exploring TangiTime, a tangible tabletop installation designed considering socioenactive approach to tangible artefacts. The selected method evaluated aspects of the experience related to emotional aspects such as satisfaction or pleasure. Also, it evaluated functional aspects grouped as pragmatic attributes and whether the installation was perceived as hedonic providing stimulation and identification. We have identified some needs for attributes to evaluate a socioenactive experience, especially related to dimensions such as embodiment, coupling and social. Further research questions on design considerations in a socioenactive scenario involve:

The Embodiment Dimension. There is a need for attributes to address experience with body involvement. How computational systems can incorporate design considerations that allow physical body involvement in the interaction? How to evaluate these design considerations in a socioenactive scenario?

The Coupling Dimension. There is a need for attributes to integrate physical artefacts and digital processes. How computational systems can incorporate design considerations towards integrating physical artefacts and digital processes. How to evaluate the ubiquity of these computational systems?

The Social Dimension. There is a need for attributes to address the experience of groups. How computational systems can incorporate design considerations to provide ways for a participant's action to influence the sequences of actions of other participants? How to evaluate these design considerations in a socioenactive scenario?

Acknowledgments. This work is supported by the São Paulo Research Foundation (FAPESP) (grant #2015/16528-0), National Council for Scientific and Technological Development (CNPq) (grant #306272/2017-2), Coordination for the Improvement of Higher Education Personnel (CAPES) (grant #2017/173989) and a Technical Training Program (grant #2020/03503-7). The authors thank the members of the InterHAD group for their collaboration in different phases of the study and the NIED for providing us the location to conduct the study.

References

1. Weiser, M.: The Computer for the 21st Century. SIGMOBILE Mob. Comput. Commun. Rev. **3**(3), 3–11 (1999)
2. Varela, F.J., Thompson, E., Rosch, E.: The Embodied Mind: Cognitive Science and Human Experience (Revised Edition). MIT Press (2016)
3. Kaipainen, M., Ravaja, N., Tikka, P., Vuori, R., Pugliese, R.: Enactive systems and enactive media: embodied human-machine coupling beyond interfaces. Leonardo **44**(5), 433–443 (2011)
4. Baranauskas, M.C.C.: Socio-Enactive systems: investigating new dimensions in the design of interaction mediated by information and communication technologies. FAPESP Thematic Project (2015/165280) (2015)
5. Ishii, H.: Tangible bits: beyond pixels. In: Proceedings of the Second International Conference on Tangible and Embedded Interaction (TEI 2008), pp. 2175–2185. ACM, New York (2008). https://doi.org/10.1145/1347390.1347392
6. Hassenzahl, M., Burmester, M., Koller, F.: AttrakDiff: Ein Fragebogen zur Messung wahrgenommener hedonischer und pragmatischer Qualitat. In: Szwillus, G., Ziegler, J., Mensch & Computer 2003: Interaktion in Bewegung, pp. 187–196. Vieweg+Teubner Verlag, Wiesbaden (2003)
7. Mendoza, Y.L.M., Baranauskas, M.C.C.: TangiTime: Designing a (Socio)enactive Experience for Deep Time in an Educational Exhibit. In: XVIII Simpósio Brasileiro sobre Fatores Humanos em Sistemas Computacionais (IHC 2019). ACM, New York (2019). https://doi.org/10.1145/3357155.3358451

8. Bérigny, C., Gough, P., Faleh, M., Woolsey, E.: Tangible user interface design for climate change education in interactive installation art. Leonardo **47**, 451–456 (2014). https://doi.org/10.1162/LEON_a_00710
9. Chu, J.H., Clifton, P., Harley, D., Pavao, J., Mazalek, A.: Mapping place: supporting cultural learning through a Lukasa-inspired tangible tabletop museum exhibit. In: Proceedings of the Ninth International Conference on Tangible, Embedded, and Embodied Interaction (TEI 2015), pp. 261–268. ACM, New York (2015). https://doi.org/10.1145/2677199.2680559
10. Ma, J., Sindorf, L., Liao, I., Frazier, J.: Using a tangible versus a multi-touch graphical user interface to support data exploration at a museum exhibit. In: Proceedings of the Ninth International Conference on Tangible, Embedded, and Embodied Interaction (TEI'15), pp. 33–40. ACM, New York, USA (2015). https://doi.org/10.1145/2677199.2680555
11. Morita, Y., Setozaki, N.: Learning by tangible learning system in science class. In: Kurosu, M. (ed.) HCI 2017. LNCS, vol. 10272, pp. 341–352. Springer, Cham (2017). https://doi.org/10.1007/978-3-319-58077-7_27
12. Loparev, A., et al.: BacPack: exploring the role of tangibles in a museum exhibit for bio-design. In: Proceedings of the 11th International Conference on Tangible, Embedded, and Embodied Interaction (TEI 2017), pp. 111–120. ACM, New York (2017). https://doi.org/10.1145/3024969.3025000
13. De Raffaele, C., Smith, S., Gemikonakli, O.: An active tangible user interface framework for teaching and learning artificial intelligence. In: 23rd International Conference on Intelligent User Interfaces (IUI 2018), pp. 535–546. ACM, New York (2018). https://doi.org/10.1145/3172944.3172976
14. Díaz-Oreiro, I., López, G., Quesada, L., Guerrero, L.A.: Standardized questionnaires for user experience evaluation: a systematic literature review. In: Proceedings of the 13th International Conference on Ubiquitous Computing and Ambient Intelligence (UCAmi), vol. 31, no. 1, p. 14 (2019). https://doi.org/10.3390/proceedings2019031014
15. Brennand, C.V.L.T., Baranauskas, M.C.C.: Evaluating UX - case studies in socio-enactive scenarios. In: Sánchez, J. (ed.) TISE 2018, Nuevas Ideas en Informática Educativa, vol. 14, pp. 260–271. ACM (2018)
16. AttrakDiff. http://www.attrakdiff.de/index-en.html. Accessed 2019

Habitar: A Collaborative Tool to Visualize, Distribute, Organize and Share Domestic Tasks Towards Reducing the Gender Gap in Household Labor

Axel Alonso García[1]([✉]) [iD], Alondra Ayala Ramírez[1] [iD], Laura Vázquez Navarrete[1] [iD], and Rocío Abascal-Mena[2] [iD]

[1] Master in Design, Information and Communication (MADIC), Universidad Autónoma Metropolitana – Unidad Cuajimalpa, Avenida Vasco de Quiroga 4871, Colonia Santa Fe Cuajimalpa, 05300 Del. Cuajimalpa de Morelos, Mexico
raxelonso@gmail.com, alondraar@gmail.com,
lauravazquez.mn@gmail.com
[2] Department of Information Technologies, Universidad Autónoma Metropolitana – Unidad Cuajimalpa, Avenida Vasco de Quiroga 4871, Colonia Santa Fe Cuajimalpa, 05300 Del. Cuajimalpa de Morelos, Mexico
mabascal@cua.uam.mx

Abstract. Household work and domestic labor are an integral part of keeping up and maintaining a home. Nevertheless, traditional gender roles are still prevalent in a way that women often spend significantly more time and effort than men doing household chores as a form of unpaid labor. Habitar is a tool proposed to take on this complicated subject, developed through User-Centered Design, it distributes and organizes domestic chores between the inhabitants of a house while promoting active and continuous participation of men and children at home. The interactive and collective platform would allow its users to organize, distribute, visualize and share domestic work with each other, as it frames individual effort in a larger context of collective well-being for those involved.

Keywords: Human computer-interaction · Collaboration · Domestic work · User-centered design · Habit tracking · Gender gap

1 Introduction

Distribution of domestic chores between women and men in most Mexican homes is extremely uneven in terms of both time and effort. According to statistics from the National Institute of Statistics and Geography (INEGI) [1], in 2018 women dedicated an average of 39.4 h per week to domestic and care work for other members of the family, while men only spent 4.2 h per week on the same activities. Outdated notions of gender, such as men being providers who exclusively work outside of home while women must solely take care of family members and housework, are still an important

© Springer Nature Switzerland AG 2020
V. Agredo-Delgado et al. (Eds.): HCI-COLLAB 2020, CCIS 1334, pp. 136–145, 2020.
https://doi.org/10.1007/978-3-030-66919-5_14

part of Mexican gender-based social order, which directly leads to lack of involvement in domestic work from the male population.

Within most homes and pertaining all social classes, women bear a disproportionate and overwhelming burden in domestic work, which constitutes a cornerstone in gender inequality. This gender gap negatively affects individual women's physical and mental health, but also has structural consequences, such as: less time for learning, leisure and political involvement, greater obstacles to find a job outside the household, significant limitations to advance academically and professionally, and a greater partaking in informal economies, sacrificing social security and the benefits of formal labor structures in exchange for greater flexibility and more control of personal time [2].

As an interdisciplinary team, we've decided to address the need to work towards a fairer distribution of domestic labor and help create awareness about the importance of active involvement in housework and family care by all genders. According to our research, care and domestic work demand time and physical, emotional and mental effort that needs to be recognized and shared by all members of a household in order to relieve primary caretakers from the overwhelming stress of these tasks.

This paper proceeds as follows. To help us understand our proposal better, in Sect. 2 we revise thematically related applications. This section also entails the different approximations we explored about goal completion rewarding systems.

In Sect. 3, we explain how we identified the main needs our tool aims to satisfy, and elaborate on the creation of user profiles obtained through the *Persona* models suggested by Cooper, Reimann and Cronin [3]. We also describe the development of a "fake door pretotype", a Facebook page for our tool, to gauge potential interest in our project and how different users planned to interact with it.

In Sect. 4, we share our experience planning and developing a functional prototype and the feedback we obtained from some of our test subjects. Finally, some conclusions are given as well as insights towards further work.

2 Related Work

Despite some improvement in women's participation in the workforce and public life (according to INEGI, 42.6% of women older than 15 years old are part of the Economic Active Population, and 73% of them has at least one child) [4], their participation in non-remunerated labor is still greater than that of the male population. These circumstances harm the well-being and health of women, and perpetuate stereotypes about male involvement in domestic chores and their dependence on their mothers, partners, and women in general inside or outside their household, to whom domestic labors and caring work are usually outsourced.

There are some apps in the market intended to help in the organization and distribution of domestic chores. As part of our research we took on the gamification apps *Choremonster*[1] and *Habitica*[2], both try to translate the dynamics of achievements and experience points of Role-playing Video Games (RPGs) to create and stimulate habits in

---

[1] Available at http://choremonster.mx.aptoide.com/app.

[2] Available at http://habitica.com/static/home.

their users. However, these household management apps have an individualistic behaviorist approach, rewarding single task completion with prizes, points and other positive external reinforcement. We believe that this approach is restrictive and doesn't generate an authentic awareness of the shared responsibilities in a home environment. For that reason, we propose a tool that uses the chores assigned to family members to generate graphs and charts explaining the work of each member of the house, similar to apps like Tody[3] and Unf*ck your habitat[4]. We also believe that communication between partners, families and household members is key to make our users aware of their impact in the amount of care and work involved in collective environments through graphs and shared tips from users.

In this way, our proposal seeks to build a lasting involvement of its users in taking care of themselves, their surroundings and the people they share them with, by contextualizing individual work within the collective needs of a home, allowing them to visualize the time and effort they and their peers are putting in, and framing domestic work as a form of self-care.

3   Methodology

In order to detect needs and focus on the development of a solution, we followed the User-Centered Design (UCD) methodology [5]. UCD is a multitudinous approach in which the design process puts the user at its center from the beginning and all throughout, allowing for the construction of **pertinent** interactive systems. The first step of our development consisted of analyzing different challenges aggravated by the COVID-19 pandemic and the consequent shutdown of everyday activities in México. We identified gender gap in domestic work as a structural problem amplified by circumstances like confinement related stress, unemployment and an increased load of domestic work since many people remain in lockdown. We chose to address the lack of involvement of all family members, specially men, in domestic chores and the impact it has on the physical and mental health of the women they live with as the main need to attend.

3.1   Interviews and Detection of Needs

Each member of the team did informal interviews and observations with selected users to look for design problems, needs and opportunities. With the answers that we got from about two dozen men and women from various backgrounds and in different living arrangements, we learned about everyday experiences related to the disproportion in time assigned to housekeeping and cleaning between women and men, cohabitating issues, and the overall perception of male involvement at home. Some needs we identified are:

- Even when men take on household chores, they aren't aware of the total workload involved in housekeeping and often rely on constant reminders and instructions from women to complete domestic or care work.

---

[3] Available at http://todyapp.com/.

[4] Available at http://www.unfuckyourhabitat.com/.

- Women are required to not only organize and schedule all of the household work that needs to be done but also to distribute chores and tasks within the inhabitants of the home in a way that feels non-threatening, fair and evenly distributed.
- This often leads to emotional and mental stress in women and anger and frustration in men and sometimes retaliation from them.
- Women are responsible for doing their share of workload and often are also in charge of the duties of other members of the family.
- Women find it hard to talk about this gap with their male peers, which results in difficulties to renegotiate the established division of workload and causes strain in their relationships.
- We decided these problems or needs could be addressed through the following tools:
- Graphs and measurements of home-related tasks available to all family members to make them aware of the amount of time and effort domestic work entails.
- Tools to equally assign domestic chores and, by doing so, help reduce the guilt provoked in women.
- Alarms, lists and notifications to remember and organize chores assigned to each family member.
- Support networks inside and outside of home.
- Clearer and more assertive communication within home.

Through these observations, we obtained useful information about women's habits and the impact of unequal share of housework in their lives. We also learned more about the reasons that keep many men apart from domestic responsibilities, such as: negative feedback from members of their household and lack of experience, self-care notions and networks to address these issues with their male peers.

The User-Centered Design (UCD) methodology offers a greater understanding about users' needs and requirements in order to guarantee a better product or solution. This is of special importance given the complex social and cultural issues involved in gender relations, as well as pertaining to the consideration of all types of individuals in a household to offer a possible design solution.

3.2 User Profiles and Personas

We chose to work with methodologies for behavioral analysis that allowed us to gain more detailed knowledge of our users. With the *Personas* model proposed by Cooper, Reimann and Croninr [3], we created a group of four *personas* to represent the most likely active members of a household –female homemakers, women who work outside of home, men and children– to guide our thought process during development. Having two women *personas* allowed us to take into consideration the differentiated experiences of those who have to attend and solve problems at their houses and those who also perform that role at their workplaces. However, we found out both female *personas* have the goal of gaining more recreational time and getting more rest, and wish to better their communication with their male peers. The male *persona* allowed us to identify ways in which men lessen their involvement in domestic work, e.g. the notion that there are inherently "manly" or "unmanly" chores. We also identified their need to be acknowledged as part of family dynamics. Our fourth *persona* took on the children of the home, who are learning their role in domestic care and how to be responsible for themselves.

3.3 Storyboards

Once we created our *Personas*, we set out to develop a more detailed insight of the key demographic that would interact with our proposal and the expected reaction to it. Each one of us created a storyboard of our tool being used without sharing them between us. Then, we set ourselves to find the common issues that ran amongst them: the constant presence of an overwhelming physical and emotional burden on women and the need for a fairer share of domestic work and active involvement of all members of the household. Differences aside, all our storyboards also addressed the lack of involvement from men on these tasks. These observations let us define the main need of our project as the development of a notion of self-care and family involvement by all members of the household, encouraged by awareness of shared effort. Our perspective is: *domestic work demands effort and time, but with good self-management, shared responsibility, care and participation of every inhabitant of the household, this work can be less of a burden for women.*

3.4 Inspiration Board

Next, we made an inspiration board to collect references and key themes for our suggested solutions. These include: community, communication, equity, compromise, self-care, caring, well-being, self-management, responsibility (shared and individual), organization, awareness and mindfulness.

The items and references selected in our board were explained broadly in Sect. 2, but it is important to mention we explored various studies about gender inequality at work, self-management apps, and methods of reward for task completion. As mentioned, we believe that our goal of a deeper involvement in domestic chores –mainly from children and men– require organic learning, acknowledgement of responsibilities and a profound understanding of the need for domestic work. Because of that, we chose not to award points or give rewards at task completion, instead our system produces information about performance, time spent and allows users to share tips amongst themselves to instill a notion of responsibility within them.

3.5 Prototype: Fake Door

To gauge public interest in our proposed tool, we made a pretotype according to one of Alberto Savoia's techniques [6]: the Fake Door. This allowed us to test the Initial Level of Interest in a product in development, yet inexistent, by creating artifacts that suggested its availability. The data we gathered using this technique let us evaluate if our shared proposal deserved further development, as well as test our target audience and their first reaction to our pitch.

We created a Facebook page[5] with mock-ups of *Habitar,* the name given to our tool. It features descriptions and usages of our proposed tool through images: a desktop site

---

[5] Available at http://www.facebook.com/HabitarApp.

landing page (Fig. 1), mobile device screens (Fig. 2), and diagrams and illustrations of the system's main features. We purposely didn't explicitly state whether *Habitar* was a web tool or a mobile app, since we wanted to gain insight on this topic from potential users themselves.

Fig. 1. Desktop landing page

Fig. 2. Mobile device screens

The Facebook page itself (as shown in Fig. 3) contains a general explanation of what our tool would do and some of its affordances. *Habitar*'s main Facebook page got 38 followers within a 12-hour period, 81% were women and 18% men; the main post explaining the concept behind the tool reached 5,969 people in the same period, according to Facebook metrics.

Using a social media platform as our main pretotyping tool lets us obtain qualitative feedback about our proposal directly form users' comments in various posts. As such, we could confirm that people from all genres and backgrounds liked the general idea of assigning domestic work more equitable between men and women. But most importantly, we could confirm that there is a clear gender gap in the distribution of domestic work that harms women systematically.

Furthermore, the Facebook page includes a button that redirects users to a feedback survey[6], where they can express their opinions and grievances, and through which we

---

[6] Available at http://forms.gle/MMYkLmGgXVvhX4G19.

Fig. 3. *Habitar* Facebook page (PC version)

are able to gather data on our audience and identify common trends in people interested in our tool. As it happened in the Facebook page, there was a bigger interest from female users but (see Fig. 4) the gender gap is smaller in the feedback survey: 58.1% for female users, 38.7% for male users and 3.2% who preferred not to answer that question. We also discovered that 74% of this sample comes from the 25–34 year old demographic, this was an insight that our tool could be of interest to people who began living on their own for the first time, whether it be alone, with roommates or partners.

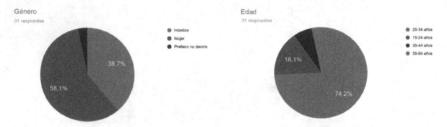

Fig. 4. Survey results of interested users by gender and age

Other relevant information we gathered were the reasons people were interested in our tool, the top two were "to self-organize" and "to know how much time I allocate to my home", both confirm our initial findings. Finally, we discovered that more than 70% of users who expressed interest in *Habitar* were accessing our site through mobile devices, this reach gave us the insight to decide on a mobile version of the tool. With this information, we started developing a functional digital prototype.

3.6 Digital Prototype

The next logical step in the development process would have been to employ a face-to-face technique to propose potential interfaces for our users to evaluate in a quick and accessible way (i.e. a paper prototype), but due to COVID-19 related circumstances, we instead worked directly on a digital prototype. The proposed tool in our prototype is the mobile version of *Habitar*.

To create this prototype, we first built a wireframe to understand the possible structure, organization and flow of information within and between the elements in the tool, pertaining to the main tasks most likely to serve our users according to our analysis, while taking into consideration their needs and the suggestions obtained in previous steps. While building the wireframe and designing the individual screens, we relied on the ten usability heuristics for user interface design defined by Jacob Nielsen [7, 8].

Next, based on the design and architecture information decisions made in the wireframe, we proceeded to create a digital functional prototype (Fig. 5). Even though the majority of the core tasks and related actions relevant for our users were considered in this wireframe—as well as certain interactions and information flows—the digital prototype focused on what we thought as the most pertinent screens and functions of the app based on the research presented above.

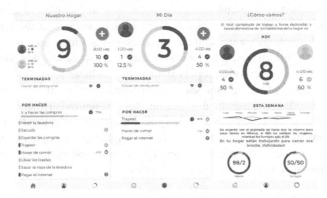

Fig. 5. Prototype main screens

The tool selected to develop the digital prototype was InVisionApp[7] for its convenience to work with hotspots and pre-made screens, which allowed us to better simulate a mobile application user experience. The first version of the prototype was evaluated by users to obtain feedback and suggestions, thus leading us to update it regarding the graphic representation of shared metrics between users.

4 Main Results

Once our prototype was developed, we selected four users off our main demographic to assess how they interacted with the app and to test our implementation of Nielsen's heuristics. For that purpose, we designed a trial run that would specifically require our subjects to understand and go through the main functions and points of inference in the prototype in order to achieve a result. Since one of our key project goals was to visualize and highlight domestic work distribution, we first asked our subjects to identify what certain key graphic elements within the prototype represented, to test if they could easily find, understand and make use of such information. Then, we asked them to perform a

---

[7] Available at http://www.invisionapp.com/.

specific task that would require multiple steps and actions to be completed, in this way, we managed to test different parts of the prototype in the same run, and to not only see if they worked by themselves, but in relation to one another and as part of a unified system.

We observed and took notes while our subjects performed the trial run. Due to the personal and often emotional nature of the themes involved in our work, we thought it extremely important to know the sentiments and personal thoughts subjects had while interacting with our prototype, so we created a survey[8] they could fill on their own and performed casual interviews with them to gain some insights about their experiences. According to the survey, while all of our test users considered the prototype aesthetically pleasing, they generally thought our system didn't provide them with enough feedback to let them understand what some of the data meant at first use, and as consequence, encountered trouble in performing some actions without additional instructions. Some specific issues to address were the lack of user identification, the need for a clearer indication of assigned chores and instructions on how to complete a given chore; in addition, a number of subjects perceived a lack of achievement at the comfortability heuristic level and they also suggested an improvement at functions pertaining the use of language to better match our system with the way users speak in a day-to-day context.

On the other hand, users also reported that they believe some core functions of *Habitar*, like the option to assign the same chore to many users, the core visual design and the potential to be an aesthetically pleasing tool to help visualize domestic needs and distribute them, were ways that directly address their main needs and concerns. Other suggestions include the introduction of a landing or splash page for simplicity and clarity, improving some of the interaction and the intuitiveness of the app, and a broader capability to customize background and text options.

5 Conclusions and Further Work

Through User-Centered Design methods we propose a tool to help users distribute and manage chores, keep track of the specific nuances required to perform them, generate alerts to signify completion and monitor and compare the involvement of all the inhabitants of the house. The main users of our tool are working women and female homemakers who need to reduce their workload, men who need to understand and practice self and collective care and want to take an active role participating in household activities, and children learning responsibility, autonomy and collaboration.

Our prototypes were developed taking into consideration those ideal users, while we used social networks and online surveys to test the interest in a tool that helps in the organization and assignment of domestic work. The feedback we got was mostly positive and gave us some insight to update our prototype. The test with actual users gave us specific feedback about the information disposition and display, the need to make an intuitive navigation between screens and the need of providing more explicit help to the user.

The feedback we obtained makes it clear that, while the core idea or our tool is useful to our users, there are things that still need to be refined in terms of IA, instructions and

---

[8] Available at http://forms.gle/9C5tXvvBcP5onRv18.

colloquial language. We hope to continue our work on this project and perform more user tests to assure a tool that can be used by all interested parties, especially as a collaborative tool between people from different ages and genders who share a home, as we believe this is a key issue in Mexican families.

References

1. Instituto Nacional de Estadística y Geografía (INEGI): Trabajo no Remunerado de los Hogares (2018). https://www.inegi.org.mx/temas/tnrh/
2. ONU Mujeres: Trabajo doméstico y de cuidados no remunerado. ONU Mujeres México, Mexico (2015). https://www2.unwomen.org/-/media/field%20office%20mexico/documentos/publicaciones/2016/trabajo%20dome%CC%81stico%20serie%20transformar%20nuestro%20mundo.pdf?la=es&vs=1057
3. Cooper, A., Reimann, R., Cronin, D.: About Face 3. The Essentials of Interaction Design. Design Wiley, Indianapolis (2007). ISBN 978-0-470-08411-3
4. Instituto Nacional de Estadística y Geografía. Comunicado de prensa número 243/19: Estadísticas a propósito del Día de la Madre (10 de mayo), May 2019. https://inegi.org.mx/contenidos/saladeprensa/aproposito/2019/madre2019_Nal.pdf
5. Norman, D.: The Design of Everyday Things. Basic Books, New York (1988)
6. Savoia, A.: Pretotype it: make sure you are building the right it before you build it right. (2011). https://www.pretotyping.org/uploads/1/4/0/9/14099067/pretotype_it_2nd_pretotype_edition-2.pdf
7. Nielsen, J., Molich, R.: Heuristic evaluation of user interfaces. In: Proceedings of the ACM CHI 1990 Conference, Seattle, WA, 1-5 April, pp. 249–256 (1990). https://doi.org/10.1145/97243.97281
8. Nielsen, J.: Enhancing the explanatory power of usability heuristics. In: Proceedings ACM CHI 1994 Conference Boston, MA, 24–28 April, pp. 152–158 (1994). https://doi.org/10.1145/191666.191729

Human Body AR: A Mobile Application for Teaching Anatomy for Elementary Students Using Augmented Reality

Briseida Sotelo-Castro[✉] and Diego Iquira Becerra

Universidad Nacional de San Agustín de Arequipa, Arequipa, Peru
{bsoteloc,diquira}@unsa.edu.pe

Abstract. When the children arrive at the educational institution, they have prior knowledge of the world around them. These previous knowledge's are the product of their experiences, games, among other activities, and based on this knowledge, they can explain facts and natural phenomena. Traditional teaching methods do not allow adapting to the learning that students need, therefore the use of technological tools in education provides different learning opportunities for both students and teachers. The present research evaluates at the usability level an application that we have developed for the use of augmented reality to improve the anatomy teaching process, the use of this technology allowed us to improve the learning process, the validation of this research was carried out using a methodology to evaluate the didactic value of educational software, and this evaluation was carried out in a group of teachers.

Keywords: Augmented reality · Usability · Education · Anatomy

1 Introduction

This research focuses on carrying out a case study from the perspective of the educational usability of an augmented reality application for teaching anatomy. Usability is the degree to which users interact with an application that must be effective, efficient, and easy to learn. In the design of the application, we have taken as a basis the traditional method of teaching anatomy where different activities are used, which describe the different parts of the human body and begin with a general approach reaching specific topics. On the other hand, the use of augmented reality is carried out through the recognition of surfaces where after establishing reference points, either horizontal or vertical surfaces are created, and on these surfaces, 3D models of the different parts of the body will be generated. Finally, the case study was carried out with different participants who conducted a survey measuring the usability of the application at an educational level.

2 Augmented Reality

Augmented reality (AR) is a variation of virtual environments (VE) or virtual reality (VR). Figure 1 shows a vision of the continuity between virtuality and reality defined by

© Springer Nature Switzerland AG 2020
V. Agredo-Delgado et al. (Eds.): HCI-COLLAB 2020, CCIS 1334, pp. 146–154, 2020.
https://doi.org/10.1007/978-3-030-66919-5_15

Milgram in 1995 [1], where VE technologies completely immerse the user in a synthetic environment (right of the Fig. 1), not being aware of the real world that surrounds.

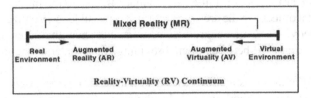

Fig. 1. Milgrams reality-virtuality continuum [2]

In contrast, AR allows the user to view virtual objects overlaid in the real world. Therefore, AR complements reality rather than completely replacing it [2]. Thus, Azuma defines AR as a technology that meets 3 characteristics [3]:

a. Combine virtual and real content.
b. Interactivity in real-time.
c. A union between a 3D environment of real and virtual objects.

There are different investigations of the use of augmented reality in education, of which we can highlight the following: In an investigation they analyzed the educational usability in the use of augmented reality and gamification for the teaching of zoology [3]. In another study, they proposed the use of tools such as the Kinect for the creation of educational virtual environments to teach anatomy concepts [4].

3   Teaching Anatomy

The Ministry of Education of Peru (MINEDU) proposes the use of learning routes to guide the correct teaching to students, as well as the faculty of articulating, integrating, and transferring knowledge through the exercise of a set of abilities and skills that allow the development of operations mental or actions on reality [5]. The indicators that children are expected to learn about the area of anatomy are:

1. Characteristics of the organs of the human body.
2. Functioning of the organs of the human body.
3. Identification of the systems of the human body.

For this reason, to achieve this learning, teachers make use of materials such as:

1. Metallic board and illustrated plates of the systems of the human body.
2. Cards with descriptions of the organs.
3. Paper, markers and adhesive tape.
4. Colored cards.
5. Science and Environment Book provided by MINEDU.

Biology, anatomy, physics and astronomy are important areas of study but difficult to teach since traditionally texts and images are used, but this type of content does not generate a correct immersion of the course towards the student. That is why through the use of AR, new learning opportunities are obtained thanks to the interaction of the real world with digital objects, in the area of anatomy it is possible to visualize the 3D models of the human body which may contain animations that show the different systems and the relationships that exist between them, providing greater interactivity in the student's learning process.

There are different investigations focused on the use of technologies for teach- ing anatomy, of which we can highlight: The development of a simple, light, and inexpensive three-dimensional visualization device based on MR, where doctors can see radiological examinations [6]. Other research focused on creating an interactive AR system to learn the structure of human anatomy [4]. An inves- tigation was also carried out on an AR mirror prototype [7], allowing intuitive viewing of realistic anatomical information. Another investigation was focused on a system that offers a real-time 3D representation of the human heart in an interactive VR environment [8]. Blum presents an AR mirror for teaching anatomy [9], which uses a depth camera to follow the posture of a user standing in front of a large screen, generating the illusion of being able to see the inside of a person's body and uses a gesture control with which it is possible to un- derstand the spatial relationships between the body and the virtual interaction plane. Another research focused on the effectiveness of VR-based learning in early childhood students [10].

4 Methodology

The tests were carried out on 20 children of 5 years old, their actions and attitudes towards the application were observed. With the help of the teacher in charge, the children were asked questions about each heuristic. The results were collected and a table of the level of usability of the application was built.

4.1 Stages of Heuristics

To develop a proposal for Heuristics based on Nielsen but focused on applications with AR, the Rusu Methodology [10, 11] was followed, who gradually defines a series of six stages to establish new usability heuristics.

1. Exploratory Stage: Serves to compile bibliography; A review of the literature related to usability evaluation, AR, and applied heuristics was made, considering the importance of the research according to the results and the problems faced.
2. Descriptive Stage: It serves to highlight the most important characteristics of the information previously collected; concepts of the heuristics used for the usability evaluation of an interface were refined and formalized.
3. Correlational Stage: It serves to identify the characteristics that the usability heuris- tics should have for specific applications; The main characteristics that a proposal for usability heuristics for an augmented reality application should consider were identified, based on Nielsen heuristics.

4. Explanatory Stage: The set of proposed heuristics is formally identified; Using a template, the proposed heuristics were specified with the following fields: Code, name, definition, and example of compliance or violation of heuristics.
5. Validation stage (experimental): An evaluation experiment is carried out to verify the new heuristics against the traditional heuristics; The evaluation was carried out with the proposed and traditional heuristics in the augmented reality application.
6. Refinement stage: A refinement of the proposed heuristics is carried out based on the validation stage.

4.2 Heuristics Specification

After performing the stages of Rusu's methodology [12], eighteen heuristics were obtained. The names of the proposed heuristics to evaluate the usability of an AR application is presented [11, 13, 14].

- HRA1-Confidence
- HRA2-Friendliness
- HRA3-System Status Visibility
- HRA4-Familiarity
- HRA5-Clarity
- HRA6-Accessibility
- HRA7-Interactivity
- HRA8-Navigability
- HRA9-User Control
- HRA10-Consistency and Standards
- HRA11-Error prevention
- HRA12-Minimize memory load
- HRA13-Visibility
- HRA14-Flexibility
- HRA15-Efficiency of use
- HRA16-Minimize irrelevant information
- HRA17-Ease and efficiency of Use
- HRA18-Help and documentation

5 Proposal

In recent years, applications allow students to improve their cognitive, intellectual, and personal skills, as well as other skills, beyond the technological and inclusive contribution provided by said educational support systems, it offers a possibility to enhance the acquisition of knowledge in different educational areas. Therefore, the objective of this system is to provide and reinforce educational knowledge based on augmented reality to ensure the inclusive education process for 5-year-old students on the anatomy course.

5.1 Functionalities

Login Window. The student must create an account to be able to use the application, with this account the progress of the activities can be saved, it is also possible that more than one person can enter the application with different accounts and be able to have different progress.

Missions Window. The application allows you to establish different missions that focus on activities to be carried out from the application, the progress of each mission is shown and the reward for completing it, if the mission has not yet been completed, a padlock icon is shown as seen in Fig. 2, additionally, at the top, you can see a diamond that indicates how many missions are still available.

Fig. 2. Missions window

Profile Window. The application displays student data such as name, score, coins, completed missions, and completed levels.

Connect Activity. In this activity, at the start, the human body, skeleton or muscle is visualized in a complete way where you can recognize the different parts that conform it and how they connect with each other, then the different parts are separated, and one must drag the different parts in the shaded image as seen in Fig. 3.

Fig. 3. Connect activity and auditory information activity

Auditory Information Activity. In this activity, you must click on the different red circles to obtain a greater description of the different concepts of anatomy, with which a description will be heard, a sound that characterizes it and the name of the body part will be shown. If the button is pressed again, the audio is heard again as shown in Fig. 3.

AR Activity. In this activity, AR is used to show the different parts of the human body through the device's camera. First, the physical environment where one is located must be analyzed to determine the surface. A list of reference points will be generated, with which a surface is determined where we can place the 3D models, after having created the surface, click on a point on the surface to make the 3D models appear as shown in Fig. 4.

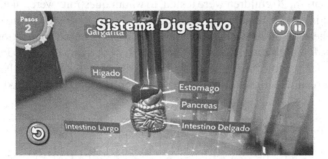

Fig. 4. AR Activity completed

To complete the activity it is necessary to click on the different parts of the 3d model, which means that it is necessary to physically move in the area where the model is located and click on the different elements, after clicking on an element the name is displayed and its location is indicated, additionally the number of steps to complete the activity is reduced as seen in Fig. 4.

5.2 Implementation

The application was developed for mobile devices with the use of the camera to recognize the surfaces of the environments, reference points are used to find the surfaces, this application is aimed at initial students, where students through different activities interact with the parts of the human body which appear as 3D models Fig. 4.

6 Results

The sample size was the total test population (20 initial 5-year-olds).

Concerning the adaptation of Nielsen's heuristics [15], to evaluate the us- ability of the "Human Body AR" application, a scale has been developed that shows the measurement values that will be evaluated in each heuristic as seen in Fig. 5, taking into account Sánchez´[16] who carried out a website usability evaluation.

VALUE MEASUREMENT OBSERVATIONS

1	Strongly disagree	They do not perform the activity or do not understand the content.
2	Disagree	They carry out the activity or understand the content, but it is not useful.
3	Neutral	They do the activity or understand the content easily, but could be better.
4	Agree	They carry out the activity or understand the content with ease.
5	Strongly agree	They perform the activity or the content meets or exceeds theuser's expectation.

Fig. 5. Heuristics measurement scale value measurement

In the evaluation, 20 children were tested, to whom questions were asked about each heuristic, for this reason, a table was elaborated that provides value to the total of each heuristic and the total of the evaluation, the usability level of the application.

The scores for each question of the heuristics were synthesized in Fig. 6, which contains the total value of each heuristic and the total percentage of the evaluation, obtaining, as a result, the level of usability of the application "Human Body AR".

HRA	Total	Answers																			
		1	2	3	4	5	6	7	8	9	10	11	12	13	14	15	16	17	18	19	20
1	10	6	6	9	7	8	9	9	7	7	9	7	7	8	5	8	8	5	8	8	9
2	10	9	8	5	7	5	8	5	7	8	8	8	8	10	6	10	8	5	9	6	8
3	5	5	4	3	3	2	3	4	5	2	2	4	5	2	4	5	4	5	3	4	4
4	5	5	3	2	4	5	3	3	4	5	3	3	4	2	2	3	3	4	3	4	5
5	20	16	16	14	14	13	17	13	15	15	14	15	12	14	13	14	17	13	16	12	17
6	10	8	6	5	4	4	7	6	9	5	8	4	7	9	6	6	6	8	7	8	8
7	10	8	7	4	7	5	6	9	6	4	3	7	9	5	6	6	7	3	7	5	6
8	10	10	9	6	6	4	7	9	8	7	6	4	8	8	7	7	6	5	9	7	6
9	15	13	11	9	11	8	11	13	13	13	9	7	10	15	11	11	14	10	11	14	8
10	20	18	17	14	14	13	13	15	14	18	15	16	14	18	14	16	13	16	13	15	15
11	15	9	8	11	11	7	10	7	8	11	15	12	8	10	8	9	10	8	11	10	13
12	20	14	12	14	13	11	14	8	13	17	13	10	14	12	15	15	14	13	12	15	13
13	5	3	4	4	3	2	3	3	2	3	3	1	2	3	3	4	2	2	4	5	2
14	5	3	4	5	3	3	4	2	2	1	2	3	4	4	1	3	4	3	3	3	5
15	5	3	3	5	3	4	3	1	3	3	2	2	5	3	2	3	2	2	2	4	4
16	5	4	5	5	4	3	4	2	3	3	2	3	4	4	2	2	3	1	4	3	2
17	5	3	3	3	5	2	3	1	2	2	1	1	2	3	3	4	2	2	4	2	2
18	25	11	17	13	16	12	15	13	10	13	12	10	14	13	10	11	14	10	15	14	16
Total	200	148	143	131	135	111	140	123	131	137	127	117	137	143	118	137	137	115	141	139	143

Fig. 6. Results of the evaluation

The results show that, of the 20 evaluations, 16 obtained the value "Good", which means that there is no total satisfaction, so it was proposed to implement new improvements to the heuristics that had lower scores:

- Minimize the memory load: in this heuristic, it was observed that some users did not clearly identify the objects and the actions they performed, the screen is in simple form but the users cannot distinguish it by some images that distract them.

- Error prevention: users made mistakes when entering the application so they immediately left the application and their information was not saved, as well as when they wanted to return to the main menu they left the screen completely.
- Ease of use: the application expresses error messages through sounds, however, it does not suggest a solution for the user so they should ask an adult for help.
- Help and documentation: The user does not have a series of steps to follow to provide help in the application, likewise the application does not have tutorials that imitate the lessons in the classroom.

7 Conclusions and Future Work

7.1 Conclusions

The heuristics proposal provides a more efficient usability evaluation compared to traditional heuristics.

During the evaluation carried out in the development of the applications, several design problems were found including the use of AR techniques in the application. When the end-user of the application is children, it is advisable not to use markers for the recognition of 3D elements, it was difficult to keep their attention in pointing to the marker and at the same time seeing the recognition image. Therefore, it is concluded that choosing the interaction techniques depends on the requirements of the application. The same set of techniques will not work well in all situations.

The physical environment used for the usability evaluation was controlled. The tests were carried out in the classroom of the 5-year-old children, then they executed the applications with the supervision of the evaluators. One of the methods used was the Laboratory evaluation, which made it possible to record the actions and attitudes of the children when they used the application to later discuss what was observed, improving the specification of the problems found by the evaluators.

The heuristics proposal provides a more efficient usability evaluation com- pared to traditional heuristics.

7.2 Future Works

It is important to consider the unfulfilled heuristics such as error prevention, ease of use, help, and documentation according to the proposed Heuristics, so that they are addressed and the child's development is improved when interacting with objects superimposed in the real world in size, avoiding spatial problems and location in the child's environment.

Carry out tests using the evaluation proposal presented to evaluate new virtual contents and the use of other types of 3D interactivity techniques or sensors.

Acknowledgment. Our research is part of the project TIM-003-2018-UNSA "Use of mixed reality as an alternative for learning anatomy in 5-year-old children" and it was possible due to the funds granted by Unsa Investiga and "Universidad Nacional de San Agustín de Arequipa".

References

1. Milgram, P., Takemura, H., Utsumi, A., Kishino, F.: Augmented reality: a class of displays on the reality-virtuality continuum. In: Telemanipulator and Telepresence Technologies, vol. 2351, pp. 282–292. International Society for Optics and Photonics (1995). https://doi.org/10.1117/12.197321
2. Schaeffer, S.E.: Usability evaluation for augmented reality (2014). http://hdl.handle.net/10138/136421
3. Becerra, D.A.I., Castro, B.D.S., Conislla, M.M.F., Corrales-Delgado, C.: Augmented reality applied in the design of learning activities in zoology. In: 2018 XIII Latin American Conference on Learning Technologies (LACLO), pp. 121–126. IEEE (2018). https://doi.org/10.1109/LACLO.2018.00036
4. Chien, C.-H., Chen, C.-H., Jeng, T.-S.: An interactive augmented reality system for learning anatomy structure. In: Proceedings of the International Multiconference of Engineers and Computer Scientists, vol. 1, pp. 17–19, International Association of Engineers Hong Kong, China (2010). http://citeseerx.ist.psu.edu/viewdoc/download?doi=10.1.1.302.6410rep=rep1type=pdf
5. Minedu, M.: Currículo nacional de la educación básica (2016)
6. Ferrari, V., Megali, G., Troia, E., Pietrabissa, A., Mosca, F.: A 3-d mixed-reality system for stereoscopic visualization of medical dataset. IEEE Trans. Biomed. Eng. 56(11), 2627–2633 (2009). https://doi.org/10.1109/TBME.2009.2028013
7. Meng, M., et al.: Kinect for interactive ar anatomy learning. In: 2013 IEEE International Symposium on Mixed and Augmented Reality (ISMAR), pp. 277–278. IEEE (2013). https://doi.org/10.1109/ISMAR.2013.6671803
8. Falah, J., et al.: Virtual reality medical training system for anatomy education. In: 2014 Science and Information Conference, pp. 752–758. IEEE (2014). https://doi.org/10.1109/SAI.2014.6918271
9. Blum, T., Kleeberger, V., Bichlmeier, C., Navab, N.: Mirracle: an augmented reality magic mirror system for anatomy education. In: 2012 IEEE Virtual Reality Workshops (VRW), pp. 115–116. IEEE (2012). https://doi.org/10.1109/VR.2012.6180909
10. Merchant, Z., Goetz, E.T., Cifuentes, L., Keeney-Kennicutt, W., Davis, T.J.: Effectiveness of virtual reality-based instruction on students' learning outcomes in k-12 and higher education: A meta-analysis. Comput. Educ. 70, 29–40 (2014). https://doi.org/10.1016/j.compedu.2013.07.033
11. Fierro Díaz, N.Y.: Heurísticas para evaluar la usabilidad de aplicaciones web bancarias (2016)
12. Jiménez, C., Rusu, S., Roncagliolo, S., Inostroza, R., Rusu, V.: Evaluating a methodology to establish usability heuristics. In: 2012 31st International Conference of the Chilean Computer Science Society, pp. 51–59. IEEE (2012). http://repositorio.unap.edu.pe/handle/UNAP/8879
13. Sutcliffe, A., Gault, B.: Heuristic evaluation of virtual reality applications. Interact. Comput. 16(4), 831–849 (2004). https://doi.org/10.1016/j.intcom.2004.05.001
14. Giraldo, F.D., Arango, E., Cruz, C.D., Bernal, C.C.: Application of augmented reality and usability approaches for the implementation of an interactive tour applied at the university of quindio. In: 2016 IEEE 11th Colombian Computing Conference (CCC), pp. 1–8. IEEE (2016). https://doi.org/10.1109/ColumbianCC.2016.7750798
15. Nielsen, J.: The usability engineering life cycle. Computer 25(3), 12–22 (1992). https://doi.org/10.1109/2.121503
16. Sánchez, J.: Evaluación usabilidad de sitios web: Método de evaluación heurística, Universidad de Chile (2000). https://doi.org/10.21556/edutec.2011.37.39

Mixed Reality Infotainment Simulator, Work in Progress

F. Cristian Beltrán(ID), Alejandro Aponte(ID), and Wilson J. Sarmiento(✉)(ID)

Grupo de Investigación en Multimedia-GIM-Facultad de Ingeniería, Universidad Militar Nueva Granada, Bogota, Colombia
{u1201945,u1201940,wilson.sarmiento}@unimilitar.edu.co

Abstract. The use of driving simulators to evaluate different aspects from the interaction with aspects is an extended practice, which is the case of assessing interaction with infotainment system. However, when these systems are evaluated, the testbed does not consider Latin American drivers' mental models. Thus, It is necessary for developing tools that allow performing those evaluations in driving conditions of our own countries. This work shows preliminary advances in developing a driving simulator equipped with an infotainment system using mixed reality elements. This work presents the actual state of development and reflections of the findings found.

Keywords: Infotainment systems · Mixed reality · Simulator

1 Introduction

The automotive industry has relevant advanced in recent years, and any various directions. Is the case of infotainment systems, these are In-car entertainment/information multimedia applications that allow access to the state of the vehicle and traffic while providing some entertainment services. So at this moment is possible to access to advantages of the actual world, as communication through phone, access to social networks, multimedia content reproduction while we drive an automotive [1]. However, that has produced that the task of driving may be more complex. Usually, a driver has multiple possibilities of interaction that could distract him, activate windshield, raise windows, adjusting the air conditioning, and talk to companions. The distractions can increase considerably with an infotainment system; if your interface is not designed correctly [2], even these systems can generate stress and additional anxiety to the driver [3], which simultaneously are the psychological factors that cause more traffic accidents [4].

For this reason, the use of simulators to drive is an important tool in the automotive industry. However, it has been identified that the current infotainment systems had not been designed for the mental model of Latin American drivers, which increases the risks of accidents in our region. For this reason, it has proposed the necessity of build

This work is a result of the research project INV-ING-2994 funded by the Office of the Dean of Research of Militar Nueva Granada University and INSA/Lyon (execution period 2019).

© Springer Nature Switzerland AG 2020
V. Agredo-Delgado et al. (Eds.): HCI-COLLAB 2020, CCIS 1334, pp. 155–159, 2020.
https://doi.org/10.1007/978-3-030-66919-5_16

tools that allow evaluating these systems in Latino American variables [5, 6]. This work presents an advance in this direction, showing preliminary results in working a driving simulator equipped with infotainment systems. Section 2 shows a review of previous work. Section 3 describes the developed process and actual results. By last, Sect. 4 presents some short consideration of the findings found and future work.

2 Previous Work

As already mentioned, driving a vehicle is an activity that involves having all the attention focused on the road and what happens here. However, inside of any automotive, some elements may be distracting to drivers from this activity. Is the case of infotainment systems, which in theory have been designed to facilitate the interaction of the driver and passengers with digital media [2]; nevertheless, it has been proved that these elements can cause accidents on the road [3, 4].

For this reason, the use of driving simulators in virtual environments to evaluate and test interaction interface is an alternative that has shown important advantages. For example, Fernandes et al. [1] assert that evaluating a computer simulation is a more viable solution compared to the costs of a test in real scenarios; while Galarza et al., highlight the importance of the use of simulators being able to evaluate the design principles and carry out traceability of the system variables and user response [7, 8], even alternatives are using free software are various [9].

Specifically, infotainment systems have been evaluated in simulators, such as the work of Medenica et al. [10], who performed a simulation of different models of personal navigation device system and proved the impact these have on visual attention and conduction performance. They validated the use of augmented reality and the impact that have the manipulation of the navigation system on visual attention and conduction performance in a simulated system [10]. Ricardo et al. [10], carried out a simulation of different models of personal navigation device systems and the impact these have on visual attention and conduction performance.

Galarza et al. [8] evaluated user performance and acceptance in the scene of real driving, taking into account several variables that in under different conditions, complicate the use of the infotainment system, such as radio tuning, navigation, etc. Rodriguez Garzon et al. [1] developed an infotainment system prototype to evaluate the customization interface according to the context. They validated yours results in the user simulation while driving and using the infotainment system's functions, through the questionnaire Nasa Task Load Index [11], which have been designed to evaluate physical and mental conditions, such as performance, effort, frustration in a driving simulator. A steering wheel controls the simulator, and two pedals connected using a united interface to complement on Google Earth, which allowed measuring workload in conduction [1].

3 Preliminary Results

As mentioned above, this paper shows the first findings of a work in progress. The final target is developing an infotainment system simulator that allows carry out testbed with users of the Latin America region. For this, our approach is to extend a virtual reality driving simulator, including components of mixed reality. This approach supposes that incorporate physical interaction very closed with real environment increase user engagement in the immersion system and allow test with suitable quality. Figure 1 shows the main architecture of the proposal. The infotainment simulation run in embedded hardware (for example, a raspberry). Physical and electronics components will provide mixed reality interactions. In order to build a modular system, the communication with the Virtual Reality driver simulator will be using wireless network protocol (IEEE 802.11, Bluetooth, among others).

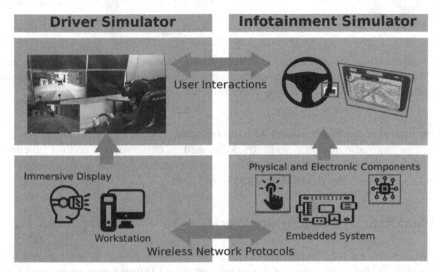

Fig. 1. The general architecture of the system. In the left column, the driver virtual reality simulator. In right column Infotainment Simulation. It is possible to see closed in blue line the components that allow a Mixed Reality interaction.

This paper shows the result of the first stage, identifies the main elements of physical interaction in an infotainment system. Seeking that the developed tools can be used to evaluate interaction with Infotainment systems present in the country, the best-selling automobile in the last years in Colombia was identified. This is the *"Renault Duster"*, which has an Infotainment system called *"MEDIA-NAV Evolution"*.

A detailed analysis process to the user manual and official support videos of the automobile manufacturer allowed identified two elements of interaction that use the Infotainment system integrally. The first element is the infotainment system's main interface, which has a touch screen and some buttons that allow access to basic functions. The second element is a control located under the steering wheel that provides shortcut functionality. The two elements of interaction can be seen in Fig. 2 to include real interaction elements in the driving simulator (Mixed Reality), 3D models of the previously identified interaction elements were made. The goal is to implement physical models scale 1:1 that will be used to simulate the automobile environment. These models will later be printed in 3D, and basic embedded electronics will be developed too, which will allow the interaction of each bottom. In this way, the function of the Infotainment system

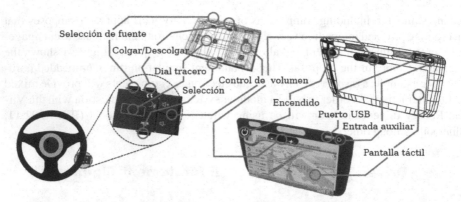

Fig. 2. 3D models of the interaction elements of the Infotainment system "MEDIA- NAV Evolution". In the top, It is possible to see a wire-frame render, and in the lower part a render that allows visualizing the aesthetics of these elements in the automobile.

will be simulated, such: interaction with the navigator (GPS), receiving and hanging up calls, changing radio station o audio track, as well as basic volume control functions, etc. Figure 2 shows the 3D models developed; it is clarified that the images correspond to renders of the models developed in this work.

4   Final Remarks and Future Work

This work presents preliminary results in developing a simulation with mixed reality elements designed to carry out future evaluations of Infotainment systems in Latin American countries' driving conditions. For this, the interaction elements of devices with which the infotainment system will be manipulated were identified, and 3D models were made to later print and integrate them as physical elements in the simulator. Thus, the work evidenced the large number of elements that can distract the driver and the need to include them in a driving simulator. The way to interact with the infotainment system and the need to build real interaction elements (Mixed Reality) in this type of simulators was also identified. The work will continue with the 3D printing of the designed models and the design of electronic elements that simulate interaction with the virtual vehicle.

References

1. Rodriguez Garzon, S.: Intelligent in-car-infotainment systems: a contextual personalized approach. In: 2012 Eighth International Conference on Intelligent Environments, pp. 315–318 (2012)
2. Platten, F., Milicic, N., Schwalm, M., Krems, J.: Using an infotainment system while driving - a continuous analysis of behavior adaptations. Transp. Res. Part F: Traff. Psychol. Behav. **21**, 103–112 (2013)
3. Vicente, E.S., Egeda, R.B., MonteagudoSoto, M.J.: Exploration of the anxiety by novice and professional drivers. Ana. Psicol./Ann. Psychol. **13**(1), 67–75 (1997)

4. Li, X., Oviedo-Trespalacios, O., Rakotonirainy, A., Yan, X.: Collision risk management of cognitively distracted drivers in a car-following situation. Transp. Res. Part F: Traff. Psychol. Behav. **60**, 288–298 (2019)
5. Luna García, H., et al.: Front-end design guidelines for infotainment systems. Dyna 1–9 (2017)
6. Luna García, H., et al.: Mental models associated to voice user interfaces for infotainment systems. Dyna **93**, 245 (2018)
7. Fernandes, R., Vieira, F., Ferreira, M.: VNS: an integrated framework for vehicular networks simulation. In: 2012 IEEE Vehicular Networking Conference (VNC), pp. 195–202, November 2012
8. Galarza, M.A., Bayona, T., Paradells, J.: Integration of an adaptive infotainment system in a vehicle and validation in real driving scenarios. Int. J. Veh. Technol. (2017)
9. Vargas, J.S., Casanova, N., Carrillo, O., Sarmiento, W.J.: Open source tool for vehicular traffic simulation at virtual environments, study case. In: Proceeding of 2nd Workshop Cata? (2019)
10. Medenica, Z., Kun, A., Paek, T., Palinko, O.: Augmented reality vs. street views: a driving simulator study comparing two emerging navigation aids. In: Proceedings of the 13th International Conference on Human Computer Interaction with Mobile Devices and Services, MobileHCI 2011, pp. 265–274 (08 2011)
11. Hart, S.G., Staveland, L.E.: Development of NASA-TLX (task load index): results of empirical and theoretical research. Adv. Psychol. **52**, 139–183 (1988)

Mobile Application to Improve Reading Habits Using Virtual Reality

Estefany Chavez-Helaconde$^{(\boxtimes)}$ ⓘ, Cristian Condori-Mamani$^{(\boxtimes)}$ ⓘ,
Israel Pancca-Mamani$^{(\boxtimes)}$ ⓘ, Julio Vera-Sancho$^{(\boxtimes)}$ ⓘ, Betsy Cisneros-Chavez$^{(\boxtimes)}$ ⓘ,
and Wilber Valdez-Aguilar$^{(\boxtimes)}$ ⓘ

Universidad Nacional de San Agustín de Arequipa, Arequipa, Peru
{echavezhe,ccondorimama,ipancca,jveras,bcisnerosc,
wvaldez}@unsa.edu.pe

Abstract. Education is changing rapidly, so emerging technologies are being used to improve this process. One of these technologies is the Virtual Reality (VR), whose field of action is increasingly broad, so it has been incorporating new methods in teaching having a great positive impact in recent years, but the applicability in the area of communication is minimal. Seeing the challenges faced by the Ministry of Education in the development of reading skills and strengthening the capabilities of students in our country. In the this research a new alternative is proposed, to improve the beginnings of the habit of reading in students of second grade of Elementary School having to use of a mobile application with VR named *Diverticuentos* that generates scenes of the readings in 360° besides being connected to a databases like firebase that allows us to see the progress of each student verifying that it is possible to integrate this new technology in the sessions and to generate a beginning of habit of reading of the students.

Keywords: Virtual reality · Reading habits · M-Learning · Unity

1 Introduction

In this research, we propose to improve the beginnings of reading habits in second graders of Elementary School, through the use of educational software that helps students to be motivated and read with pleasure and enthusiasm [1].

The educational system has been incorporating new tools that bring students closer to new knowledge in a dynamic and interactive way. However, the knowledge and applicability of this digital tool in reading habits is still emerging in the field of teaching [2].

In 2018, the Ministry of Education carried out an evaluation in the area of communication for the second grade of Elementary School. The results in reading were evaluated according to the performance at different levels of achievement, which were initiated, in process, and satisfactory. These data show us the levels of achievement and percentages. Compared to 2016 and 2018, there was no significant progress. In the reading tests conducted in 2016, 6.3% of students were at the beginning of learning achievement, 47.3%

V. Agredo-Delgado et al. (Eds.): HCI-COLLAB 2020, CCIS 1334, pp. 160–170, 2020.
https://doi.org/10.1007/978-3-030-66919-5_17

were in progress, and 46.4% were satisfactory. In 2018, reading test results showed 5.8% of students were at the beginning of learning achievement, 56.4% were in progress, and 37.8% were satisfactory. Therefore, it is important for teachers to provide opportunities for students to read different types of texts and reading genders [3].

2   Related Works

Ariston Harianto in his research "Strengthening the reading habits of young people through text based games" The game has a good story, interesting enough for the player to immerse himself in the game and therefore want to explore and discover more. The design to complete the game has multiple paths, each path is totally different from the other, therefore, the user experience is different. The experience of a different story and options motivates them more to keep reading and concluding the text. It is concluded that text-based games can have a significant impact as a means of learning and directly improve reading habits among young people [4].

Pei-Luen Patrick Rau in his research "Speed reading on virtual reality and augmented reality" proposes that the reading performance in Virtual Reality (VR) and Augmented Reality (AR) can be different from that of a traditional desktop screen, because the reading and the performance generally depends on the device that displays the texts, in its research concludes that answering multiple choice questions in Virtual Reality (VR) and Augmented Reality (AR) is approximately 10% longer than in LCD, so, for example, teachers should give students 10% more time if they are given tests or other word processing tasks through virtual reality (VR) or augmented reality (AR) [5].

According to the authors Lamas, Loizides, Nacke, Petrie, Winckler and Zaphiris in their research "Using virtual reality to enable individuals with severe visual disabilities to read books" they present us with a main platform compatible with virtual reality, along with the programming language the goal is to enable the application to read standard UTF-8 formats and translate them into a virtual reading panel for users to make their own reading settings. They use the Project, which is displayed in front of the user through a floating panel in a dark screen environment. Graphic distractions are kept to a minimum to avoid accessibility. The user manipulates the environmental variables through voice control, which allows him to change the letter number in this virtual world [6].

3   Theoretical Framework

3.1   Virtual Reality

The term Virtual Reality (VR) is associated with images found in three dimensions generated by a computer and the interaction of users with this graphic environment [7]. This implies the existence of a complex electronic system to project visual spaces in 3D and send and receive signals with information about the user's performance [8].

We also found that virtual reality is a technology that allows users to interact with virtual environments, simulated by a computer or a mobile device. In general, the virtual reality environment presents a visual experience on a stereo device screen [9].

A virtual reality system can be considered an interface that is capable of creating a simulation involving all the senses, generated by a computer, that can be explored, visualized and manipulated in real time in the form of digital images and sounds, giving the sensation of presence in the computer environment [10].

3.2 Reading Habit

The reader's habit is to promote and propagate the repetitive activity of reading until it becomes an intrinsic and natural need, using various existing or innovative mechanisms or strategies [11]. It is advisable to create this habit and the reader's sensitivity through imagination, which causes a better connection with the text, which characterizes the act of reading [12]. The pleasure produced by aesthetic values generates motivates and captures the interest in reading [13]. Therefore, an average of more than two months is calculated to generate a new behavior that becomes automatic, to be exact 66 days and, in addition, can vary widely depending on the behavior of the person and the circumstances so indicates Phillippa Lally in 2010 [14].

4 Materials and Methods

For the implementation of the application we use the following platforms and services:

- **Unity:** Unity3D is a cross-platform integrated game development tool developed by Unity Technologies that allows players to easily create interactive content such as 3D, etc. [15]
- **Fungus:** Is a free open source project, used to create 2D and 3D narrative games [16].
- **Firebase:** Is an API for saving and synchronizing data in the in real time [17, 18].
- **Google Analytics:** Is an analytical tool that analyzes the behavior of users when they enter the application, either web or app, this web analyzer pro- vides simple statistics and simple on the website [19].

5 Proposal

5.1 Application Usage

For the use of the application, it is necessary for the mobile device to be midrange and the screen is enlarged so that the user, when using the cardboard, has a wide view in the virtual environment, for the tests we use a Huawei P30 and a cardboard VR-BOX. The Fig. 1. shows the simulation in virtual and external mode, showing the repre-sentation of the X, Y and Z axes.

(a)   (b)

Fig. 1. (a) Virtual panorama, (b) External panorama of the 3 dimensions

The Figs. 2, 3 and 4 are the views for 2D mode

Fig. 2. Reading.   **Fig. 3.** Questionnaire.   **Fig. 4.** Outcome.

6   Methodology

The methodology used in the research is of an applicative nature, being a demonstrative explanatory research. The design of the research will be pre-experimental because we will have an experimental group, the results will be measured in time, the technique used to collect the information will be through a questionnaire applied before and after the use of the app. A quantitative data analysis technique was used because we used statistical techniques for the representation of the results having as hypothesis "The use of virtual reality improves the reading habits in second grade students of the San Francisco de Sales Private Educational Institution". In the study, 25 students of 2nd grade of primary school with an average age of 7 to 8 years participated in the application of the instrument during the second two-month period in the months of August and September with a pre-test and a post-test that obtained results that were codified to obtain the statistical data. In the learning sessions, literal questions were also asked in the app in order to verify that each student carried out the readings.

6.1   Pre-evaluation

In this first stage, a questionnaire was taken from second grade students in Regular Basic Education (EBR), to measure their frequency, time and consistency in reading before applying the activities and use of the Funny Stories application. The questionnaire is divided into three dimensions: desire, which consists of 10 items; knowledge, which consists of 12 items; and ability, which consists of 8 items. These are based on the dimensions proposed by the author Covey Salazar Bustamante, who defines habit as an intersection of knowledge (what to do?/why?); ability (how?) and desire (motivation/wanting to do) [20].

6.2 Selection of Readings

The selection of readings is defined according to the contents that are worked in the area of communication, according to the Ministry of Education where narrative readings were selected that include: stories, fables, myths and legends; it was considered pertinent to select the legends of Peru to revalue our oral customs and traditions, using the competence "Read various types of texts in your mother tongue", in this way the student will give his opinion and recommend readings according to his interest, enjoying his readings as a main objective and generating the beginning of a reading habit. The selected readings are the following:

As shown in Table 1, the readings that were selected to be taken to virtual reality are shown:

Table 1. Readings

3d reading	Time	Genre
El Puente del diablo	17 min	Narrative
El tuturutu	17 min	Narrative
La leyenda de la casa embrujada	17 min	Narrative
La sirena del Puente de fierro	17 min	Narrative
Duendes arequipeños	17 min	Narrative
Los Subterr´aneos de la Catedral	17 min	Narrative

6.3 Selection of the Models

After selecting the readings, we look for 3D models that resemble the characters in the texts, using free model download platforms such as mixao, free3d, some models bought in unity 3D and sketchfab. The selected models have animation and movement, so the scenes shown are more interactive, users can walk and visualize the characters in movement and feel the immersion in 360 in all the scenes shown with the VR viewer.

6.4 Application Description

The mobile application called "Diverticuentos", has as main objective to generate the beginnings of the reading habit in second grade students, using the application to have a selection of 7 stories in 3D with VR and 20 stories in 2D. The students can access the application through a smartphone that uses the Android operating system.

The functionality of the mobile application "Diverticuentos" is done through a register that stores the information constantly, this way there will be a register of entry and exit of the APP in real time. Users must register, completing their name and surname, grade they belong to, ID number and password. To enter the application, their user name and password will be placed by accessing a general 2D AND 3D history screen. The 3D stories will be used in the classroom along with the learning sessions and the 2D stories will be done at home, using the APP and the Internet. Each learning session that was done at the school with VR was in a time of 17 min for each session done. Each student will have a database that will be monitored showing the progress that each student, during the use of the application, for both 2D and 3D readings. At the end of the reading of each learning session, the student will be able to visualize some scenes of the texts, then he/she will have to answer 3 to 4 questions of literal level to corroborate that the student carried out the reading. Finally, they will have a satisfaction question for each reading done. The information obtained was used to analyze the time of use of the application and the time it took for each reading.

The Table 2 of events and parameters is shown:

Table 2. Events and Parameters the application

Events	Parameters
Start of the game	Start of the game
Game completed	Saved score, type of reading (2D or 3D)
Reading in the app	Reading time
Reading questionnaire	Time to answer the reading

6.5 Learning Session

The learning sessions were carried out respecting the structure and the moments of each session according to the communication area, before, during and after the reading. The sessions carried out had two pedagogical hours of dictation per session, using VR for 17 min twice a week in which characters and the place where the stories were developed were visualized, all of them with VR. At the beginning of the reading session, the students were asked if they knew any of the characters they had seen. What will happen to the characters? They knew the purpose of the session "Today we will know the legend of the Bolognesi Bridge".

As in the beginning of the session the students visualized the characters in 3D with VR and contextualized the scenes and characters so they could answer the questions, during the reading all the students were asked to do a silent reading as well as a choral reading, after the reading we verified that the questions were correct from the beginning of the learning session by also asking some additional questions such as what new things did they find? what was the text about? As feedback we used the app "Funny Stories" to verify if the reading was done through 3 literal questions, to end the session we asked the following questions: What did we learn today? Did we like the topic what we worked on? The sessions were held over a month and a half.

7 Results

The research was carried out with a population of 25 students of 12 girls and 13 boys of second grade of primary school of regular basic education (EBR), between the ages of 7 and 8 years. Obtaining the results that support the hypothesis the students was considered to compare the results of the pre-test and post- test the two-dimensional longitudinal perimeter test was considered because the samples are related to the same experimental group. Obtaining the results which show that the levels of reading habits in the post-test are better than in the pre-test, we proceeded to contrast, to know if they have significant differences:

H_0: The use of virtual reality does not improve reading habits in second grade students of the San Francisco de Sales Private Educational Institution.

H_1: The use of virtual reality improves reading habits in second grade students of the San Francisco de Sales Private Educational Institution.

7.1 Result of Reading Habit

Analyzing the entire questionnaire of the 25 students according to the Fig. 5. and the Table 3 in the pre-test 16.00% is at the high level and 76.00% is at the low level, for the post-test 88.00% rose to the high level and at the low level it was found at 12.0%. No one was found at the very high and very low level. The student's t test was performed considering the confidence level of 95% and an error margin of 5% (0.05), as it is a variable of categorical origin, therefore the corresponding test was performed.

Table 3. Reading habits results

	Pre test		Post test	
	f	%	f	%
Very high	0	0.0%	0	0.0%
High	4	16.0%	22	88.0%
Low	19	76.0%	3	12.0%
Very low	2	8.0%	0	0.0%
Total	25	100.0% 25	100.00%	25

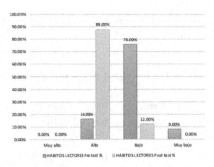

Fig. 5. Result of reading habit

Table 4. Normality test

pretest = 0.585 <Alfa = 0.05
postest = 0.980 <Alfa = 0.05

Table 5. Shapiro-wilk

Static gl Sig
Pretest 0,968 25 0,585
Postest 0,987 25 0,980

Calculate the p-Value of the Normality Test. To be able to apply the instrument, the alpha shapiro wilks statistical reliability test was performed, with our population being less than 30 students, which allows us to measure the normality test.

Thus, the data was submitted, as shown in the Tables 4, 5, the results being.

According to the table of paired differences, it is concluded that the normality test passed as shown in the Table 6.

Table 6. Testing of paired samples.

	Average	Desviation	Error average	95% confidence interval of the difference		t	gl Bilateral
				Lower	Higher		
Par 1 prestest postest	−0,50333	0,22339	100.00%	−0,59554	−0,41112	−11,266	240,000

Decision of the Statistical Test. As p-value = 0.000 alpha = 0.05 H0 is rejected and H1 is accepted Conclusion: There is a significant difference in the mean before and after the learning sessions which were based on virtual environments.

The t-studen tests will be carried out for paired samples as observed in the Table 7.

Table 7. Paired sample statistics

		Average	N	Desv. Deviation	Desviation Average error
2*Par 1	Pre-test	2,2650	25	0,32137	0,06427
	Pos-test	2,7683	25	25 0,21384	0,04277

In fact, students increased their reading habit average from 2.26 (AV) to 2.76 (CS).

8   Conclusions

In this research, a significant difference was presented in the beginnings of the reading habit in the students before and after using the application with virtual reality. Therefore, it is concluded that virtual reality has significant effects, in the pre-test it was found in 16.00% the high level and 76.00% the low level, for the post-test 88.00% went up to the high level and in the low level it was found in 12,0%. No one was found at the very high and very low level. It has been verified how the sessions carried out in the students, have con- tributed in the beginnings of the reading habits also in the attraction to read and to finish each one of them motivating them to read more. It also generates interactivity, motivation and interest of the students in the readings. We must not forget that technology is a support for student learning that must be used effectively and usefully in the classroom. This way, technology will have a positive impact on student learning.

Acknowledgment. A special recognition to the Universidad Nacional de San Agustín de Arequipa, UNSA that through the contract of subsidy IAI-005-2018-UNSA of the project "Animación a la lectura con M-Learning, creando situaciones reales y virtuales", is that it was possible to make the investigation of the proposal presented in this article.

References

1. Tondeur, J., van Braak, J., Ertmer, P.A., Ottenbreit-Leftwich, A.: Understanding the relationship between teachers' pedagogical beliefs and technology use in education: a systematic review of qualitative evidence. Educ. Technol. Res. Dev. **65**, 555–575 (2016). https://doi.org/10.1007/s11423-016-9481-2
2. Howard, S., Lewin, K.: Virtual reality content for higher education curriculum (2018). https://eprints.qut.edu.au/116132/
3. MINEDU: Resultados de la evaluación censal de estudiantes 2016 (2017). http://umc.minedu.gob.pe/resultadosece2016/
4. Harianto, A., Nugroho, E., Fredericco, R.: Reinforcing youth reading habits through text-based games. In: 2015 4th International Conference on Interactive Digital Media (ICIDM), pp. 1–5. IEEE (2015). https://doi.org/10.1109/idm.2015.7516344
5. Rau, P.L.P., Zheng, J., Guo, Z., Li, J.: Speed reading on virtual reality and augmented reality. Comput. Educ. **125**, 240–245 (2018). https://doi.org/10.1016/j.compedu.2018.06.016
6. Weir, K., Loizides, F., Nahar, V., Aggoun, A.: Using virtual reality to enable individuals with severe visual disabilities to read books. In: Lamas, D., Loizides, F., Nacke, L., Petrie, H., Winckler, M., Zaphiris, P. (eds.) INTERACT 2019. LNCS, vol. 11749, pp. 680–684. Springer, Cham (2019). https://doi.org/10.1007/978-3-030-29390-1_62
7. Ambrosio, A.P.: Una aposta pel canvi en les sèries de ficció. La realitat virtual com a estratègia narrativa al servei de la immersió de l'espectador. Anàlisi: Quaderns de Comunicació Cult. (57), 1–14 (2017) https://doi.org/10.5565/rev/analisi.3105
8. Obrist Bertrand, V.U., Martínez Jara, E.A.: Application of virtual reality in a learning experience. In: XXI Congreso Argentino de Ciencias de la Computación, June 2015
9. Maulana, H., Khansa, R.: Virtual reality application for educational interactive media "3 historical monuments of yogyakarta". In: Journal of Physics: Conference Series vol. 1193. IOP Publishing (2019). https://doi.org/10.1088/1742-6596/1193/1/012019
10. Avendaño Rodríguez, L.A., Hernández Perilla, J.M.: Comunicación y experiencia mediada por la realidad virtual. Nexus (1900–9909) (24) (2018). https://doi.org/10.25100/nc.v0i24.7693
11. Vivanco Tinco, M.C.: Aplicación del plan lector para fomentar el hábito lector en los estudiantes del tercer grado de primaria de la IEP "Fraternidad universal" del distrito de ate–2017 (2018). http://repositorio.unfv.edu.pe/handle/UNFV/2604
12. Villota, M.F.E., Escobar, M.F., Velásquez, F.G.: Una revisión general a los hábitos y técnicas de estudio en el ámbito universitario. Psicogente **18**(33), 166–187 (2015). https://doi.org/10.17081/psico.18.33.64
13. Álvarez Martínez-Iglesias, J.M., Rabal Alonso, J.M., Molina Saorín, J.: Unidades didácticas de lengua y literatura basadas en las TIC. In: Congreso Internacional de Investigación e innovación en educación infantil y primaria, March 2020
14. Lally, P., Van Jaarsveld, C.H., Potts, H.W., Wardle, J.: How are habits formed: modelling habit formation in the real world. Eur. J. Soc. Psychol. **40**(6), 998–1009 (2010). https://doi.org/10.1002/ejsp.674
15. Unity.com: Documentacion de unity (2019). https://unity3d.com/es/unity

16. Fungus: Documentacion de fungus (2019). http://fungusgames.com/
17. Client, R.: Documentación de rest client (2019). https://assetstore.unity.com/packages/tools/network/rest-client-for-unity-102501
18. Albertengo, G., Debele, F.G., Hassan, W., Stramandino, D.: Sobre el rendimiento de los servicios web, la mensajería en la nube de Google y la mensajería en la nube de firebase. http://hdl.handle.net/10486/688897
19. Sharma, M., Joshi, S.: Online advertisement using web analytics software: a comparison using AHP method. Int. J. Bus. Anal. (IJBAN) 7(2), 13–33 (2020). https://doi.org/10.4018/IJBAN.2020040102
20. Salazar Ayllon, S.: Claves para pensar la formación del hábito lector. Allpanchis (66) 13–46 (2006). http://hdl.handle.net/10760/8551

Model for Pervasive Social Play Experiences

Ramón Valera Aranguren[1]([⊠])(iD), Patricia Paderewski Rodriguez[2]([⊠])(iD),
Francisco Luis Gutiérrez Vela[2]([⊠])(iD), and Jeferson Arango-López[3]([⊠])(iD)

[1] Universidad Centroccidental "Lisandro Alvarado", Barquisimeto, Lara, Venezuela
rvalera@ucla.edu.ve
[2] Universidad de Granada, Granada, Spain
{patricia,fgutierr}@ugr.es
[3] Universidad de Caldas, Manizales, Colombia
jeferson.arango@ucaldas.edu.co

Abstract. Game-inspired applications use fun to motivate user participation in activities designed to achieve specific objectives. In this sense, there is a spatial, temporal, social framework, and a set of rules that guide user participation and interaction. Recently, pervasive computing has become a key element to explore new interaction schemes in game inspired applications. By making the concept of space and time ambiguous and confusing, it allows building new mechanics that engage the participant with innovative elements and consequently produce a different, in some cases, more interesting and entertaining experience. This research describes the social expansion as a strategy to enhance game experiences supported by pervasive computing, thus exposing a conceptual model that shows its components, how they relate, and what is the flow of interaction that a user experiences when he or she gets involved; among the most important aspects to consider is the incorporation of a new role to the traditional game mechanics, the spectator. The incorporation of the spectator offers us the opportunity to promote communication schemes with the players, strengthen the affinity ties between spectator-player and expose a series of premises to build pervasive game mechanics.

Keywords: Pervasive games · Social gaming experience · Pervasive computing

1 Introduction

The philosopher Huizinga, already in 1938 in his book "Homo ludens" [1] offers an important concept to analyze the process of playing, which he calls the Magic Circle. As he describes it, "this is the space to play, it is a place of dreams and fantasy created to escape from the daily routine and the daily problems, it is delimited in advance materially and ideologically and the events that happen in the real world have a special meaning inside it, there you get special rules that mark the accomplishment of actions, they are temporary worlds inside the ordinary world".

This metaphor of Huizinga's magic circle is a voluntary and contractual structure that circumscribes the space and time where the participant has fun, there he develops diverse activities, mainly playing. Game designers can break these boundaries or expand

© Springer Nature Switzerland AG 2020
V. Agredo-Delgado et al. (Eds.): HCI-COLLAB 2020, CCIS 1334, pp. 171–180, 2020.
https://doi.org/10.1007/978-3-030-66919-5_18

them to reproduce a new generation of emotions, for example, at a spatial level the place where the game is played is confusing or unlimited and the physical world is confused with the virtual space of the game. At a temporal level, there is the sensation that every moment of the person's life is connected to game action, it is not known with certainty when it begins or when it ends. And at a social level, it is related to involve in the gaming experiences people that traditionally are not part of the games, such as the audience (people who observe the game but do not actively participate in it), additionally, it is played with the level of awareness about the role that the participant plays in the game and the possibilities of interaction that he or she has, among many other things.

The temporal and spatial expansion has been enabled by pervasive computing environments that provide technological devices with high levels of computing power, miniaturization, and connectivity. A user can take them anywhere without complications and they perform tasks of different nature and complexity. The constant connectivity to the Internet, a very fast speed, along with its interoperability with other devices and its geolocation capability makes it possible to develop play activities not previously seen in traditional games [2–6], anywhere and at any time the actions of the game are confused with the daily activities of the player.

It is considered important to determine the essential characteristics of a social gaming experience within a pervasive computing environment. This will give the designer important information about the elements that a game-inspired application should have to activate pervasive social mechanics based on cooperation and communication, which will help keep participants engaged and motivated in various fields of application, such as education, health, and sports.

In this work we propose a conceptual model that allows us to show the elements that promote the development of game experience with social expansion, taking into account that it is developed in a game inspired application that is being supported by pervasive computing. Special attention is given to the audience since it becomes a very important role when building pervasive social mechanics, for this, we start by reviewing the definition of Pervasive Games, then we pay special attention to social expansion by exposing the elements that make it possible, which will serve as input to formulate the components of the model and how these relate, finally we have the section of conclusions and future work where we summarize the essential knowledge gained in research and the direction it will take in the immediate future.

2   Pervasive Games

There is no consensus to define a Pervasive Game, however, what stands out in all the definitions found, is that it promotes a different gaming experience than the one offered by traditional games, mainly because the game is developed along with the player's daily life, in this sense:

- The Pervasive Games is a genre of games that emerge to break the social and physical limits of traditional games [7].
- Pervasive Games are designed with mechanics that are in opposition to the rules of the environment in which they are played, having as a sole objective to provide players with new experiences [8].

– The objectives with Pervasive Games are based on generating a greater attraction for players at a higher level than that presented by traditional computer games and board games, in a physical and social context [9].

One of the biggest problems when analyzing pervasive games is that the concept of pervasiveness can be used for many types of experiences (live role-playing games, geolocalized games, ...). To solve this problem, we are going to use the work done by the GEDES research group at the University of Granada related to the conceptualization and characterization of pervasive games [10] that have been carried out within the research project entitled DISPERSA (Design of Pervasive Games Based on Context-Sensitive Learning Experiences) where the problem of developing geolocalized pervasive game experiences is addressed [11].

After analyzing the geolocalized pervasive experiences [11], it was possible to evidence that GPS devices integrated into mobile equipment with high computing power opens a range of options for designing context-sensitive game mechanics, that is, mechanics with the ability to translate direct or indirect, voluntary or involuntary actions of participants within a given physical space, the possibility of knowing at any moment the current position of the player together with the possibility of displaying contextualized content allows to delimit geographical areas and display physical devices (temperature sensors, movement, lighting) and virtual elements to collect the user's actions, these are interpreted as tangible facts that have a meaning in the designed user experience.

Taking as a reference the Pervasive Games projects studied [2, 4, 6, 12–14] and the classification of Kasapakis, Gavalas, and Bubaris [15] that takes into account the environment where the experience is developed, we can establish a set of characteristics and behaviors that surround the pervasive games, in this way:

– The player interacts with the game through a set of sensors arranged in a physical space or with a pervasive computing device.
– There is a narrative that sets the scene for the experience, sets the tone for the chronological order in which the mechanics are activated.
– The game world that faces a player is full of traditional game elements, augmented reality can be important to make interaction with them more attractive.
– The computing power of mobile devices allows the development of game mechanics supported by augmented reality. This expands the amount of fantasy and artificial elements that can be superimposed in the physical space of the game.
– Sensitivity to the context where the experience takes place is a highly valuable element so that the experience is made on a par with a person's everyday activities.
– The wide range of communication possibilities offered by pervasive computing allows the definition of collaboration and cooperation processes among participants.
– You can create game mechanics in a real physical space, what happens in the experience is intertwined or confused with the everyday life of the player, its duration in some cases is ambiguous, it is possible to create a scenario where you have the perception that is continuous game experience, without specific limits of beginning and end.

3 Social Expansion in Gaming Experiences

The social aspect in a game experience refers to the interaction that participants make, through individual or group actions, within the framework of mechanics designed to achieve specific objectives. Communication, collaboration, and competition are some of the most used mechanisms to implement it. The social expansion has to do with the incorporation of strategies and elements that play with the participant's state of consciousness to motivate him/her to participate in the mechanics of collective work designed to achieve certain objectives. Technology can be a key factor to support this and make it possible.

Socially expanded games depend on temporal and spatial expansion. Montola [16] warns that games that do not break the barrier provided by the area and the play session will hardly break the social barrier. This implies that the pervasive social gaming experiences that are the subject of this research will require spatial and temporal expansion supported by pervasive computing technologies.

In the specific case of games with social expansion, there are some interesting case studies, Montola [16] for example gives great importance to the role played by the spectator and the degree of awareness that this has about their role and impact on the mechanics of prepared games. In this way, the spectator may become an obstacle for the player, a witness of a game event, the receiver of a message or an object to be collected by the participating players.

A participant can engage in a gaming experience consciously, i.e., with full knowledge of the role they play and how their actions influence the objectives, or they may do so with little or no clarity about it. Everything begins with an invitation that may be adorned with different subliminal elements to hide in some cases the true intention of the proposal. The participant is introduced by the designer into a role with a state of consciousness about his or her function in the experience, thus beginning a life cycle for the participant, which in some cases starts from an unconscious state about his or her role and ends in a conscious state, sometimes passing through states of confusion or ambiguity.

The construction of social game experiences supported by pervasive computing elements constitutes an important opportunity for the construction of novel game mechanics that involve non-traditional elements of interaction. All this implies important challenges to handle moral and ethical aspects related to the management of consciousness of the role that a participant plays in the experience and how he is introduced and involved in it. It is very important to take care of the details associated with how to incorporate the participant without producing a perception of invasion or coercion, to preserve the privacy of the participants in an environment where it is not known exactly what other people are interacting with and to what degree they are collaborating with them.

4 Model for Pervasive Social Play Experiences

Given the advantages that pervasive computing offers for the construction of game experiences, especially in terms of the possibility of expanding the boundaries of space and time and its use in the construction of new mechanics of a social nature that increase a participant's engagement, we present a "Model for Pervasive Social Game Experiences", a summary of the elements that make social expansion in the game experience possible.

The conceptual model considers that any experience that occurs in applications inspired by games starts from the definition of a set of objectives and the corresponding mechanics to achieve them. There is a thread (narrative) centered on a historical period, a booklet with a world populated by fictional characters and other elements produced by the imagination, to direct the deployment of interaction and activities of participants, so that everything takes place in a game world that is driven by pervasive computing technology, can be in real world geolocated with the presence of sensors, a virtual world created by technologies such as virtual reality or augmented reality or a mixture of both. Participants communicate, work in teams, or individually to execute collaborative or competitive processes, which contribute to the achievement of the designed objectives. (See Fig. 1).

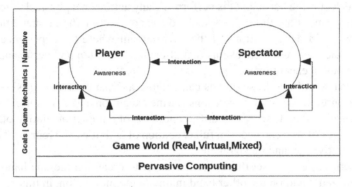

Fig. 1. Components of a pervasive social game experience.

The model consists of three layers, superimposed one over the other, in such a way that the services of one layer are exposed as specific functionalities to the layer immediately above it. In this way, the lower layer called "Pervasive Computing" represents all the technological elements that support the construction of the "Game World" which in turn offers the necessary services for the "Participants" to interact on it, also in the latter, different types of interaction occur among the participants. The transversal layer "Objectives, Mechanics, and Narrative" represents the fact that all the activities of the overlapping layers are directed by the rules and definitions formulated therein.

Next, we will give more detail about each of the layers and the activities and functionalities that are executed in them.

4.1 Goals, Game Mechanics and Narrative

When the designer builds a game experience, he does it within the framework of a specific knowledge area (Education, Health, Fun) and proposes a set of objectives that he expects the participants to achieve to awaken a set of specific feelings. Within the proposal, the objectives are defined as a hierarchical structure, in which high-level objectives, called strategic, and low-level objectives, called operational, are distinguished. The highest level objectives are decomposed until reaching the operational objectives that are achieved with the execution of one or more game mechanics, the latter establishes the coordination mechanisms between participants so that, in a cooperative way and under communication processes advance in their achievement.

The objectives must be measurable, so indicators should be built to provide information about the effectiveness with which players act to achieve them, these are generated from metrics related to the execution of the mechanics of games and the state of the objects arranged in the game world. The value of an indicator can be used to establish how far you are from achieving an objective, what deviation exists between the expected and actual value, and whether it is necessary to act to fulfill it according to what has been planned.

In the proposed model, context-sensitive game mechanics are executed that include different types of social interaction among participants. These "Pervasive Game Mechanics" are designed to react to changes in the position of the participants, determine some movement, detect if the participant is performing any action on a physical object present in the environment, either through a specific device or through direct interaction. In this way, any change in the conditions of the environment where the experience is taking place is translated into concrete events that affect the evolution and performance of the game mechanics in execution.

The mechanics of pervasive games can acquire a dynamic behavior, since the participants can agree in real-time conditions for the execution and terms of calculation of different elements such as scores, boards, conditions of completion among others, likewise, the changes of role can occur in full execution of activities and represent important elements of motivation and engagement.

The experience can be set through a narrative, to create on the one hand an initial interest in the game and on the other hand maintain the motivation, in this way you can resort to various narrative resources such as mystery, plot twists, to make the experience more entertaining.

4.2 Pervasive Computing

Pervasive Computing refers to the set of technological elements that support the development of the game experience, including all the advances related to connectivity, miniaturization, and computing power that once deployed in a physical space serve as intermediaries between the participant and the real world, to, for example, determine changes in the environment, establish the position of each participant in a game space, receive interactions from participants.

This layer of the model also includes all the technological advances that serve to create worlds based on virtual reality and augmented reality, intending to increase immersion and thus help in the motivation to participate.

The application inspired by Games can run on a computer device provided with features of high mobility, computing power, and connectivity, so that the experience can be developed in a shared way between the environment and the virtual world that is presented in it, the device thus becomes a tool for the participant to execute specific actions that lead to the alteration of the environment and feel its consequences.

4.3 Game World

The game experience takes place in a world supported by various advances in pervasive technology, It can be about:

- A real geo-located physical space in which different sensors are distributed to detect user actions, participants interact among themselves and on the environment while they are involved in different game mechanics.
- A Virtual World created mainly with virtual reality technology or augmented reality, in this case, the user interacts with the world through a mobile device or devices specially designed for the experience.
- A world in which the real and the virtual are mixed, in this way there is a geo-located physical space in which real and virtual objects are displayed, the participant interacts with both using direct action or pervasive computing devices, such as a cell phone.

4.4 The Participants

The game experience exists because the participants make it possible, in this sense, converge in a game world that is defined in a real physical space, virtual or a mixture of both, then there they execute actions regulated by a set of rules and conditions using different types of interaction, so we can see interaction:

- Among the Participants, communication, collaboration, cooperation, and competition activities are traditionally carried out.
- Between Participants and Game World, in this case, the participant acts on the pervasive computing devices deployed in the game world and the game responds accordingly.

In the model, there are two types of participants, "The Player" who intervenes with their actions to directly achieve the objectives proposed by the designer and "The Spectator" with a more passive role, focused on supporting and monitoring the actions of the "Player" and to know the status and progress of the game experience.

The level of knowledge that a participant has about what he can or cannot do within the game and what type of role he plays in a moment, is called level of awareness, and can be used in different ways in various game mechanics, to generate new attractions to the experience, so you can alternate the level of knowledge for different aspects such as:

- The design objectives of the experience.
- Knowledge about the rest of the people who participate.
- Knowledge about how you can interact with the elements of the game.

The "Spectator" as it has happened with the "Player" in other areas of research, is a type of participant that we can profile, this to generate a map of interests, which allow understanding the factors that motivate him to interact, this would serve the designer to incorporate in early stages of design motivators to ensure their participation. In a determined moment of the experience a Participant can be a "Player", but at any moment of the history, he can transform himself into a "Spectator", and vice versa.

5 Conclusions and Future Work

Social expansion is a strategy that the designer has to build game experiences, incorporating non-traditional roles to socialize, collaborate, and cooperate is a powerful element to improve motivation and add new elements of fun.

Pervasive computing supported gaming experiences that focus on social expansion is a reality that requires a set of elements:

- There are two types of participants, some whose efforts are aimed at achieving the objectives (Players) and others who reinforce them indirectly (Spectators).
- Different levels of awareness can be managed for participants in terms of what they can do, what their purpose is in the experience, and who else is participating.
- The story is the discourse that directs the development of all the activities in the experience, it establishes the thread in which the mechanics of the game are developed. Augmented reality, for example, can help introduce fantastic elements into the story, and together with the advances in high definition multimedia resources can make the experience more alive and real.
- Pervasive game mechanics are a key element to direct the activities of players and spectators, their sensitivity to the environment allows us to detect actions and intentions of participants either through direct interaction on pervasive computing devices or through devices designed or configured for the experience.
- The participant's experience becomes a structured process based on what is called the participant's journey, is formed by phases in which are introduced at convenience game mechanics aimed at producing different sensations.

In the proposed conceptual model it has been shown how the audience becomes a preponderant factor to support indirectly the achievement of the objectives and how this happens as a consequence of their interaction with the players in the framework of game mechanics supported by pervasive computing, of all this, The need to know the motivating aspects that lead to participation is derived and since based on these factors spectator profiles can be made that allow the designer to direct his efforts to guarantee the motivation and hooking to the mechanics of constructed games, it is expected to develop a model to typify the spectator profiles in such a way that it addresses the characteristics of each one and the factors that lead to staying motivated.

A key aspect within this research is to identify the software architecture needed to support the viewer's participation in-game mechanics that are context-sensitive, i.e. mechanics that can identify changes and alterations in the environment and can act accordingly. The components must have the ability to integrate with the advances in sensors and electronic devices available in pervasive computing, thus making the game experience more real and motivating.

After identifying the technical and functional characteristics to support the pervasive social game mechanics is to identify some patterns of game mechanics based on UML modeling language that allows collecting successful cases of experiences with social expansion so that they can be reused in projects inspired by game applications to exploit the social expansion and thus improve the engagement of players.

Acknowledgements. This work has been funded by the Ministry of Economy and Competitiveness of Spain as part of PERGAMEX-ACTIVE (RTI2018-096986-B-C32) project.

References

1. Huizinga, J.: Homo Ludens. A Study of Play Element in Culture. Maurice Temple Smith Ltd., London (1970)
2. Nevelsteen, K.J.: A Suvey of Characteristic Engine Features for Technology-Sustained Pervasive Games. SpringerBriefs in Computer Science. Springer, Cham (2015). https://doi.org/10.1007/978-3-319-17632-1
3. Magerkurth, C., Engelke, T., Memisoglu, M.: Augmenting the virtual domain with physical and social elements: towards a paradigm shift in computer entertainment technology. In Proceedings of the 2004 ACM SIGCHI International Conference on Advances in computer entertainment technology, pp. 163–172. ACM (2004). http://dx.doi.org/10.1145/1067343.1067363
4. Gentes, A., Guyot-Mbodji, A., Demeure, I.: Gaming on the move: urban experience as a new paradigm for mobile pervasive game design. Multimed. Syst. **16**(1), 43–55 (2010). https://doi.org/10.1007/s00530-009-0172-2
5. Akribopoulos, O., et al.: Developing multiplayer pervasive games and networked interactive installations using ad hoc mobile sensor nets. In: Proceedings of the International Conference on Advances in Computer Enterntainment Technology, pp. 174–181. ACM (2009). http://dx.doi.org/10.1145/1690388.1690418
6. Sanneblad, J., Holmquist, L.E.: "Why is everyone inside me?!" Using shared displays in mobile computer games. In: Rauterberg, M. (ed.) ICEC 2004. LNCS, vol. 3166, pp. 487–498. Springer, Heidelberg (2004). https://doi.org/10.1007/978-3-540-28643-1_63
7. Caon, M., Mugellini, E., Abou Khaled, O.: A pervasive game to promote social offline interaction. In: Proceedings of the 2013 ACM Conference on Pervasive and Ubiquitous Computing Adjunct Publication, pp. 1381–1384. ACM (2013). http://dx.doi.org/10.1145/2494091.2497359
8. Linehan, C., Bull, N., Kirman, B.: BOLLOCKS!! designing pervasive games that play with the social rules of built environments. In: Reidsma, D., Katayose, H., Nijholt, A. (eds.) ACE 2013. LNCS, vol. 8253, pp. 123–137. Springer, Cham (2013). https://doi.org/10.1007/978-3-319-03161-3_9
9. Åhlén, M., Winbjörk, M., Hietala, S.: Conquest - outdoor based games enhanced with sensors. In: Hervás, R., Lee, S., Nugent, C., Bravo, J. (eds.) UCAmI 2014. LNCS, vol. 8867, pp. 68–71. Springer, Cham (2014). https://doi.org/10.1007/978-3-319-13102-3_13
10. Arango-López, J., Vela, F.L.G., Collazos, C.A., Moreira, F.: Modeling and defining the pervasive games and its components from a perspective of the player experience. In: Rocha, Á., Adeli, H., Reis, L.P., Costanzo, S. (eds.) WorldCIST'18 2018. AISC, vol. 746, pp. 625–635. Springer, Cham (2018). https://doi.org/10.1007/978-3-319-77712-2_58
11. Arango, J., Gallardo, J., Gutiérrez, F.L., Amengual,E., Collazos, C.: GeoPGD: proposed methodology for the implementation of geolocated pervasive games. In: Proceedings of the XIX International Conference on Human Computer Interaction, ACM Digital Library (2018). https://dx.doi.org/10.1145/3233824.3233862
12. Piekarski, W., Thomas, B.: ARQuake: the outdoor augmented reality gaming system. Commun. ACM **45**(1), 36–38 (2002). https://doi.org/10.1145/502269.502291

13. Magerkurth, C., Engelke, T., Memisoglu, M.: Augmenting the virtual domain with physical and social elements: towards a paradigm shift in computer entertainment technology. In: Proceedings of the 2004 ACM SIGCHI International Conference on Advances in Computer Entertainment Technology, pp. 163–172. ACM (2004). http://dx.doi.org/10.1145/1067343. 1067363
14. Akribopoulos, O., et al.: Developing multiplayer pervasive games and networked interactive installations using ad hoc mobile sensor nets. In: Proceedings of the International Conference on Advances in Computer Entertainment Technology, pp. 174–181. ACM (2009). http://dx. doi.org/10.1145/1690388.1690418
15. Kasapakis, V., Gavalas, D., Bubaris, N.: Addressing openness and portability in outdoor pervasive role-playing games. In: 2013 Third International Conference on IEEE Communications and Information Technology (ICCIT), pp. 93–97 (2013). http://dx.doi.org/10.1109/ ICCITechnology.2013.6579529
16. Montola, M., Stenros, J., Waern, A.: Pervasive Games: Theory and Design. Morgan Kaufmann Publishers Inc., Burlington (2009). https://doi.org/10.1201/9780080889795

Model-Driven Multidisciplinary Production of Virtual Reality Environments for Elementary School with ADHD

Héctor Cardona-Reyes[1]([⊠]), Jaime Muñoz-Arteaga[2], Lorena Barba-González[3], and Gerardo Ortiz-Aguiñaga[3]

[1] CONACYT Research Fellow, CIMAT Zacatecas, Zacatecas, Mexico
hector.cardona@cimat.mx
[2] Autonomous University of Aguascalientes, Av. Universidad #940, Cd. Universitaria, 20131 Aguascalientes, Mexico
jaime.munoz@edu.uaa.mx
[3] Center for Research in Mathematics, Quantum: Knowledge City, Zacatecas, Mexico
{maria.barba,Gerardo.ortiz}@cimat.mx

Abstract. This work proposes a multidisciplinary model based on models for the production of interactive environments as technological support to the needs of children with ADHD who often present specific educational needs. So, a multidisciplinary team composed of technologists, psychologists and teachers can collaborate for the production of these environments as a technological solution as school support. Under the proposed approach, an interactive environment in virtual reality is presented to support the educational development of children with ADHD in basic education, which also allows for specific adaptations to be carried out for each case. The development of the current proposal is presented along with the artifacts of the proposed model.

Keywords: Model-driven development · ADHD · Elementary school · Interactive environments · Virtual reality

1 Introduction

Attention deficit hyperactivity disorder (ADHD) is a neurobiological and developmental disorder characterized by symptoms of inattention, impulsivity, and hyperactivity that causes problems in multiple areas of functioning and hinders the person's cognitive, emotional and social development, as well as some consequences in the family and school system are frequently diagnosed in childhood and may persist in adulthood [1].

According to Wolraichet et al. [2], approximately 10% of children aged 4 to 17 have a diagnosis of ADHD, i.e., in a classroom with 30 probably children 2 or 3 of them may have this disorder. ADHD has a worldwide prevalence of 5%, in the United States 7 to 9% in people under 18 years old [3] and in Mexico ADHD affects between 4 and 12% of the school population, it is estimated there are approximately 33 million children and adolescents, of which 1.5 million could be diagnosed with ADHD [4].

© Springer Nature Switzerland AG 2020
V. Agredo-Delgado et al. (Eds.): HCI-COLLAB 2020, CCIS 1334, pp. 181–192, 2020.
https://doi.org/10.1007/978-3-030-66919-5_19

1.1   ADHD in the School Context

ADHD approach in the school context is complex, there are few works where a systemic approach includes teachers, parents, and classmates [5, 6]. Traditionally the student is referred by his teacher to the psycho-pedagogical department for presenting behaviors such as inattention, misbehavior, not following directions, being out of place, etc. And depending on the institution, if they have specialists diagnosed or derivative to an institution for diagnosis. In the case of being diagnosed with ADHD, you will receive treatment according to the professional who was channeled, which can be a pharmacological treatment, cognitive behavioral therapy or combined. The activities within the interactive environment will aim to positively influence the problems of inattention, hyperactivity, and impulsivity, classified in the diagnostic criteria of mental disorders [1].

1.2   Interactive Environments in Virtual Reality and ADHD

Virtual reality is a technology that allows the user to interact with computer-simulated environments and is a means to create a personalized reality [7]. Riener and Harders [8] identify two main components, which are the user environment and the virtual environment, these two environments communicate to exchange information, including physical information that the user receives through the use of additional devices, such as motion sensors, audio devices, controls, etc. In order to increase the quality of presence and provide the user with a realistic experience [8, 9].

Fig. 1. Keys to adopt virtual reality. Statistics are taken from Gilbert [10].

Today the adoption of virtual reality has reached a large number of users with diverse needs and their orientation to various applications, these include education, entertainment, video games, militia, medicine, and other large numbers that are incorporated every day.

However, there are several barriers to be addressed, which over time have been decreasing, among the most significant barriers, according to a report by Gilbert [10], we have the poor user experience that is offered with 26%, that as this percentage has been reduced because the new devices on the market that are increasingly oriented to the user. In second place is the content barrier with a 24%, this percentage has gradually gone down, because every time there is content-oriented to various applications, quality is improved and even exists at a commercial level, as is the case of video games and simulation applications in medicine, robotics, among others. As the main benefits of virtual reality for the development of the workforce can be mentioned, which provides information in real-time (49%), facilitates the simulation and training in real-life experiences and aspects of the industry that could be risky, impossible, or expensive (49%) and allows an improvement in creativity in the design and development of products (48%), among other benefits that can be seen in Fig. 1.

This work is oriented towards the use of virtual reality in the field of psychiatric disorders prevalent in childhood such as attention deficit hyperactivity disorder, with the aim of supporting cognitive restructuring and classical intervention techniques through a virtual environment highlighting the psycho-therapeutic principles involved in ADHD therapy [11]. This work is composed of 5 sections, in the following section a literary review of works is presented in which various treatments are supported through virtual reality. In Sect. 3 the proposed multidisciplinary model is presented and the elements that comprise them are described. A case study in Sect. 4 is presented, which describes the stages of the proposed multidisciplinary model for the implementation of an interactive environment in virtual and augmented reality for primary school children, and finally, a section of conclusions and future works are presented.

2   Literary Review

This section presents a literature review of works that propose various approaches aimed at providing solutions to treatments related to ADHD. It is important to know these approaches and related technologies in addition to virtual reality and know how the human factor is taken into account for the design of solutions focused on the field of therapy, particularly ADHD. The multidisciplinary factor, the proposed approach and the human factor are key pieces for the proposed technological solutions to be adequate to the users' needs.

As can be seen in Table 1 most of the proposals include solutions based on virtual and augmented reality [11, 13, 18, 19] whose proposed approaches are based on providing techniques for the assessment, diagnosis, design and implementation of the application and exploration of the limitations of the human factor. Other works use additional devices such as sensors, EEG devices and cloud-based solutions [12, 14, 16, 17] to support virtual reality whose focus is more oriented to courseware, use of cognitive tests and serious games. Finally, approaches based on design pattern extraction for mobile applications and therapeutic intervention and validation with serious games are also presented [15, 20].

This analysis allows us to propose a multidisciplinary approach, that is, to be able to involve the family, the educational institution, the counselors or psychologists and pediatricians together with the technologists to incorporate technology-based solutions to assist the child from the early stages of the therapeutic process of suspicion and treatment of ADHD and to offer interactive environments in virtual reality and identify the implementation platforms according to the needs of treatment and school context.

The following section describes the stages of a multidisciplinary model for the production of these interactive environments for the support of ADHD.

Table 1. Virtual and augmented reality applications and their approaches to ADHD.

Reference	Platform	Treatment	Description	Multi-disciplinary	Approach
Ab Aziz et al. [12]	AR and Cloud Computing	ADHD	AR based courseware for ADHD students	–	Courseware via cloud computing
Van Krevelen and Poelman [13]	AR characteristics	–	Describes limitations regarding human factor in the use AR Systems	–	Survey the known limitations regarding human factors in the use of AR
Alchalcabi et al. [14]	Wearable EGG & Serious Games	ADHD/ADD	The design of a virtual reality serious game to improve the focusing ability of people with ADHD and ADD	–	Serious games, BCI
Anton et al. [11]	Virtual Reality	ADHD	The implementation of the psychotherapeutic principles involved in ADHD therapy in a VirtualClassroom environment	–	Assessment & diagnosis
Hashemian and Gotsis [15]	VideoGames Based	ADHD	Mini-game mechanics targeting ADHD diagnosis	✓	Intervention based on VR, a therapeutic tool of high ecological validity
Othmer and Kaiser [16]	Wearable EGG/VR	ADHD, seizures and mood disorders	EEG biofeedback on cognitive test	–	Assessment & diagnosis
Rohani et al. [17]	Brain Computer Interface	ADHD	Games designed to challenge the sustained visual attention and visual discrimination abilities that are hard for ADHD subjects	–	Serious games, BCI

(*continued*)

Table 1. (*continued*)

Reference	Platform	Treatment	Description	Multi-disciplinary	Approach
Yeh et al. [18]	Virtual Reality	ADHD	Virtual Classroom that includes visual and auditory distractions of different intensity levels, durations, and sequence	✓	Assessment & diagnosis
Li et al. [19]	Augmented Reality	–	AR-Based Applications for Enhanced Engagement for Math Education	✓	Design and implementation AR-based social game
Villareal-Freire et al. [20]	Mobile, Android	ADHD	Reverse engineering for the Design Patterns Extraction of Android Mobile applications for ADHD	✓	Design Patterns

3   Model Driven Multidisciplinary Production

The proposed multidisciplinary model is based on existing algorithms in the literature for suspicion, diagnosis, and treatment of ADHD [21–25], in Fig. 2 each of the stages that compose it is presented and each of them is described below.

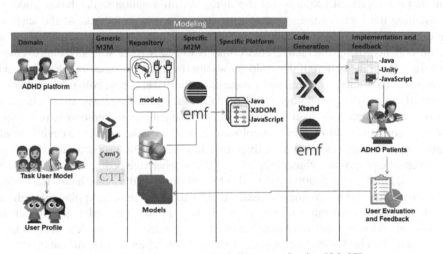

Fig. 2. Model-driven multidisciplinary production [26, 27].

The proposed model begins with the stage domain where, the technologists, working together with the educational institution, psychologists, family and pediatrician to obtain information about the user profile of the child (age, diagnosis, treatment, special considerations, etc.) and begin with the definition of a task model of the child with ADHD and obtain a natural language scenario using different notations, such as Concur Task Trees (CTT), UML, etc. [26–28]. At this stage technologists also define interactions with the interactive environment, is included here, the use of motion sensors such as Leap Motion, to interact with gestures. Targets used in augmented reality applications, that combine elements of the real world to the virtual, and virtual reality headsets sophisticated, such as Google Cardboard, Oculus Rift, etc. This stage will allow the educational institution and psychologists to assess the child's school situation based on the use of interactive environments produced, with which they allow the child to navigate in immersive graphics environments in order to stimulate their concentration and motivation [29].

During modeling, technologists with the elements of the previous stage perform a series of transformations and definition of model-to-model (M2M) rules using tools, such as specific domain language (DSL), Eclipse Modeling Tools, which also includes the language of ATL transformations, etc. [30, 31]. A repository allows adapting and reusing the models produced to create new interactive environments according to the needs of children with ADHD. It is noteworthy that this is because the educational institution, psychologists and pediatricians perform ongoing assessments to the child and monitor their progress. In the specific platform and code generation stages, these begin from models obtained in the domain stage represented in an abstract notation and that require a specific platform notation to continue the production of the interactive environment. Tools like Xtend help generate the abstract syntactic structure (AST) [27] to define an objective platform, which at the implementation stage is transferred toa video game engine such as Unity, Unreal, etc.

One of the advantages of model-based development is the ability to set rules for moving from a source model to a model destination and generate different portions of code that can represent solutions for the storage of information in databases, code for representing the logic of the interactive environment, among others. At the stage of implementation and feedback, educational institutions and psychologists analyze information obtained using interactive environments to see if there was any improvement and take appropriate action. If the child shows improvement, the use of interactive environments is continued as a treatment measure, otherwise, a psychological evaluation is carried out by the psychologist and pediatrician, and a diagnosis and therapeutic proposal are determined. With the information obtained a new iteration is performed modeling abstraction domain by technologists to produce new interactive environments to give support to this new stage of diagnosis and therapeutic proposal. Derived from the therapeutic proposal, a clinical report is obtained where the pediatrician may include behavioral, family, and pharmacological interventions. On the other hand, the educational institution and psychologists create an educational intervention plan through the use of interactive environments, this plan will help monitoring and evaluation at the educational and user-level to obtain feedback and generate new models according to the needs of the child to produce new interactive environments and continue treatment.

Next, a case study is presented for the implementation of interactive environments under the proposed model.

4   Case Study

The proposed model was implemented through a case study conducted during 6 months by teachers from Support Units for Regular Education (USAER, by its acronym in Spanish) and a group of students of second level of elementary school from Aguascalientes City in Mexico. In fact, USAER team conforms a multidisciplinary team compose of a psychologist, a special education teacher and a pedagogue. Next, the phases of the proposed model are described through the production of the interactive environment in virtual and augmented reality called Puzzle City in primary school children in Aguascalientes, Mexico.

4.1   ADHD in the School Context

USAER teachers have proposed to apply an initial assessment to students of a group of the second level of an elementary school from Aguascalientes city in Mexico. "Jane" was the only one student has been identified with ADHD symptom with a minimum rescue of impulsivity. Until that moment, Jane has not accessed the reading-writing, nor achieved the count from 1 to 9 with concrete material; she had low communication skills and she had low motivation to study. Then an ICT team (an analyst, a designer, and a programmer) is added to the USAER teachers, this new team is proposed to the family in order to help the learning need of the student.

Puzzle City mobile application was designed to be easily accessible and inexpensive for teachers and family, uses virtual reality technology based on Google Cardboard [32] and augmented reality offered by the Vuforia SDK [33, 34]. The advantage of its implementation is only required a mobile phone-based on Android, a headset compatible with Google Cardboard and targets, which are codes that can be printed in the desired size. Figure 3 shows the basic equipment for Puzzle City interactive environment.

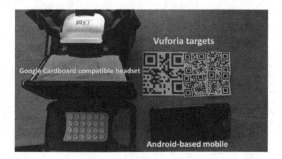

Fig. 3. Puzzle City set.

The use of the mobile application Puzzle City in children is primary education(as can be seen in Fig. 4) starts when the teacher installs the application on his mobile device and places it in the virtual reality headset, then places and adjusts the headset in the child's head and shows him the 9 printed targets. The teacher instructs the child how the city should look and the child must accommodate the targets according to the teacher's instructions, the child must focus his attention on the details contained in each element of the city, such as trees, animated characters, streets, buildings, etc. While the teacher gives feedback to the child. This activity promotes the child's ability to hold the attention, capture and conceptualize new knowledge through learning situations [32].

4.2   Modeling

The ICT team working together with the psychologist has proposed the use of interactive artifacts with the virtual reality in the learning activities required to do by the student with the ADHD. An interactive mobile application has designed to help the student to build and identify the components of a city. A UML model (see next Fig. 5) specifies the software structure and the virtual reality resources that compose the interactive Puzzle City application.

Fig. 4. Mobile VR/AR application Puzzle City for ADHD children.

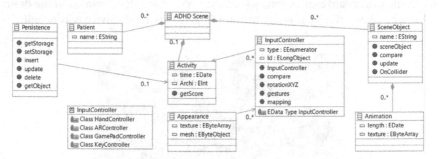

Fig. 5. UML diagram system design.

4.3   Code Generation

For code generation, a set of important rules to mention is those that allow transformations of the models to a context of data persistence, with the possibility of mapping the model Classes in Tables, Attributes in Fields and the Operation sin Functions. It is, moving off a class-model which is under a meta-model UML class diagram for a model defined by the user using the EMF tools, as a result, obtain a model in XMI format (XML Metadata Interchange) for its subsequent coding [35]. These advantages within the production of interactive environments allow the storage, adaptation, and reuse these models according to changes in the treatments ruled by health experts, or the incorporation of new platforms for the user with ADHD.

4.4 Implementation and Feedback

The next evaluation of skills of Jane's development was in charge of the psychologist, who by means of the application of the tests classified in the diagnostic criteria of mental disorders [1], has confirmed that the student has presented symptoms of ADHD. As first feedback, a work team was formed among the community; the psychologist and teacher of USAER. The ICT team, incorporating the pediatrician and the mother of the student, who is, in fact, the head of his family. Stakeholders perform a psychologist, pediatrician, and teacher evaluation and the evaluation report, in order to know and identify the special educational needs presented by the student and the ICT team have evaluated the process of technological insertion. In addition, the ICT team will propose a set of applications for specific purposes, which have been selected by the intervention teams according to the initial diagnosis of the student and will be configured and chosen for its use, according to their progress throughout the intervention process. At this stage of feedback it is also important to evaluate the user experience, so we propose a series of assessments with the aim of knowing how children and specialists perceive the proposed reality environments for ADHD therapies, in addition to identifying further improvements the models generated for new needs. Below are some of the proposed instruments for the evaluation of user experience and usability.

- User Experience Questionnaire (UEQ)[1] [36]: measures both classical aspects of usability (efficiency, clarity, reliability) and aspects of user experience (originality, stimulation).
- System Usability Scale (SUS)[2] [36]: provides an overview of subjective us-ability evaluations.
- AttrakDiff[3] [37]: helps you to understand how users personally rate the usability and design of your interactive product.

As a result of this stage, the first impressions of "Jane" when using the Puzzle City application were known. In this sense, it was possible to observe that the application is motivating, the child keeps his attention at all times when carrying out the task of searching, identifying and putting together the pieces of the puzzle of the city, although an instructor is present to give instructions, the child works on the aspects of attention by being immersed under the virtual reality glasses and listening to the indications at the

---

[1] https://www.ueq-online.org/.

[2] https://www.usabilitest.com/.

[3] http://attrakdiff.de/index-en.html.

same time. On the other hand, it allows the specialists to get involved in the development of the therapy task using this type of applications in the sessions.

5 Conclusions and Future Works

This work presents a model based on multidisciplinary models for the production of interactive virtual reality environments that support the process of detecting and diagnosing ADHD in children's basic education. The objective of this production of environments is to have the elements of a multidisciplinary group of experts to capture the appropriate requirements according to the needs of the child with suspicion and diagnosis of ADHD, and that these interactive environments can also adjust to the treatment needs. While the various stakeholders play an important role in defining the user profile and therapy needs and the assessments of the various therapy experts, the model-oriented approach allows to bring all this together and take it to a computational context in which virtual reality environments can be produced according to the specific needs of ADHD therapy and to put together mechanisms to evaluate the user experience for future improvements. As was shown in this work, virtual reality is a technology that allows re-creating simulated environments and delivers immersive experiences where they can treat the symptoms associated with ADHD. Although in this work the production process is presented under the proposed model of a virtual and augmented reality application, the first registered impressions of the implementation are shown with a case study where there are learning needs in a school context. Future work has the challenge of considering new experiments in which the creation of new models can be strengthened, identifying new user profiles with ADHD, and obtaining relevant statistical information regarding the use and user experience of virtual reality environments produced. In addition, to designing strategies to make the applications produced available and can be used with low-cost devices to all those involved in the therapeutic process of ADHD.

Acknowledgments. The authors appreciate the support provided for this research to the National Council of Science and Technology (CONACYT) Mexico.

References

1. Association, A.P., et al.: DSM 5. diagnostic and statistical manual of mental disorders—fifth version (2013)
2. Wolraich, M.L., et al.: The prevalence of ADHD: its diagnosis and treatment in four school districts across two states. J. Attent. Disord. **18**(7), 563–575 (2014). https://doi.org/10.1177/1087054712453169
3. Polanczyk, G., De Lima, M.S., Horta, B.L., Biederman, J., Rohde, L.A.: The worldwide prevalence of ADHD: a systematic review and met regression analysis. Am. J. Psychiatry **164**(6), 942–948 (2007). https://doi.org/10.1176/ajp.2007.164.6.942
4. Palacios-Cruz, L., Peña, F.D.L., Valderrama, A., Patiño, R., Calle Portugal, S.P., Ulloa, R.E.: Conocimientos, creencias y actitudes en padres mexicanos acerca del trastorno por déficit de atención con hiperactividad (TDAH). Salud Ment. **34**(2), 149–155 (2011)

5. Segura, A.B.J.: El TDAH, trastorno por déficit de atención con hiperactividad, en las clasificaciones diagnosticas actuales (CİE 10, DSM IV–R y CFTMEA–R 2000). Norte Salud Ment. **8**(35), 30–40 (2009)
6. Pedreira Massa, J., de Dios, J.G.: Evidencias diagnosticas en el trastorno por déficit de atención con hiperactividad en la infancia y la adolescencia. Pediatría Atención Primaria **19**(76), 147–152 (2017)
7. Mandal, S.: Brief introduction of virtual reality & its challenges. Int. J. Sci. Eng. Res. **4**(4), 304–309 (2013)
8. Riener, R., Harders, M.: Virtual Reality in Medicine. Springer, Heidelberg (2012). https://doi.org/10.1007/978-1-4471-4011-5
9. Heeter, C.: Being there: the subjective experience of presence. Presence: Teleoper. Virtual Environ. **1**(2), 262–271 (1992). https://doi.org/10.1162/pres.1992.1.2.262
10. Gilbert, N.: 62 Virtual reality statistics you must know in 2019 & 2020: adoption, usage & market share, December 2019. https://financesonline.com/virtual-reality-statistics/#adoption. Accessed 18 Dec 2019
11. Anton, R., Opris, D., Dobrean, A., David, D., Rizzo, A.: Virtual reality in rehabilitation of attention deficit/hyperactivity disorder the instrument construction principles. In: 2009 Virtual Rehabilitation International Conference, pp. 59–64. IEEE (2009). https://doi.org/10.1109/ICVR.2009.5174206
12. Aziz, NA.A., Aziz, K.A., Paul, A., Yusof, A.M., Mohamed Noor, N. S.: Providing augmented reality based education for students with attention deficit hyperactive disorder via cloud computing: its advantages. In: 2012 14th International Conference on Advanced Communication Technology (ICACT), PyeongChang, pp. 577–581 (2012)
13. Van Krevelen, D., Poelman, R.: A survey of augmented reality technologies, applications and limitations. Int. J. Virtual Reality **9**(2), 1–20 (2010)
14. Alchalcabi, A.E., Eddin, A.N., Shirmohammadi, S.: More attention, less deficit: wearable eeg-based serious game for focus improvement. In: 2017 IEEE 5th International Conference on Serious Games and Applications for Health (SeGAH), pp. 1–8. IEEE (2017). https://doi.org/10.1109/SeGAH.2017.7939288
15. Hashemian, Y., Gotsis, M.: Adventurous dreaming highflying dragon: a full body game for children with attention deficit hyperactivity disorder (ADHD). In: Proceedings of the 4th Conference on Wireless Health, p. 12. ACM (2013). https://doi.org/10.1145/2534088.2534101
16. Othmer, S., Kaiser, D.: Implementation of virtual reality in EEG biofeedback. Cyberpsychol. Behav. **3**(3), 415–420 (2000). https://doi.org/10.1089/10949310050078878
17. Rohani, D.A., Sorensen, H.B., Puthusserypady, S.: Brain-computer interface using p 300 and virtual reality: a gaming approach for treating ADHD. In: 2014 36th Annual International Conference of the IEEE Engineering in Medicine and Biology Society, pp. 3606–3609. IEEE (2014). https://doi.org/10.1109/EMBC.2014.6944403
18. Yeh, S.C., Tsai, C.F., Fan, Y.C., Liu, P.C., Rizzo, A.: An innovative ADHD assessment system using virtual reality. In: 2012 IEEE-EMBS Conference on Biomedical Engineering and Sciences, pp. 78–83. IEEE (2012). https://doi.org/10.1109/IECBES.2012.6498026
19. Li, J., van der Spek, E., Hu, J., Feijs, L.: See me roar: self-determination enhanced engagement for math education relying on augmented reality. In: Extended Abstracts Publication of the Annual Symposium on Computer-Human Interaction in Play, pp. 345–351. ACM (2017). https://doi.org/10.1145/3130859.3131316
20. Villareal-Freire, A.P., Aguirre, A.F.A., Ordonez, C.A.C.: Reverse engineering for the design patterns extraction of android mobile applications for attention deficit disorder. Comput. Stand. Interfaces **61**, 147–153 (2019). https://doi.org/10.1016/j.csi.2018.07.001

21. Palacio, J.D., la Peña-Olvera, D., Palacios-Cruz, L., Ortiz-León, S., et al.: Algoritmo lati-noamericano de tratamiento multimodal del trastorno por déficit de atención e hiperactividad (TDAH) a través de la vida. Rev. Colombiana Psiquiatría (2009)
22. Fundacioncadah.org: Proceso de detección, valoración e intervención en personas con TDAH en la Comunidad Autónoma de Cantabria, December 2019. https://www.fundacioncadah.org/web/articulo/proceso-de-deteccion-valoracion-e-intervencion-en-personas-con-tdah-en-la-comunidad-autonoma-de-cantabria.html. Accessed 4 Nov 2019
23. de Salud, S.M.: Protocolo de coordinación de actuaciones educativas y sanitarias en la detec-ción y diagnóstico del trastorno por déficit de atención e hiperactividad TDAH. Revisión 2012. Consejería de Sanidad y Política Social, Consejería de Educación, Formación y Empleo (2012)
24. Compains, B., Alvarez, M., Royo, J.: The child with attention deficit hyperactivity disor-der (ADHD). Hyperkinetic multi-disciplinary therapeutic approach. In: Anales del sistema sanitario de Navarra, vol. 25, pp. 93–108 (2002). https://doi.org/10.23938/assn.0834
25. Montoya-Sanchez, E., Herrera-Gutiérrez, E.: Manifestaciones del tdah en la etapa de edu-cación infantil y cómo afrontarlas. In: Navarro, J., Gracia, Ma. D., Lineros, R., Soto, F.J. (eds.). Claves para una educación diversa (2014)
26. Jung, B., Lenk, M., Vitzthum, A.: Model-driven multi-platform development of 3D applica-tions with round-trip engineering. Softw. Eng. (2013)
27. Bettini, L.: Implementing Domain-Specific Languages with Xtext and Xtend. Packt Publish-ing Ltd. (2016)
28. Paternó, F.: Concur task trees: an engineered notation for task models. The Handb. Task Anal. Hum.-Comput. Interact. 483–503 (2004)
29. Delgado Pardo, G., Moreno García, I.: Aplicaciones de la realidad virtual en el trastorno por déficit de atención con hiperactividad: Una aproximación. Anuario Psicol. Clín. Salud **8**(2012), 31–39 (2012)
30. Steinberg, D., Budinsky, F., Merks, E., Paternostro, M.: EMF: Eclipse Modeling Framework. Pearson Education, London (2008)
31. Jouault, F., Allilaire, F., Bézivin, J., Kurtev, I.: ATL: a model transformation tool. Sci. Comput. Program. **72**(1), 31–39 (2008). https://doi.org/10.1016/j.scico.2007.08.002
32. Lee, S.H., Sergueeva, K., Catangui, M., Kandaurova, M.: Assessing Google card-board virtual reality as a content delivery system in business classrooms. J. Educ. Bus. **92**(4), 153–160 (2017). https://doi.org/10.1080/08832323.2017.1308308
33. Boonbrahm, S., Kaewrat, C., Boonbrahm, P.: Using augmented reality technology in assisting English learning for primary school students. In: Zaphiris, P., Ioannou, A. (eds.) LCT 2015. LNCS, vol. 9192, pp. 24–32. Springer, Cham (2015). https://doi.org/10.1007/978-3-319-206 09-7_3
34. Xiao, C., Lifeng, Z.: Implementation of mobile augmented reality based on Vuforia and rawajali. In: 2014 IEEE 5th International Conference on Software Engineering and Service Science, pp. 912–915. IEEE (2014). https://doi.org/10.1109/ICSESS.2014.6933713
35. Quintero, J.B., Anaya, R.: Mda y el papel de los modelos en el proceso de desarrollo de software. Rev. EIA (8), 131–146 (2007)
36. Devy, N.P.I.R., Wibirama, S., Santosa, P.I.: Evaluating user experience of English learning interface using user experience questionnaire and system usability scale. In: 2017 1st Interna-tional Conference on Informatics and Computational Sciences (ICICoS), pp. 101–106. IEEE (2017). https://doi.org/10.1109/ICICOS.2017.8276345
37. Walsh, T., Varsaluoma, J., Kujala, S., Nurkka, P., Petrie, H., Power, C.: Axe UX: exploring long-term user experience with iScale and AttrakDiff. In: Proceedings of the 18th international Academic Mindtrek Conference: Media Business, Management, Content & Services, pp. 32–39 (2014). https://doi.org/10.1145/2676467.2676480

Recommendations and Challenges for Developing English Vocabulary Learning Games

Diana Toro(✉) ⓘ, Aldemar Rodríguez ⓘ, Miguel Velasco ⓘ, Edwin Gamboa ⓘ,
and María Trujillo ⓘ

Universidad del Valle, Cali, Colombia
{toro.diana,aldemar.rodriguez,velasco.miguel,edwin.gamboa,
maria.trujillo}@correounivalle.edu.co

Abstract. English Vocabulary Learning Games (EVLG) are suitable to help motivate students in learning a second language. Therefore, knowing the EVLG's developmental recommendations or challenges is relevant when starting a developmental process. Due to the lack of related information about EVLG development from the perspective of developers, students, and teachers, and in order to explain the elements that should be considered before beginning this process, in this document, we present recommendations and identify challenges for EVLG development. Through a series of interviews with a group of EVLG developers, English teachers, and recreation professionals, we have been able to identify and address these challenges. We employed a Thematic Analysis to study the data collected. We found that recommendations and challenges are related to aspects of motivation, development tools and processes, the story of a game and its vocabulary, the availability and limitations of resources, and EVLG developers and users. The findings show that EVLG development should include collaborative design among students, teachers, and developers. Have previous experience with development tools to facilitate the process, including those with a low learning curve. EVLGs should be an educational and motivational tool. In addition, include a story and vocabulary that is attractive to end users.

Keywords: Tales of Etrya · Video game · Incidental learning ·
Recommendations · Challenges · Development · Vocabulary

1 Introduction

The use of digital games in education today has helped to motivate students to participate in learning processes [1–3]. Educational games need to create an immersive world that motivates and engages students in play activities, and this generates incidental learning [4]. In many schools in Colombia, English lessons do not provide the expected results of learning a new language [5]. English Vocabulary Learning Games (EVLG) are suitable to help motivate students in learning a second language. But the use of EVLG comes with some challenges that limit the achievement of its goal of teaching and motivating

© Springer Nature Switzerland AG 2020
V. Agredo-Delgado et al. (Eds.): HCI-COLLAB 2020, CCIS 1334, pp. 193–202, 2020.
https://doi.org/10.1007/978-3-030-66919-5_20

learners [6, 7]. For example, there is no consistency between the game and the story or that the objective of the game is not clear [7], also, visual or performance aspects [6]. To our knowledge, these challenges have not yet been identified by involving the perspective of development experts, students, and teachers of English in a comprehensive manner. Therefore, in this document, we identify recommendations and challenges for developing EVLG. We conducted a qualitative study that includes the perspectives of a group of EVLG developers, English teachers, and recreation professionals. We found eight recommendations and eleven challenges of developing EVLG. Also, we present related papers and Tales of Etrya as our case studies.

2 Related Works

Strong Shot [6] is a 2D shooter digital game whose propose is to convey basic English vocabulary to secondary school students. It was developed using a collaborative scheme, involving 20 students from a secondary school in Cali, Colombia who supported the process of designing the game story, characters, world, and rules. Strong Shot uses game context (i.e. game world, game tasks, locations, and story) to deliver vocabulary to students. It incorporates three *English Challenges* (EC), which are mini-games or puzzles that players can access at any time. Thus, vocabulary evaluation is voluntary since players decide when to play health packs or vehicles to go through game levels easily. Moreover, Strong Shot keeps a record of the words that a player has seen/interacted with throughout his journey. In this way, incidental learning is promoted to allow students to understand the meaning of a word [8].

Ruby Rei [9] is an educational game for language learning, created by Wibbu [10] in collaboration with Cambridge Assessment [11]. Ruby Rei is an explorer, adventurer, curious, respectful and a good person. Especially suitable for beginners or learners with a low-intermediate level, the game is also suitable for those who need extra motivation with the language and for those who want to experience a language immersion in an interactive way [12].

Trace Effects is a 3D video game for learning the English language. Players interact and solve puzzles in a virtual world filled with diverse English-speaking characters. In the game, students take a dynamic journey through the United States. Aimed at young people, Trace Effects exposes users to American society [13].

I-FLEG (Interactive French Language Learning Game) is a serious 3D game designed to learn French as a second language [14]. It consists of an avatar that can move around a house and touch elements it finds in it. The study was commissioned to look at the impact of the video game on the acquisition of a second language, evaluating six 9-year-old children from a German primary school, with one year of schooling in French. I-FLEG developers designed a test where a group of students would have both auditory and visual feedback, and another group would only have visual feedback, the results of this test concluded that students could keep more information with both visual and auditory feedback [15].

Due to the lack of documentation regarding EVLG's developmental issues, this study is being conducted.

3 Tales of Etrya

This document is based on the development of the video game Tales of Etrya (ToE), formerly called Strong Shot. A project that has taken approximately three years of development. ToE is a digital non-violent adventure game for smartphones that transmits basic English vocabulary using context. Our goal is to motivate and involve students in the English learning process. ToE is being designed using a collaborative scheme, involving high school students and an English teacher from the *Institución Educativa Multipróposito*. The design process was constrained by a requirement from the principal and teachers at that school. They asked for any component that promotes violence to be reduced or preferably eliminated. Since the name, gender, mechanics, and history of Strong Shot contain violent elements, a new history was constructed. The game is being designed incrementally using the approach presented in [16]. A user-centered design, in which the development team along with students and a teacher from the educational institution were constantly involved in the design of the EVLG. ToE is made up of two levels and a series of mini-games each dealing with a set of vocabulary. The first level of ToE (in Fig. 1) requires the user to follow the clues and instructions to find a set of objects.

Fig. 1. First level Tales of Etrya

4 Methods

This study aims to identify the recommendations and mention the challenges of developing EVLG as mentioned by developers, English teachers and Recreation Professional.

4.1 Participants

7 ToE developers were interviewed, along with 1 English teacher and 2 students from last year's class of recreation professionals. They participated voluntarily, knowing the objective of the study. The characteristics of the participants are presented in Table 1.

Table 1. Participants' characteristics

Id	Title	Years of Experience*	Role in ToE
D1	Systems Engineer Student	1	Developer
D2	Master of Engineering in Computer Science	5	Project Leader
D3	Technology in Software Development Student	–	Developer
D4	Systems Engineer	0.5	Developer
D5	Systems Engineer	0.7	Developer
D6	Technology in Software Development Student	–	Developer
D7	Systems Engineer Student	–	Developer
P1	Classroom Teacher	13	English Language Teacher
P2	Recreation Professional Student	–	Product owner
P3	Recreation Professional Student	–	Product owner

*As game developers and/or products owner

4.2 Data Collection and Analysis

Data were collected through a semi-structured interview with questions to identify EVLG recommendations and developmental issues. Each participant was interviewed individually. The collected data were transcribed into a spreadsheet and analyzed using the thematic analysis method [17].

5 Findings and Discussion

After coding and grouping the data collected iteratively, we found that the recommendations relate to 8 categories and the challenges related to 11 categories illustrated in Fig. 2 and explained in detail below. Also, based on our findings, we propose some recommendations to be considered when developing EVLG targeted at school students.

5.1 Recommendations

The participants mentioned the following aspects.

Collaborative Design. Participants consider that spaces for designing activities or iterations facilitate getting feedback. Iterations between developers and teachers help to obtain validated vocabulary sets that are correct and appropriate for students. Development ownership involves students and teachers in the development stages of the EVLG.

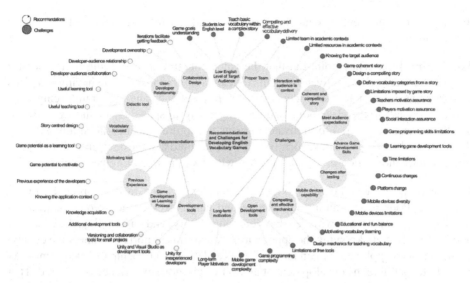

Fig. 2. Recommendations and challenges for developing English vocabulary learning games

They become designers with their ideas and their tastes are reflected in the game. Therefore, that is important there must be a collaborative design between students, teachers, and the developers of the video game. To include users' ideas and make them feel part of the design process. Also, by including teachers, they can validate the chosen vocabulary.

User-Developer Relationship. Participants mentioned that the developer-audience relationship is very good, motivating, friendly, fantastic, and enjoyable. Allowing active participation generates good communication between developers, teachers, and students during the game design process. Also, they mention that developer-audience collaboration allows us to contribute ideas for the vocabulary and mechanics of the game. The teacher's willingness and help were available. Consequently, it is important in the user-developer relationship, to have a good deal between students, teachers, and developers. This facilitates communication by finding new mechanics to include them in the video game, making the work environment more enjoyable.

Didactic Tool. They report that the Useful Learning Tool allows incidental learning so that the student acquires vocabulary in English. It is easy to use regardless of the difficulty levels of the game. It is also a useful teaching tool for teachers as it allows them to give students language tools so that they can play the game while learning. As a result, video games should be a didactic tool within an academic context, allowing students to learn English vocabulary while playing and having fun, which makes it a very useful tool in education.

Vocabulary Focused. Developers and teachers say that story-centered design allows the design of an EVLG to be focused around a story. This helps with ideas of which vocabulary can be taught and which cannot, in which contexts the student will need to apply those words. Therefore, it is important to add a story in the development of a game to help when including the vocabulary, because it tells us how to adapt it and under what context to use it.

Motivating Tool. They point out that the game potential as a learning tool generates support for teachers to motivate students to learn autonomously while having fun. This generates an interest in the students to acquire a second language, reinforcing their knowledge outside the classroom, and creating a playful space. By including students' needs, the game potential to motivate helps us to capture students' attention and keep them focused on a topic. Consequently, it should be noted that the development of EVLG must achieve motivation in the student. Allowing them to learn English autonomously.

Previous Experience. For developers, previous experience in developing EVLG is important. Prior programming knowledge and language skills are required. In addition to having experience with development tools (Unity) and having played a variety of games. For teachers knowing the application context, it is important to know the context of the intended application to understand users and their relationship to video games. As a result, to facilitate the development of an EVLG, previous experience is required. That is, you must have the basic concepts of programming, a basic command of English, and a previous knowledge of the context to which the video game is going to be directed.

Game Development as a Learning Process. For developers, knowledge acquisition allows them to learn agile practices, relate to a new language, and see things from the player's perspective. Also, to improve the use of the development tools. They say that learning from additional development tools for example to use planning, project organization and design tools are useful. Therefore, the development of an EVLG is also a learning process, new knowledge is acquired, such as the language being taught and new development practices, this are all skills required for a working stage.

Development Tools. The developers highlight the versioning and collaboration tools for small projects that Unity Collaborate allows to work on the project in a collaborative way and with version control. Taiga allows them to track project progress and deliveries. Regarding Unity and Visual Studio as development tools, they say that Unity has video tutorials with the most common problems of the games, plus attractive documentation. Its main language (C#) is quite easy to learn and understand, while the Visual Studio code being an editor allowed the development of the project scripts. Finally, for them, Unity for inexperienced developers facilitates learning because the unit a game engine is widely used for video game development. Unity is based on component-based programming that facilitates its use, in addition to its great community and the capacity to support multiple platforms. Consequently, EVLG's development tools have a low learning curve, allowing for prototyping, collaborative development, and easy integration of new developers. Also, collaborative tools help developers stay in control of everything that is happening in game development.

5.2   Challenges

The participants mentioned the following aspects.

Long-Term Motivation. The participants point out that to achieve a long-term motivation player, a constant interest in the player must be obtained. This can be through playing time, which is enough to engage the player, although all this does not guarantee a constant motivation of the player. And about the mobile game development complexity they say that developing a game with history in a world that includes different scenarios, generates a challenge for the developers. As a result, it is important to consider that the video game must have a structure capable of providing the player with a story that appeals to him, different scenarios within the game so that he has multiple options when playing. This provides a video game that helps students for a good time.

Open Development Tools. For developers the game programming complexity is due to some issues with Unity like its graphical user interface (GUI) system is a bit difficult to understand. Concerning Visual Studio, it is exaggeratedly heavy on a computer with little capacity. For them, the limitations of free tools are because the free version of Unity Collaborate or Taiga prevents adding space, members, or collaborators to the project. Therefore, it should be considered that free development tools are very useful for videogame development but they have limitations since not all their resources are available, and this way you can't have a result like a professional development team would have. If you need to have a large capacity for storage of the project you should take this into account.

Compelling and Effective Mechanics. For the participants, the design mechanics for teaching vocabulary includes finding mechanics and dynamics according to the game. This is to allow students to acquire vocabulary while interacting with the game. For them motivating vocabulary learning requires looking for more graphic and intuitive alternatives for the player. Giving the student a purpose or reason to use certain vocabulary. And even for them, there must be an educational and fun balance to obtain a game that helps the reinforcement or learning of the English language. It is indispensable to find a path that is not so evident or that the player doesn't feel like he is being taught. On the contrary, it should combine interesting mechanics with educational content, which achieves a balance between fun and learning. And finally getting the player's motivation to keep playing the game. Consequently, for the mechanics to be effective, the video game must be able to integrate mechanics and game dynamics that can attract the player's attention, and that, in turn, has a balance between learning and fun.

Mobile Devices Capability. For the participants, the diversity of mobile devices is about getting an adequate game performance. To be able to run the game on different mobile devices. To make this possible, several platform optimizations had to be performed. And they even mention that mobile device diversity is a limitation due to the lack of student devices. Achieving compatibility on different mobile devices. As well as the variety of operating systems that limited access to the game while testing sessions with students. As a result, the capacity of mobile devices must be considered, since there is a great variety of mobile devices and their characteristics. This creates a major challenge, since not all users can access the game, nor will their performance be the same.

Changes After Testing. For the developers, the changes from desktop to a mobile platform is a challenge, because the context of the game had to be changed. In addition to the continuous changes, because the students didn't like the graphic aspect, the design had to be changed again. In each retrospective and the test sessions with the students, changes were generated that consisted of adjusting or replacing some functionality or mechanics. All this because the students didn't understand or found it too complicated to interact with the game. Therefore, it should be noted that the changes after each test, is a relevant challenge for developers because it can generate a partial or total change of what was being implemented. Due to changes related to the objectives or preferences of end-users or even in the early stages of prototyping.

Advance Game Development Skills. The developers mention that time limitations influence to have something coherent and elaborated. Besides the little experience that developers had with development tools. In addition to this, the learning game development tools required additional time and work, because you had to learn how to use the tools, in this case, Unity. Finally, they say the game programming skills limitations influence that when it is required of a little more complex functionalities of the game the lack of experience or domain of the tool makes difficult the process of development. For example, bugs, problems related to the change of 2D and 3D or rotation movements of the game character. Consequently, it is important to take into account the advanced capacity of game development because of the lack of knowledge of the tools can generate difficulties in the development process.

Meet Audience Expectations. The teachers indicated that social interaction assurance can be given by allowing the video game to be connected to the Internet generating the student to be in constant learning and interaction with other students. For the participants, the players' motivation assurance is to get the attention of the users, that the game is eye-catching, interesting, intuitive, and easy to understand. Also, they indicate that teacher's motivation assurance can be affected because the requests can be difficult for the development team. Besides the fact that they are very meticulous with their do in search of the student to find a game that has correct vocabulary writing and not a traditional English class. In short, one that meets the needs and expectations of the user. For them, the limitations imposed by the game's story is in knowing how to develop a game with a story. Mixing different genres with a real vocabulary that the student can use in everyday life, makes the components very specific and difficult to reuse in other parts of the game. Besides the modeling of the characters and the elements of the game. As a result, the public's expectations should be considered. There are differences in the expectations of students and teachers. While students look for something more attractive and visually interesting, teachers look for a more educational video game.

Coherent and Compelling Story. For developers defining vocabulary categories from a story can be a challenge because the story can restrict the inclusion of a vocabulary set. Preventing the teaching of these. And even design a compelling story that fits a variety of vocabulary, because this story requires that it be attractive to players and that the vocabulary is consistent with each other. That's why a coherent game story must fit well with the theme of the game. Therefore, it should be taken into account that when developing a video game under a story, it becomes a challenge to make the story coherent and convincing, to include the vocabulary related to it, and to make it appealing to the end-users.

Interaction with the Audience in Context. For the participants knowing the target audience, it should be considered that all students are not willing to participate in the development stage. In many cases in the test activities, you do not have the required number of students. It is necessary to carry out a good process of participative diagnosis, to know key elements of the reality of the final users. For the developers, having limited resources in academic contexts implies another challenge for the EVLG, because it is not only economic but also of the personnel necessary for the development of the games. Consequently, it must be considered that interaction with the context of the audience. The video game must be friendly to the population it is aimed at, and that is where one of the greatest challenges lies since not all users have the same condition or vision of what is happening around them.

Proper Team. Developers mention that the limited team in academic contexts for EVLG's development affects because a large team is needed, to perform development stages such as design or testing. Problems you see when you don't have the experts. As a result, it must be considered that what is important is to have an adequate team, which includes all the professionals related to the development stages.

Low English Level of Target Audience. For the participants compelling and effective vocabulary delivery influences that one should look for a vocabulary that is easy to understand. Also, it allows us to teach basic vocabulary within a complex story and that the student understands within that learning strategy. This can cause students to lack game goals understanding because it is difficult to explain a game in a language unknown to the player. In addition to the fact that we are dealing with Students with a low English level. Therefore, knowing the English level of the public in which the learning is going to be developed is really important since this implies doing a much more concrete work so that the user does not feel overwhelmed with the information that is "taught".

6   Conclusion

We found that recommendations and challenges are related to aspects of motivation, development tools and processes, the history of a game and its vocabulary, the availability and limitations of resources, and EVLG developers and users. The study included the perspective of a group of developers, English teachers, and recreation professionals, leading to a comprehensive overview of EVLG's development. These participants were able to overcome the challenges by adapting to the resources available for EVLG development. Based on the experience gained from the development of EVLG, they provide the recommendations presented in this study in order to avoid or overcome the challenges encountered during the development process. However, it is necessary to include the perspective of the students regarding the EVLGs, to know the opinion and the factors that motivate them to use this type of tool for the learning of English.

References

1. Arnseth, H.C.: game studies - learning to play or playing to learn - a critical account of the models of communication informing educational research on computer gameplay. http://gamestudies.org/06010601/articles/arnseth. Accessed 12 July 2020
2. Godwin-Jones, R.: Games in language learning: opportunities and challenges. Lang. Learn. Technol. **18**(2), 9–19 (2014)
3. Prensky, M.: Listen to the Natives. Marc Prensky. **63**(4), 8–13 (2005)
4. Llach, M.D.P.A.: Dinámica del aprendizaje incidental de léxico en lengua extranjera. Nation (1997)
5. Education Intelligence: English in Colombia: An examination of policy, perceptions and influencing factors May 2015 (2015)
6. Gamboa, E., et al.: Strong shot, a student centred designed videogame for learning english vocabulary. Tecnol. Educ. **3**(3), 29–43 (2016)
7. Suaza, J. et al.: Tales of etrya: a digital game for motivating students to learn and rehearse English vocabulary. In: Ciencias Computing Memorias 13 Congress on Colombia Computing, pp. 264–280, May 2018
8. Wood, J.: Can software support children's vocabulary development? (2001)
9. FUN with Ruby Rei. https://fun.rubyrei.com/. Accessed 21 June 2020
10. Juegos educativos que conectan el mundo – Wibbu. https://wibbu.com/. Accessed 21 June 2020
11. The University's international exams group I Cambridge Assessment. https://www.cambridgeassessment.org.uk/. Accessed 21 June 2020
12. Ruby Rei convierte en un juego el aprendizaje de idiomas. www.efeescuela.es, https://www.efeescuela.es/noticias/ruby-rei-convierte-juego-aprendizaje-idiomas/. Accessed 21 June 2020
13. Trace Effects I American English. https://americanenglish.state.gov/resources/trace-effects. Accessed 21 June 2020
14. I-FLEG: A Serious Game For Second Language Acquisition. https://www.seriousgamemarket.com/2013/04/i-fleg-serious-game-for-second-language.html. Accessed 22 June 2020
15. Amoia, M., et al.: Learning a second language with a videogame. In: Proceedings of the 2011 ICT Language Learning Conference, May 2011
16. Padilla-Zea, N., et al.: Proceso de diseño para videojuegos educativos con actividades colaborativas. Dyna **82**(193), 223–232 (2015). https://doi.org/10.15446/dyna.v82n193.53498
17. Burnard, P., et al.: Analysing and presenting qualitative data. Br. Dent. J. **204**(8), 429–432 (2008). https://doi.org/10.1038/sj.bdj.2008.292

Reference Framework for Measuring the Level of Technological Acceptance by the Elderly: A Virtual Assistants Case Study

Manuel Bolaños[1]([⊠]) [iD], Cesar Collazos[2] [iD], and Francisco Gutiérrez[3] [iD]

[1] Nariño University, San Juan de Pasto, Colombia
mbolanos@udenar.edu.co
[2] Cauca University, Popayan, Colombia
ccollazo@unicauca.edu.co
[3] Granada University, Granada, Spain
fgutierr@ugr.es

Abstract. The elderly people often have problems with the use of technology. That is why today there are and are being generated a diversity of systems and applications adapted to this kind of user, to facilitate communication with their social environment, and serve as support for their daily tasks. Motivation and technological acceptance are very important and key aspects to ensure the usability of technological systems by the elderly. Issues related to such a situation can be solved with a good definition of requirements, which allows identifying the true characteristics and functionalities that this kind of user expected to find in these products. Technology developed for the elderly must meet their essential expectations so that they accept and adopt it in their daily lives. This paper shows the results of a study developed to identify the intention of a group of the elderly to use intelligent virtual assistants, and the activities in which they consider these devices would be useful.

Keywords: Technology acceptance · Smart virtual assistant · Elderly · Usability

1 Introduction

The elderly represents a growing proportion of the world population. According to the United Nations report, 9% of the population corresponds to people 65 years of age and older in 2019, and such a percentage is becoming higher due to the increase in age in life expectancy, so it is expected that by 2050 this kind of people reaches 16% of the world's population, as shown in Fig. 1[1].

Today, cultural stereotypes about aging have led people to experience some fear of the arrival of this stage of the natural lifecycle. Such a situation can cause episodes of depression and even social and emotional isolation [2]. Therefore, understanding how the elderly use technology products, also understanding how are their environments, in order to respond with innovative design can help meet the challenges of an aging population [3]. In consequence, using rapidly advancing technology as a tool to provide user-friendly devices and applications can benefit the elderly's lifestyle [4].

© Springer Nature Switzerland AG 2020
V. Agredo-Delgado et al. (Eds.): HCI-COLLAB 2020, CCIS 1334, pp. 203–212, 2020.
https://doi.org/10.1007/978-3-030-66919-5_21

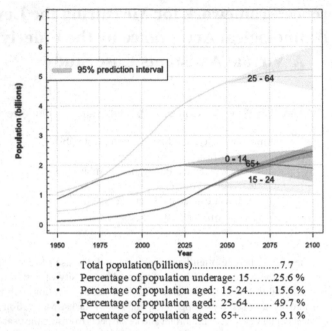

- Total population(billions)..............................7.7
- Percentage of population underage: 15.......25.6 %
- Percentage of population aged: 15-24......... 15.6 %
- Percentage of population aged: 25-64......... 49.7 %
- Percentage of population aged: 65+............. 9.1 %

Fig. 1. World population projection by age groups [1].

The increase in the elderly has led to the development of appropriate solutions for this kind of user, and although there are some ICT-based services designed to help and improve their quality of life, there is not an entire relationship between services and ease of use, which reduces its usefulness. It should be noted that technological products developed for the elderly must be accessible, attractive, and easy to use.

Most software development initiatives target users with technological abilities and skills, leaving aside a great potential of possible users. They are motivated to learn, to keep their brains active, and to be able to interact in the digital society in which they are immersed [5].

When applications are developed or systems are built for the elderly, they are generally sought to be robust, stable, and reliable; however, it cannot be guaranteed that these requirements are those that the elderly require for their acceptance and use. Implementing characteristics such as the size or the colors used in the interface does not guarantee its usability and acceptability. In this vein, this kind of users must perceive valuable services and usefulness, because the simple offer of services does not guarantee it [6]. Also, it is important that technologies for the elderly provide different functionalities to carry out daily activities, and not focus only on solving medical problems [7].

Technology products developed for the elderly must meet the essential expectations of users to be accepted and adopted in their daily lives. Besides, the elderly must not be intimidated by the complexity of installing and using applications, as they may feel unmotivated to use them [7].

The making of a study to determine the intention of the elderly to use technology can determine the elements and characteristics they expect to find when interacting with technological devices and systems, which will be reflected in the future design and implementation of solutions for this kind of users, and this particular case, in the design of playful experiences supported by smart virtual assistants.

2 Smart Virtual Assistants

Virtual assistants are technological tools created to facilitate different processes and activities of daily life, and they can generate an experience closer to the interaction with people in their social environment.

The elderly can have pleasant experiences when interacting with virtual assistants since they could reduce certain problems that such users have in terms of technology acceptance; Virtual assistants are usually systems based on interaction paradigms such as voice, they do not require much learning, they are easy to use, and they integrate well with their usual social environment which facilitates their acceptance.

Virtual assistants in the market, such as the Echo Dot Alexa, Siri, Google Assistant, Cortana, and Bixby, shown in Fig. 2, have become a great help to integrate and keep the elderly active, in addition to facilitating the different tasks that are done daily [8].

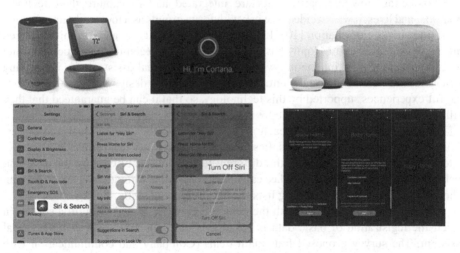

Fig. 2. Smart virtual assistants.

Virtual assistants offer different functionalities for users, and they have useful features that allow them to be easily and quickly integrated into so-called smart homes. These devices have some functionalities such as: turning the lights on and off, adjusting the temperature, and turning on or interacting with other technological devices; Also, they can search for information online, consulting about the weather status, set reminders, play music, make restaurant reservations, manage emails, and make calls, among others [9]. Thus, smart virtual assistants have gradually become an indispensable element for the development of daily activities of any kind of people.

3 Development Methodology

The objectives of the study were to know the intentions of using smart virtual assistants by the elderly and to identify the characteristics that they as users would like to find when interacting with this kind of devices so that the information obtained serves to contribute to the design of playful experiences supported by virtual assistants.

For the development of the study, there was a group of 24 older adults from Pasto city (in southern Colombia), who have prioritized certain daily activities depending on their roles, so they were integrated into the following four groups:

- A first group made up of people who created a club more than 20 years ago with public sector employees.
- Another group that meets periodically for physical and sports activities.
- A third group made up of professionals who are and were active in university teaching full and emeritus professors.
- The last group is made up of the elderly who develop their activities in a nursing home.

Considering how the participants are integrated and to capture their feelings, thoughts, and lives, it was decided to work with focus groups as a tool to obtain accurate, clear, and simple information [10]. In order to do that, a survey and a semi-structured interview were prepared to know basic information about each of the participants and their expectations after interacting with an intelligent virtual assistant, for identifying preferences and elements to take into account in the future design and development of playful experiences supported by this technology, so that it can be guaranteed that they will have a high level of acceptance by the elderly.

An induction was made with each group about what the smart virtual assistant is, about its purpose, and how it works. In such a case, Echo Dot® from Amazon was used. Later, the elderly interacted with the different functionalities offered by the assistant, such as the administration of agendas, calendars, scheduling reminders, interaction with other devices, scheduling shopping lists, and entertainment skills, among others.

After the elderly interacted with the device, they were invited to fulfill a survey, in which the registration of basic data is requested, and their interest in using a virtual assistant. The survey proposed four main items (Company and communication with family and friends, reminders, help with housework, and help with medical procedures).

Once the survey was completed, an interview was conducted with each of the groups, with three main points: *How comfortable did you feel when interacting with the virtual assistant? How do you consider the interaction with the device? And describe your experience, highlighting the positive aspects and the aspects that you consider should be improved.*

Finally, the analysis of the information collected was developed following the objective of the research.

4 Results

The information recorded in the surveys and that collected with the interviews allows to show the perception of the participating older adults towards the acceptance of the virtual assistant and the interest in using it to carry out different activities of their daily life.

Table 1 shows the results corresponding to the basic information recorded by the 24 participants, which allows knowledge of relevant data for the research.

Table 1. General information of participants.

Gender	Self-sufficient	Any disease?	Require medication	Live alone	Income	Work	Age
Male	Yes	Yes	Yes	No	Yes	No	83
Female	Yes	No	No	No	Yes	Yes	72
Male	Yes	No	No	No	Yes	No	85
Female	Yes	No	No	No	Yes	Yes	72
Male	Yes	Yes	Yes	No	Yes	No	85
Male	Yes	No	No	No	Yes	No	83
Female	Yes	Yes	Yes	No	Yes	Yes	75
Female	Yes	Ycs	Yes	No	Yes	Yes	62
Female	Yes	Yes	Yes	No	Yes	No	69
Male	Yes	Yes	Yes	No	Yes	Yes	61
Female	Yes	Yes	Yes	No	Yes	No	70
Female	Yes	Yes	Yes	No	Yes	No	78
Male	Yes	No	No	No	Yes	Yes	74
Male	Yes	No	No	No	Yes	Yes	63
Male	Yes	No	No	No	Yes	Yes	64
Male	Yes	No	No	No	Yes	Yes	62
Male	Yes	No	No	No	Yes	Yes	68
Male	Yes	No	No	No	Yes	Yes	61
Male	Yes	Yes	Yes	No	No	No	68
Female	Yes	Yes	Yes	No	No	No	71
Male	Yes	Yes	Yes	No	Yes	No	81
Female	Yes	No	No	No	No	No	70
Female	Yes	No	No	No	No	No	72
Male	Yes	No	No	No	Yes	Yes	68

According to the above, it can be observed that all participants show self-sufficiency to do their daily activities; This makes it possible to anticipate that for the moment, some type of help or special activity is not necessary for the elderly to interact in the following stages of the research.

The recorded data indicates that 45.83% of the participants have at least one disease and are taking medications, which opens the picture to think about using virtual assistant functionalities such as reminders about names, dosage, and time of taking medications, as well as scheduling medical appointments.

100% of the participants live with other people, close relatives, who provide accompaniment and help. This information is important if it is taken into account that support can be had in those companions to fulfill one of the fundamental objectives of the recreational experiences that they want to design, which is to promote and generate collaborative environments so that the elderly could interact with the device in group activities with greater confidence, also allowing them to integrate socially, and have help with the use of technology in case of being necessary.

In the economic aspect, it can be seen that 83.33% of the elderly receive income and 50% are currently working, which allows them to have a certain level of freedom and autonomy in making decisions regarding investing in the acquisition of technology. Besides, they are people who can use virtual assistants for daily activities at home and tasks related to their work, so they could induce co-workers and their friends to use these types of devices if their experience of use is positive.

Table 2 shows the preferences of the participating older adults regarding the activities for which they would use a virtual assistant, and in Table 3, the total and the percentages regarding the preferences of the participants can be observed.

It is important to register that 79.16% of the participants consider that they would use the virtual assistant for at least one of the four proposed activities, which is an important percentage if one takes into account that all of them are self-sufficient in terms of performing their daily tasks, and their preference is not associated with an imperative need.

When observing that 62.5% register that they would use a virtual assistant for company and communication, it allows inferring the need for this type of people to integrate and avoid social isolation.

50% of the participants would use virtual assistants to do some medical procedures, which can enhance the use of some of the functionalities offered by these devices, such as the creation of agendas and lists of activities.

Housework, with a 45.8% preference, shows that nearly half of the participants find an opportunity in virtual assistants to have control within their daily work circle; It should be noted that these self-imposed itineraries constitute unavoidable operations for their well-being.

The reminders with 29.16% have the lowest percentage preference, which is the reflection that the group of participants consider themselves self-sufficient in terms of doing their daily activities, and they feel having full use of their cognitive and memory skills.

The information obtained allows us to show that before developing playful strategies supported by virtual assistants, it is necessary to deepen the research to define strategies that make it possible to equate somehow the different activities in which adults consider they can use virtual assistants.

Table 2. Preferences in the activities that virtual assistants could use.

	Company and communication	Reminders	Housework	Medications
Group 1	X			X
	X	X	X	X
				X
	X		X	X
Group 2	X	X	X	X
	X	X	X	X
	X		X	
	X		X	X
	X	X	X	X
	X	X	X	X
Group 3	X			
	X		X	X
				X
	X			
Group 4		X	X	
			X	
	X	X		X
	X			
	X			

Table 3. Consolidated preferences in the use of a virtual assistant.

	Company and communication	Reminders	Housework	Medications
Group 1	3	1	2	4
Group 2	6	4	6	5
Group 3	3	0	1	2
Group 4	3	2	2	1
	62,50%	29,16%	45,83%	50%

Table 4 shows the most important positive aspects and the recommendations of the participants after their interaction with the virtual assistant. Also, some research notes are recorded, which are important aspects and must be considered in the design of the recreational experiences to be developed.

Table 4. Positive aspects, recommendations, and elements to consider in the future.

	Positive aspects	Recommendations	Research notes
Group 1	It is a device that can greatly help the elderly to remember things to do like medical appointments, meetings	The device should be wireless for portability The device should be smaller and lighter	Identify strategies to strengthen reminder functionalities Consider the design and portability of the device
Group 2	Alexa is very useful, especially to remind the elderly about things, since we are very prone to forgetting, and it also serves as a company	The device is very useful when one is at home, but it would be much more useful if it were portable, not dependent on the electrical current It would be nice to be able to personalize it, have it in a more friendly way, including a more familiar voice	Consider that it should be strengthened in the functionalities related to reminders, and tasks related to games, curiosities, and entertainment
Group 3	It is very useful for people who have memory problems, as it can remind them of different things like taking medicine, or simply that they require the company to keep their cognitive abilities active	It would be important that the device could be carried everywhere because the elderly are not going to stay at home all the time	Identify strategies that help maintain active cognitive skills Strengthen functionalities related to reminders Consider the design features of the device
Group 4	It would be very useful to remember things like where a receipt was left or when it should be paid. It serves as a company and serves to facilitate some activities	It must always be connected to the electrical current. It would be nice if it had a rechargeable battery to be able to carry it to activities like going out to exercise. It could be used as a decorative element if it had another shape	Consider allowing access to Web apps related to the provision of services Consider the design features and portability of the device

The results obtained both in the responses recorded in the survey and the interview with each group are satisfactory about the acceptance of the virtual assistant and its functionalities. Likewise, important information was obtained about certain characteristics that the participants would like to be implemented in this type of device to improve their level of acceptance and adaptability.

In the positive aspects and recommendations, it is appreciated that the elderly, in their expressions without realizing much, learn some new habits and learn habits from their friends and family, which are gradually incorporated in order to create favorable circumstances in the development of their activities at different times and situations. This input for research puts on the table the willingness of the participants to learn new ways of doing things; they can follow a cognitive process that leads them to see the usefulness of the technology.

The appraisals made by the participating the elderly and listed in Table 4 can be seen as added in Fig. 3, which expresses the context before and after the acceptance of technology, where ergonomics is made between tastes and the range of functions offered by the virtual assistant.

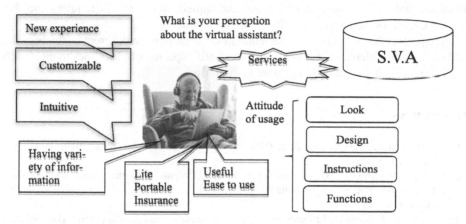

Fig. 3. Contexts before and after the acceptance of technology by older adults.

Focusing the descriptive analysis on the graph, the devices must conform to the physical characteristics required by the user. From this, it can be inferred that the user has prior knowledge, is interacting with information, and has developed a habit of use. The ergonomics represented in the service connects the user with the services offered by the Web through virtual assistants, to promote the incorporation of the daily activities of the elderly in an experience of using technology, which is acquired little by little as a habit with a view to adaptability, so that real-life activities are complemented with virtual activities in terms of efficiency and effectiveness.

5 Future Work

In order to have a specific tool that allows the development of technological acceptance studies by the elderly, it is necessary to analyze each of the existing technology acceptance models in order to determine if any of them include the elements necessary to guarantee that its application will allow having clear and precise results, or if, on the contrary, it is necessary to define a new technology acceptance model to be applied specifically for older adults.

6 Conclusions

The recommendations made by the elderly are the basis for proposing and designing playful strategies with the characteristics that this kind of user would like to find.

It is necessary to develop a technology acceptance study aimed specifically at the elderly so that each of the necessary factors can be precisely identified so that they perceive valuable services and usefulness in technological products, which can guarantee their usability and acceptability.

Smart virtual assistants facilitate the development of work, recreational, and even health-related activities for the elderly thanks to their oral interface, their ease of use, and the level of acceptance they have among users.

Considering the particularities of older adults, it is necessary to define strategies that allow technology developers to understand and implement the specific requirements that facilitate their use and acceptance by these types of users.

Technology has become a fundamental pillar of help in the different contexts of the daily life of the elderly, so it is necessary to identify specific product lines to meet each of the needs of this large and important kind of users.

References

1. United Nations: Perspectivas de la Población Mundial 2019, New York (2019). https://population.un.org/wpp/
2. Carbajo, M.: Mitos y estereotipos sobre la vejez. Propuesta de una concepción realista y tolerante. Rev. Fac. Educ. Albacete 87–96 (2009). https://dialnet.unirioja.es/servlet/articulo?codigo=3282988
3. Weintraub, R., Colucci, J.: Design Thinking can improve care for the elderly. Harverd Bus. Rev. (2015). https://hbr.org/2015/12/design-thinking-can-help-improve-care-for-the-elderly
4. Syeda, M., Kwon, Y.: Photo alive! Application and method for intergenerational social communication. In: International Conference on Advanced Communication Technology, ICACT, pp. 326–332 (2017). https://doi.org/10.1007/978-3-540-39850-9_30
5. Guo, P.: Older adults learning computer programming: motivations, frustrations, and design opportunities. In: Conference on Human Factors in Computing Systems- Proceedings, 2017-May, pp. 7070–7083 (2017). https://doi.org/10.1145/3025453.3025945
6. Rodríguez, F., Ochoa, S., Gutierrez, F.: Seamlessly mediation of social interaction services respecting communication preferences In: Proceedings, vol. 2, pp. 1249 (2018). https://doi.org/10.3390/proceedings2191249
7. Shore, L., Power, V., de Eyto, A., O'Sullivan, L.: Technology acceptance and user-centred design of assistive exoskeletons for older adults: A commentary. Robotics 7, 1–13 (2018). https://doi.org/10.3390/robotics7010003
8. McLaughlin, M.: What a virtual assistant is and how it works. https://www.lifewire.com/virtual-assistants-413853
9. Reis, A., Paulino, D., Paredes, H., Barroso, J.: Using intelligent personal assistants to strengthen the elderlies' social bonds. In: Antona, M., Stephanidis, C. (eds.) UAHCI 2017. LNCS, vol. 10279, pp. 593–602. Springer, Cham (2017). https://doi.org/10.1007/978-3-319-58700-4_48
10. Kitzinger, J.: Qualitative research: introducing focus groups. BMJ 311, 299 (1995). https://doi.org/10.1136/bmj.311.7000.299

Relaxing and Familiar, Guidelines to Develop Interactive Applications for Dementia Patients

Diana Millares[(⊠)] [ID], Andrés Serrato [ID], Juan Castro [ID], Nathalia Ceballos [ID], Edwin Gamboa [ID], and María Trujillo [ID]

Universidad del Valle, Santiago de Cali, Colombia
{diana.millares,andres.serrato,juan.castro.vasquez,
nathalia.ceballos.hurtado,edwin.gamboa,
maria.trujillo}@correounivalle.edu.co

Abstract. Dementia describes a group of symptoms affecting memory, thinking and social abilities. Treatments aim to improve levels of functionality of patients with dementia. Some patients may experience catastrophic episodes during their treatment, these episodes are characterised by excessive emotions or physical response. Psychiatrists have used supportive tools and therapies to improve patients' levels of functionality, trying to prevent and decrease catastrophic episodes. In this study, we present *Memento*, an application designed for catastrophic episodes management in patients with dementia through Information Technology. To develop *Memento*, we identified design aspects that should be considered when developing an application to reduce catastrophic episodes. Our main contribution is the classification of these aspects. To do this, we have analysed our findings in specifications which include the patient needs and characteristics; therapy guidelines; area or environment of interaction; dementia action protocol; and user interface navigation. Our findings may serve as guidelines for the design and development of interactive applications targeted at patients with dementia.

Keywords: Dementia · Development · Treatment · Application · Design · Catastrophic episodes

1 Introduction

Dementia is a syndrome that mainly affects memory, thinking, orientation, comprehension, calculation, learning capacity, language, and judgement. It is caused by diseases and injuries that affect the brain, such as Alzheimer's disease or stroke [1]. Dementia symptoms can be classified into three stages: early, middle and late; early-stage includes forgetfulness, losing track of the time and becoming lost in familiar places [1]. Treatments for patients with dementia are primarily aimed at achieving an improvement in levels of functionality, these treatments may include occupational therapy sessions, music therapy, multi-sensorial stimulation or reality orientation therapy [2]. Some patients may experience catastrophic episodes during the treatment, also known as catastrophic reactions or agitation. These episodes are characterised by the excessive and abrupt emotional

V. Agredo-Delgado et al. (Eds.): HCI-COLLAB 2020, CCIS 1334, pp. 213–222, 2020.
https://doi.org/10.1007/978-3-030-66919-5_22

or physical response, such as anger, verbal and physical aggression [3]; and can be generated by aspects related with changes in behaviour or delirium, medication, environmental stressor(s), unmet needs, inexperienced or intrusive care-giving or aspects of the cognitive disturbance [4].

Recently, there has been an increasing development of interactive applications focused on dementia, the main idea of these applications is to delay the health decline, help patients to maintain autonomy and social relationships, as well as promote a relaxed state of mind [5]. Therefore, we developed *Memento* as an application to support therapies for patients with dementia at a local hospital. *Memento* comprises two main components. First, a web-based application that includes the discussion of activities, events and past experiences, using tangible stimuli such as photographs. Second, a scenario editor, in which a patient can create different scenarios using the objects available, three base scenarios (the house, the garden, the lake) are available to start editing. Both components are intended to be used always under psychiatrist supervision, who is responsible for personalising a session according to a patient's personal needs. *Memento* was developed following an incremental, iterative and user-centred methodology. Thus, a group of psychiatrists were engaged in the whole development process to make health-related decisions and validate each prototype.

2 Related Work

Several serious games and interactive applications for different aspects of dementia have been developed [5], e.g. virtual reality has been implemented to show relaxing scenes for dementia patients. One of these applications is *ImmersiCare*, which has a high control of what happens in each scene [6].

There are also applications for people with dementia that focus on the person's inhibition capacity, physical activity using virtual reality, and reminiscence therapy [7–9]. Some aspects to be taken into account, as well as the technical requirements, for the development of applications for dementia are mentioned, but they are not completely clear from medical personnel and developers point of view.

Barriers to Co-Designing Mobile Technology with Persons with Dementia and Their Carers, an article that adopted a qualitative exploratory case study design with people involved in the co-design of 'My House of Memories', a mobile app. The results obtained showed difficulty in becoming familiar with the application and learning how to use it due to the skills of the diseased patients. Other issues founded were inaccurate perceptions of how people with dementia or carers would use technology which meant many initial design ideas had to be scrapped or significantly changed [10].

Factors Influencing the Adoption of Smart Health Technologies for People with Dementia and Their Informal Caregivers: Scoping Review and Design Framework, a study that focuses on the technology adoption factors of dementia patients and their caregivers. The results revealed a list of factors influencing the adoption of technologies. Four domains were found to consider for the design and development of technologies for this population: cognitive decline domain, physical decline domain, social domain, and development domain [11].

In the design area, it was concluded that patients with dementia respond better to devices that have a familiar aspect. Regarding the design of the user interface, it has to be simple and easy to use. This includes considerations such as appropriate colours, background styles, text font and size, and sounds to adapt to patients' hearing and vision [11].

3 Design and Development Guidelines Identification

Based on the results obtained from the development of *Memento*, we conducted a qualitative study to identify a set of relevant guidelines to consider during the design and development of applications for early-stage dementia patients. All or most of the guidelines could be considered to improve the user experience.

3.1 Participants

Two health professionals specialised in psychiatry, both belong to a local hospital, and two systems engineering students, have participated in the study conducted. Their characteristics are presented in Table 1.

Table 1. Characteristics of the participants.

Title	Years of experience	Role
Systems engineering student	–	Programmer, designer
Systems engineering student	–	Programmer, designer
Psychiatrist 1	24	Tester
Psychiatrist 2	2	Tester

3.2 Procedure

Data is collected through semi-structured interviews[1], asking psychiatrists about the characteristics of the activities they normally conduct to treat patients, the information they are interested to collect and the results they expect to obtain with the use of *Memento*. Data collected from the developers was regarding what scenarios should be included, what colours should be used, the devices where the application should be available and the dementia stage it is focused on. The session has a duration of approximately one hour.

3.3 Analysis

The collected data were transcribed into a spreadsheet and analysed using the thematic analysis method [12]. We produced a list of statements related to the objective of the study, then assigned a code to each statement, the codes are then grouped into categories. This method is performed with a total of two iterations, the first iteration individually by the study members and the second one in a group manner.

---

[1] https://cutt.ly/ByuUNEq.

3.4 Obtained Classification

During the development of the thematic analysis, categories were found related to the therapeutic meaning, approach, interactive area, action protocol and the user interface navigation, which will be explained in the following section.

4 Findings

We found 33 statements regarding the design aspects of the application. These statements are grouped into Therapeutic Meaning (6 statements), User Interface Navigation (8 statements), Interactive Area (5 statements), Approach (4 statements), Action Protocol (10 statements) which is divided into Characterisation (2 statements) and Tracking (8 statements). A summary of the findings is presented in Fig. 1. Additionally, a *persona* model was created from the information to characterise the target audience.

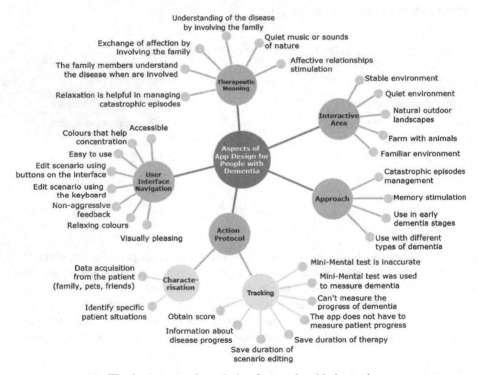

Fig. 1. Aspects of app design for people with dementia.

4.1 Therapeutic Meaning

According to the participant statements, it is suggested to include quiet music or sounds of nature that allow a state of relaxation, which is useful for managing catastrophic episodes. Additionally, the stimulation of emotional relationships through the exchange of affection helps patients progress significantly. Thus, involving the family is an important factor, since family members understand the situation better when they are involved in it, which in turn generates a better understanding of the disease.

4.2 User Interface Navigation

Participants expect the application to meet both patient and psychiatrist friendly aspects such as accessibility criteria, to be easy and intuitive to use, and to be visually pleasing, ideally including a colour palette that stimulates patient concentration as well as providing non-aggressive feedback. Besides, the scenarios can be edited using different interfaces; e.g. graphic interface or keyboard in the case of applications running on a computer.

4.3 Interactive Area

It is important that the interactive area or play area, in which a patient is immersed, provides a space for relaxation. The use of outdoor nature-related environments (e.g. ocean, beaches, farms, ocean, lakes) and familiar surroundings are ideal settings to use.

4.4 Action Protocol

Participants consider it important to include aspects related to specific patient situations; that is, the application has to allow the collection of information associated with everyday aspects of their lives (e.g., family members, pets, friends). Similarly, participants mention that the application should focus on the degree of dementia through the *Mini-mental* test [13], which despite not being an exact test, allows a first approach to the patient's level of dementia. Additionally, it is important to collect usage data (e.g. time of editing the scenario, score, duration of therapy).

4.5 Approach

The participants mentioned that the application may help different types of dementia, by controlling the catastrophic episodes that patients present, and in particular patients who are in the early stages of dementia. It also stimulates memory, which is useful in treating dementia.

4.6 Persona Model Characterising Dementia Patients

We were able to create four *persona* models[2] for the application, with the information obtained from the interviews and doing research. These models have common symptoms, characteristics and needs that people with dementia can experience; the skills that are most affected in the early stage; besides the factors that can lead to dementia.

---

[2] https://cutt.ly/fa2RDRo.

5 Discussion

This paper aims to identify relevant guidelines that should be considered when developing an application for the treatment of patients with dementia. The aspects involved in carrying out this study are related to the action protocol, the approach, the interactive area, the characteristics of the patients and the navigation in the user interface.

According to our findings, when developing applications for dementia patients, the whole visual section of the application (both within the interaction area and within the interface) should be built to generate a relaxing environment (quiet sounds and light colours). In particular, the dynamics included in the application should also be constructed, ideally including the family environment, so that family members understand the situation and have greater participation in the therapies. The above is important because excessive noise or stimulation, new or unfamiliar surroundings, or disruption in the patient's daily routine are common causes of catastrophic episodes in dementia [4]. Besides, the selected dynamics should contribute to the recovery of abilities that tend to be lost or have been affected by dementia (e.g. orientation, memory, understanding).

Our findings show that to approach or treat dementia through digital resources, it is necessary to take into account two key stages in the action protocol. The first stage deals with the characterisation of the patient, which allows us to identify specific situations. Also, to acquire information that will allow us, in later stages, to carry out a follow-up taking into account the information collected previously. Likewise, in the second stage, we can provide an approach to the level of dementia of the patient when starting the use of the application. The data collected during each session allows to provide information on the progress of a patient. Treatment follow-up may help identify even undiagnosed medical conditions [4].

Also, pleasant feedback is important to provide, and therefore, avoid any information that could be aggressive to a patient. Furthermore, the second part of the application, *Memento Builder*, was developed to be used with web technologies, to provide an alternative for patients who may be affected by the possible side effects of the use of virtual reality technology (e.g., dizziness, discomfort, etc.).

6 Prototype

Memento is an application to support therapies for dementia patients to avoid or reduce catastrophic episodes. The application is composed of some activities to offer a personalised experience to patients and support specific neuropsychiatric symptoms in dementia. In *Memento*, therapies are intended to be conducted under professional psychiatric supervision. This way, psychiatrists will be able to support therapies; also to manage and visualise data associated with therapy sessions. The application is divided into two main sections: *Memento Web App* and *Memento Builder*.

- *Memento Web App*: This section aims to work memory, including the patient emotional relationships and follow-up the patient with some activities of the *Mini-mental* test [13]. This section is shown in Fig. 2. It is composed of:

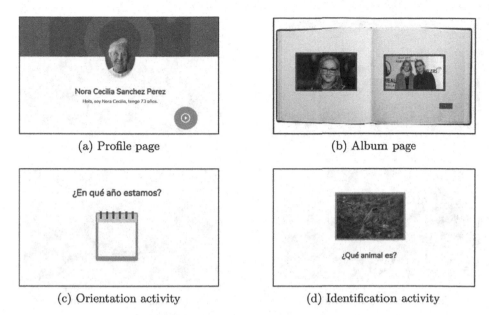

(a) Profile page   (b) Album page

(c) Orientation activity   (d) Identification activity

Fig. 2. Modules in *Memento Web App*

1. Profile page: In Fig. 2.a). Chosen based on possible therapeutic effects to keep a patient up to date with his/her life. When a patient is created in the application, it starts with a form to collect personal information. The form is filled out by the caregivers to keep them involved in the process.
2. Album page: In Fig. 2.b). Suggested by the psychiatrists so that the patient remembers and stimulates their emotional relationships, it can include pets and even caregivers. After seeing the whole album, which is focused on one of the patient affective relationships. We try to stimulate the memory, making a test about the relationship that the patient has just observed.
3. Activities Page: In Fig. 2.c) and d). Suggested by the psychiatrists, these activities based on the *Mini-mental* test, are intended to follow the patient in addition to strengthening him/her in memory, calculation, attention and language. Patients get a score from each of these activities. In this module, when the patient makes a mistake, friendly messages are displayed, to prevent any kind of inconvenience.

- *Memento Builder*: This section aims to distract the patient and work on memory. This section is shown in Fig. 3. It is composed of:

1. Base scenarios:
a) The house: In Fig. 3.b). Suggested by the psychiatrists for the patient to remember how is the distribution of the rooms in a house, that is, in which room do the objects go. The objects included to create the scenario are divided into five different categories, as of kitchen objects, living room objects, bedroom objects, home appliances and bathroom objects.

(a) Tutorial

(b) House Scenario Editor

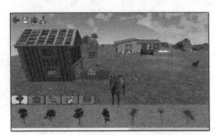

(c) Garden Scenario Editor

(d) Lake Scenario Editor

Fig. 3. Scenario editor in *Memento Builder*

b) The Garden: In Fig. 3.c). Chosen based on the possible therapeutic effects of a nat-
    ural outdoor landscape, for people with dementia, by spending time in this environ-
    ment [14]. The objects included to create the scenario are divided into five different
    categories, as trees, flowers, wild animals, domestic animals and decoration.

c) The Lake: In Fig. 3.d). Chosen taking into account that incorporating a landscape
    with green and blue components, like trees and lakes, rivers or the sea, can be
    regarded as a specific subset of therapeutic landscapes [14]. The objects included to
    create the scenario are the same as the Garden scenario.

2. Scenario Editor: With the editor, the user can create a scenario with the objects
    available in the object bar, in this bar the objects are classified by categories. Each
    object can be moved from its position with the position editor, or with the directional
    arrow keys, and can be rotated on itself with the rotation editor, or with using the
    keyboard.

3. Tutorial: In Fig. 3.a). It explains the actions that can be performed within the Scenario
    Editor, e.g. move the objects in the scenario.

7 Limitations and Future Work

The main limitation of this study is its qualitative approach, besides this, within the
framework of this study we do not have a perspective of the patients, ideally, more
psychiatrists should be included to have a greater number of statements and find new
aspects to take into account. Therefore, future work should be carried out considering the
patients' perspective and including a greater number of associated psychiatrists. Besides,
user experience evaluation has to be conducted for evaluating if *Memento* allows patients

to avoid or reduce catastrophic episodes by offering a compelling and personalised experience and distracting from their clinical condition. Also, the guidelines identified could be classified according to the relationships that can be determined between these aspects, and also according to the stage in which the application development is set.

8   Final Remarks

Design applications for dementia patients should take into account the visual aspect, the proper use of colours and sound that allow the patient to feel calm and relax, due to the disease and related symptomatology. Additional, it is important to focus on building a personalised environment, involving the family of the patient and stimulating their emotional relationships. Furthermore, collecting information that has been worked on in each session by the patient to track the disease helps to identify new symptoms and specific situations.

The study carried out presents certain criteria for the design of applications for people with dementia, which can be taken into account during the implementation. For this case study, corrections should be made in the future to include the criteria that have not been taken into account in the first version. The development of applications for people with dementia cannot be taken lightly, the design is one of the main factors, for the operation and incorporation of technology, as well as the long-term engagement of patients and caregivers.

References

1. World Health Organization: Dementia (2013). https://www.who.int/news-room/fact-sheets/detail/dementia. Accessed 24 Mar 2020
2. Servicio Canario de la Salud y Gobierno de Canarias: Manual de actuación en la enfermedad de alzheimer y otras demencias. Canarias: Gobierno de Canarias, Consejería de Sanidad (2011)
3. del Pino, A.C.S., Arqués, M.A.G., Martín, A.M.: Alteraciones conductuales en la enfermedad de alzheimer. Semergen: revista española de medicina de familia (11), 541–545 (2005). https://doi.org/10.1016/S1138-3593(05)72987-7
4. Kimchi, E.Z., Lyketsos, C.G.: Management of agitation in dementia. In: Halter, J.B., Ouslander, J.G., Studenski, S., High, K.P., Asthana, S., Supiano, M.A., Ritchie, C. (eds.) Hazzard's Geriatric Medicine and Gerontology, 7e., chap. 74. McGraw-Hill Education, New York (2017)
5. McCallum, S., Boletsis, C.: dementia games: a literature review of dementia-related serious games. In: Ma, M., Oliveira, M.F., Petersen, S., Hauge, J.B. (eds.) SGDA 2013. LNCS, vol. 8101, pp. 15–27. Springer, Heidelberg (2013). https://doi.org/10.1007/978-3-642-40790-1_2
6. Immersicare. https://www.immersicare.com/. Accessed 29 Mar 2020
7. Tong, T., Chan, J.H., Chignell, M.: Serious games for dementia. In: Proceedings of the 26th International Conference on World Wide Web Companion, pp. 1111–1115 (2017). https://doi.org/10.1145/3041021.3054930
8. Eisapour, M., Cao, S., Boger, J.: Participatory design and evaluation of virtual reality games to promote engagement in physical activity for people living with dementia. J. Rehabil. Assist. Technol. Eng. 7 (2020). https://doi.org/10.1177/2055668320913770
9. McCallum, S.: Gamification and serious games for personalized health. In: pHealth, pp. 85–96 (2012). https://doi.org/10.3233/978-1-61499-069-7-85

10. O'Connor, S., Bouamrane, M.M., O'Donnell, C.A., Mair, F.S.: Barriers to co-designing mobile technology with persons with dementia and their carers. Nurs. Inform. **225**, 1028–1029 (2016)
11. Guisado-Fernández, E., Giunti, G., Mackey, L.M., Blake, C., Caulfield, B.M.: Factors influencing the adoption of smart health technologies for people with dementia and their informal caregivers: scoping review and design framework. JMIR Aging **2**(1) (2019). https://doi.org/10.2196/12192
12. Burnard, P., Gill, P., Stewart, K., Treasure, E., Chadwick, B.: Analysing and presenting qualitative data. Br. Dent. J. **204**(8), 429–432 (2008). https://doi.org/10.1038/sj.bdj.2008.292
13. Folstein, M.F., Robins, L.N., Helzer, J.E.: The mini-mental state examination. Arch. Gen. Psychiatry **40**(7), 812 (1983). https://doi.org/10.1001/archpsyc.1983.01790060110016
14. Motealleh, P., Moyle, W., Jones, C., Dupre, K.: Creating a dementia-friendly environment through the use of outdoor natural landscape design intervention in long-term care facilities: a narrative review. Health Place **58** (2019). https://doi.org/10.1016/j.healthplace.2019.102148

Rivit: A Digital Game to Cognitively Train and Entertain Heart Failure Patients

David Crespo$^{(\boxtimes)}$ ⓘ, Melissa Fuentes ⓘ, Edwin Gamboa ⓘ, Kevin Franco ⓘ,
Kevin Domínguez ⓘ, and Maria Trujillo ⓘ

Universidad del Valle, Cali, Colombia
{david.crespo,melissa.fuentes,edwin.gamboa,franco.kevin,
kevin.dominguez,maria.trujillo}@correounivalle.edu.co

Abstract. People with heart failure tend to develop cognitive impairments, anxiety and constant boredom due to the time they have to wait to get surgery while being hospitalised. Serious games may assist these in improving their cognitive abilities and get distracted while waiting for surgery. In this paper, we present Rivit, a collection mini-games aimed at improving cognition and mood of heart failure patients, which is still under development. We present the current state of the game and a preliminary user experience evaluation. The aim of this evaluation is to identify the strengths and weaknesses of Rivit so that it can be tested with real patients at a later stage. Although the evaluation was not conducted with real heart failure patients, we found that elderly people may need more effort than young people to understand game goals. Our work may serve as a basis for developers of games aimed at heart failure patients during early development stages.

Keywords: Serious game · User experience evaluation · Heart failure · Cognitive training

1 Introduction

Cognitive functions play a fundamental role in the processing of information that affects our perception of reality. The deterioration of these functions may be due to lifestyle, substance abuse, or disease such as cardiovascular disease, which affects blood flow to the brain. Among these diseases is heart failure, one of the most common heart diseases around the world. Almost one up to three people of 55 years of age will develop this syndrome at some point in their remaining lifespan [1]. Cognitive impairment is common in heart failure patients and shares an independent relationship [2]. There is an incidence that varies from 25% to 50%, and even up to 80% among heart failure patients in cognitive areas such as working memory, concentration, and executive function [2–4]

Heart failure patients have to remain hospitalized while waiting to get their required surgery. Depending on the hospital's capacity, they may have to wait even months before being operated. In some cases, they are barely able to do any other activity other than stay on bed all day. During this time, patients tend to develop anxiety, constant boredom, and even depression. According to [5], there is a relation between some mental illnesses and

© Springer Nature Switzerland AG 2020
V. Agredo-Delgado et al. (Eds.): HCI-COLLAB 2020, CCIS 1334, pp. 223–232, 2020.
https://doi.org/10.1007/978-3-030-66919-5_23

hearth failure. In a sample of 153 heart failure patients, 36% have depression according to the Beck Depression Inventory-II [6], and 45% have anxiety according to the State-Trait Anxiety Inventory [7].

Games, in general, are associated with unconscious learning and allow an increase in the probability of learning [8]. Among the sub-categories of games, there are serious games. Recent years have seen considerable growth in the application of serious gaming in various areas, including health [9], and several types of research suggest that serious games have a positive impact on health and well-being of elder people [10]. A suitable solution is the development of a serious game that centers on stimulating cognitive functions. The design of the game will take into account the user's situation. This paper will present the current state of the project named Rivit. The project is in an early phase of development by the authors of this publication. Rivit is meant to improve cognitive abilities and improve the wellness of heart failure patients. Additionally, will present preliminary usability and user experience evaluation. This paper is structured as follows: Sect. 3 presents Rivit and the mini-games created to date. Section 4 explains about the preliminary user experience evaluation, Sect. 5 presents the results obtained, and Sect. 6 presents the discussion and final remarks.

2 Related Work

This section will present some relevant works for the development of this project. We reviewed papers that address issues such as the impact of serious gaming on the cognitive performance of older people.

The work [11] mentions the development of 3 games to evaluate the cognitive performance of older people. To test the games they worked with 2 groups of people over 50. The first group was composed of 55 people with high cognitive ability, and the other group consisted of 51 patients with cognitive impairment. Cognitive performance was verified using the Montreal Cognitive Assessment (MoCA). It concludes that games can be used to evidence variations in the cognitive performance of people with cognitive pathologies.

In the work [12], to measure the cognitive performance of older people, they developed a whack-a-mole game. It presents conclusions regarding the usability and viability of this type of tool. The usability study was conducted with 24 healthy, non-elderly participants. Because of this, it is unclear how viable it is for the older population.

[13] found that *MentalPlus* might be an effective game to evaluate cognitive dysfunction in heart failure patients.

Ballesteros et al. [14] found that a group of older people obtained an improvement in cognitive abilities such as memory and concentration after using the commercially available cognitive training platform *Lumosity*[1]. Also they found a slight improvement in the participants' well-being. The study involved two groups of healthy older people: the participants of the first group trained with selected Lumosity games for 20 sessions over 10–12 weeks, while the second group just attended three meetings. However it was not possible to conclude that the skills trained could be transferred to daily skills. There was no improvement in executive control or spatial working memory.

---

[1] https://www.lumosity.com/. Accessed: July 24 2020.

Similarly, Anguera et al. [15] identified an improvement in working memory and concentration in elderly people, who were trained for a month with *NeuroRacer*.

The papers mentioned above support the possibility of improving cognitive skills with serious gaming, especially in the elderly, which is one of the objectives of Rivit.

Also, serious games have been demonstrated to be a source of motivation for patients in other health areas such as physical rehabilitation [16].

3 Rivit

Rivit is a collection of casual non-action mini-games targeted at heart failure patients to be used while they are hospitalized waiting for a heart transplant surgery. Since patients are usually on a bed while being hospitalised due to their health condition, it was decided to develop it for mobile devices. Thus, facilitating their use without having to relocate patients, or requiring complex devices settings, e.g. personal computers or game consoles with joysticks. Also, mobile games might be more accessible than other platforms. The reason it was chosen to be a library of casual non-action mini-games is that although there is evidence that action games also stimulate cognitive skills, older people have a preference for reasoning games [17]. Besides, the game is planned to be used for an extended time, so providing a diverse catalogue of mini-games can help avoid monotony. It is developed iteratively using agile methodologies with two week development cycles.

3.1 Mini-games

Rivit's mini-games are intended to enhance cognitive skills. The mini-games were designed based on other similar casual reasoning games. Each mini-game has a variety of game modes to choose from. Each game mode follows a core game-play but differs in some parameters making the difficult vary, al- lowing players to choose the difficulty that best suits them. Furthermore, all mini-games follow a uniform user interface design that comprises the three main components (See Fig. 1). An instructions screen that explains the gameplay and rules of the current mini-game. A mode selection screen to choose a game mode, check a brief description of the game mode and the highest achieved score. And a results screen, which appears after a game session is over. Here, players can check the final score and a ranking containing the top 5 achieved high scores. All mini-games can be accessed from the Rivit's Home screen. Rivit is being developed with Unity using C#. Its source code is available under an MIT license online[2].

The current four mini-games (See Fig. 2) are the next:

Melody Choir. A choir director will teach the player a melody. Then, the player must repeat the melody in the same. The player must repeat the melody by pressing the six frogs on screen in the same order as shown. Once the player has repeated the entire tune correctly, it will be displayed once more but with the addition of one more note. This process is repeated until the player has made a mistake in the order of the melody.

---

[2] github.com/MCV-Univalle/Rivit

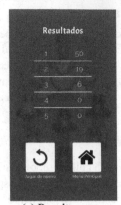

(a) Instructions screen   (b) Mode selection screen   (c) Results screen

Fig. 1. Rivit's mini-games common components

Bug Eater. In this game, a large number of insects will appear moving from left to right, and there is a hungry frog that sticks out its tongue in the direction pressed by the player. The player must nimbly press the insect that matches the frog's desired insect. The game ends if the player takes too long to eat the right insect, or eats many times consecutively the wrong insect.

Dragonfly Chasing. A dragonfly will fly over some items on the screen, and the player must follow the route taken by the dragonfly.

Frog Counter. The player must count the number of frogs left inside a bush in a certain amount of time. During that time, there will be several frogs jumping in and out of the bush simultaneously. As the player succeeds, the speed and number of frogs jumping increases, making the game more challenging.

4   Preliminary Evaluation

Since Rivit is still under development, we conducted a preliminary evaluation involving a group of healthy people. The goal of this evaluation is to identify issues regarding the user experience offered by the game and to assess how intuitive it is so far.

4.1   Participants

21 participants (13 Females, 8 Males) of different age ranges participated voluntarily in this evaluation. All participants are acquaintances of the authors of this paper, and none of them suffered from heart failure. The only requirement to participate was to

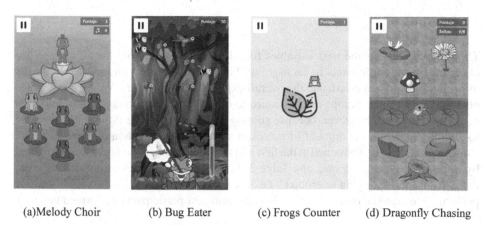

(a)Melody Choir   (b) Bug Eater   (c) Frogs Counter   (d) Dragonfly Chasing

Fig. 2. Rivit's minigames

never have tested the mini-games before. Participants were classified into 3 age ranges: group A containing participants under 30, group B containing participants between 30 and 60 years old, and group C containing participants being 60 or older. The profile of the participants is summarized as in Table 1.

Table 1. Participants' grouping and characteristics

	Total	Male	Female	Have experience with digital games
Group A	7	3	4	4
Group B	7	3	4	3
Group C	7	2	5	0

4.2 Procedure

First, the evaluation facilitator presents the goal and instructions of this evaluation to the participants. Then, the participants play each one mode of each mini-game 5 times. After that, they answer an online questionnaire composed of 21 questions, 3 for demo- graphic data, 12 for reporting their performance at first and fifth attempt and the highest archived score (3 per mini-game), 3 to assess their experience with each mini-game and for the overall experience. The questionnaire is available online[3]. No details were provided to the participants about how to play in order to observe the intuitiveness of the game and to check how well the users would interact without any instruction.

---

[3] Evaluation questionnaire: https://bit.ly/2RbpYBP.

5   Results

This section presents the next variables found from the evaluation: the average scores obtained by the participants in each group, how understandable and how difficult the mini-games were perceived, and the overall experience by the users. We used the scores obtained in the three groups as a measure to compare the performance between them in each mini-game. However, because scoring in each mini-game differs, it is possible to obtain a much higher amount of scores in some mini-games than in others. Table 2 shows the mean scores obtained at the first and fifth attempts and the highest score earned by each group per mini-game, and Table 3 shows the standard deviation. As observed, the participants belonging to group C, i.e., the elderly people, had a considerably worse performance than the other groups. Also, the youngest participants performed better.

Table 2. Performance achieved by the participants grouped by age range

Participants' mean scores									
	Group A			Group B			Group C		
	1er	5th	Best	1er	5th	Best	1er	5th	Best
Melody choir	43	45.1	76.2	16.2	21	28.2	9.3	10.8	29.8
Bug eater	45.3	125	135	80	212	240	22.1	68.5	83.8
Frog counter	7.5	4.5	5.7	3	3.2	3.6	0.6	4.6	4.6
Dragonfly chasing	11.2	14	20	3	3	3	1.6	1.5	1.5

Table 3. Standard deviation of the scores achieved grouped by age range

Standard deviation									
	Group A			Group B			Group C		
	1er	5th	Best	1er	5th	Best	1er	5th	Best
Melody choir	38.3	41.4	43.5	26.1	17,04	23.3	16.3	12.9	33.4
Bug eater	31.6	104.5	102.1	73.5	123.9	93	30.2	103.6	111.6
Frog counter	10.03	1.7	2.05	1.2	1.4	1.7	0.81	5.4	5.4
Dragonfly chasing	19.01	22.02	33.9	0	0	0	1.9	1.6	1.6

Those results are confirmed by perceived difficulty to understand the goal of each mini-game (Fig. 3). Most of the participants from group A reported to have understood three of the mini-games easily. Again, the elderly participants indicated to have difficulties to understand the mini-games. Frog Counter was the best rated mini-game, while Dragonfly Chasing was difficult to understand for most of the participants.

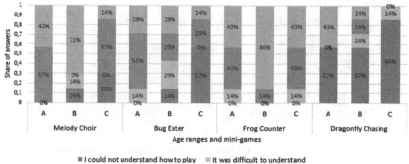

Fig. 3. Results regarding understanding of mini-games' goal

Regarding gameplay difficulty, all of the mini-games were rated rather normal to hard (Fig. 4). Additionally, except for Dragonfly Chasing, the participants rated the experience offered by all the mini-games as positive (Fig. 5). Bug Eater was considered as the most enjoyable by the participants (Fig. 6). Regarding the user interface, the participants to rate their experience from 1 to 5. The obtained mean scores were 4.5, 4.0 and 3.5 for group A, B and C respectively.

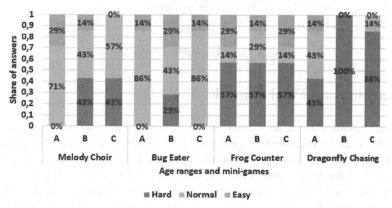

Fig. 4. Results for mini-games' gameplay difficulty

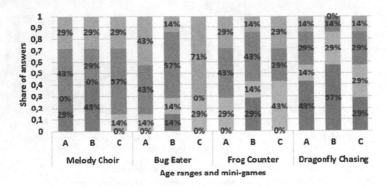

Fig. 5. Overall-experience results

Fig. 6. Most enjoyable mini-game

6 Discussion and Final Remarks

This paper presented Rivit, an open-source collection of mini-games targeted a heart failure patients and a preliminary evaluation. It was developed taking into account the conditions proposed by the professionals of the cardiology area of a local hospital. They highlighted that the mini-games had to stimulate basic functions of the brain, due to the lack of blood circulation produced by the heart failure. Therefore, each mini-game should support training cognitive skills and improving emotional state. However, at this stage of development of Rivit, it is not yet possible to say whether it is achieving those goals or not. Except for one of the mini-games, the participants' feedback was positive regarding understanding, difficulty, experience and user interface. Also, all participants improved their performance after some gameplay sessions. Although the difficulty of the mini- games was considered normal to hard, the positive rated experience may indicate that the participants may perceive the difficulty as a challenge, which may be a source of motivation. As mentioned previously Rivit is still under development, the negative feed- back regarding Dragonfly Chasing may due to the lack of continuous feedback, i.e. to reinforce correct actions and unclear instructions.

We found that most of the people belonging to the youngest group had experience with digital games, while no person from the elderly group did. This may be the reason for elderly participants to have the lowest performance. Thus, new alternatives to make the mini-games more intuitive and appealing for them should be identified. Also, the collection of mini-games for Rivit should be expanded to offer more variety. Additionally, we plan to include a mood record option to allow patients registering their current mood every day. Also, an activity record, where scores and spend playtime for each mini-game will be recorded. Additionally, we plan to allow patients to customize Rivit's mascot as a source of motivation. The main limitations of this work are related to the development maturity of Rivit and the lack of a representative audience in the participants. However, we decided to conduct an initial evaluation before moving to the next development stage. This fact and the current pandemic led us to exclude heart failure patients from this evaluation. We plan to conduct more evaluations in the future following an iterative approach. Although our results are not entirely conclusive, our work may shed light on the design and development of digital games for improving cognitive skills in heart failure patients. However, further research may be conducted to address the issues identified by elderly people. Also, the long term effects of these games on patients should be identified.

References

1. Bleumink, G.S., et al.: Quantifying the heart failure epidemic: prevalence, incidence rate, lifetime risk and prognosis of heart failure: the rotterdam study. Eur. Heart J. **25**(18), 1614–1619 (2004). https://doi.org/10.1016/j.ehj.2004.06.038
2. Vogels, R.L., Scheltens, P., Schroeder-Tanka, J.M., Weinstein, H.C.: Cognitive impairment in heart failure: a systematic review of the literature. Eur. J. Heart Fail. **9**(5), 440–449 (2007). https://doi.org/10.1080/13803395.2012.663344
3. Bennett, S.J., Sauve´, M.J.: Cognitive deficits in patients with heart failure: a review of the literature. J. Cardiovasc. Nurs. **18**(3), 219–242 (2003)
4. Pressler, S.J.: Cognitive functioning and chronic heart failure: a review of the literature (2002-july 2007). J. Cardiovasc. Nurs. **23**(3), 239–249 (2008). https://doi.org/10.1097/01.JCN.0000305096.09710.ec
5. Friedmann, E., et al.: Relationship of depression, anxiety, and social isolation to chronic heart failure outpatient mortality. Am. Heart J. **152**(5), 940–e1 (2006). https://doi.org/10.1016/j.ahj.2006.05.009
6. Beck, A.T., Steer, R.A., Brown, G.: Beck depression inventory–ii. Psychol. Assess. (1996). https://doi.org/10.1037/t00742-000
7. Spielberger, C.D.: State-trait anxiety inventory. The Corsini Encyclopedia of Psychology, pp. 1–1 (2010)
8. Marcano La´rez, B.E., et al.: Juegos serios y entrenamiento en la sociedad digital (2008)
9. Wattanasoontorn, V., Boada, I., García Hernandez, R., Sbert, M.: Serious games for health. Entertain. Comput. **4**, 231–247 (2013). https://doi.org/10.1016/j.entcom.2013.09.002
10. Nguyen, T.T.H., et al.: Impact of serious games on health and well-being of elderly: a systematic review. In: Proceedings of the 50th Hawaii International Conference on System Sciences (2017). https://doi.org/10.24251/HICSS.2017.447
11. Neto, H.S., Cerejeira, J., Roque, L.: Cognitive screening of older adults using serious games: an empirical study. Entertain. Comput. **28**, 11–20 (2018). https://doi.org/10.1016/j.entcom.2018.08.002
12. Tong, T., Chignell, M., Lam, P., Tierney, M.C.: Designing serious games for cognitive assessment of the elderly. In: Proceedings of the International Symposium of Human Factors and Ergonomics in Healthcare, vol. 3 (2014). https://doi.org/10.1177/2327857914031004

13. Pereira, V.F.A., Valentin, L.S.S.: The mentalplus R digital game might be an accessible open source tool to evaluate cognitive dysfunction in heart failure with preserved ejection fraction in hypertensive patients: a pilot exploratory study. Int. J. Hypertens. **2018** (2018). https://doi.org/10.1155/2018/6028534

14. Ballesteros, S., et al.: Brain training with non-action video games enhances aspects of cognition in older adults: a randomized controlled trial. Front. Aging Neurosci. **6**, 277 (2014). https://doi.org/10.3389/fnagi.2014.00277

15. Anguera, J.A., et al.: Video game training enhances cognitive control in older adults. Nature **501**(7465), 97–101 (2013). https://doi.org/10.1038/nature12486

16. Gamboa, E., Ruiz, C., Trujillo, M.: Improving patient motivation towards physical rehabilitation treatments with playtherapy exergame. Stu. Health Tech. Inf. **249**, 140–147 (2018). https://doi.org/10.3233/978-1-61499-868-6-140, http://www.ncbi.nlm.nih.gov/pubmed/29866970

17. Cota, T.T., Ishitani, L., Vieira, N.: Mobile game design for the elderly: a study with focus on the motivation to play. Comput. Hum. Behav. **51**, 96–105 (2015). https://doi.org/10.1016/j.chb.2015.04.026, http://www.sciencedirect.com/science/article/pii/S0747563215003131

Smartphones, Suitable Tool for Driver Behavior Recognition. A Systematic Review

Jovan F. Fernández Joya[1] (ID), Gabriel Ávila Buitrago[1] (ID),
Huizilopoztli Luna-García[2] (ID), and Wilson J. Samiento[3](✉) (ID)

[1] Facultad de Ingeniería, Diseño e Innovación, Institución Universitaria Politécnico
Grancolombiano, Bogota, Colombia
{jofernandez9,gavilabu}@poligran.edu.co
[2] Centro de Investigación e Innovación Automotriz de México (CIIAM),
Universidad Autónoma de Zacatecas, Zacatecas, Mexico
hlugar@uaz.edu.mx
[3] Grupo de Investigación en Multimedia -GIM, Facultad de Ingeniería,
Universidad Militar Nueva Granada, Bogota, Colombia
wilson.sarmiento@unimilitar.edu.co

Abstract. A current reality is the increase in the number of road traffic accidents caused mainly by incorrect driving habits. For this reason, the development of different approaches that can help reduce accidents on the road is imperative. A strategy is the use of smartphones as a tool to identify driving behaviors, which is documented in the state of the art. This paper presents a systematic review focused on the strategies used to recognizing driving behaviors with sensors that are part of smartphones. The review was carried out on the *Scopus* database, included studies published in the last 4 years (2017–2020) that allowed identifying a total of 22 relevant results. This paper presents a report of the most used sensors, algorithms, driving events and driving patterns. It includes result discussion and considerations of future work on this topic, additional to the bibliometric report.

Keywords: Smartphones · Driving behavior · Recognition · Systematic review

1 Introduction

The task of driving an automobile is a complex and dynamic process that involves three main elements: the vehicle, the environment and the driver. However, only one of these elements that can make decisions and take actions, the driver (in the case in cars without technological aids) [1]; for this reason, the 90% of traffic accidents around the world are attributed to the driver. About this issue, driving behavior is a learned way to behave that a person and evolve in a habit. Martinez et al. [2] assert that two factors influence driving behavior. The first is human factors, such as emotions, age, gender, personality, attitude, the ability to take risks, demographic origin, decision-making skills, familiarity with the vehicle, driver's experience, substance abuse, among other conditions. The second is the environmental factors, such as traffic, the season of the year, the weather, the road type,

© Springer Nature Switzerland AG 2020
V. Agredo-Delgado et al. (Eds.): HCI-COLLAB 2020, CCIS 1334, pp. 233–242, 2020.
https://doi.org/10.1007/978-3-030-66919-5_24

other drivers, visibility, the road conditions, the moment of the day, pedestrians, cyclists and illumination conditions. In this way, accurate recognition of driving behaviors would help reduce road traffic accidents, and for this reason, interest in this research field has been increasing in recent years [3, 4].

Driving behavior can be identified by the use of sensors placed in three locations, 1) Roads, 2) Vehicles, and 3) Smartphones (from the driver or one of the passengers) [5]. The first case requires a special infrastructure, usually related to smart cities. The second case is related to the automobile with advanced and expensive features. Both of these cases present challenges in the context of Latin American countries because cities in this region don't have a suitable infrastructure, and the vehicle fleet is comprised of cheaper or outdated cars. For this reason, approaches oriented to detecting driving behaviors by using sensors in smartphones are convenient to this region because they have the advantage of being low-cost strategies, with broader possible applications in different types of cities or vehicle fleets.

A survey published in 2017 shows the importance of this last approach as a viable alternative [5]. However, the review mentioned above is not focused on articles which only use sensors present in smartphones. This document presents a contribution in that sense, by doing a literature review that includes a compilation of studies made in the last four years, specifically focused on identifying driving behaviors using sensors in smartphones. This work provides information about detection methods, sensors used for data capturing, driving behaviors detected, and bibliometric information related to the research.

The remaining sections of this article are structured as follows. Section 2 presents methodological details that were used for the development of the literature review. Section 3 shows the obtained results regarding the sensors that were used, detection methods and algorithms, and driving events that were detected. Finally, Sect. 4 includes an analysis of the results and a brief discussion for future work.

2 Materials and Methods

This systematic review was conducted by an adaptation of standard protocol [6] consisting of five stages showed in Fig. 1. The first stage consisted of the formulation of the research questions, which would help define the parameters for the search process. In the second stage, the search equation was executing, allowing the identification of the target publications. The third stage is a fine- tuning the search equation in an iterative process between 2 and 3 stages to optimize the last search. In the fourth stage, exclusion criteria

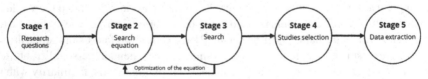

Fig. 1. Stages of this systematic review. Figure emphasis is in iterative process between 2 and 3 stages that allow optimizing the search equation

were applied to the results, and finally, in the fifth stage, the extraction and information analysis was conducted. The next sections describe the details of each stage.

2.1 Research Questions

The first stage of a systematic review consists of identifying the target of the research. In this case, the aim was to identify the type of sensors and machine learning algorithms being used. Also, it was important to find contributions in Latin America regarding this subject. This process is summarized in the following research questions:

P1. Which studies have been published where smartphones are used to identify driving behaviors?
P1.1 What is the state of Latin America regarding the use of smartphones for the identification of driving behaviors?
P2. Which smartphone's sensors that have been used as a support for the identification of vehicle driving behaviors?
P3. What machine learning methods have been used as a support for the identification of vehicle driving behaviors?

2.2 Search Equation

Once clarified the bibliographic research objectives, the next step consisted of defining the different terms and keywords used in the search equation. The initial search string was written with three seed words "Smartphone AND Driving behavior AND Identification". Afterward, a synonym search was conducted for each seed word, allowing for a larger number of publications.

Table 1 shows the full list of terms, each column containing the synonyms that were used. The equation was then formulated by concatenating all the possible combinations with an "OR" connector. The equation includes a date and sources filter, where only were included documents published since January 2017 in scientific journals and conferences.

Table 1. Terms or words used in the search equation

Smarthphone	Driving behavior	Identification
Mobile	Driving pattern	Recognition
Cellular phone	Driving mode	Classification
	Driving behavior	Characterization
	Driving comportment	Characterisation
	Driving kind	Detection
	Driving type	Learning

2.3 Search

The search was carried out on the Scopus database, which was mainly chosen because of its wide editorial coverage, high recognition among the scientific com- munity, and considering that the research team had access to the search engine. The most recent search corresponds to July 5th, 2020, which generated 73 documents; 17 published in 2017, 15 in 2018, 34 in 2019, and 7 in 2020.

2.4 Studies Selection

Afterward, a filtering of the resulting publications was conducted by applying a set of exclusion criteria. At first, three duplicated publications were eliminated. The next step was to review the titles and abstracts, including those documents that were allowed to solve the research questions that were proposed previously. Twenty-two (22) articles were removed because the smartphone was used passively or because it was not used for information extraction for the driving behavior recognition process. A similar procedure was then performed by reading the introduction section of the articles, which allowed for excluding 20 documents. Finally, the remaining publications (25) were read in full. A quality assessment was undertaken to determine if an article added value to the process, which allowed for the exclusion of three publications. Table 2 shows the number of excluded publications at each step, with information of the publication year.

Table 2. Detail of the publication filtering process and the exclusion criteria. The last row presents the number of documents at the end of each stage.

Year	Initial search	Repeats	Abstract	Introduction	Quality
2017	17	0	−5	−1	−2
2018	15	−2	−3	−9	0
2019	34	−1	−14	−4	−1
2020	7	0	−3	−6	0
Total	73	70	45	25	**22**

2.5 Data Extraction

The final stage was the information extraction process to the selected publications to obtain the following data: 1) Country and affiliations publication, 2) Sensors of smartphone used to driver behaviors recognition, and 3) Machine learning methods implemented driver behavior recognition.

3   Findings

The methodology that was followed allowed identifying the evolution of smartphones used as capturing devices of the maneuvers that occur in a vehicle to determine driver behaviors. In a general way, it is possible to state that the research field has been growing during the period analyzed, passing from 4 articles in 2017 to 9 in 2019. It's worth mentioning that 3 of the selected documents were published in the current year. The selected papers also have many citations, which concludes that the topic is active and with a growing interest from research teams. Those above can be noticed in Fig. 2, where the blue columns show the number of documents published per year, and the orange columns show the number of citations that those publications have received. This information answers the first research question and also identifies that it is a topic in a growing tendency. Concerning the country of origin, it is possible to assure that Greece, The United States and China have the highest number of publications, represented graphically in Fig. 3. It should be noted that none of the 22 final publications was done in Latin America; for this reason all initial 73 publications were reviewed again to check for information about the country of origin, obtaining the same results, and this way provide an answer to the question 1.1. The previous point is a call for attention to the need to develop studies in our region focused on this topic.

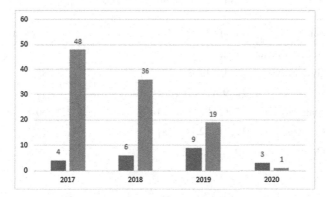

Fig. 2. The figure shows the number of publications per year (blue), and total citations of publications were made in the same year (orange). (Color figure online)

In response to the second question, it was possible to confirm that, of the sensors found in smartphones, the most frequently used in the publications studied are the accelerometer, the gyroscope, the GPS, the magnetometer and the camera. The use of additional sensors such as the microphone, the rotation sensor and the illumination sensor was also demonstrated. Table 3 shows the list of publications that include the use of these sensors. The last column contains the percentage of these publications about the total.

About for the third research question, regarding machine learning algorithms used in state of the art, a great diversity could be demonstrated, even many of them where only used in one or two publications. Among the methods that stand out for their most widespread utility are vector support machines (SVM), random forest, decision trees

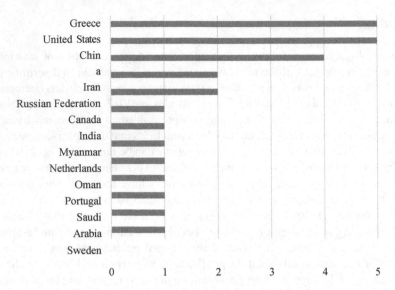

Fig. 3. Country of origin of the selected publications.

Table 3. Publications by sensor.

Sensor	Publications	Percent
Accelerometer	[7–25]	85%
Gyroscope	[7–15, 17–20, 22–26]	82%
GPS	[8, 9, 11, 13–16, 19, 20, 23–25, 27]	59%
Magnetometer	[7, 8, 10, 11, 13, 14, 16, 19, 22, 24, 25]	50%
Camera	[9, 18, 22, 25, 28]	23%
Others	[9, 22]	9%

C4.5, multilayer perceptrons (MLP) and Naıve Bayes and K nearest neighbor algorithms. It was also noted that most publications employ more than one algorithm in order to improve pattern identification. It is important to mention that 6 publications incorporated cross-validation of the results [8, 12, 16, 17, 21, 23]. Table 4 indicates the list of algorithms and the corresponding publications that report the use of these.

It is relevant to say that definition and recognition of particular driving behavior can be ambiguous since many aspects can be taken into account. An important finding while conducting this research was the identification of a general process that can be used to recognize driving behaviors. At first, it was expected to find a direct application of different machine learning approaches over the signals that were being measured from the sensors. However, most of the analyzed works followed a similar methodology, oriented at recognizing driving events as indicators of driver behaviors. For example, recognizing how a driver takes a right turn can identify aggressive driving behavior. The

Table 4. Publications by machine learning algorithm.

Algorithms	Publications	Percent
SVM	[8, 16–18, 21, 22, 24]	32%
Random forest	[8, 12, 17, 24, 26]	23%
C4.5	[8, 16, 17, 23]	18%
MLP	[10, 12, 16, 23]	18%
Naïve Bayes	[8, 12, 16, 17]	18%
K – NN	[8, 15, 16, 22]	18%
Net Bayes	[8, 12, 22]	14%
Fuzzy Inference	[10, 16]	9%
Others	[12, 13, 16, 18, 19, 22–24, 26–28]	50%

publications' analysis resulted in five different driving behaviors identified, as shown in Table 5.

Table 5. Publications by driving behavior.

Driving behavior	Publications	Percent
Aggressive driving	[7, 9–12, 15, 17, 27]	36%
Distracted driving	[7, 9, 11, 18, 22, 28]	27%
Normal driving	[13, 14, 23, 25, 26]	23%
Abnormal driving	[9, 13–15]	18%
Other driving behaviors	[7, 16, 24]	14%

The main events used as driver behavior indicators were turns (right, left, and U -turn), acceleration, braking, lane changing, speed, head, and eye movement. Table 6 presents a list of publications that recognize the six (6) main driving events captured by smartphones.

Finally, regarding the use of smartphone sensors for the detection of the events mentioned above, it was found that the accelerometer is used for the identification of acceleration, braking and speed processes. The gyroscope for lane changing, left, right and U-turns. The magnetometer, combined with the gyroscope, is employed to recognize turns and the forces generated in these events. The GPS allows for the identification of speed and vehicle location in a given road. The frontal camera is used for driver analysis and can help determine fatigue and drowsiness. The back camera is used for keeping

Table 6. Driving behaviors identified in the systematic review.

Event	Publications	Percent
Acceleration	[7, 9, 11–15, 17, 19–21, 23, 25–27]	68%
Braking	[7, 9, 11–15, 17, 19–21, 23, 25–27]	68%
Turns	[8, 10–14, 16, 17, 19, 26]	45%
Speed	[7, 9, 11, 14–16, 24, 25, 27]	41%
Lane change	[8, 10, 16, 17, 21, 23]	27%
Using the smartphone	[7, 11, 14, 15, 18]	23%

track of the road and other vehicles. The microphone can help identify noise inside the cabin of a car to determine distracting sounds (such as conversations with other passengers) or silence. The light sensor indicates how dark the cabin is and possible to use the frontal camera. Additionally, various authors point out that GPS has the highest battery consumption among the different sensors, and therefore its use is recommended only for very specific scenarios.

4 Conclusion and Further Work

This paper shows the results of a systematic search carried out on the Scopus database, aiming at identifying the sensors and algorithms used for driving behavior recognition by smartphone usage. It can be concluded that the most used sensors are the accelerometer, the gyroscope and the GPS; the more recurring algorithms are SVM, random forests and the C4.5 decision tree. An important finding was a driving behavior recognition method based on events, using the different sensors found in smartphones and the application of machine learning algorithms. It is possible to assert that this topic is currently of high interest, based on the increase in publications and citations. However, regarding the search for works being conducted in Latin America, a lack of publications was found. Therefore, there is an opportunity to develop research in this area in the regional context. Finally, highlight that recognition of driver behaviors can be used by different sectors, such as traffic authorities, regulatory organizations, insurance companies, and others interested in all road actors' well-being.Sample Heading (Third Level). Only two levels of headings should be numbered. Lower level headings remain unnumbered; they are formatted as run-in headings.

References

1. Khan, M.Q., Lee, S.: A comprehensive survey of driving monitoring and assistance systems. Sensors **19**(11), 2574 (2019)
2. Marina Martinez, C., Heucke, M., Wang, F.Y., Gao, B., Cao, D.: Driving Style Recognition for Intelligent Vehicle Control and Advanced Driver Assistance: A Survey IEEE Trans. Intell. Transp. **19**(3) (2018)

3. Le, V.H., den Hartog, J., Zannone, N.: Security and privacy for innovative automotive applications: a survey. Comput. Commun. **132**, 17–41 (2018)
4. Breitschaft, S.J., Clarke, S., Carbon, C.C.: A theoretical framework of haptic processing in automotive user interfaces and its implications on design and engineering. Front. Psychol. **10**, 1470 (2019)
5. Karaduman, M., Eren, H.: Smart driving in smart city. In: ICSG 2017 - 5th International Istanbul Smart Grids and Cities Congress and Fair, pp. 115–119 (2017)
6. Torres-Carrion, P.V., González-González, C.S., Aciar, S., Rodríguez-Morales, G.: Methodology for systematic literature review applied to engineering and education. In: 2018 IEEE Global Engineering Education Conference (EDUCON), pp. 1364–1373 (2018)
7. Vlachogiannis, D.M., Vlahogianni, E.I., Golias, J.: A reinforcement learning model for personalized driving policies identification. Int. J. Transp. Sci. Technol. **9**(4), 299–308 (2020)
8. Ouyang, Z., Niu, J., Liu, Y., Liu, X.: An ensemble learning-based vehicle steering detector using smartphones. IEEE Trans. Intell. Transp. Syst. **21**(5), 1964–1975 (2020)
9. Kashevnik, A., Lashkov, I., Gurtov, A.: Methodology and mobile application for driver behavior analysis and accident prevention. IEEE Trans. Intell. Transp. Syst. **21**(6), 2427–2436 (2020)
10. Eftekhari, H.R., Ghatee, M.: A similarity-based neuro fuzzy modeling for driving behavior recognition applying fusion of smartphone sensors. J. Intell. Transp. Syst.: Technol. Plan. Oper. **23**(1), 72–83 (2019)
11. Papadimitriou, E., Argyropoulou, A., Tselentis, D.I., Yannis, G.: Analysis of driver behaviour through smartphone data: the case of mobile phone use while driving. Saf. Sci. **119**, 91–97 (2019)
12. Rahman, A.A., Saleem, W., Iyer, V.V.: driving behavior profiling and prediction in KSA using smart phone sensors and MLAs. In: 2019 IEEE Jordan International Joint Conference on Electrical Engineering and Information Technology, JEEIT 2019 - Proceedings pp. 34–39 (2019)
13. Lourenco, N., Cabral, B., Granjal, J.: Driving profile using evolutionary computation. In: 2019 IEEE Congress on Evolutionary Computation, CEC 2019 - Proceedings (Ml), 2466–2473 (2019)
14. Tselentis, D.I., Vlahogianni, E.I., Yannis, G.: Driving safety efficiency benchmarking using smartphone data. Transp. Res. Part C: Emerg. Technol. **109**, 343–357 (2019)
15. Mantouka, E.G., Barmpounakis, E.N., Vlahogianni, E.I.: Identifying driving safety profiles from smartphone data using unsupervised learning. Saf. Sci. **119**, 84–90 (2019)
16. Bejani, M.M., Ghatee, M.: A context aware system for driving style evaluation by an ensemble learning on smartphone sensors data. Transp. Res. Part C: Emerg. Technol. **89**, 303–320 (2018)
17. Guo, Y., Guo, B., Liu, Y., Wang, Z., Ouyang, Y., Yu, Z.: CrowdSafe: Detecting extreme driving behaviors based on mobile crowdsensing. In: 2017 IEEE SmartWorld Ubiquitous Intelligence and Computing, Advanced and Trusted Computed, Scalable Computing and Communications, Cloud and Big Data Computing, Internet of People and Smart City Innovation, Smart World/SCALCOM/UIC/ATC/CBDCom/IOP/SCI 2017, pp. 1–8 (2018)
18. Nambi, A.U., et al.: Demo: HAMS: Driver and driving monitoring using a smartphone. In: Proceedings of the Annual International Conference on Mobile Computing and Networking, MOBICOM, pp. 840–842 (2018)
19. Tahmasbi, F., Wang, Y., Chen, Y., Gruteser, M.: Poster: Your phone tells us the truth: R identification using smartphone on one turn. In: Proceedings of the Annual International Conference on Mobile Computing and Networking, MOBICOM (October), pp. 762–764 (2018)
20. Kang, L., Banerjee, S.: Practical driving analytics with smartphone sensors. In: IEEE Vehicular Networking Conference, VNC 2018-January, pp. 303–310 (2018)

21. Al-luhaibi, S.K., Said, A.M., Najim Al-Din, M.S.: Recognition of driving maneuvers based accelerometer sensor. Int. J. Civil Eng. Technol. **9**(11), 1542–1547 (2018)
22. Streiffer, C., Raghavendra, R., Benson, T., Srivatsa, M.: DarNet: A deep learning solution for distracted driving detection. In: Middleware 2017 - Proceedings of the 2017 International Middleware Conference (Industrial Track), pp. 22–28 (2017)
23. Vlahogianni, E.I., Barmpounakis, E.N.: Driving analytics using smartphones: Algorithms, comparisons and challenges. Transp. Res. Part C: Emerg. Technol. **79**, 196–206 (2017)
24. Xu, X., Yin, S., Ouyang, P.: Fast and low-power behavior analysis on vehicles using smartphones. In: 2017 6th International Symposium on Next Generation Electronics, ISNE 2017 (2017)
25. Cho, W., Kim, S.H.: Multimedia sensor dataset for the analysis of vehicle movement. In: Proceedings of the 8th ACM Multimedia Systems Conference, MMSys 2017, pp. 175–180 (2017)
26. Wang, R., Xie, F., Zhang, B., Liu, W., Qian, W., Xian, W.: Detecting abnormal driving behaviors by smartphone sensors based on multi-feature convolutional neural network. In: Chinese Control Conference, CCC 2019-July(2), pp. 6639–6644 (2019)
27. Mon, T.L.L., Thein, T.L.L.: Design and implementation of smart alert system for reducing road traffic accidents in Myanmar. In: AIP Conference Proceedings, vol. 2129, July 2019
28. Lashkov, I., Kashevnik, A., Shilov, N., Parfenov, V., Shabaev, A.: Driver dangerous state detection based on OpenCV & dlib libraries using mobile video processing. In: Proceedings - 22nd IEEE International Conference on Computational Science and Engineering and 17th IEEE International Conference on Embedded and Ubiquitous Computing, CSE/EUC 2019, pp. 74–79 (2019)

State of the Art of Business Simulation Games Modeling Supported by Brain-Computer Interfaces

Cleiton Pons Ferreira[1,2,3]($\boxtimes$) (iD) and Carina Soledad González González[1] (iD)

[1] Universidad de La Laguna, San Cristóbal de La Laguna, Spain
{alu0101382166,carina.gonzalez}@ull.edu.es
[2] Universidade Federal do Rio Grande, Rio Grande, Brazil
[3] Instituto Federal de Educação Ciência e Tecnologia do Rio Grande do Sul, Rio Grande, Brazil

Abstract. The use of Business Simulation Games in education is becoming very common as a training strategy offered by companies and universities. However, the real-time monitoring and analysis of the use of these resources has not been sufficiently studied. The aim of this work is to present the state of the art of simulators of organizational environments, from the point of view of Neuroscience, through the support of two data collection devices during the user experience: electroencephalography and eye tracking. The study points out relevant aspects that the physiological and neuroscientific interfaces can offer in monitoring the use of these tools, contributing to the definition of what is important in their conception and modeling for meaningful learning.

Keywords: Simulation · EEG · Eye-tracking · Learning · Neuroscience

1 Introduction

Preparing and improving people to deal with the everyday situations of a company requires continuous training. If, on the one hand, including this training during university studies can be hindered by the distance from the reality of organizations, letting these professionals learn in practice, after being hired, can bring costs or risks to the business's heritage, safety or environment, often due to just wrong or poorly thought out decision. For this reason, companies and universities have been looking for new alternatives for business learning, and, in this scenario, serious games or simulators appear, for allowing them to develop knowledge, skills, and competences that can be transferred to the real world using interactive virtual environments. In them, apprentices are the protagonists of decisions that can be reflected during the experience in the simulated environment. The possibility of playing several times and making different decisions, in addition to applying previous experiences in new challenges, allows the practice and improvement of learning. However, studies show that to meet the learning requirements, the development of serious games or simulators goes beyond the tool's resources as interactivity, immersion, engagement, and loyalty to the real situation [1] and includes aspects such as: clear objectives of the game, experimental challenges, constant evaluation of the

© Springer Nature Switzerland AG 2020
V. Agredo-Delgado et al. (Eds.): HCI-COLLAB 2020, CCIS 1334, pp. 243–252, 2020.
https://doi.org/10.1007/978-3-030-66919-5_25

learner's performance and feedback during the game and at the end, which makes the evaluation complex, as there is no pre-defined object, but an experimentation environment with the possibility of mistakes and successes, in which it is necessary to evaluate the process beyond the result [2]. Besides, there are few studies about the contribution of these tools for the cognitive and socioemotional aspects to their users, nowadays considered relevant for the 21st-century professional [3, 4]. Thus, the proposal of this work arises when presenting a multidisciplinary study involving areas of Computing, Game Design, Education, and Neuroscience so that together, it can provide subsidies for the development of Business Simulation Games more efficient and effective.

2 Business Simulation Games and Neuroscience of Learning

The study, development, and improvement of skills necessary for the current generation of professionals, has been recommended by companies, governments, and institutions around the world. Studies such as the one published by the Organization for Economic Cooperation and Development [4], highlighting the importance of developing aspects such as high-level thinking, creativity, collaboration and the ability to analyze problems and make decisions for professional success, also have motivated research for the application of new methodologies that provide training in line with the needs of the labor market. The current business context has also been influenced by the digital transformation process, which, due to its revolutionary and evolutionary characteristics, has required significant management knowledge. Thus, another important aspect in the development of professional characteristics for those who exercise some strategic function in the company, regardless of their area of training, is the ability to manage a business for the continuous improvement and maintenance of competitiveness [5]. Research on skills and competencies for the management of organizations has discussed the relevance of this knowledge for future professionals [6]. The great and current challenge of teaching business management is to establish the balance between practice and theory, as normally the knowledge developed in academia is limited to a static view of organizations and as an ordered set of activities, without considering any possible changes in business models. A solution that presents itself to solve the problem is the Business Simulation Games, designed to improve the learning experience for students [7]. On the other hand, according to a study of over 2600 students, an average of only 20% of the knowledge students acquire in the classroom can be skillfully applied in professional life [8]. This disconnect between what students know and how skillfully they can apply such knowledge has been called in the educational environment as the "knowing-doing gap". To reverse this scenario the Simulation Games are gaining more and more space in learning environments, including Business. In these virtual systems, the learner can experience situations in specific business environments, addressing internal or external aspects of the organization, in whole or in part; or build organizational models and simulations of these models, allowing them to learn through a process in which they act as a key actor, so that the result is not the most important, but the exercise of planning and decision making [9]. It is also associated with the use of simulation games, the development of skills such as motivation, problem solving - analytical thinking, knowledge transfer, greater knowledge retention, adaptive learning, behavioral and attitude change

[10]. Concerning a Business Simulation, as a practical class, it offers a context similar to the real one, which may favor the acquisition and future evocation of the content, as it offers elements that can support the reconstruction of a scenario, a context. When dealing with something new, the brain seeks to connect to an existing network, in which the information received will be integrated. When connecting new information to experiences, the student increases the complexity of neuronal connections and the potential for retaining information, as new information makes sense, or has meaning, when it fits an existing neuronal pattern [3, 11, 12]. In everyday life, each of us is trapped in the chain of emotions, an important component of behavior. It is well known that there is a close correlation between brain functions and emotions. In particular, the limbic system, the paralimbic system, the vegetative nervous system, and the reticular activating system are involved in processing and controlling emotional reactions [13]. From affective perspective, simulation game helps in developing technical, professional and managerial skills. Through simulation, the development of intellectual capabilities is achieved through integration of various functional areas and the platform of dynamic environment reinforces learning integration, and the group level learning is achieved through team dynamics that makes learning independent and helps develop interpersonal skills [10]. Specific scientific studies by neuroscientists have helped to create models and give great insights about simulation to support advanced learning, such as an increase in brain volume and plasticity with its use [14–16], and also highlight the development of skills such as coordination, memory and visual acuity.

3 Definition of Business Simulation Game (BSG)

Simulators are digital tools designed for a purpose other than entertainment and fun, involving the use of electronic gaming technologies and methodologies to deal with real-world problems. The purpose is to teach or train, but may include elements of play and entertainment. According to [17], "A simulation is a working representation of reality; it may be an abstracted, simplified or accelerated model of a process. It purports to have a relevant behavioral similarity to the original system". The author also defines that "A simulation game combines the features of a game (competition, cooperation, rules, participants, roles) with those of a simulation", and concludes that "A game is a simulation game if its rules refer to an empirical model of reality". In the specific field of business and administration, and as the object of this study, BSGs constitute a well-known example of an e-learning method in management training [18] because presents virtual representations of real business situations that allow students to manage companies in risk-free environments and provide an overall view of corporate strategic functions and allow students to address educational contents in interactive and enjoyable ways [19]. Each business game that incorporates any of the critical features of the "business world" should be considered a BSG. All business game could be considered a BSG and should be included in the "simulation game" category, except in case that the tool offers erroneous teaching and virtual environments that manifest professedly unrealistic reactions to a player's choices [20]. A graphical representation of this understanding is shown in Fig. 1.

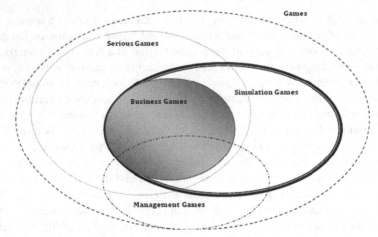

Fig. 1. A graphical representation of the set of games and its subsets. Source: [20]

A BSG can be used as training tool, simulate market trends in order to improve the capacity to face changes, or provide an overall strategic view of a corporation [21].

4   Elements of Business Simulation Games

The first classification established for the BSGs [21], considered that this tool under the design point of view can present itself as: total enterprise or functional, interacting or noninteracting, and computer or noncomputer; and according to their expected use: as a part of a general management training program; for selling new techniques or procedures, or for conducting research. To be effective as learning methods, simulators must develop and/or improve skills, in addition to supporting the assessment of results and providing feedback to learners [22], what does it mean include aspects related to the fidelity, verification and validation of the model and of the tool itself, such as interactivity, non-linearity and immersion [23], and also others like sequential nature of decisions, appearance and user interface [20]. With regard to the systematization of research on the modeling of a simulator, the Taxonomy of Computer Simulations [24] and then adapted for the BSG [20] considers five macro-categories: Environment of application; Design elements of user interface; Target groups, goals objective & feedback; User relation characteristics; Characteristics of the simulation model. Given this complexity and multiplicity of requirements, it is important to consider the possibility of contributing with new methodologies to support the design and analyze the efficiency of the BSG as a learning resource.

5   Physiological and Neuroscientific Methods of Data Collection

The use of brain-computer interfaces (BCIs) applying physiological and neuroscientific techniques has been allowing studies involving the disciplines of psychophysics, cognitive neuroscience, and computer science, to understand aspects of human-technologies interaction, including learning with the support of simulators and games. A recent research addressed the most prominent methods in this field [25], highlighting the Electroencephalography (EEG) and Eye-tracking (ET) considered the support techniques most used in the business area [26–29].

5.1 Electroencephalography (EEG)

Electroencephalography has been one of the most used methods for capturing and analyzing non-invasive brain signals, using EEG data. To capture the signals, a cap is inserted in the individual's head, and electrodes are attached to it, which easily make contact and send brain stimuli, from very small changes in the electrical activity inside the brain during a certain activity. The moment the neuron is activated, it becomes polarized, generating an action potential that can be propagated to other neurons, thus generating the circulation of information and showing the electrical activity of the brain, which in turn is captured by the electrodes and sent for equipment that performs data filtering and treatment [30]. The records obtained through the electrodes show the intensity of the brain waves recorded from the scalp, Modern EEG devices have a high temporal resolution, capable of to measure activity every millisecond, and a reasonable spatial resolution. The devices are portable and are currently sold at relatively affordable prices in some models [31]. The use of EEG in the areas of emotion recognition and mental work has been used in many types of research. The temporal resolution of EEG is high, meaning that changes in brain activity can be detected milliseconds after they occur. However, the spatial resolution of EEG is limited, but it is possible to identify the general source of EEG, providing information about the types of mental processes that are occurring [25]. In one investigation [32], several methods were proposed to extract useful information from the observed human EEG activities. EEG measurements have been used to research the users response to games [33, 34]. In a study [35], field experts discussed the methodological advancements within player experience and playability research considering EEG as a good measure for cognitive processing.

5.2 Eye-Tracking (ET)

ET is a method that can directly and continuously record visual attention, is often employed to explore the attention bias, utilizing a device that emits infrared rays into the user's eyes, allowing accurately calculate where the person is looking and also measure eye movements such as fixations, views, and regressions. The ET systems have been used in diagnostic applications, through the extraction of data from record eye movements and process, and can give a diagnosis very fast. [36]. The following metrics can be collected through ET, during system evaluation of a task [37], for performance measures: Efficiency and Effectiveness; for process measures: Number of fixations and Fixation, Attentional switching and Scanpath similarity. This is an indicator of position and sequence similarity among different viewers, e.g., suitable especially for expert and novice comparisons. The study of monitorated tasks by ET provide patterns of activity that reflect the interactions among the stimulus, the receptive-field activating region, the temporal response characteristics of the neuron, and the retinal positions and image motions imparted by eye movements. The diversity of the activity patterns suggests that during natural viewing of a stationary scene some cortical neurons are carrying information about saccade occurrences and directions whereas other neurons are better suited to coding details of the retinal image, offers the dual benefit of monitoring brain activity as well as oculomotor function [37]. For this reason, currently the eye-tracking systems have been used in fields such as marketing [28, 29], analysis of the usability of a system [38], and more recently in human behavior and Neuroscience studies [37, 39], including the use of EEG and ET interfaces in a joint and complementary way [38].

6 Business Simulation Games Researches and Discussion

To understand the current stage of research on BSG, a consultation was carried out in the scientific database Web of Science (WOS), using compositions of the keywords of this work. As the term Business Simulation can also be found in the literature as a Business Game, this variation was considered too. The results of consulting the database by descriptors, without other inclusion criteria, are shown in Table 1.

Table 1. Results of the key words and compositions about BSG consulting at WOS

Descriptor	Results WOS
Business Simulation+Education	198
Business Simulation+EEG or Business Simulation+Eye-tracking	0
Business Game+Education	119
Business Game+EEG or Business Game+Eye-tracking	0

Source: Web of Science (WOS). http://webofscience.com/ Accessed in: 05/22/2020.

A BSG can lead to one or both of the following results: the training of players in hard or soft business skills or the quantitative or qualitative evaluation of players.

From an analysis of the abstracts of the articles listed in response to queries from the database (Table 1), when the objective of the research is to evaluate constructive aspects or the use of BSGs for education, as a learning resource, it was found that it has a qualitative bias. This means that the results presented by the existing studies

Table 2. Results at WOS of the composition of key words about Simulation EEG/ET

Descriptor	Results WOS
Simulation+Education+EEG	52
Simulation+Education+Eye-tracking	84
Game+Education+EEG	35
Game+Education+Eye-tracking	17

Source: Web of Science (WOS). http://webofscience.com/ Accessed in: 05/22/2020.

with BSGs consider only aspects of evaluation from the point of view of their users or instructors, corroborating the fact that currently there are no studies developed with the support of brain-computer interfaces, with the real-time data collection while using the tool. Other aspect identified is the lack of BSG researches using EEG and ET interfaces, demonstrating that human-computer interfaces have not been used in studies to measure the experience in BSG. So, in the search for some approximations, a new less restrictive consultation was carried out, removing the descriptor "Business". The results are shown in Table 2.

The objective of considering the descriptor Education was to identify specific contributions in this topic, considering that currently there are researches on simulators and games in others areas less relevant for this study. Selecting, from the results of the Table 2, only the studies that present results on the contribution of EEG or Eye-tracking BCI's in learning processes, available in Open Access format and in the last 3 years of publication, four documents were identified. All of them have important results that can be replicated for the BSG study, starting with a recent investigation on the building of neurocognitive models of the internal mental and brain processes of children using a novel adapted combination of existing computational tools using EEG data to validate the models [40]. The result shows that the neurocognitive modeling could be integrated in closed-loop brain training to induce the desired optimal psychological state prior to learning experience. In another paper, a comparative study classifies emotions, using a EEG dataset for Emotion Analysis, presenting a future applicability in the field of affective computing in the context of education, marketing, recommender systems and games [13]. The other two results evolving Simulation/Game and ET in Education also presents very interesting studies with possible applications for BSG. It is the case of a research developed on the influence of prior knowledge on the use, by professionals and students, of a computer-based simulation game in the medical field to train complex problem-solving skills, using eye-tracking as an analysis tool [41]. Another study addresses the contribution of the use of ET to dynamically monitor students' problem-solving tasks in a learning environment based on games for teaching microbiology [42]. The results suggest that, in seeking a deep understanding of what is happening to better absorb the content on the theme of the game, the learner uses a combination of accurate metacognitive monitoring and cognitive knowledge strategies. In fact, researches on the use of simulators and games supported by the EEG and ET interfaces has been showing significant results that have supported to the development of these tools to improve the learning, including BSGs.

7 Conclusions

In general, research supports that simulation can facilitate learning, but it is difficult to draw stronger conclusions about the educational impact of these tools at this time, especially in a business environment, due to the lack of definitions, methodologies. research and learning approaches. On the other hand, advances in research in the field of Neuroscience have demonstrated the unmatched capacity of the human brain to learn and adapt, including the study of the practical impact of learning through simulators and games. Although these experiences are somewhat complex, they offer new insights into what differences between traditional and new training methods. Following in the steps of what has been happening with research with games for entertainment, simulation in the health, mobile and web applications, correlations between physiology, neurology, and behavior, along with the introduction of the technology of data collection, can aid our understanding of the mechanisms underlying user experience, potentially leading to increasing the effectiveness of simulators. This approach, proven from these studies already carried out in other segments, can be transferred directly to business simulation environments, where information, activities and tasks can be applied at a level appropriate to the learner's reality, and the neurofeedback can be used to support the practice of key aspects of executive functions, attention, actions and emotions aspects, contributing in the design of these tools. Thus, this study gave an overview of the importance of using simulators for business learning based on the contribution of the ET and EEG interfaces. Compared to self-reporting, these measures are generally impartial and therefore provide a more complete and informative measure of these virtual environments contributing to a better understanding of the relevant aspects in the development of BSGs. It is also important to note that a combination of these measures may be more appropriate to unravel complex cognitive and behavioral mechanisms. It is expected from this discussion to motivate more research in the area of business simulation that can go a little further than analyzing the perception of users and instructors, considering qualitative and quantitative aspects of its use, adding and complementing results that can contribute to more organizations use these instruments in the preparation of your (future) professionals with the security of significant learning results, and present subsidies so that developers can create more effective and engaging BSGs.

References

1. McGlarty, K.L., Orr, A., Frey, P.M., Dolan, R., Vassileva, V., McvAy, A.: A Literature Review of Gaming in Gaming, pp. 1–36 (2012). http://www.pearsonassessments.com/hai/Images/tmrs/Lit_Review_of_Gaming_in_Education.pdf%5Cnpapers3://publication/uuid/32BC44F8-5E69-43C6-9E62-5C00DF0E540F
2. Ratwani, K.L., Orvis, K., Knerr, B.: Game-Based Training Effectiveness Evaluation in an Operational Setting, pp. 34 (2010). http://oai.dtic.mil/oai/oai?verb=getRecord&metadataPrefix=html&identifier=ADA530660
3. Lent, R.: Cem Bilhões de Neurônios: Conceitos Fundamentais de Neurociência. Atheneu, São Paulo (2001)
4. Santos, D., Primi, R.: Desenvolvimento socioemocional e aprendizado escolar: Uma proposta de mensuração para apoiar políticas públicas, pp. 87 (2014). https://doi.org/10.1017/cbo9781107415324.004
5. Bontinck, G., Isik, Ö., Van den Bergh, J., Viaene, S.: Unlocking the potential of the process perspective in business transformation. In: La Rosa, M., Loos, P., Pastor, O. (eds.) BPM 2016. LNBIP, vol. 260, pp. 161–176. Springer, Cham (2016). https://doi.org/10.1007/978-3-319-45468-9_10
6. Prifti, L., Knigge, M., Löffler, A., Hecht, S., Krcmar, H.: Emerging business models in education provisioning: a case study on providing learning support as education-as-a-service. Int. J. Eng. Pedagog. 7(3), 92 (2017). https://doi.org/10.3991/ijep.v7i3.7337
7. Monk, E.F., Lycett, M.: Measuring business process learning with enterprise resource planning systems to improve the value of education. Educ. Inf. Tech. 21(4), 747–768 (2014). https://doi.org/10.1007/s10639-014-9352-6

8. Baldwin, T.T., Pierce, J.R., Joines, R.C., Farouk, S.: The elusiveness of applied management knowledge: a critical challenge for management educators. Acad. Manag. Learn. Educ. 10(4), 583–605 (2011). https://doi.org/10.5465/amle.2010.0045

9. Barçante, L.C., Pinto, F.C.: Jogos de Negócios: Revolucionando o Aprendizado Nas Empresas. Impetus, Rio de Janeiro (2003)

10. Abdullah, N.L., Hanafiah, M.H., Hashim, N.A.: Developing creative teaching module: business simulation in teaching strategic management. Int. Educ. Stud. 6(6), 95–107 (2013). https://doi.org/10.5539/ies.v6n6p95

11. Gazzaniga, M., Heatherton, T., Halpern D.: Ciência Psicológica. Artmed Editora (2005)

12. Izquierdo, I.: Memória. ArtMed, Porto Alegre (2002)

13. Bălan, O., Moise, G., Petrescu, L., Moldoveanu, A., Leordeanu, M., Moldoveanu, F.: Emotion classification based on biophysical signals and machine learning techniques. Symmetry (Basel) 12(1), 21 (2019). https://doi.org/10.3390/sym12010021

14. Green, C.S., Bavelier, D.: Exercising your brain: a review of human brain plasticity and training-induced learning. Psychol. Aging 23(4), 692–701 (2008). https://doi.org/10.1037/a0014345.Exercising

15. Kühn, S., Romanowski, A., Schilling, C., et al.: The neural basis of video gaming. Transl. Psychiatry 1, e53 (2011). https://doi.org/10.1038/tp.2011.53

16. Kühn, S., Gleich, T., Lorenz, R.C., Lindenberger, U., Gallinat, J.: Playing super mario induces structural brain plasticity: gray matter changes resulting from training with a commercial video game. Mol. Psychiatry 19(2), 265–271 (2014). https://doi.org/10.1038/mp.2013.120

17. Ruohomaki, V.: Viewpoints on learning and education with simulation games. In: Riis, J.O. (ed.) Simulation Games and Learning in Production Management, pp. 14–28. Chapman & Hall, London (1995)

18. Siddiqui, A., Khan, M., Akhtar, S.: Supply chain simulator: a scenario-based educational tool to enhance student learning. Comput. Educ. 51(1), 252–261 (2008). https://doi.org/10.1016/j.compedu.2007.05.008

19. García, J., Cañadillas, I., Charterina, J.: Business simulation games with and without supervision: an analysis based on the TAM model. J. Bus. Res. 69, 1731–1736 (2016). https://doi.org/10.1016/j.jbusres.2015.10.046

20. Greco, M., Baldissin, N., Nonino, F.: An exploratory taxonomy of business games. Simul. Gamin. 44(5), 645–682 (2013). https://doi.org/10.1177/1046878113501464

21. Eilon, S.: Management games. J. Oper. Res. Soc. 14(2), 137–149 (1963). https://doi.org/10.1057/jors.1963.22

22. ABNT: NBR ISO 10015: Gestão da qualidade - Diretrizes para treinamento, p. 12 (2001)

23. Benyon, D.: Designing interactive systems: a comprehensive guide to HCI, UX and interaction design (2013). http://catalogue.pearsoned.co.uk/educator/product/Designing-Interactive-Systems-A-comprehensive-guide-to-HCI-UX-and-interaction-design-3E/9781447

24. Maier, F.H., Größler, A.: What are we talking about? - A taxonomy of computer simulations to support learning. Syst. Dyn. Rev. 16(2), 135–148 (2000). https://doi.org/10.1002/1099-1727(200022)16:2%3c135:AID-SDR193%3e3.0.CO;2-P

25. Bell, L., Vogt, J., Willemse, C., Routledge, T., Butler, L.T., Sakaki, M.: Beyond self-report: a review of physiological and neuroscientific methods to investigate consumer behavior 9, 1–16 (2018). https://doi.org/10.3389/fpsyg.2018.01655

26. Arico, P., Borghini, G., Di Flumeri, G., Sciaraffa, N., Babiloni, F.: Passive BCI beyond the lab: current trends and future directions. Physiol. Meas. 39(8) (2018). https://doi.org/10.1088/1361-6579/aad57e

27. Teo, J., Chia, J.T.: EEG-based excitement detection in immersive environments: an improved deep learning approach. In: Nifa, F., Lin, C., Hussain, A., (eds.) 3RD International Conference on Applied Science and Technology (ICAST 2018). American Institute of Physics, Georgetown, Malaysia (2018). https://doi.org/10.1063/1.5055547

28. Burger, C.A.C., Knoll, G.F.: Eye tracking: possibilidades de uso da ferramenta de rastreamento ocular na publicidade. Front - Estud midiáticos **20**(3), 340–353 (2018). https://doi.org/10.4013/fem.2018.203.07

29. Oliveira, J.H.C., Giraldi, J.M.E.: Neuromarketing and its implications for operations management: an experiment with two brands of beer. Gest e Prod. **26**(3) (2019) https://doi.org/10.1590/0104-530x3512-19

30. Eysenck, M.W., Keane, M.T.: Manual de Psicologia Cognitiva. Artmed, Porto Alegre (2010)

31. Kugler, M.: Uma contribuição ao desenvolvimento de interfaces cérebro-computador utilizando potenciais visualmente evocados (2003)

32. Wolpaw, J.R., Birbaumer, N., Heetderks, W.J., et al.: Brain-computer interface technology: a review of the first international meeting. IEEE Trans. Rehabil. Eng. **8**(2), 164–173 (2000). https://doi.org/10.1109/tre.2000.847807

33. Salminen, M., Ravaja, N.: Oscillatory brain responses evoked by video game events: the case of super monkey ball 2. Cyberpsychol. Behav. Impact Internet Multimed. Virtual Real Behav. Soc. **10**(3), 330–338 (2007). https://doi.org/10.1089/cpb.2006.9947

34. Sheikholeslami, C., Yuan, H., He, E.J., Bai, X., Yang, L., He, B.: A high resolution EEG study of dynamic brain activity during video game play. In: Annual International Conference of the IEEE Engineering in Medicine and Biology Society (EMBC), pp. 2489-2491. https://doi.org/10.1109/iembs.2007.4352833

35. Nacke, L.E.: Affective ludology: scientific measurement of user experience in interactive entertainment. Ph.D. Thesis, Blekinge Institute of Technology (2009). http://www.bth.se/fou/forskinfo.nsf/Sok/ca7dff01c93318fdc1257646004dfce1/$file/Nacke_diss.pdf%5Cnhttp://phd.acagamic.com/

36. Li, J., et al.: An improved classification model for depression detection using EEG and eyetracking data (2020). https://doi.org/10.1109/TNB.2020.2990690

37. Duchowski, A.T.: Eye Tracking Methodology (2017). https://doi.org/10.1007/978-3-319-578 83-5

38. Cuesta-cambra, U., Rodríguez-terceño, J.: El procesamiento cognitivo en una app educativa con electroencefalograma y «Eye Tracking». Comunicar **XXV**(52), 41-50 (2017)

39. Carvalho, M., Oliveira, L.: Emotional design in web interfaces. Observatorio **11**(2), 14–34 (2017). https://doi.org/10.15847/obsobs1122017905

40. D'Angiulli, A., Devenyi, P.: Retooling computational techniques for eeg-based neurocognitive modeling of children's data, validity and prospects for learning and education. Front. Comput. Neurosci. **13** (2019). https://doi.org/10.3389/fncom.2019.00004

41. Lee, J.Y., Donkers, J., Jarodzka, H., van Merrienboer, J.J.G.: How prior knowledge affects problem-solving performance in a medical simulation game: using game-logs and eyetracking. Comput. Hum. Behav. **99**, 268–277 (2019). https://doi.org/10.1016/j.chb.2019.05.035

42. Emerson, A., Sawyer, R., Azevedo, R., Lester, J.: Gaze-enhanced student modeling for game-based learning. In: UMAP 2018 – Proceedings of the 26th Conference on User Modeling, Adaption and Personalization, pp. 63–72 (2018). https://doi.org/10.1145/3209219.3209238

Tales of Etrya: English Vocabulary Game

Juan José Salazar Salcedo$^{(\boxtimes)}$ ⓘ, Diana Katherine Toro Ortiz ⓘ, Edwin Gamboa ⓘ,
and María Trujillo ⓘ

Universidad del Valle, Cali, Colombia
{salazar.juan,toro.diana,edwin.gamboa,
maria.trujillo}@correounivalle.edu.co

Abstract. Video games are an adequate tool for teaching and learning since they are engaging, motivating and meet new generation preferences and needs. Consequently, video games may be a suitable strategy to use when learning vocabulary of a second language. However, this is only possible when players are in constant practice and interested in playing. Furthermore, attractive aesthetics improve the quality of the game and makes it more compelling to players. In this paper, the first level of Tales of Etrya (ToE) is presented. ToE is a user-centred mobile game focused on teaching English vocabulary in context. Additionally, we present an optimisation technique based on Level of Detail (LOD) and Culling Optimisation to achieve an acceptable performance in mobile devices. The game was validated with English teachers and tested by a group of students for validation purposes using the Player Experience Inventory (PXI). Our findings show positive results regarding important aspects for the students' motivation such as interest, immersion, aesthetics and game performance. Meanwhile, the testers showed a slightly positive attitude about mastery, autonomy and difficulty of ToE. Finally, we found that the low English level of the testers is an obstacle for achieving incidental learning through a video game. Our work contributes to the development of motivating educational games.

Keywords: Serious games · English vocabulary learning · User centred development · Digital games development

1 Introduction

Video games have taken root in children and teenagers' lives around the world since they consider these as one of the most enjoyable activities [1]. Although several authors highlight some problems or a negative impact of video games (e.g. the potential harm related to violence, addiction and depression), others have identified some benefits that result from playing (e.g. cognitive, motivational, emotional and social benefits) [2]. According to [3], video games are an adequate tool to be used along a learning process, improving cognitive skills, increasing motivation and making knowledge acquisition easier. Additionally, video games enhance children general development by allowing them to try out social rules and attitudes and their capabilities and limitations [3]. Furthermore, [4] claims that an attractive graphic aspect and a favorable sound environment improves

© Springer Nature Switzerland AG 2020
V. Agredo-Delgado et al. (Eds.): HCI-COLLAB 2020, CCIS 1334, pp. 253–262, 2020.
https://doi.org/10.1007/978-3-030-66919-5_26

the quality of the game and makes it more compelling to players. Game aesthetics are considered an important aspect by children and young people.

In this paper, we present Tales of Etrya, an educational game to assist secondary students in learning and rehearsing English vocabulary. The game was co-designed with a group of secondary students and an English teacher. Player Experience (PX) evaluations have shown users' positive interest and motivation towards the game.

2   Related Work

Strong Shot [5] is a 2D shooter digital game whose purpose is to convey basic English vocabulary to secondary students. It was developed using a collaborative scheme, involving 20 students from a secondary school in Cali, who supported the process of designing game story, characters, world, and rules. Strong Shot uses game context (i.e. game world, game tasks, locations and story) to deliver vocabulary to players. It incorporates *English Challenges* (EC), which are mini games or puzzles that players can access at any time. ECs help players obtain game money to upgrade his current arsenal, buy health packs, or vehicles to go through game levels easier. Moreover, Strong Shot keeps a record of the words that a player has seen/interacted with in a Vocabulary menu; each menu item contains an image and a text explaining the meaning of the corresponding word. This way, *incidental* learning is promoted to allow players to understand the meaning of a word [6].

LingQ [7] is a web platform for learning English through texts that the player has to read and translate. LingQ can help develop the four core language skills: listening, reading, speaking and writing. Also, LingQ has a library where the new words that are found during the texts are stored, so that players can review the meaning of a word like in a dictionary.

Memrise [8] is a free online language learning tool. The learning process is based on three different pillars Science, Fun, and Community. Memrise creates lived memories, limits the amount of exercises to avoid overloading the user's memory and periodically reviews the vocabulary learned. Finally, Memrise exercises are built in conjunction with the community, so that a learning network is created between Memrise users [9].

2.1   Player Experience and Motivation in Video Games

The PXI is a scale designed to assess player experience based on two levels, dynamics and aesthetics, [10]. The dynamics level assesses the functional consequences of a game-play episode; i.e., the facility to understand the controls of a game. Meanwhile, the aesthetics level evaluates the psychological consequences; i.e., the feeling of mastery regarding the game controls.

Motivation of the players can be evaluated using the PXI since some of the aspects of the scale can be related to Self-Determination Theory SDT [11]. According to [12], the SDT consists of 3 motivators. First, *Competence or mastery*, which is the sensation of being effective in dealing with the external environment. This aspect is assessed using 3 questions in the PXI. Second, *Autonomy*, which is the innate need to feel in charge of life, while doing what is considered meaningful and in harmony with the values of each person. This aspect is assessed using 3 questions in the PXI. And third, *Relatedness*, which involves social connection with family, friends and others.

3 Development of Tales of Etrya

ToE (in Fig. 1) is a non-violent adventure mobile game aimed at conveying basic English vocabulary using context. It takes the ideas and addresses the motivation problems presented in [5]. Our goal is to incorporate new elements, improve game story, aesthetics and vocabulary delivery means. The goal of ToE is to motivate and engage players in a learning process. ToE is being developed using a collaborative user-centred approach, involving secondary students and an English teacher from *Institución Educativa Multipropósito*. These students participate contribute with ideas and making corrections to the game. The design process was restricted by a requirement from the head and teachers from that school. They asked to reduce or preferably eliminate any violence.

Fig. 1. Tales of Etrya.

3.1 User-Centred Design

The game was designed incrementally using the approach presented in [13]. First, the development team co-designed the educational content of the game with an English teacher. Then, entertaining content and its relationship with educational content was co-designed with a group of secondary students and the English teacher during two workshops. To develop the game, we proposed the following two rules to the students while designing game challenges: (1) the game must not contain any acts that could possibly lead to violent situations, racism, or sexual content. Contrary to this, students must design novel combat strategies or game mechanics to distract enemies, and (2) the situations must occur on a map designed by them.

To design the map, the development team proposed to the students to recreate the neighbourhood where they live. The students highlighted places where they usually spend their leisure time or popular places they often visit. At the end of the workshop, a complete map with the most common places and a possible route to visit them was designed.

3.2 Game Story

The story features an explorer called Jhonny. One day, Jhonny was in the unexplored jungle of *Albya*. In his path, Jhonny found a building like a shrine. Inside this place, a strange rock was mysteriously floating over an altar. Jhonny decided to grab it. As the rock was lifted, it glowed and took Jhonny to another realm. Once there, Jhonny fall on the floor of what looked like a forest. There, he found another shrine that looked more destroyed than the one he saw before. Jhonny looked to the shrine and saw the rock floating again. He run, trying to grab the rock, but the rock avoided him, broke into two pieces and flew away from him. Jhonny tried to follow the flying pieces but was unable to keep the pace. After running a few meters away from the shrine, Jhonny saw a small city over a mountain, and the rocks were flying to the city, so Johnny run following the pieces.

Once in the city Jhonny should find the rock pieces. After that, he is going to be challenged by Aradis, a magician who was a guardian of the forest in past times.

3.3 Mechanics

The first level of ToE consists in following clues and directions to find a set of objects. It was designed by the students of *Institución Educativa Multipropósito*. In this level, players help an old woman who feared the enemies that appear in the first level zone. These enemies made her run, dropping some personal objects in the whole city. When players talk to her, she asks for help to find her things. The old woman gives the player three magic jewels so he can escape from the enemies.

The group of students designed game mechanics with the purpose of creating a set of actions that players could use to face enemies. As stated before, the combat system must not be violent (i.e. shooting, killing, exploding). Instead, students proposed a set of gemstones that could be picked up during game interaction or purchased in a local store of the game. Each gemstone can be thrown at enemies, or near them, and each type has a unique effect on enemies. Three gems were presented, a blue one to freeze the enemies, a red one to separate them and a yellow one to damage them over time.

A clue for each personal object was composed to help players locating the lost objects in different places of the city. The clues contain an image representing the personal object, an image representing the place where the object can be located and a text that specifies the location of the personal object in relation to the important place. An example of this clue is presented in Fig. 2.

Fig. 2. Clue presentation.

4 Performance Improvement Strategy

In order to improve the performance of the game, optimising it for mobile devices, two video game optimisation techniques were implemented:

4.1 Level of Detail

To reduce the house's models' number of vertex, four layers of LOD were added to each model. This technique consists in reducing the details of the models as the player moves away from them, each layer represents a LOD, being the layer 0 the most detailed one. The LOD technique improves performance because it reduces the number of vertices that the engine needs to render. This reduction of vertices also reduces the quality of the model, but this is unnoticed because of the distance of the object to the game camera. Figure 3 present the fourth layer of one model LOD layers of a house model in which a reduction of 33.64% is reached.

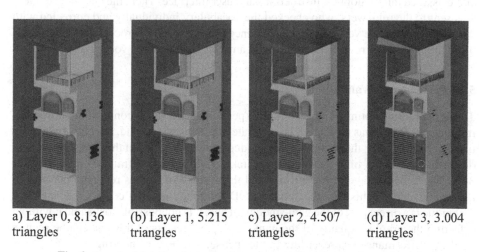

a) Layer 0, 8.136 triangles   (b) Layer 1, 5.215 triangles   c) Layer 2, 4.507 triangles   (d) Layer 3, 3.004 triangles

Fig. 3. Level of detail optimisation layers comparison for one house model

4.2 Culling Optimisation

A Culling Optimisation technique was applied in order to reduce the workload of the rendering process, this technique improves the game performance by hiding (i.e. not rendering) the elements that are not visible by players, thereby reducing the workload of the render engine. This process is illustrated in Fig. 4.

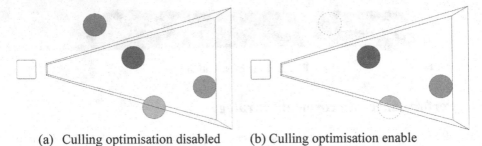

    (a) Culling optimisation disabled   (b) Culling optimisation enable

Fig. 4. Culling optimisation technique illustrated. The square represents the player's point of view.

5 Preliminary Validation

5.1 English Content Validation

To assess the quality of the vocabulary presented during the game, two English teachers and one native English speaker were invited to validate each sentence shown in the game. They validated the correctness and properness for English learners. To evaluate the vocabulary of the game, all the words and sentences delivered in the game were extracted and classified into dialogues, instructions and user interface. Then, the classified content was sent to the reviewers, who checked the vocabulary individually and corrected with the most appropriate version of each sentence according. This process was carried out three times until the reviewers did not find any corrections in the vocabulary set.

5.2 Performance Validation

To test the Culling optimisation technique, a performance test was conducted. The rendering time per frame was measured; i.e., the rate of frames per second, which is frequently used when analysing the performance of video games. To perform this test, Culling was deactivated, and the time that the engine takes to render each frame is measured for 30 s. Then, the average of these times and the average of frames rendered per second are calculated. For this test, the applied LOD technique was not considered since this technique is a direct part of the game models. Thus, it is not possible to disable it without affecting the graphics quality of the game. Complete results of this test can be seen in Table 1. Performance test regarding frames per second (FPS) rendering.

6 Player Experience and Motivation Evaluation

A PX evaluation was conducted in the post-production phase of the project in order to identify if the motivation aspects are addressed correctly. For this evaluation the players filled out a demographic questionnaire. Then, they were asked to play the first level of ToE. Finally, the players answered the Player Experience Inventory (PXI) to evaluate different aspects of the game (e.g. controls, aesthetics, difficulty).

Table 1. Performance test regarding frames per second (FPS) rendering

Android device	Average FPS Without culling	Average FPS With culling	Improvement
Huawei Y6II	3.01	3.2	6%
Motorola Moto G5	7.51	10.54	40.31%
Xiaomi Redmi 4X	5.86	10.29	75.39%
Huawei Mate 9	11.70	20.51	75.26%
Xiaomi MI A2	14.39	26.15	81.64%

Furthermore, the challenge of the game is an important aspect to consider when assessing motivation. The Flow Channel is defined as the point in which boredom and frustration are balanced [14]. That is, challenge should be according to players skills to avoid lack of motivation due to frustration or boredom. To assess whether the players remain in the flow channel, we analyse the results of the challenge and immersion aspects of the PXI. Additionally, players who show a moderate level of interest tend to show a positive impact on their motivation as well [15]. Therefore, we also consider this aspect of the PXI as a motivator when evaluating the game. Finally, in this project, the aesthetics of the game, the clarity of the objectives and the performance of the game are important aspects that contribute to players' experience, that's why we also consider the audio-visual appeal and clarity of goals aspects of the PXI.

6.1 Participants

20 (7 F, 13 M) tenth grade students from *Institución Educativa Multipropósito* were selected by the English teacher to participate in the test. Regarding their game preferences and habits, 75.0% started playing video games at least three years ago. Their favourite game genres are action (24.2%), adventure (16.7%) and sports (13.6%). Moreover, mobile devices (45.00%), PC (20.00%) and Play Station (20.00%) are their preferred game consoles. Finally, six students (30.00%) play video games more than 4 days per week, six students (30.00%) play between 2 and 4 days per week, seven students (35.00%) plays less than two days per week and the rest of them (5.00%) never plays video games.

6.2 Results and Discussion

Regarding interest, the players showed a positive attitude. They were interested in the game from the beginning of the test, which may be a result of using a user-centred methodology. The results regarding mastery are not consistent. Although some of the participants (55.00%) considered themselves good at playing, only 20.00% of them considered that they could master the evaluated level, which may be caused by the limited amount of time that players invested on the level. When asked if they felt capable while playing the game, they answered in a neutral way, which may be related to the limited mechanics offered in the level to face the enemies and explore the game world. Regarding autonomy, the participants showed a neutral attitude. 40.00% of the students felt that they have the freedom to interact with the world. However, they expected to be able to explore different city locations, which is planned to be included in future iterations. Immersion, the students gave positive feedback. Most of the students (70.00%) were fully focused on the game. Showing that a video game might be an effective tool to focus players on learning content. The negative results (15.00%) may be due to distractions caused by the presence of another student testing another game scenario simultaneously.

The results regarding to challenge, the test showed negative aspects, half of the students (50.00%) consider that the game challenge is not properly balanced, this may be due to the difficulty of players to evade enemies, who chased the player all over the map. Another possible factor for these results could be the low level of English of the players, who did not understand correctly the objectives of the level. Audio-visual appeal, 55.00% of the players enjoyed the style of the game. These results may be due to having a unified game visual style, which was supervised by a professional in arts. Additionally, the feedback received from the players during the prototypes tests was considered as much as possible. The feedback gathered about clarity of goals are negative. Most of the students (55.00%) found that the objectives were not clear, and only 30% of them understood the objectives of the game. This is might be due to the low level of English proficiency of the students that prevents understanding the game goals. Some of the participants suggested to include a "Switch to Spanish" option to be used when some text/word is confusing. These results lead us to think that the way in which the objectives are displayed is not the most suitable for the audience and should be studied and modified (e.g. using animated clues). Considering the immersion and challenge results, we can say that the students, with respect to motivation, stayed focused on the game most of the time, but some of them not knowing how to respond to enemy attacks, this difficulty in reacting to enemies may have caused players to perceive the game as very difficult. This perception of difficulty was reflected in the lack of immersion of some of the players, who asked the evaluators how to avoid them and commented on the difficulty.

Reviewing the mastery aspect, it was found that the players felt good playing the game without reaching the point of having mastered it, this is possibly due to the limited time the players had to play the game. More playing time can help players feel motivated to improve their skills in the game. Additionally, for the autonomy aspect, the players showed mainly neutral results, this can be due to the scarcity of elements that allow interacting with the game world, adding more elements of this class can help the player to understand that their actions can affect the game world. According to the positive results found in the aspect of interest, we can also say that most of the students were motivated to continue playing, these positive results may be due to the inclusion of students in the development process, encouraging their curiosity about the finished project. The results observed in visual aspect clearly demonstrate a positive opinion on the part of the students. This improvement was possible thanks to the inclusion of a professional in visual arts and the design of the first level in conjunction with the students, allowing to accelerate the creative process and to polish a unified style for the game.

Finally, the performance test shows that the game has a positive performance in medium (Xiaomi mi A2) and high (Huawei Mate 9) range cell phones and none of the students expressed dissatisfaction with the performance of the game during the user experience tests. On the other hand, some of the students complained and expressed frustration at the difficulty in understanding the dialogues or the objectives of the game.

7   Final Remarks and Future Work

In this work, the first level of a video game called ToE was presented. This video game assists learning and rehearsing of English vocabulary. It is targeted at school teenagers with a low English proficiency level. It was developed using an iterative user-centred methodology involving the students and teachers of *Institución Educativa Multipropósito*, which allowed to adapt to the changes that happened during the development of the project. That is, we could identify problems and possible enhancements in the game play and to improve the interaction of players with the game; thereby, improving player experience.

A user experience evaluation was conducted to assess the quality of the first level of ToE and evaluate the motivators mentioned in subsection 2.1. It was found that most of the students enjoyed the game and were interested in exploring the rest of the level. The students felt a neutral sense of mastery, possibly due to the short time they played the level. Regarding the autonomy motivator, the results showed a lack of autonomy from the students, this may be due to the limited actions that players have to interact with the game world. Although half of the students showed that the game was too difficult, most of them were focused on the game, without expressing frustration. About the interest motivator, positive results were found. Also, the students found the aesthetics of the game attractive. Although a goals system, a map and visual aids were included in the developed level, the limited English knowledge of the students is still an obstacle that prevents them to understand game goals clearly. Thus, the way to deliver the objectives in the developed level may not be the most appropriate and should be improved (e.g. using animated instructions).

Based on the results of the performance tests shown in Subsect. 5.2, we can say that the Culling Optimisation technique is effective, especially when applied to devices with high graphics processing capacity, reaching up to twice as many frames per second in devices such as the Xiaomi Mi A2 (82% increase) and the Huawei Mate 9 (75% increase). Nevertheless, this technique is quite moderate in mobile phones with low graphics processing, such as the Huawei Y6II where the increase in frames per second was minimal (6%).

ToE is open for future work. First, the use of spaced repetitions techniques may allow rehearsing vocabulary in a more effective way. For this purpose, a new location (represented as a gym) could be added to the main city, where a student would be able to rehearse the topics he needs. Similarly, ToE has currently 1 mini-game in the first level. Thus, including new mini-games would cover a larger vocabulary range and increase the offered game-play time, which is also important to develop long-term motivation. Finally, an evaluation to assess the effectiveness of ToE to assist vocabulary learning should conducted. Such evaluation may imply monitoring the use of the game as part of an English learning process (e.g., in an English course at the *Institución Educativa Multipropósito* during one academic period.

References

1. Vigotsky, L.: El desarrollo de los procesos psicológicos superiores, p. 136. Crítica, Barcelona (1979)
2. Granic, I., Lobel, A., Engels, R.C.M.E.: The benefits of playing video games. Am. Psychol. **69**(1), 66–78 (2014)
3. Zea, N.P., Sanchez, J.L.G., Gutierrez, F.L.: Collaborative learning by means of video games: An entertainment system in the learning processes. In: 2009 9th IEEE International Conference on Advanced Learning Technologies, pp. 215–217 (June 2009). https://doi.org/10.1109/ICALT.2009.95
4. Pirovano, M.: The design of exergaming systems for autonomous rehabilitation. Ph.D. thesis, Italy (2015)
5. Gamboa, E., Trujillo, M., Chaves, D.: Strong shot, a student-centred designed videogame for learning english vocabulary. Tecnologa Educativa Revista CONAIC **3**(3), 29–43 (2016)
6. Wood, J.: Can software support children's vocabulary development? (2001)
7. Lingq. https://www.lingq.com
8. Memrise. https://www.memrise.com/es/
9. Memrise FAQ team: About memrise (2012). https://www.memrise.com/es/about/
10. Vanden Abeele, V., Nacke, L., Mekler, E., Johnson, D.: Design and preliminary validation of the player experience inventory, pp. 335–341 (October 2016). https://doi.org/10.1145/2968120.2987744
11. Pink, D.H.: Drive: The Surprising Truth about What Motivates Us. Penguin (2011)
12. Werbach, K., Hunter, D.: For the Win: How Game Thinking can Revolutionize your Business. Wharton Digital Press (2012)
13. Padilla-Zea, N., et al.: A design process for balanced educational video games with collaborative activities. Dyna **82**(193), 223–232 (2015)
14. Csikszentmihalyi, M.: Beyond Boredom and Anxiety: Experiencing Flow in Work and Play. Jossey-Bass (2000)
15. Katz, I., Assor, A., Kanat-Maymon, Y., Bereby-Meyer, Y.: Interest as a motivational resource: feedback and gender matter, but interest makes the difference. Soc. Psychol. Educ. **9**(1), 27–42 (2006). https://doi.org/10.1007/s11218-005-2863-7

Towards a Process Definition for the Shared Understanding Construction in Computer-Supported Collaborative Work

Vanessa Agredo-Delgado[1,2](✉) ⓘ, Pablo H. Ruiz[1,2] ⓘ, Alicia Mon[3] ⓘ,
Cesar A. Collazos[2] ⓘ, and Habib M. Fardoun[4,5] ⓘ

[1] Corporación Universitaria Comfacauca - Unicomfacauca, Popayán, Colombia
{vagredo,pruiz}@unicomfacauca.edu.co
[2] Universidad del Cauca, Popayán, Colombia
ccollazo@unicauca.edu.co
[3] Universidad Nacional de La Matanza, Buenos Aires, Argentina
alicialmon@gmail.com
[4] Information Systems, Faculty of Computing and Information Technology,
King Abdulaziz University, Jeddah, Saudi Arabia
hfardoun@kau.edu.sa
[5] Computer Science Department, College of Arts and Science, Applied Science University,
Al Eker, Bahrain

Abstract. In Computer-Supported Collaborative Work - CSCW, there are factors that affect the collaboration achievement, as for example, the difficulty of having all group members participate effectively in the development of an idea, for this, it is necessary to go beyond having the activity and the technological tools. A deeper approach must be taken through some external factors' analysis, among them, cognitive processes. One of these cognitive processes is shared understanding, which refers to the degree to which group members concur on a topic, its interpretation, when they share a perspective (mutual agreement), or can act in a coordinated manner. This is why, this paper presents a process proposal initial for the shared understanding construction in a problem-solving activity, where the aim is to achieve, before starting the executing process of the task, way a shared understanding of the objective, that is, the whole group knows what is to be achieved at the end of the activity. This paper is intended to show an initial version of this process, where was validated its viability and usefulness in shared understanding construction, through an experiment with students from two Latin American Universities. For this work, a substantial body of research was consolidated using the multi-cycle action-research methodology with a three-cycle bifurcation. According to the results, it can be said that the process is feasible and useful for the shared understanding construction since the application of the process allows achieving it, however, it was discovered that it has aspects to improve from the viewpoint of high cognitive load that generates its use and the need to monitor and assist maintain the shared understanding.

Keywords: CSCW · Shared understanding · Problem-solving activity · Process

© Springer Nature Switzerland AG 2020
V. Agredo-Delgado et al. (Eds.): HCI-COLLAB 2020, CCIS 1334, pp. 263–274, 2020.
https://doi.org/10.1007/978-3-030-66919-5_27

1   Introduction

In many situations, it has been believed that having a technological infrastructure guarantees effective collaboration [1], however, in CSCW, the collaboration is hard to achieve [2], since, there are factors that affect its achievement [3]. This is why, for guarantees effective collaboration, it is necessary to go beyond [4], must analyze some external factors such as people group, activities, technological infrastructure and cognitive processes [5]. Some research has been conducted to improve collaboration among group members [6–9], but these and other authors have in common that they pay special attention to the processes followed and the tools provided to help to the communication and interaction among team members; but the critical cognitive aspects that ensure that the team works effectively and efficiently toward a common objective, are frequently absent [7, 10]. One of these cognitive processes is shared understanding, which is known that its existence in the collaborative work process among all involved actors is one prerequisite for its successful implementation [11–13]. In general terms, shared understanding refers to the degree to which people concur on topics, the interpretation of the concepts, is when group members share a perspective (mutual agreement) or can act in a coordinated manner [14]. The idea is to achieve, before starting the task execution, way a shared understanding of the objective, that is, that the whole group knows what is to be achieved at the end of the problem-solving activity [15]. This is why this paper presents a process proposal initial for the shared understanding construction in a problem-solving activity, where was validated its viability and usefulness in shared understanding construction, through an experiment with students from two Latin American universities. For this work, a substantial body of research was consolidated using the multi-cycle action-research methodology with a three-cycle bifurcation [16]. According to the results, it can be said that the process is feasible and useful for the shared understanding construction since the application of the process allows achieving it, however, it was found that it has aspects to improve from the viewpoint of high cognitive load that generates its use and the need to monitor and assist maintain the shared understanding.

This paper is structured as follows: Section 2 contains related works. Section 3 contains the methodology for defining the process proposal. Section 4 has conclusions and future work.

2   Related Work

Most researches have focused on the shared understanding measurement, but not on how we can construct it [15, 17, 18]. Below, some researches about shared understanding measurement are presented: Smart [19] used a cultural model, where the nodes of the model represent concepts and their links reflect the ideas of each group member, in addition, to measure shared understanding, it is necessary to measure the shared skills that the participants have. Similarly, Rosenman et al. [20] worked with interprofessional emergency medical teams, where they measure the shared understanding through team perception and a team leader effectiveness measure. On the other hand, White et al. [21], describe a range of techniques, the use of concept maps, relational diagrams, and word association tests, by adopting them for specific application contexts, might obtain measurements of understanding that can then be compared across multiple individuals. Sieck et al. [22] determined that the similarity of mental models might provide a shared understanding measure. Bates et al. [23] developed and validated the Patient Knowledge Assessment tool questionnaire that measured a shared clinical understanding of pediatric cardiology patients.

The previous works show different methods for the shared understanding measurement, but none is related to build shared understanding in collaborative activities, in such a way that they do not guide its materialization, that is why in this work, an initial process is proposed that supports this construction.

3   Methodology

This research was developed following the multi-cycle action-research methodology with bifurcation [16], for which cycles were followed: conceptual cycle, methodological cycle, and evaluation cycle.

3.1   Conceptual Cycle

This cycle consisted of conducting a review and literature analysis, which is showed briefly shown in this paper. The review was aimed to identify the existing elements in the literature that could be included in the initial process definition, in addition, to keep in mind the needs of the context of collaborative problem-solving activities, computer-supported collaborative work, and heterogeneous groups.

To characterize and identify according to the literature the different approaches (process, activities, phases or steps, techniques, and strategies) that allowed the process definition. The literature review work was addressed through the next research questions: What approaches have been reported for executing computer-supported collaborative work? Do the approaches found consider the shared understanding construction in their definitions? Do the approaches use some formal measuring to validate shared understanding achieve?.

As data sources for literature review development were used: IEEE Computer Society Digital Library and Scopus. In the search strategy, the keywords were identified with their respective synonyms and plurals, and through combining these key-words and their association, the search string was developed. Then, the identification and selection of the primary studies were based on two main steps: *Step 1,* the search in data sources and *Step 2,* the apply inclusion and exclusion criteria were defined that allowed to verify their quality and guarantee that they were studies related to the context need.

Step 1: Consisted of applying on each of the data sources the search string, in this way, we obtained for IEEE = 10 papers and for Scopus 263 papers, eliminating repeated papers.

Step 2: In order to reduce the application subjectivity of the inclusion and exclusion criteria, in this step participated several researchers (Two from the Universidad de la Plata and another from the Universidad del Cauca). In the first iteration of this step, the criteria application was done by reading for each one paper its title, abstract, keywords, and conclusions. As a first iteration result, 30 papers were obtained as possible primary studies. In the second iteration, the criteria application was done by reading all the papers' content. As the result was obtained a set of 12 papers classified as primary studies.

From all this process it was evidenced that in the most of the literature found there is no complete approach that ranges from the design of the activity to the complete verification of compliance with it, in addition to not considering shared understanding, as a strategy to improve collaboration, an aspect that will be taken into account in this work, including the what and how to achieve it. With these 12 primary papers, it was possible to identify elements that served as the basis for the creation of the first version of the process proposed here.

3.2 Methodological Cycle

This cycle consisted of analyzing the information obtained previously, allowing to create the initial version of the process, that contains phases, activities, tasks, and steps that will allow executing a collaborative work in problem resolving activities seeking to achieve a shared understanding. For defining the collaboration process, we followed the collaboration engineering design approach [24], which addresses the challenge of designing and deploying collaborative work practices for high-value recurring tasks and transferring them to practitioners to execute for themselves without the ongoing support from a professional expert in collaboration [25]. To model the process, we use the conventions based on the elements and stereotypes proposed by SPEM 2.0 meta-molding (Software Process Engineering Meta-Model) [26].

In this work, what we refer to as "Shared understanding" is both an important determinant for performance. Group members might be using the same words for different concepts or different words for the same concepts without noticing [25]. We aim to address this challenge by providing a structured collaboration process based on theory grounded design guidelines that can be used to support heterogeneous groups to develop a shared understanding of a task. With this, we contribute to making the construction of shared understanding in more predictable and manageable.

According to our proposed process, the computer-supported collaborative work we divide it into 3 phases, Pre-Process, Process, and Post-Process, which were taken from Collazos' work [27], phases that were updated and adapted to collaborative work. The first phase Pre-Process begins with the activity design and specification, in the Process phase, the collaboration activity is executed to achieve the objectives based on the interaction among group members and with necessary resources. At the end of the activity, in the Post-Process phase, the activity coordinator (the person in charge of guiding the activity) performs an individual and collective review to verify the achievement of the proposed objectives (See Fig. 1).

For the first Pre-Process phase, the activities proposed by Collazos' [27] were updated and adapted, to each one of them was assigned with the respective description, the responsible person, the inputs and outputs of such activity (See the phase activities in Fig. 2):

This research focuses mainly on the Process phase since it is here where the collaborative work interactions take place, where we can obtain shared understanding through

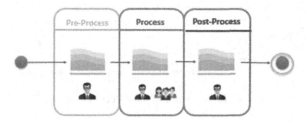

Fig. 1. Computer supported collaborative work phases.

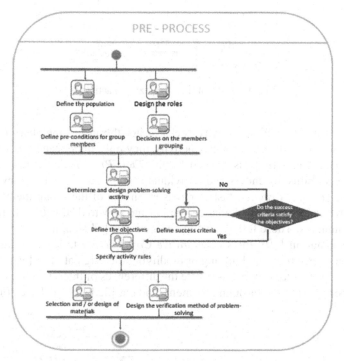

Fig. 2. Activities of the Pre-process phase

different strategies. For this phase, the following activities were defined (See Fig. 3). Each of these activities has defined tasks, steps, roles, inputs, and outputs. This document shows in detail the activities of *Organization* and *Shared Understanding*, the latter, which was validated to verify if it was possible to construct shared understanding, and with this activity validated in a later version of the process, with new validations and investigations, it is expected that the other activities will be detailed with their respective information.

The Organization activity was defined so that the coordinator organizes all the elements necessary to start the collaboration activity (See the tasks of Organization activity in Fig. 4).

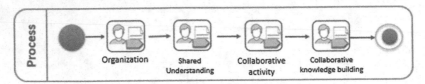

Fig. 3. Activities of the Process phase

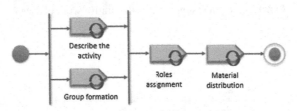

Fig. 4. Tasks of the Organization activity

The Shared understanding activity seeks to get the group members to agree on what the problem is in the collaborative activity, they must understand it before starting its development, this activity is formed by the *Tacit Pre Understanding* task which is, the people's ability to understand individual representations when they make use of them [28], The *Construction* task happens when one of the group members inserts meaning by describing the problematic situation and how to deal with it, hereby tuning in fellow teammates. These fellow teammates are actively listening and trying to grasp the given explanation [29], the *Collaborative Construction* task is a mutual task of building meaning by refining, building or modifying the original offer [30], and finally, *Constructive Conflict* task, which is where the differences of interpretation between the group members are treated through arguments and clarifications [14] (See Fig. 5).

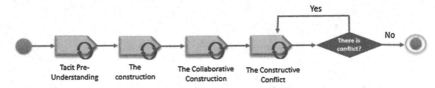

Fig. 5. Tasks of Shared understanding activity

Considering these tasks, we define for each a series of steps that will allow achieving the objectives (See Table 1).

In this work, only is detailed and show until the shared understanding activity of the proposed process, due to that construction of the process obeys an iterative and incremental approach where portions of processes are proposed and then evaluated. In this way, seek is to progressively improve and validate both the structure of the process and its semantics. With this, it is sought that the proposed process be fully validated, in addition to verifying whether it is complete and supports the shared understanding

Table 1. Steps of the Shared Understanding

Activity	Steps	Description
Tacit pre-understanding	1: Appropriation - tacit knowledge	Read the task individually
	2: Express – explicit knowledge	Each member writes what they understood
	3: Clarify pre-understanding	Each member writes questions
Construction	4: Construction of meaning	Share their individual understanding
	5: Listening to others	Listen to the understanding of the others
	6: Understanding others	Write the questions or disagreements about what you hear from others
Collaborative construction	7: Clarifying different understandings	Each member asks clarification questions
	8: Identifying conflicts	Classify their own questions in conflicting and non-conflicting
Constructive conflict	9: Solving conflicts	Discuss conflict differences until everyone agrees
	10: Group voting	Voting to agree with the shared description
	11: Expressing the shared understanding	The group writes a new understanding where everyone agrees

construction in such a way that it improves the CSCW. For the next increases, the other missing activities in the workflow will be evaluated.

3.3 Evaluation Cycle

This cycle allowed us to achieve the objective of inquiring about the feasibility and utility of the proposed initial process for the shared understanding construction, through an experiment, It is important to clarify that, the process was subjected to several revisions in which two members of the IDIS research group of the Universidad del Cauca and a member of the GIS group of the Universidad de la Matanza participated, also, we conducted a focus group with two experts on group work and collaboration engineering to review the process, before they should be implemented in practice. The experiment is presented in a summary way in the following sections.

Experiment Context
The experiment was conducted in a university environment in which participated: 45 last semester students of Universidad de la Matanza - UM (Argentina) with a well level of experience in the activity topic, for this group the proposed process was applied. Moreover, participated 15 students of Universidad Nacional de la Plata - UP (Argentina), enrolled in the last year, with a well level of experience in the topic, to which the proposed process was not applied. The groups were formed using a software tool called Collab [31] that analyzes the learning styles and organizes the group through an algorithm Genetic described in [32], where heterogeneous groups of 5 participants were formed and allowed learning styles to complement each other and thus obtain better results.

The problem-solving activity consisted of each group assuming that they were part of the process engineering team of a company, where they had to establish the software development processes that best adapt and support the projects in the company. To solve the problem, they had to follow an execution guide called SpeTion-SPrl, where information about the projects and processes is defined, and with this determine the scope of each one of them.

Experiment Planning
The research question was defined as: How feasibility and useful is this proposed process? This study had one analysis unity, which was the academic context, where a problem-solving activity about the Scope definition in Software Process Line carried out.

Hypothesis. Considering the objective, it is intended to evaluate the following hypotheses:

- The proposed initial process is feasible for the construction of shared understanding in a problem-solving activity
- The proposed initial process is useful for achieving the objectives of the problem-solving activity.

For the experiment, instruments were designed that would allow applying the proposed process. Table 2 summarizes the phases planned for the experiment development and specifies its planned duration and the support instruments that were used for its development.

Execution of the Experiment
The UM groups applied the entire process, while the UP groups simply met to develop the proposed activity. Therefore, the UM in the Pre-Process phase for each activity used a software tool MEPAC [33], which provided the step by step through forms, with the design and definition of necessary elements. In the Process phase used a software tool Collab [31] for group formation, in this phase also was used formats for to write the individual understanding about the problem, to write the questions or disagreements, to classify the understanding of the other members, to classify their own understanding, the group also wrote the understanding where everyone agreed, the groups solve the problem and used a survey format with 24 questions for analyzing the results.

Table 2. Phases, duration and instruments

Phase	Duration	Support instruments
Pre-Process	1 h 25 min	A software tool MEPAC [33] that, through forms, provides the step-by-step for the design and definition of the elements necessary for the subsequent execution of each activity
Process	2 h	Software tool Collab for group formation [31], formats for role assignment, to execute the activity, to assess individual and group understanding, to analyze questions and disagreements, to analyze understandings and participant survey
Post-Process	1 h	MEPAC that will guide the execution of the activities with forms

The time used for applying the proposed process in UM was 3 h 55 min, and for the UP it was 2 h and 40 min.

Results Analysis

With the observation made by the researchers while the activity was being carried out, it was possible to determine that those groups that obtained poor results in the evaluations were those that did not perform well in the application of the process, did not generate internal discussions to resolve doubts. it was observed that following the process was exhausting for the participants and that this generated a lack of commitment to the rest of the activity and a high cognitive load. On the other hand, to guarantee that the results found are not only observational and apparent but statistically significant was used the student's t-distribution [34], which allowed validating the hypotheses (The details of the results obtained in the validation can be seen in [35]). With this statistical analysis, the specific hypotheses that were accepted were:

- There is a statistically significant difference in grade point average between individual and group descriptions, and for group descriptions between UM and UP participants.
- The percentage of perception about the level of understanding and opinion that the participants have in front of the descriptions of other participants in the group, is greater than or equal to 60%.
- There is a statistically significant difference in the average of the results obtained from the homogeneous understanding of the group before and after the use of the proposed process, and between the UM and UP groups.
- There is a statistically significant difference in the average of the results obtained from the differences in individual knowledge versus group knowledge, before and after the use of the proposed process, and between the UM and UP groups.
- There is a statistically significant difference in the average of the results obtained from the construction, co-construction, and constructive conflict activities between the UM and UP groups.

With all the specific alternative hypotheses accepted, it can be determined that the process is feasible to build a shared understanding.

- There is a statistically significant difference in the average of the notes from the results after applying the guide between the UP and UM groups.
- There is a statistically significant difference in the number of questions asked to the activity coordinator between the UM and UP groups.
- There is a statistically significant difference in the average of results obtained from satisfaction perceived by the participants about the attainment of the objectives between the UM and UP groups.
- There is no statistically significant difference in the average of the results obtained from the satisfaction perceived by the participants about process items between the UM and UP groups, and about activity outcomes between the UM and UP groups.

With 3 of the 4 specific alternative hypotheses accepted, it can be determined that the process is useful for achieving the objectives of the problem-solving activity.

With the statistical comparison of the results with the use of the process and without its use, it was verified that the process used, improves the participants' individual understanding, improve the group understanding about the activity, generate a homogeneous understanding of the activity, it does not generate a discrepancy of each participant regarding the group understanding, the shared understanding activities generated better results and were better fulfilled among the participants. Also determined that the use of the process generates final products with better quality levels. The process allowed to obtain better achievement participants' satisfaction with the objectives proposed by the activity. Conversely, it cannot be determined that the elements of the process are satisfactory for the participants and in the same way, with the outcomes of the activity.

4   Conclusions, Future Work and Limitations

This paper presents the first version of a process for the shared understanding construction of problem-solving activity, which was constructed from elements found in the literature review, the analysis of the context, and its needs. The validation consisted of an experiment in which the results obtained from the statistical analysis allowed us to conclude that it is a feasible process for shared understanding construction and is useful for achieving its objectives. However, according to the specific null hypotheses that were accepted, it cannot be determined that the perception of the participants' satisfaction with the elements of the process and the results of the activity improve. In addition, the need was found to improve the process in a way that is lighter and easier to carry out, to avoid the cognitive burden at the beginning of the activity.

As future work, it was possible to identify that, although we use existing measurement elements for shared understanding, there is a need to include in the process, the use of more advanced instruments to identify all of its categories, in addition to including monitoring and assistance mechanisms that allow it to be maintained throughout the activity. In the same way, it is necessary to carry out a greater investigation of the mechanisms that must be incorporated into the process, that allows achieving a better-shared understanding and that is easier to use, developing techniques and elements to take advantage of their benefits for more effective group work. Elements such as more specific templates that guide the creation of an activity that builds a shared understanding, specific roles, and the additional that can be incorporated into the process for said construction.

As limitations of the work carried out, the research does not include the analysis of all the complete phases of the process, and its specification, in addition to a lack of computational support to facilitate the execution and tracing of the process, elements that are expected to be completed in later phases of the investigation.

References

1. Dillenbourg, P.: What do you mean by collaborative learning? In: Dillenbourg, P. (ed.) Collaborative Learning: Cognitive and Computational Approaches, pp. 1–19. Elsevier, Oxford (1999)
2. Grudin, J.: Why CSCW applications fail: problems in the design and evaluation of organizational interfaces. In: Proceedings of the 1988 ACM Conference on Computer-Supported Cooperative Work, pp. 85–93 (1988)
3. Persico, D., Pozzi, F., Sarti, L.: Design patterns for monitoring and evaluating CSCL processes. Comput. Hum. Behav. **25**(5), 1020–1027 (2009)
4. Rummel, N., Spada, H.: Learning to collaborate: an instructional approach to promoting collaborative problem solving in computer-mediated settings. J. Learn. Sci. **14**(2), 201–241 (2005)
5. Scagnoli, N.: Estrategias para motivar el aprendizaje colaborativo en cursos a distancia (2005)
6. Garcia, A.S., Molina, J.P., Martinez, D., Gonzalez, P.: Enhancing collaborative manipulation through the use of feedback and awareness in CVEs. In: Proceedings of the 7th ACM SIGGRAPH International Conference on Virtual-Reality Continuum and its Applications in Industry (2008)
7. DeFranco, J.F., Neill, C.J., Clariana, R.B.: A cognitive collaborative model to improve performance in engineering teams—a study of team outcomes and mental model sharing. Syst. Eng. **14**(3), 267–278 (2011)
8. Leeann, K.: A Practical Guide to Collaborative Working. Nicva, Belfast (2012)
9. Barker Scott, B.: Creating a Collaborative Workplace: Amplifying Teamwork in Your Organization, pp. 1–9. Queen's University IRC (2017)
10. Lara Pachón, J.A.: Cognición distribuida y trabajo colaborativo en contexto Blended Learning. Universidad Autónoma de Mainizales, Manizales (2014)
11. Oppl, S.: Supporting the collaborative construction of a shared understanding about work with a guided conceptual modeling technique. Group Decis. Negot. **26**(2), 247–283 (2017)
12. Kleinsmann, M., Valkenburg, R.: Barriers and enablers for creating shared understanding in co-design projects. Des. Stud. **29**(4), 369–386 (2008)
13. Jentsch, C., Beimborn, D.: Shared understanding among business and it - a literature review and research Agenda. In: Proceedings of the 22nd European Conference on Information System (ECIS), Tel Aviv (2014)
14. Van den Bossche, P., Gijselaers, W., Segers, M., Woltjer, G., Kirschner, P.: Team learning: building shared mental models. Instr. Sci. **39**(3), 283–301 (2011)
15. Christiane Bittner, E.A., Leimeister, J.M.: Why shared understanding matters–engineering a collaboration process for shared understanding to improve collaboration effectiveness in heterogeneous teams. In: 46th Hawaii International Conference on System Sciences (HICSS), pp. 106–114 (2013)
16. Lencinas, V., et al.: Investigacion-accion: una oportunidad para generar conocimiento desde la práctica profesional de bibliotecatios y archiveros, Cordoba (2017)
17. Gomes, D., Tzortzopoulos, P., Kagioglou, M.: Collaboration through shared understanding in the early design stage. In: 24th Annual Conference of the International Group for Lean Construction, Boston (2016)

18. Johnson, T., O'Connor, D.: Measuring team shared understanding using the analysis-constructed shared mental model methodology. Perform. Improv. Q. **21**(3), 113–134 (2008)
19. Smart, P.R.: Understanding and Shared Understanding in Military Coalitions. Web & Internet Science, Southampton (2011)
20. Rosenman, E.D., et al.: A simulation-based approach to measuring team situational awareness in emergency medicine: a multicenter, observational study. Acad. Emerg. Med. **25**(2), 196–204 (2018)
21. White, R., Gunstone, R.: Probing Understanding. The Falmer Press, London (1992)
22. Sieck, W.R., Rasmussen, L.J., Smart, P.: Cultural network analysis: a cognitive approach to cultural modelling. In: Network Science for Military Coalition Operations: Information Exchange and Interaction, pp. 237–255 (2010)
23. Bates, K.E., Bird, G.L., Shea, J.A., Apkon, M., Shaddy, R.E., Metlay, J.P.: A tool to measure shared clinical understanding following handoffs to help evaluate handoff quality. J. Hosp. Med. **9**(3), 142–147 (2014)
24. Kolfschoten, Gwendolyn L., de Vreede, G.-J.: The collaboration engineering approach for designing collaboration processes. In: Haake, J.M., Ochoa, S.F., Cechich, A. (eds.) CRIWG 2007. LNCS, vol. 4715, pp. 95–110. Springer, Heidelberg (2007). https://doi.org/10.1007/978-3-540-74812-0_8
25. de Vreede, G.-J., Briggs, R.O., Massey, A.P.: Collaboration engineering: foundations and opportunities: editorial to the special issue on the journal of the association of information systems. J. Assoc. Inf. Syst. **10**(3), 7 (2009)
26. OMG: Software & Systems Process Engineering Metamodel (SPEM) (2007)
27. Collazos, C.A., Muñoz Arteaga, J., Hernández, Y.: Aprendizaje colaborativo apoyado por computador, LATIn Project (2014)
28. Stahl, G.: Group cognition in computer-assisted collaborative learning. J. Comput. Assist. Learn. **21**(2), 79–90 (2005)
29. Web, N., Palincsar, A.S.: Group Processes in the Classroom. Prentice Hall International, Upper Saddle River (1996)
30. Baker, M.: A model for negotiation in teaching-learning dialogues. J. Interact. Learn. Res. **5**(2), 199–254 (1994)
31. Lescano, G., Costaguta, R.: COLLAB: conflicts and sentiments in chats. In: Interacción 2018 Proceedings of the XIX International Conference on Human Computer Interaction, Palma de mayorca (2018)
32. Lescano, G., Costaguta, R., Amandi, A.: Genetic algorithm for automatic group formation considering student's learning styles. In: 2016 8th Euro American Conference on Telematics and Information Systems (EATIS), Cartagena (2016)
33. Agredo, V., Ruiz, P., Collazos, C., Fardoun, H.: Software tool to support the improvement of the collaborative learning process. In: Colombian Conference on Computing (2017)
34. Neave, H.R.: Elementary Statistics Tables. Routledge, London (2002)
35. Agredo-Delgado, V., Ruiz, P., Mon, A., Collazos, C., Moreira, F., Fardoun, H.: Validating the shared understanding construction in computer supported collaborative work in a problem-solving activity. In: 8th World Conference on Information Systems and Technologies, WorldCist 2020, Budva (2020)

Towards to Usability Guidelines Construction for the Design of Interactive Mobile Applications for Learning Mathematics

Carlos Andrés Casas Domínguez[1](✉) ⓘ, David Oidor Mina[1] ⓘ,
Vanessa Agredo-Delgado[1,2] ⓘ, Pablo H. Ruiz[1,2] ⓘ, and Deema M. AlSekait[3] ⓘ

[1] Corporación Universitaria Comfacauca - Unicomfacauca, Popayán, Colombia
{carloscasas,davidoidor,vagredo,pruiz}@unicomfacauca.edu.co
[2] Universidad del Cauca, Popayán, Colombia
[3] Princess Nourah Bint Abdulrahman University, Riyadh, Saudi Arabia
DMAlSekait@pnu.edu.sa

Abstract. There is a wide variety of approaches to establish usability in different types of applications and contexts, in order to achieve effectiveness, efficiency, and satisfaction in users. Given this diversity and the absence of clear rules on how to apply such usability in specific contexts. This paper proposes a set of usability guidelines that provide adequate elements for software development in the specific context of the design of interactive mobile applications for learning mathematics in children aged 6–7, which were derived from existing general usability guidelines, of context analysis and its needs. This paper is intended to show an initial version, where were validated its completeness, suitability, ease of use, and ease of learning, through expert judgment. For this work, a substantial body of research was consolidated using the multi-cycle action research methodology with a three-cycle fork: conceptual, methodological, and evaluation. According to the results, it can be said that the guidelines are complete, easy to learn, moderately usable and moderately suitable; it determines that there is a need to continue improving their description in such a way that they can adequately satisfy the purpose for which they were created, however, we believe that the resulting guidelines represent a good contribution to the usability engineering knowledge field in this context.

Keywords: Usability · Guidelines · Usability guidelines · Design of interactive mobile applications

1 Introduction

In recent years the use of the mobile device (phones, portable audio players, personal digital assistants, GPS (Global Positioning System) navigators, tablets, digital cameras, etc.) has increased considerably, which is why it is important to have methodologies, elements, and tools that allow to carry out specific usability studies for applications developed for this type of devices [1], specifically for applications that were developed to run on mobile phones. The term mobile refers to being able to access data, applications,

© Springer Nature Switzerland AG 2020
V. Agredo-Delgado et al. (Eds.): HCI-COLLAB 2020, CCIS 1334, pp. 275–284, 2020.
https://doi.org/10.1007/978-3-030-66919-5_28

and devices from anywhere. [2], for this reason, to software development of this kind, certain restrictions that the hardware has and the context where it will be used must be taken into account, however, the methods, metrics, and guidelines currently used to define usability have been created for desktop applications or web, which may not be directly suitable or appropriate for mobile environments [3], besides, there is an absence of clarity on how to apply this usability in more specific contexts [4]. One of the main challenges is to identify the additional variables related to the use environment and the context, which can impact the usability of a mobile application so that when designing, these variables can be included [3].

This is why this paper focuses on defining a set of usability guidelines for software development in the specific context of the design of interactive mobile applications for learning mathematics in children aged 6–7 years, which were derived from existing usability guidelines, an analysis of the context and its needs. Taking into account that the field of education is incorporating new supports, tools, or technologies that favor student learning processes [4, 1]. However, each application has its own particularities in relation to human-machine interaction that affects the handling and design of its interfaces, as well as the function and uses they may have in a given environment. [4]. For this reason, this paper intends to show an initial version of the set of guidelines to which their completeness, suitability, ease of use and ease of learning were validated, through the judgment of experts, using the multi-cycle action research methodology with a branch of three cycles. According to the results, it can be said that the guidelines are completeness, easy to learn, moderately usable and moderately suitable; determining that there is a need to continue improving its description so that they can adequately satisfy the objective for which they were created, however, we believe that the resulting guidelines represent a good contribution to the usability engineering knowledge field.

This paper is structured as follows, section two: related works, section three: the methodology that was carried out, section four: validation and finally, section five: the conclusions and future work.

2   Related Work

The objective of research of Videla et al. [5], was to determine the elements, components, and factors that are key when designing interactive interfaces for augmented reality environments, focusing in particular on the development of virtual environments for educational applications. For this study two applications of augmented reality of educational content were carried out and tested and whose purpose was to be a complement to the textbook, which were designed for non-tactile interfaces and in which the use of a Webcam and a computer.

On the other hand, Collazos et al. [6], define a guide to correctly include usability in interactive television, and shows evaluation methods to verify its good design. This work described and structured a set of guidelines that can be followed by user interface designers to achieve services clearly adapted to the interactive environment of television. Similarly, there was a project in the UTM (University Technical of Manabí) that focused on the development of educational applications for mobile devices called Edumóvil. It is a project that was born in the UTM and had as its objective: to improve the teaching-learning process of basic level children through the incorporation of mobile technology in the classroom [7], It was focused on developing applications for PDAs (Personal Digital Assistant) and cell phones that covers primary subjects, such as Spanish, Mathematics, History and Natural Sciences, this development an application consisting of a collaborative game for the subject of Natural Sciences and a story viewer aimed at the subject of Spanish [7].

From the viewpoint of education, there are projects such as the one defined by Ocsa et al. [8], which aimed to systematize the design and development of m-learning applications through two types of applications, the first one inter-active in comic format about the foundation of the Inca Empire and the second in book format Interactive about the main tourist sites of Peru, which was intended to reduce the complex development of these applications through encapsulations of native code for mobile operating systems, allowing to establish design and development guidelines for high quality mobile educational applications, in addition, to Consider elements of human-computer interaction, user-centered design as the basis for the development of case studies in order to reflect the scope of applications from a pedagogical and technological viewpoint. Similarly, Tello and Yautibug [9], took into account the current influence of Virtual Learning Environments (VLE), where its development and design is of great relevance for its context of use, therefore, they identified and implemented criteria of good usability practices to detect design errors in the VLE of the National University of Chimborazo and thus increase its level of usability.

The previous works show different methods to evaluate usability in various contexts and applications, but none are related to a specific context of usability guidelines for the design of interactive mobile applications for learning mathematics in children from 6 to 7 years old, that is why in this work, a set of these guidelines is proposed to further guide this process.

3   Methodology

This research was developed following the multi-cycle action-research methodology with bifurcation [10] for which cycles were followed: conceptual cycle, methodological cycle, and evaluation cycle.

3.1   Conceptual Cycle

This cycle consisted of carrying out an analysis of the literature, to identify the existing usability guidelines, as well as to gather important information about concepts, design guidelines, guidelines and elements necessary to include usability in this context. This process showed that most of the guidelines were focused on a web context and desktop applications regardless of context, and lacked a clear explanation for their application. For the development of this cycle, the following activities were carried out as shown in Table 1 Conceptual cycle.

Table 1. Conceptual cycle

Number	Activity
1	To collect information in the literature regarding usability guidelines for application design
2	To Identify the characteristics of end-users of interactive mobile applications
3	To analyze the information collected to identify a set of guidelines, rules or elements appropriate for the design of interactive mobile applications
4	To select the relevant information from the previous analysis
5	To select the guidelines that meet the design needs of interactive mobile applications in this context

3.2 Methodology Cycle

This cycle consisted of analyzing the information obtained previously, selecting the useful elements and defining the necessary ones that allowed to create a first version of the guidelines for the context of this paper. Table 2 shows the activities carried out in this cycle.

Table 2. Methodology cycle

Número	Actividad
1	To realize an interview with math teachers, where needs, difficulties and important elements of the specified context are identified
2	To determine if the usability needs of the users were met with the guidelines analyzed in the previous activities
3	To build the usability guidelines that meet the needs not contemplated in existing studies
4	To generate the guide or list of usability guidelines, obtained in the previous analyzes for later implementation
5	To classify usability guidelines according to usability standard 9241-11

For this cycle, a survey was conducted with 9 teachers from the municipality of Puerto Tejada and 1 teacher from the city of Popayan. The survey consisted of 7 open questions, in this way, more than questions, a dialogue was held with each teacher. These questions were developed in order to obtain information on the topics in which the most difficulties are presented among students, the topics that seek to be supported by the application, in the same way, to socialize the idea and see the opinions and ideas of teachers that will help to solve the missing needs that had not been identified.

After analyzing the data obtained, it was determined that the strongest needs in mathematics on the part of the children were in the sum, which is why it was defined as the topic to be treated of the applications to be designed, in addition to defining that these applications must be used by the child for an approximate time between 10 to 15 min. From the survey, some missing guidelines were also defined in order to meet the unidentified or missing needs related to the context.

As a result of this activity, the definition of a format necessary to describe each guideline is obtained, which contains an identifier, a name, a category, a brief description, the steps to be followed, and an illustrated example of applying the guideline. In addition, the first version of the list of guidelines is obtained with a total of 56.

To improve the first version of the guidelines, the standard 9241-11 of usability is taken into account which contains 3 fundamental characteristics that are: effectiveness, efficiency, and satisfaction [11]. These characteristics were redefined for the context of this work, and each guideline was classified into each characteristic. With this classification, those guidelines that do not comply with any of the characteristics of the standard are discarded and, as a result, we obtain a second version of the list of guidelines, generating a total of 39 (See the list of guideline names on Table 3, see an example of the guideline definition on Table 4).

3.3 Evaluation Cycle

This cycle allows evaluating the completeness, suitability, ease of use and ease of learning of the second version of the usability guidelines. Table 5 the activities carried out in this cycle are shown.

For the development of this cycle, a validation of the guidelines was carried out through a survey aimed at experts in usability, validating its completeness, suitability, ease of use, and ease of learning, for the design of interactive mobile applications for learning mathematics in children aged 6–7 years.

4 Validation

The objective of this validation was to evaluate with experts in usability issues the completeness, suitability, ease of use, and ease of learning of the guidelines developed for the design of interactive mobile applications for learning mathematics in children 6–7 years. This validation was carried out with 6 experts in the area of usability, of which 66.7% have more than 5 years of experience in the area of usability and 33.3% have between 1–5 years of experience.

Each of the experts was given the compendium of the guidelines, in addition to a survey link for validation. The survey had 2 sections, the first one briefly explaining the why and for what of the completion of this survey and the evaluation method which will be conducted according to the Likert scale [12], a second section where the questions were presented in accordance with the 4 categories that are to be validated: completeness, suitability, ease of use and ease of learning.

With the evaluation of the experts, the results of the validation of the proposed guidelines were obtained (See results Fig. 1), these experts provided suggestions for a better interpretation and greater impact of the guidelines on their use, some of the most outstanding opinions by categories were the following:

Table 3. List of guideline names

Guideline title	
System status visibility	Icons
Correspondence between the system and the real world	Character and environment
Control and freedom for the user	Colors
Consistency and standards	Interaction styles suitable for children
Error prevention	Realistic math
Recognize before remembering	Interactivity
Flexibility and efficiency of use	Think like a child
Aesthetics of dialogues and minimalist design	Competitiveness
Help users to recognize, diagnose and recover errors	Foster creativity
Promotion of access to the social environment	Thematic scope
Provision of access to the natural environment	User needs
Attention resources management	Constant evaluation
Management of motivational resources	Required fields
Learning facility	Communication with aspects of the device
Processing capacity	Publication
Security	Dynamic data validation
Capacity (storage and memory)	Pop-up windows
Texts	Confirmation pages
Tabs	Estimated time
Compatibility	

Completeness:

- To include an additional section that refers to when a guideline is violated
- To improve writing and synthesize descriptions in some cases

Suitability:

- No specific guidelines for learning mathematics are identified in children between 6 and 7 years old (only guideline 36 is found)
- There are some guidelines that are generic, even heuristics such as Nielsen's have been included, so they must be filtered and specified more in the context of children and mathematics

Table 4. Guideline example

Identifier	11
Name	Provision of access to the natural environment
Category	Pedagogical strategies, content, games, web.
Description	It refers to the incorporation of elements that generate the environment in which the student will perform, and with them, it must be achieved that it identifies the tasks that must be performed in the educational application [1]
Application steps	• To include images that have educational purposes or that help the student's memory [5]. • To include animations for explanatory purposes of some content or concept [5]. • The use of a metaphor that associates a specific function with a representative image is recommended so that the child does not have to memorize them and interact in a more intuitive way.
Example	A clear example is the Duolingo application, an app dedicated to teaching the English language, which uses images that help the user understand and memorize what they want to teach.

Table 5. Evaluation cycle

Number	Activity
1	To design a mechanism for assessing completeness, suitability, ease of use, and ease of learning of the defined guidelines
2	To perform the application of the evaluation mechanism to usability experts
3	To analyze the results obtained by the experts

Easy to use:

• To define a tool (guide) that facilitates the use of the guidelines, where it is determined when and how to use each guideline

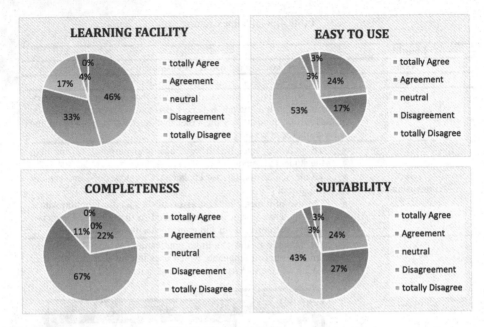

Fig. 1. Expert evaluation results

- To define a flow chart that helps to better understand the process for creating the application with the association of each guideline

Ease of learning:

- The guidelines are written for a non-developer end user, it is necessary to use a more specific and technical language, to make it suitable and easier to use
- The application steps are defined as recommendations, specific steps must be defined, in addition to including numbering, determining whether or not each step is mandatory, and the order in which they should be applied.

4.1 Analysis of the Results

According to the experts' perception, it can be said that the guidelines contain the necessary elements to affirm that they are completeness, given that more than 80% of the respondents agree with this. In addition, it can be said that they are easy of learning, since more than 70% of respondents agree with this because they structurally contain the necessary elements and these are mostly well described.

Nevertheless, since more than 40% of respondent's state that the guidelines do not consider appropriate information, it can be said that they are moderately suitable, this because all the guidelines must be based on the context of the children, mathematics and defined for the design of mobile applications specifically and some are not subject to this, they are very general guidelines that do not differentiate any context. In addition, it can be considered, where according to the experts' perception, 50% of them determine that the guidelines are not easy to use because they are too extensive, the steps are not clear to apply and the examples presented, in some cases, they do not correspond to the use in the specific context and do not give a guide for its correct application.

These results on suitability and ease of use, according to the analysis carried out, is due to the fact that it is a first version of the guidelines, guidelines that were initially created based on literature review and surveys of teachers in the area, which showed that It was not enough and it was necessary to emphasize more in the context and to generate, in addition to new more specific guidelines for said context, a way to make them easier to use and understand.

4.2 Solutions for Problems Found by Experts

According to the results obtained by the evaluation of experts and their respective analyses, it was possible to determine the following proposed solutions to improve these results and be applied in a later stage of the guidelines, in such a way that they achieve the objective for which they were created.

Easy to use:
To solve a little the difficulty of the correct use of the guidelines since they are extensive, it aims to develop a guide to show the developer an optimal way to use it in the correct order and in the appropriate way, this guide can be handled graphically or in writing.

Suitability:
As most of the guidelines are focused on a more general context, it aims to focus the examples of use to our context (mathematics) and categorize them by parts, since every application needs general guidelines, in this way they are optimized both for our context as for the general context.

Ease of learning:
To solve the deficiencies found in this category, the steps of the application will be listed, written in a better way that shows how to do it by yourself, but not how it could be done, thus showing a step by step, it also will show, what steps are required and which are not.

5 Conclusions and Future Work

This paper presents the first version of a set of usability guidelines for the design of interfaces in interactive mobile applications in the context of learning mathematics in children between 6–7 years old, which were constructed based on guidelines found in the literature review, context analysis, and children's needs.

The validation with experts allowed us to identify elements to improve the content, the structure, the form of presentation, the description of the guidelines, and their semantics. According to the expert opinion, it is determined that the guidelines were complete, easy to learn, moderately easy to use, and moderately suitable. Therefore, it is necessary to define in their description a set of elements that facilitate its use and adapt the existing elements to the specific context to improve its suitability.

From the comments obtained by the experts, it was possible to determine as possible improvements for the following stages of the investigation, the creation of a tool, which could be considered to have a guide (that determines the step by step of the design of the interfaces in the specific context and for each step which guideline to use) and a flow chart that graphically shows this process, and thus facilitate its use, in addition to the generation of a light version, that is, a new version of the guidelines that only has the identifier, name, category, and description, and apart from having the complement of the guidelines, which contains the application steps and the examples to be used, this in order to access the complement only when necessary and thus not be so extensive for its access.

As future work, the analysis and subsequent application of the suggestions made by the experts should be carried out, in order to generate a more complete version of the guidelines that must subsequently be validated in a real context, initially creating a functional prototype, using the guidelines and in this way, their application will be evaluated in the context for which they were designed, allowing the validation of useful aspects for their definition and subsequent use.

References

1. Marín, V.: La Gamificación educativa. Una alternativa para la enseñanza (2015)
2. Deloitte: Consumo movil en Colombia: Los móviles prueban ser indispensables en un mundo "siempre" conectado, Colombia (2016)
3. Zhang, D., Adipat, B.: Challenges, methodologies, and issues in the usability testing of mobile applications. Int. J. Hum.-Comput. Interact. **18**, 293–308 (2005)
4. Chimarro Chipantiza, V.L., Mazón Olivo, B.E., Cartuche Calva, J.J.: La usabilidad en el desarrollo de software. Machala, UTMACH (2015)
5. Videla Rodriguez, J.J., Sanjuan Perez, A., Martinez Costa, S., Seoane Nolasco, A.: Diseño y usabilidad de interfaces para entornos educativos de realidad aumentada (2017)
6. Collazos, C.A., Arciniegas, J.L., Mondragón, V.M., Garcia Pañeda, X.: Lineamientos de usabilidad para el diseño y evaluacion de la television digital interactiva (2008)
7. Aquino, L.: ¿Quien se come a quien? juego colaborativo para niños de primaria en palms de un ecosistema utilizando bluetooth. Tesis de ingenierar en Computacion (2006)
8. Ocsa, A., Herrera, J., Villalba, K., Suero, G.: Propuesta Para El Diseño Y Desarrollo De Aplicaciones M-Learning: Caso, Apps De Historia Del Perú Como Objetos De Aprendizaje Moviles (2014)
9. Tello Valle, J.A., Yautibug Apugllón, M.E.: implementación de mejores prácticas de usabilidad en el diseño de la interfaz del entorno virtual de aprendizaje de la universidadd de chimborazo, Riobamba (2018)
10. Nataloni, F., Hannover, S., Villanueva, T.G., Lencinas, V.: Investigacion-accion: una oportunidad para generar conocimiento desde la práctica profesional de bibliotecatios y archiveros, Cordoba (2017)
11. N. E. I. 9241-11: Requisitos ergonómicos para trabajos de oficina con pantalla de visualizacion de datos (PDV) ISO 9241-11 (1998)
12. Serzo, H.: Rensis Likert y Douglas Mcgregor. Management Today en español, pp. 33–36, enero de (1984)

Usability Evaluation over Multiplayer Games on Display Wall Systems

Marc Gonzalez Capdevila[1]([✉]) [iD], Karine Aparecida Pistili Rodrigues[1] [iD],
Valéria Farinazzo Martins[2,3] [iD], and Ismar Frango Silveira[2,3] [iD]

[1] Centro Universitário Facens, Sorocaba, Brazil
{marc.capdevila,karine.rodriguez}@facens.br
[2] Faculdade de Comptação e Informática,
Universidade Presbiteriana Mackenzie, São Paulo, SP, Brazil
{valeria.farinazzo,ismar.silveira}@mackenzie.br
[3] Programa de Pós-Graduação em Distúrbios do Desenvolvimento,
Universidade Presbiteriana Mackenzie, São Paulo, SP, Brazil

Abstract. This paper evaluates a usability study comparing different proposed controllers (Web, Accelerometer and Keyboard) of multiplayer games to discover which are the best methods to interact with display walls. A set of tasks were designed to test user experience and get feedback data from 40 participants. The results indicate that although the keyboard has best results on satisfaction compared to mobile controllers, it has scalability limitations, consequently further research is opened to improve the mobile controllers to achieve a more scalable possibility of players.

Keywords: Display wall · Games · Usability · Liquid Galaxy

1 Introduction

Nowadays, it is commonsense that Extended Reality (XR) is increasingly becoming a de facto standard for advanced human-computer interaction, despite all already known barriers and technological limitations. In this context, XR is an umbrella term that covers all types of computer-altered reality, including Augmented Reality (AR), Virtual Reality (VR) and Mixed Reality (MR). However, before all these technologies become widespread, Display Walls (DW) were the first attempt to bring some kind of immersive virtual experiences to users. A DW is a kind of LSIE (Large Screen Information Exhibits), category which includes from large-scale projections to sets of side-to-side screens.

DW applications are different compared with XR ones, for different reasons. One of them is the hardware needed for the tasks. VR applications, for instance, require users to wear special oculus – which substituted the old-fashioned Head Mounted Displays (HMD). Popular examples of these devices are OculusRift [1] or GearVR [2]. On the other hand, AR applications require cameras in notebooks or mobile devices. In the case of DW, all visualization is generated over screens or walls like CAVE [3],

© Springer Nature Switzerland AG 2020
V. Agredo-Delgado et al. (Eds.): HCI-COLLAB 2020, CCIS 1334, pp. 285–294, 2020.
https://doi.org/10.1007/978-3-030-66919-5_29

Syzygy [4], OpenSG [5], Multiprojectors [6] and Liquid Galaxy [7, 8]. It implies that one DW installation can be used for multiple people at the same time and they are not restricted to hardware controllers, which makes DW an interesting solution for collective visualization, as in the case of multiplayer games.

One of the challenges studied about multiscreen displays is how to provide users more intuitive, easy to use and enjoyable interactive experiences. These questions are related, obviously, to the type of application that will run on these devices. In the case of multiplayer games when players share the same physical – and sometimes also virtual – spaces, but with individual controllers, the challenge is to provide an immersive collective experience.

In this sense, the present study focuses on analyzing new interaction methods with multiscreen environments using multiplayer games. Tests were performed using Google Liquid Galaxy DW [7, 8], consisting of a cluster of five screens and computers running master-slave or client-server applications to provide immersive experiences to larger groups of people.

Multiplayer versions of classical games (Pong and Snake) were developed, supporting three different controlling methods (Web, Accelerometer and Keyboard). A comparative study was carried on determining which types of controllers are more suitable to be used for multiplayer gaming in DW with the aim to find a suitable interaction method for the community and future research.

This work is organized as follows: Section 2 provides a brief background on Liquid Galaxy Platform; Sect. 3 present some related works; the methods proposed to perform the usability tests are presented in Sect. 4; results related to the different tasks performed are shown in Sect. 5 with their discussion; finally, Sect. 6 presents some conclusions and further works.

2   Liquid Galaxy Platform

Liquid Galaxy is a cluster display-wall that started as a Google project, made up of a custom number of computers, where every node has a single monitor [8, 9], as seen in Fig. 1.

Fig. 1. Liquid Galaxy Platform [12]

Although the technology was initially built to run Google Earth, it is possible to create an immersive experience running other types of applications, such as video streaming [10] and video-games like Quake 3 Arena [11].

The Liquid Galaxy platform is included in the category of information display elements on long screens or LSIE (Large Screen Information Exhibits), which can vary from projections in large proportions to sets of screens arranged in what is conventionally called display wall.

User interaction with the system can be done with different types of devices, such as a mouse, keyboard, joystick, Leap Motion, Microsoft Kinect, voice controllers and others [12].

3 Related Work

On [13] it has been proposed a set of usability heuristics for information display in LSIE. When analyzing five information display systems in LSIE, the authors suggest a set of eight potential usability heuristics for those systems. Similar objective is the work of [14], but with a more targeted approach to multi-user applications.

Specifically, on the usability of the Liquid Galaxy platform, the work of [15] presents the results of usability tests in this platform, covering the three aspects (effectiveness, efficiency and satisfaction), with 27 users. In these UX tests, the users needed to complete a set of tasks, with post-tests questionnaires to measure the qualitative information. Using both system performance and user behavior information, they could observe the system performed satisfactorily for users. Also, [15] addresses a study on UX and Liquid Galaxy platform. In this work, a mixed study (survey and interviews) was carried out with 25 users using Google Earth and Google Street View in an immersive way. UX data and their emotions were collected when using the platform. Other works that bring usability studies specifically to the Liquid Galaxy platform include those pointed out by [16–19].

On the other hand, [20] presents a work that compares the performance of game controllers in two-dimensional pointing tasks using ISO 9241-9 standard [21]. This standard specifies the requirements for non keyboard input devices. For this comparison they used four games controller interface: a Logitech mouse and keyboard, a Logitech Bluetooth Touchpad and keyboard, a Sony Playstation DualShock 4 controller, and Valve's first-generation Steam controller. Also, they made an analysis about the evaluation of usability and UX with these devices during gameplay. They compared performance measurements for controllers while varying the user's exposure to the different feedback elements contained within each controller device, using the ISO 9241-9 evaluation recommendations. Besides performance testing, they measured UX with the controllers while players playing a popular first-person video game. Participants had to complete game levels for each type of controller and answer a questionnaire about their experience.

Regarding Liquid Galaxy, some usability assessments were found in the literature. Specifically, in relation to games on this platform, it is clear that it is possible to extend these evaluations for the use of this platform in the game context.

4 Methodology

This study conducts a usability test to explore best methods to interact with a display wall using different kinds of multiplayer video games. The games, the controllers and the procedure used for this study are presented in the following sections as the data collection instruments.

4.1 The Games

For this study it has been used two-pixel games for the facility on the development. The first one is the Pong [22] (Fig. 2-a) and the other is Snake [23] (Fig. 2-b). Both games have been designed taking into account the multiplayer and multiscreen environment of a display wall. Games work with a server-client structure where the master node runs the game and the other computers connect to the server to set their proper point-of-view (POV).

(a) Pong game   (b) Snake game

Fig. 2. Pong and Snake screenshots

In Pong's game the player controls a paddle and has to return a ball which is moving back and forth. According to how you hit the ball with the paddle, the ball speed increases, and the game continues until one of the players fails hitting the ball. The goal of the game is to reach eleven points. The developed version remains as the original and do not introduce changes to the game, only when more than 2 players are added to play, the color changes to identify them.

The mechanics of the game Snake are based on the player maneuvers a line which moves continuously in four different directions. The objective of the player is to "eat" or gather different squares that appear on the screen. Once it reaches one, the length of the line increases. The game finishes when the player hits himself with their own line. In our version we considered another ending game that happens when a player hits another player.

4.2 Controllers

According to the controllers, we decided to use a common keyboard and a mobile device because the first one is well-known for everybody and the second one give us the possibility to add multiple players and further scale. However, on the mobile, users interact individually with their own device. For this reason, we developed two different ways to perform the tasks with the mobile, therefore three different controllers were used:

- **Keyboard controller (Kc):** with the keyboard, each connected player can interact with a fixed set of keys, having to share the same controller with the others.
- **Web controller (Wc):** offers the main functionalities that can be performed by the user (Fig. 3-a). This includes the options to Start, Pause and Restart the game and, also, the four different movements. Main color of the game identifies the color of the player in the display wall once they are connected. Also, when a user touches any of the buttons a pulse lets the user know that some operation was done.
- **Accelerometer controller (Ac):** the mobile controller is a web application that uses the mobile accelerometer to identify the direction of the paddle (Fig. 3-b). The system has three different possible states: up, down and quiet. It identifies a range of 180° over the x-axis and as much the mobile rotates the speed of the paddle also increases. Quiet state it happens when the x-axis has a value between 20° and −20°.

To interact with the Snake game, the participants used the Keyboard and the Web controllers. On the other hand, to interact with the Pong game, the participants had the Keyboard and the Accelerometer controllers.

4.3 Experimental Design

The aim of the experiment was to compare the satisfaction results of using different controllers and gather users' feedback to learn which controller had best results. Users were provided with informative consent ensuring they continually understand the information. If they wanted, they could leave the study at any given time. All the studies were placed on the Liquid Galaxy LAB installations inside Facens University (Sorocaba). The LAB was suited with accommodations for all the users be comfortable during the test and answering the forms. Two evaluators were responsible for providing support to the users during the test. One of them was in charge to give support to the users with

(a) Web controller (Wc)   (b) Accelerometer controller (Ac)

Fig. 3. Screenshots for the Mobile controllers

the different controllers and the other was in charge to control the behavior of Liquid Galaxy infrastructure during the different tasks.

An initial pretest was used to collect subjects' information like age, sex, educational level and, also, number of hours that they spend playing video games a week.

We created four different tasks to be done by users and they were associated according to the game and controller used. Also, for every task to be completed, two different rounds were conducted. Participants start with the Pong game and Keyboard controller, then Accelerometer controller. Once they finish Pong tasks they play the Snake and we invert the order of the controllers. In this case they start with the Web controller and follow with the Keyboard. At the end of every task, users were asked to answer a form using the System Usability Scale (SUS) [24].

Once the participant has completed all tasks, user feedback is collected through a small post task form (using Likert scale) about their performance with the controllers. They have to answer about their satisfaction level using the controller on two different aspects: how comfortable was the use of the controller and if the controllers hinder their performance during the game. Also, they were asked to evaluate each controller via open-ended questioning at the end of each in-game testing block. Overall, each experimental session takes around 30 min including the test (play the games) and the fulfilment of the different forms.

5 Results and Discussion

Following sections depicts the results of our experimentation with the different participants once concluded the different tasks. We also present the data gathered from the post-task usability questionnaire and we discuss what users have commented about their experience.

5.1 Usability Test Participants

A total number of 40 users participated in the experiment aged between 17–42. They were recruited in Sorocaba (Brazil) inside a university so 72,5% of the users are students coursing a bachelor's degree and the others are a mix of professionals with different grades of studies like master's Degree or Ph.D.

We asked participants about their experience with video games in terms of how much time they spend playing and results shows that 40% of participants has a lot of experience with games who play at least every day or once per week; several times a month (30%); once a month (20%); and never plays (10%).

As our participants' distribution is not equitative we split our user data in two groups: G1 represents those users aged under 25 and G2 those over 25. Participants in G1 consist of a total number of 32 (17 Men and 15 Women), on the other hand, G2 consists of 8 (3 Men and 5 Women).

5.2 Usability Test Results

In this section we analyze the data collected from our different post-test into two sections. First, we evaluate SUS results from every task realized and then we evaluate final post-test with the different qualitative answers and also comments gathered during the usability tests. Global SUS results show us that the Accelerometer controller has the lower results (65,08%) in comparison with the other controllers (85,3% and 82,7% for Keyboard controller and Web controller respectively). In Fig. 4 we show SUS results based on the previous skills of our participants for the different controllers. As can be observed, Accelerometer controller has the lowest SUS results but it can be seen that the experience of the users has a direct impact and a positive influence into the satisfaction result. According to the results Keyboard and Web controllers do not present relevant information on this aspect, but it also shows that those users who play daily provide better SUS results.

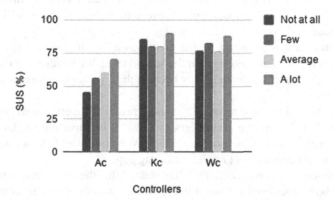

Fig. 4. SUS results for all different controllers grouped by the previous experience in video games, where Ac (Accelerometer), Kc (Keyboard) and Wc (Web) represent the analyzed interaction methods

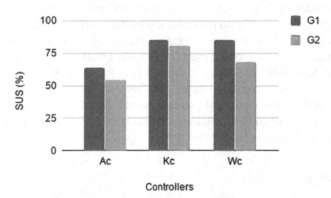

Fig. 5. SUS results for the different studied controllers grouped by age, where Ac (Accelerometer), Kc (Keyboard) and Wc (Web) represent the analyzed interaction methods

Also, Fig. 5 presents the SUS results related with the age of our participants. Data displayed show that participants from G1 give higher SUS responses (78%) than G2

(68%) for all the controllers. It is visible that the difference between both groups on Keyboard controller are smaller (SD = 3%) than in Web and Accelerometer controllers (SD = 12%, SD = 7% respectively).

Regarding if the sex has an impact role on data results, it was seen that there are no differences between female and male SUS results. Both sexes agree with the opinion that Keyboard and Web controllers are better than the Accelerometer.

Qualitative answers show us that participants on the test prefer the game Snake over the Pong. Negatives aspects that we registered during the test we have comments like: "The speed of the ball is so fast (Pong)" or "I don't understand how I lost (Snake)". On the other hand, the positive ones where related to the multiplayer activity which they say that was funnier than the original game: "I liked the cooperative and competitive modes on Pong (Pong)" and "The big space gives me time to think about how can I win against the others (Snake)".

Another thing that we noticed is that there was a big difference between the first time that they performed the task against the second time. We believe that the game user experience increases as much as they play because they master the use of the controllers and times reactions.

Related to the controllers, most of the users prefer to interact with the Keyboard (59,5%) instead of the Mobile controllers (40,5%). It is important to state that when comparing the results of the Mobile controllers, Web controller (82,4%) was preferred over Accelerometer controller (17,6%) with a big gap.

In the comments we can observe that they noticed that there is a delay with the use of the mobile in both given applications. On the Web controller one of the common errors that were done by the users was to make mistakes pressing the buttons during the game due to the fact that they have to observe the display wall and also the mobile device. Also, the design was not accurate because some players hit operational buttons (Play, Pause, Restart) instead of pressing the arrows.

In the case of the Accelerometer controller, we detected a difficulty during the learning process of understanding it. For example, instead of moving only the mobile, people move the complete arm, or they do not move it over the x-axis. Another feature that was perceived was that for the users it was hard to understand the speed of the paddle and the inclination degree of the mobile; even for the quiet position that ranges between $20°$ and $-20°$ users have difficulties to leave the paddle quiet. Positive registered comments about mobile controllers were based on the fact that they did not have to share the controller with other users and that could increase the number of players in the game. Also, other participants described that with better interactions they may prefer the use of the mobile controllers instead of the keyboard.

6   Conclusions

Guaranteeing immersive collective experiences in DW-based multiplayer gaming with individual controllers was a research challenge, considering all aspects involved in this specific situation. In this sense, the present work presented a usability evaluation for three different controllers used in multiplayer versions of Pong and Snake classical games over a DW system.

Results show that Keyboard controller and Web controller have the best satisfaction rates according to SUS test, surpassing the Accelerometer controller. One of the reasons for this could be some technical barriers regarding to Sensors API, which imposes several permissions and feature policies that are more easily solved migrating to a native application.

As further steps, a deeper focus on Web controller is meant to be carried out. In spite of Keyboard controller have provided a better UX, Web controller gives the possibility to increase the number of players, not limited to four. On the other hand, higher quantities of players that can be connected at once playing the same game bring new research challenges regarding to performance, immersion and playability. For this reason, games that are designed for two players (like Pong, for instance) will not be considered in further research; new games are meant to be explored. It is also a future objective of this research, to examine other types of controllers for DW games in relation to user satisfaction in different age groups.

Acknowledgment. This work was carried out with the support of the "Coordenação de Aperfeiçoamento de Pessoal de nível superior - Brasil (CAPES) - Programa de Excelência - Proex 1133/2019" related to Post-graduation Program in Developmental Disorders of Mackenzie Presbyterian University and also "Centro Universitário Facens", Brasil.

References

1. Goradia, I., Doshi, J., Kurup, L.: A review paper on oculus rift project morpheus. Int. J. Curr. Eng. Technol. **4**(5), 31963200 (2014)
2. Hillmann, C.: Comparing the Gear VR, Oculus Go, and Oculus Quest. In: Unreal for Mobile and Standalone VR, pp. 141–167. Apress, Berkeley, CA (2019)
3. Powell, W., Powell, V., Brown, P., Cook, M., Uddin, J.: Getting around in Google Cardboard–exploring navigation preferences with low-cost mobile VR. In: 2016 IEEE 2nd Workshop on Everyday Virtual Reality (WEVR), pp. 5–8. IEEE (March 2016)
4. Cruz-Neira, C., Sandin, D.J., DeFanti, T.A.: Surround-screen projection-based virtual reality: the design and implementation of the CAVE. In: Proceedings of the 20th Annual Conference on Computer Graphics and Interactive Techniques, pp. 135–142 (September 1993)
5. Schaeffer, B., Goudeseune, C.: Syzygy: native PC cluster VR. In: 2003 Proceedings of IEEE Virtual Reality, pp. 15–22. IEEE (March 2003)
6. Reiners, D., Voß, G., Behr, J.: OpenSG: basic concepts. In: OpenSG Symposium (February 2002)
7. Schikore, D.R., Fischer, R.A., Frank, R., Gaunt, R., Hobson, J., Whitlock, B.: High-resolution multiprojector display walls. IEEE Comput. Graphics Appl. **20**(4), 38–44 (2000)
8. Arroyo, I., Giné, F., Roig, C., Granollers, T.: Usability analysis in the Liquid Galaxy platform. In: Proceedings of the 9th International Conference on Advances in Computer-Human Interactions, ACHI 2016, pp. 345–352 (2016)
9. Google. Liquid Galaxy live demo at TED. Lecture Notes in Computer Science. Springer (2010)
10. Panoramic Video Streaming (2012). https://code.google.com/p/liquid-galaxy/wiki/PanoramicVideo. Accessed 7 Jun 2019
11. OpenArena Team. OpenArena (Quake 3 Arena) (2005). www.openarena.ws. Accessed 1 Dec 2019

12. Capdevila, M.G., Silveira, I.F., Martins, V.F.: Promovendo a Aprendizagem Ativa por meio da estratégia Jigsaw: experiências com Liquid Galaxy. Revista Ibérica de Sistemas e Tecnologias de Informação, no. E28, pp. 1–14 (2020)
13. Somervell, J.P., Wahid, S., McCrickard, D.S.: Usability heuristics for large screen information exhibits. In: INTERACT, pp. 904–907 (2003)
14. Nutsi, A., Koch, M.: Multi-user usability guidelines for interactive wall display applications. In: Proceedings of the 4th International Symposium on Pervasive Displays, pp. 233–234 (2015)
15. Tickner, A.: A Study of Users of the Liquid Galaxy Earth and Streetview Display at Davis Library (2015). https://doi.org/10.17615/889t-j659
16. Tickner, A.: The Liquid Galaxy in the library: a study of use and users of interactive digital display technology at UNC-CH. Library Hi Tech **34**(4), 657–668 (2016)
17. Arroyo, I., Giné, F., Roig, C., Granollers, T.: Analyzing Google Earth application in a heterogeneous commodity cluster display wall. Multimedia Tools Appl. **75**(18), 11391–11416 (2015). https://doi.org/10.1007/s11042-015-2859-z
18. Barbosa Costa, G.: Wikidata Liquid Galaxy visualization, Master's thesis, Universitat de Lleida (2017)
19. Arroyo, I., Giné, F., Roig, C., Granollers, A.: Performance and usability tradeoff in a cluster display wall. Comput. Stand. Interfaces **62**, 53–63 (2019)
20. Young, G.W., Kehoe, A., Murphy, D.: Usability testing of video game controllers: a case study. In: Games User Research: A Case Study Approach, pp. 145–188 (2016)
21. Natapov, D., Castellucci, S.J., MacKenzie, I.S.: ISO 9241-9 evaluation of video game controllers. In: Proceedings of Graphics Interface 2009, pp. 223–230 (2009)
22. Wolf, M.J. (ed.): The video game explosion: a history from PONG to Playstation and beyond. ABC-CLIO (2008)
23. Punyawee, A., Panumate, C., Iida, H.: Finding comfortable settings of snake game using game refinement measurement. In: Park, J.J.(J.H.), Pan, Y., Yi, G., Loia, V. (eds.) CSA/CUTE/UCAWSN -2016. LNEE, vol. 421, pp. 66–73. Springer, Singapore (2017). https://doi.org/10.1007/978-981-10-3023-9_11
24. Brooke, J.: System Usability Scale (SUS): A Quick-and-Dirty Method of System Evaluation User Information, pp. 1–7. Digital Equipment Co. Ltd., Reading (1986)

Voluminis: Mobile Application for Learning Mathematics in Geometry with Augmented Reality and Gamification

Juan Deyby Carlos-Chullo$^{(\boxtimes)}$ (ID), Marielena Vilca-Quispe (ID), and Eveling Castro-Gutierrez (ID)

Universidad Nacional de San Agustín de Arequipa, Arequipa, Peru
{jcarlosc,mvilcaquispe,ecastro}@unsa.edu.pe

Abstract. The teaching-learning process that requires the manipulation or visualization of objects has some limitations. Augmented reality and mobile devices applied to videogames make it possible to solve these deficiencies by offering the possibility of interacting with virtual objects in a three-dimensional space. The objective of this article is to analyze the effects and motivation of gamification and augmented reality using Voluminis, in sixth-grade students of the mathematics subject, in a public school. This paper's methodology are as follows: architecture of Voluminis, design and implementation of the geometry game prototype, and this was to applied is the cuasi-experimental design with 21 Peruvian 6th-grade school children. The results show that the proposed learning scheme improves learning motivation and the teaching of spatial geometry.

Keywords: Mobile augmented reality · Mathematics learning · Solid geometry · System learning · Gamification

1 Introduction

When starting a course, the most basic concepts are usually learned first. These have no direct application with real problems. That is why many of the elementary, high school students consider mathematics confusing and unnecessary [1].

Since the beginning of the digital age, video games have been very captivating, whether on a computer, a video game console, or a cell phone. These are nice for most kids and teens [2]. In recent years, mobile devices have more computing power and are more accessible by the general public. Consequently, diverse Augmented Reality (AR) games have emerged, such as Jurassic World Alive, Harry Potter: Wizards Unite, and the most popular game in AR: Pokémon GO. The use of AR can help in learning among young people [3]. Besides, the lessons learned from a respective subject can be reinforced [2]. The use of AR and gamification can bring more interest to young people. Consequently, they would learn and reinforce while playing and interacting with 3D objects.

In this study, an AR video game was developed for primary level students. They practiced spatial geometry exercises (calculation of volumes) from their cell phones. A

© Springer Nature Switzerland AG 2020
V. Agredo-Delgado et al. (Eds.): HCI-COLLAB 2020, CCIS 1334, pp. 295–304, 2020.
https://doi.org/10.1007/978-3-030-66919-5_30

teacher classification system was also developed to group students and monitor their results. The objective is to provide a complementary tool and test the influence of AR games on learning spatial geometry.

The rest of the article is organized as follows: Sect. 2, presents the related works. Section 3, presents the materials and methods used, as well as the development of Voluminis. The results obtained are presented in Sect. 4. Finally, in Sect. 5 the discussions and conclusions.

2   Related Work

Previous works has already considered the use of AR. For example, [4] demonstrated a positive impact on students' spatial ability in solving descriptive geometry exercises and spatial tests. A similar implementation [5]; their results suggest that AR applications can be used as practical learning tools in geometry courses. Additionally, [6] the incorporation of AR in mathematics education improves motivation to achieve autonomous learning and capacity and abstraction in the subject of mathematical functions.

Chang [7] suggests that AR like the digital video can enhance student learning, but that AR application can better help students retain knowledge. Second, developing an AR application is time-consuming. On the contrary, the study [8] finds that AR activities do not make a significant difference in academic performance in the biology course, but rather positively encourages motivation. It also indicates that AR helps students to develop their sense of self-efficacy. In the works [9, 10], where they found that students with learning difficulties showed interest, motivation in the learning process, the use of AR. Additionally, [11] can improve student achievement with the right resources at the right time.

In the case of gamification, there are several examples of gamification in many learning games, such as collection systems, track systems, point systems, and period time [12]. For this reason, gamification is used in learning methods. Students are becoming increasingly knowledgeable about technology, particularly video games [13].

3   Materials and Methods

Voluminis is based on AR for the visualization of information on geometric figures. The exercises are presented in levels. Each level is an exercise that the student must solve. To continue to the next level, the student must complete an exercise in the level.

To meet the needs of the ARCore[1] tool, the cell phones must have the operating system Android 7.0 or higher. Voluminis was developed on the Unity[2] game engine. Also, a real-time Firebase[3] database was used. Blender[4] was used in the design of the figures and the environment.

Voluminis has two modalities of games using the internet for saving in the Firebase database and a modality without internet use for saving in the local database, as can see in Fig. 1.

---

[1] https://developers.google.com/ar.

[2] https://unity.com.

[3] https://firebase.google.com.

[4] https://blender.org.

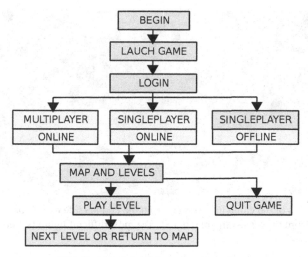

Fig. 1. Voluminis gameplay flowchart.

3.1 Augmented Reality

AR is a novel technology with additional digital information in the real world through cell phone cameras, computers, or glasses, so seeing 3D models, videos, and images. Voluminis uses ARCore, which helps project 3D models onto any surface without the need for QR codes. It can project the geometric figures and the game map on any illuminated surface, as shown in Fig. 2 and Fig. 3. With the use of two fingers, the general model can be scaled to the eye's comfort. This interaction with the model is through the screen directly with the model. A flowchart is a way of presenting the game, look at Fig. 1. This graphic organizer shows all the different components of the game that a player would take and interact with the game.

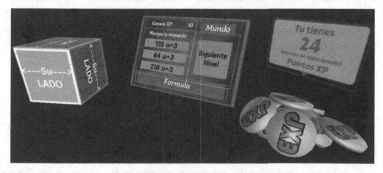

Fig. 2. Game exercise: a geometric figure, an exercise table with points to be earned, some alternatives, next level button, formula button, button to return to the main menu (game map) and total points earned.

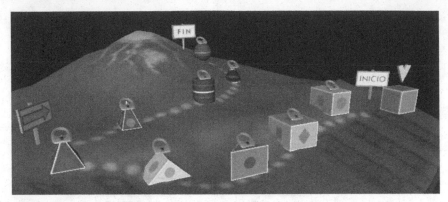

Fig. 3. The 10 levels of the game in a journey from the countryside to the volcano crater (Misti, Arequipa, Peru), from the easiest figure (cube) to the most difficult figure (sphere).

3.2 Exercises of Spatial Geometry

Students often solve many math exercises on paper. In geometry, there are three-dimensional figures; these are drawn in books, which makes the perception of the figure difficult. In Voluminis, there are ten levels with different geometric figures; from levels 1 to 10, the difficulty increases. The order of the figures in the levels is according to the formulas to obtain the volume. Some geometric figures are repeated, but these have different measures. Also, Voluminis helps the student to practice multiplying numbers.

As seen in Fig. 2 each level has a geometric figure, a menu, and coins (bonus system). The coins are related to the number of points, and these are cumulative. The measurements of the figure change value for each attempt, and the figure scales according to their measurements. Voluminis is better than a geometry book. On the other hand, the three alternatives to answer the exercise, also change the order for each attempt, thus avoiding plagiarism.

For the representation of the geometric figures' measurements, three shapes were designed, as seen in Fig. 4. Voluminis received initial feedback on the design of the geometric figures from secondary education (Prof. Juan Carlos Pulcha, professor at the Colegio De Los Sagrados Corazones - Arequipa - Peru); it was based on a teacher's experience and not on a specific textbook.

3.3 Gamification

Gamification works by making a system enjoyable, and it also increases interaction. In many serious games, there are examples of gamification such as point system, collection systems, period, and track systems [12]. In Voluminis, the bonus system is applied, accumulative, and compared with the other participants in the same group. These points are obtained by solving a level; each failed attempt the student loses 1 point, and if the students want to see the formula to solve the level loses 5 points, it is not allowed to restart the level, but if the complete game. The maximum number of points is 100 points in the game (10 points per level). Finally, gamification promotes competitiveness in students improving their learning.

Fig. 4. Three ways to represent the measurements of geometric figures. external measurements, measurements on the faces, and both, respectively.

3.4 Research Design

As a hypothesis, it is established that the integration of augmented reality applications on spatial geometry will contribute significantly to the acquisition of mathematical skills on spatial geometry in sixth-grade students. The study is developed using an experimental type design with pre-test and post-test measurements in the two groups (experimental and control), as seen in Fig. 5. Students are divided into two groups: the control group (C.G.), made up of subjects who will carry out school activities, and experimental group (E.G.), whose members will additionally use the application. Both groups were randomly selected. Following the methodological criteria of this type of research design, data is collected from each individual, before and after the intervention.

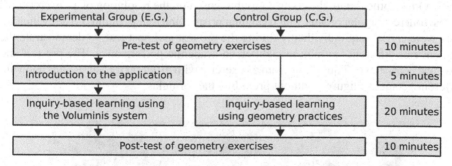

Fig. 5. Experimental procedure.

3.5 Teacher Module

This module is an administrator, which allows the teacher to create and delete groups of students. Also, the teacher can view student results with their corresponding attempts in real-time. In such a way, the teacher can identify the students with fewer skills to reinforce the subject in the next class.

After the game session, the teacher can export the results in a spreadsheet. In this document, the teacher will observe the score of each student with their respective name.

3.6 Participants

The study involved students from the Institución Educativa Señor de Huanca CIRCA (Arequipa-Perú), the sixth grade was intervened, the ages of the students range between 10 and 12 years. They had little previous experience in the use of this sort of technology. Before carrying out the study, the students got previous knowledge of basic geometry with traditional methodology. The teacher taught this class. A sample was taken at random (n = 11, of which 5 are boys and 6 are girls). After explaining the intervention, this first group called the experimental group used the application during a regular mathematics class session. In contrast, the other group (n = 10, of which 5 are boys and 5 are girls), using the traditional methodology the students did practice with exercises during the same period this group was called: control group. Girls represent 54% of the subjects in the experimental group and 50% of the control group.

3.7 Procedure

In Fig. 5 the experimental procedure is shown. The research was structured based on three stages: The first stage involves the measurement of the dependent variable (pre-test) with a duration of 10 min; in the second stage, the intervention is developed with the application of the game and a duration of 25 min; and in the third stage, the evaluation test (post-test) with a duration of 10 min.

The intervention consisted of solving the application exercises with the children of the experimental group, see Fig. 6, considering that the participants can restart the game and achieve a better score than the previous attempt, the only limitation is the time in this study. On the other hand, the control group focused on the resolution of 14 exercises (2 cubes, four rectangular prisms, four triangular prisms, and four pyramids). The evaluation tests were carried out individually during the pre-test and post-test, to demonstrate the influence of different learning modalities on academic performance. The pre-test and post-test consisted of 7 questions from an exercise with different measurements and with different geometric figures, without providing the formulas.

Fig. 6. Students using the application outside the classroom.

3.8 Analysis of Data

To check the Voluminis system's influence on the acquisition of mathematical skills on spatial geometry in schoolchildren, the analysis of the results obtained from the pre-test and post-test was carried out.

First, two normality studies were performed using the pre-test and post-test in order to compare both groups. The Shapiro-Wilk normality test was used for this study, studies similar to this as [9, 14] make use of this test. In the statistical analyzes carried out, a critical value of $p < 0.05$ is established. Subsequently, the normality study of the pre-test and post-test samples was carried out based on the scores. The Shapiro-Wilk normality test was also used.

4 Results

The data obtained[5] in the pre-test show that the groups (experimental and control), as can be seen in Table 1, do not show significant differences ($p > 0.05$). Also, in the data obtained in the post-test, it is evident that there are no significant differences ($p > 0.05$) between the experimental group and the control group, as can be seen in Table 2. In order to know the incidence of the dependent variable, it was decided to analyze the difference between the pre-test and the post-test scores for the two experimental and control groups (Table 3). There was a significant difference between post-test and pre-test ($p < 0.05$); with this, it is interpreted that the score (post-test) of the students after the traditional practices and the Voluminis system differ from the score initial (pre-test).

Table 1. Differences in the pre-test between the experimental and control group (Mann–Whitney test).

	Points
U of Mann–Whitney	44,000
W of Wilcoxon	99,000
Z	−,976
Asymptotic sig (bilateral)	,329

Some events that arose when evaluating Voluminis were the following: In the initial stage to communicate how the Voluminis application was going to be carried out, some of the students were already interacting with the game exercises, being somewhat intuitive. On the other hand, during the session with Voluminis, some students used paper and pencil to solve the exercises. Regarding the aspect of competing with their peers, they wondered about the score they were obtaining to improve their score. Additionally, participants were trying to pass the exercises by randomly marking the answer. Also, some had difficulties in recognizing the surfaces required with the cell phone to lift the game.

---

[5] https://github.com/Juandeyby/Voluminis-Mobile-Application.

Table 2. Post-test differences between experimental and control groups (Mann–Whitney test).

	Points
U of Mann–Whitney	32,000
W of Wilcoxon	98,000
Z	−1,948
Asymptotic sig (bilateral)	,051

Table 3. Analysis of the differences between post-test and pre-test (Wilconson's test).

	PostTest - PreTest
Z	−3,366
Asymptotic sig (bilateral)	,001

At the end of the session, many students showed interest in the game, the students were motivated, wanted to have more time with the application, and asked if more applications had been made to download.

5 Discussion and Conclusions

At the school, we used around 2 h to apply Voluminis. With more sessions of the application, there may be a variant of the results; however, it should also be considered that the students could practice in home.

The results of the control group and the experimental group showed similar behavior. It is suggested that this way of acting is since the two methodologies manage to impart knowledge. The student manages to capture it. However, the methodology with the use of technology leaves the student more motivated, wanting to continue learning and obtaining more knowledge.

This study shows that it is possible to increase the mathematical skills in geometry and verify the hypothesis. Considering that it had similar results to the traditional methodology.

Thanks to the use of AR, high interest and acceptance were obtained from the students during the game. The way of transmitting the concept of the three-dimensional space and the interactions with the figures, compared with the two-dimensional drawings, promoted its acceptance. About augmented reality employment, you can help students become more interested in other math topics. Concerning competition and the point system, it can be an essential motivator in a group of participants in the use of educational games. The teacher in charge was also interested in the use of the application in future class sessions.

Acknowledgements. Thanks to the "Research Center, Transfer of Technologies and Software Development R + D + i" - CiTeSoft EC-0003-2017-UNSA, for their collaboration in the use their equipment and facilities, and the Institución Educativa Señor de Huanca CIRCA (Arequipa-Perú) for the development of this research work, and Prof. Juan Carlos Pulcha - Colegio De Los Sagrados Corazones (Arequipa-Perú).

References

1. Cortés Díaz, H.D., Piáal Ramírez, O.E., Argüelles Cruz, A.J., Vicario Solórzano, C.M.: Ramath: Mobile application for math learning using augmented reality. Res. Comput. Sci. **148**(10), 261–269 (2019). https://doi.org/10.13053/rcs-148-10-22
2. Abu Bakar, J.A., Gopalan, V., Zulkifli, A.N., Alwi, A.: Design and development of mobile augmented reality for physics experiment. In: Communications in Computer and Information Science, pp. 47–58. Springer, Singapore (2018). https://doi.org/10.1007/978-981-13-162 8-9_5
3. Tezer, M.: The effect of answer based computer assisted geometry course on students success level and attitudes. Qual. Quant. **52**(5), 2321–2329 (2017). https://doi.org/10.1007/s11135-017-0666-5
4. de Ravé, E.G., Jiménez-Hornero, F.J., Ariza-Villaverde, A.B., Taguas-Ruiz, J.: DiedricAR: A mobile augmented reality system designed for the ubiquitous descriptive geometry learning. Multimed. Tools Appl. **75**(16), 9641–9663 (2016). https://doi.org/10.1007/s11042-016-3384-4
5. Ibáñez, M.B., Uriarte Portillo, A., Zatarain Cabada, R., Barrón, M.L.: Impact of augmented reality technology on academic achievement and motivation of students from public and private Mexican schools. A case study in a middle-school geometry course. Comput. Educ. **145**, 103734 (2020). https://doi.org/10.1016/j.compedu.2019.103734
6. Hernández, F.J.L., Gómez, O.L.F., Cortés, R.B.: Realidad aumentada y Matemáticas: propuesta de mediación para la comprensión de la función (2019)
7. Chang, R.-C., Chung, L.-Y., Huang, Y.-M.: Developing an interactive augmented reality system as a complement to plant education and comparing its effectiveness with video learning. Interact. Learn. Environ. **24**(6), 1245–1264 (2014). https://doi.org/10.1080/10494820.2014.982131
8. Erbas, C., Demirer, V.: The effects of augmented reality on students' academic achievement and motivation in a biology course. J. Comput. Assist. Learn. **35**(3), 450–458 (2019). https://doi.org/10.1111/jcal.12350
9. Avila-Pesantez, D.F., Vaca-Cardenas, L.A., Delgadillo Avila, R., Padilla Padilla, N., Rivera, L.A.: Design of an augmented reality serious game for children with Dyscalculia: a case study. In: Communications in Computer and Information Science, pp. 165–175. Springer, Hiedelberg (2018). https://doi.org/10.1007/978-3-030-05532-5_12
10. Tobar-Munoz, H., Fabregat, R., Baldiris, S.: Using a videogame with augmented reality for an inclusive logical skills learning session. In: 2014 International Symposium on Computers in Education (SIIE). 2014 International Symposium on Computers in Education (SIIE) (2014, November). https://doi.org/10.1109/siie.2014.7017728
11. Zhenming, B., Mayu, U., Mamoru, E., Tatami, Y.: Development of an english words learning system utilizes 3D markers with augmented reality technology. In: 2017 IEEE 6th Global Conference on Consumer Electronics (GCCE). 2017 IEEE 6th Global Conference on Consumer Electronics (GCCE) (2017, October). https://doi.org/10.1109/gcce.2017.8229353
12. van Leeuwen, J.: (ed.): Computer Science Today. Recent Trends and Developments. In: Lecture Notes in Computer Science, vol. 1000. Springer-Verlag, Berlin Heidelberg New York (1995)

13. Gamificación en Iberoamérica: Quito, Ecuador: Ediciones Universitarias Universidad Politécnica Salesiana (2018)
14. Bacca, J., Baldiris, S., Fabregat, R., Kinshuk.: Insights into the factors influencing student motivation in augmented reality learning experiences in vocational education and training. Front. Psychol. **9** (2018). https://doi.org/10.3389/fpsyg.2018.01486

Wireless Haptic Glove for Interpretation and Communication of Deafblind People

Lenin R. Villarreal[1](✉) ⓘ, Bryan J. Castro[2](✉) ⓘ, and Jefferson A. De la Cruz[3](✉) ⓘ

[1] Universidad de las Fuerzas Armadas ESPE, Sangolquí, Ecuador
lrvillarreal1@gmail.com
[2] Departamento de Ingeniería Electrónica, Universidad de las Fuerzas Armadas ESPE,
Sangolquí, Ecuador
bryanjavierespe@gmail.com
[3] Departamento de Ingeniería Electrónica, Universidad de las Fuerzas Armadas ESPE,
Latacunga, Ecuador
jadlcc@msn.com

Abstract. This article presents the construction of a low-cost assistance system to improve communication for deaf-blind people based on the universal Braille alphabet. The system is a glove that is composed of a Braille keyboard embedded in the front and vibrating micro-motors placed in the back, to write and perceive the messages respectively. The tactile switches allow the collection of digital signals to form the different Braille letters; once this information is collected it is processed and presented in a mobile application to later send a response to the haptic sensors that allow the Braille language to be coded so that the deaf-blind person can interpret it through the sense of touch. The experimental results show the correct functioning and usability of the glove for transmitting and receiving messages.

Keywords: Haptic glove · Deafness-blindness · Braille language · Fingerprint

1 Introduction

In recent years, physical therapy and technology have worked together to provide a better health service to patients with disabilities by providing greater autonomy, safety, satisfaction, teaching and usability of physical therapy devices [1]. Now, thanks to virtual environments and augmented reality, people with disabilities can not only feel the sensation of rehabilitation but also comply with the required therapy [2]. This type of rehabilitation is also implemented in people who are deaf-blind.

Deaf-blindness is a disability that results from the combination of vision and hearing impairments that generate significant difficulties in communication, access to information, education, and in coping with their environment [3]. The sensory condition of deaf-blind people varies depending on the reasons for their disability; these may be congenital or caused by accidents or illness. It is difficult for deaf-blind people to connect with the outside world because of the lack of a common language, this condition prevents

V. Agredo-Delgado et al. (Eds.): HCI-COLLAB 2020, CCIS 1334, pp. 305–314, 2020.
https://doi.org/10.1007/978-3-030-66919-5_31

them from receiving and understanding the message through the auditory channel and from supporting or understanding it through the visual channel by lip-reading which often leads deaf-blind people to social isolation and dependence on the information transmitted by the people around them [4, 5]. Depending on the extent of their hearing and vision, and their personal history of the onset of dual sensory impairment, deaf-blind people use different communication methods including alphabetic communication systems when there is total vision and hearing loss, and non-alphabetic in partial vision and hearing loss [6, 7].

The alphabetic systems used by deaf-blind people differ by country and/or region. The classification of these includes the British manual deaf-blind alphabet used in the United Kingdom; the Lorm alphabet used in Austria, parts of Germany and Poland, the Malossi alphabet used in Italy [8]. The Braille alphabet is used universally to read and write text and vice versa with letters and numbers represented by raised dots arranged in six-point Braille cells. To read information, deaf-blind people use their sense of touch to develop patterns of dots called tactile Braille formation [9, 10].

Several mechanisms for automated finger spelling or different glove systems, implementing a variety of alphabets; some of them are discontinued, there are only a few that focus on portable mobile devices and, consequently, a human-centered design approach [11]. One such system is the Mobile Lorm Glove, which uses the continuous gestures of the Lorm alphabet [12]. A similar glove system, DB-HAND, implements the Malossi alphabet [13], the WearaBraille prototype [14], which emulates typing on a keyboard. These devices perform one-way communication, i.e., either transmit or receive, but not both, they are relatively large, expensive and not portable [15]. Current devices are not accessible to all persons with dual sensory disabilities because of their higher cost and lower portability [16].

This paper presents the construction of a low-cost Braille glove. The glove used by the deaf-blind person can transmit messages using a Braille keyboard embedded in it, a Bluetooth connection transmits the glove data to a mobile application used by the communication partner. The glove receives and interprets messages sent from the mobile application, using haptic feedback patterns located on the back of the glove. It also has a long-distance communication system for deaf-blind people to transmit and receive messages in a way that is compatible with mobile communication such as sending and receiving SMS [17].

The article is organized in V Sections including the Introduction. Section 2 describes the structure of the system's operation, the composition of the haptic glove to enable transmitter-receiver communication. System construction, haptic glove instrumentation will be detailed in Sect. 3. Section 4 contains the analysis of results obtained in the present work, by means of experimental tests. Finally, Sect. 5 details the conclusions reached during the development.

2   System Structure

The device consists of a glove to be used on the user's left hand, with the palmar side as the entrance side and the dorsal side of the glove as the exit. It is connected to a microcontroller that is placed on the wrist, Fig. 1. For redact and send a message, the individual touches the touch switches in a specific sequence, on the entry side, using his right hand, which corresponds to a pattern of Braille characters. Each pulsation is confirmed with vibro-tactile feedback from a specific motor on the dorsal side of the glove; after pressing the buttons for a letter, the user presses a button to save that character and move on to the next one.

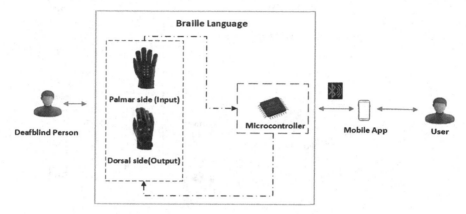

Fig. 1. Braille system.

As soon as the desired word is formed, the send button is pressed; this information is translated and transmitted to a mobile device through the Bluetooth wireless serial channel. When a character or phrase is sent from the mobile phone to the glove's microcontroller, the Braille language is simulated on the dorsal side of the glove by the simultaneous activation of the vibration motors corresponding to each character in the sequence in which the chain is introduced. Therefore, it, is achieved a translation Braille Duplex for interpretation by a deaf-blind user.

Is develops the Android application that makes it easy to use for the user to send and receive text messages. If when entering the text, the user presses 'send', the application makes sure that the message that precedes 'send' is automatically sent to the device. Besides, the application has a training mode, for users who do not know the Braille language.

3   Device Construction

The construction of the haptic glove system for the communication of deaf-blind people, goes through a process of design and implementation of hardware and software. The structure of the glove is developed with the intention of creating a comfortable and useful system for people suffering from these disabilities.

3.1   Communication Mean

The communication employ two transmission channels for the link between the haptic glove and the Smartphone; The first transmission channel uses a Bluetooth module that transmits within a maximum coverage range of ten meters, Fig. 2. The second transmission channel uses a GSM module which transmits the message as SMS and allows greater distance in the communication, the limiting in the transmission is the coverage of the network.

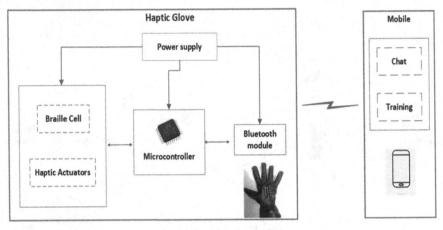

Fig. 2. Communication mean.

3.2   Data Acquisition and Control

For the control and management of sent and received messages, an ATmega 328 microcontroller is used, which is integrated in a plate Fig. 3 and is interconnected with the haptic actuators, touch switches and the communication modules GSM and Bluetooth. This electronic plate is placed near the wrist of the glove. The scattered elements in the palm and in the upper part of the glove are linked to the plate through a conductive thread that facilitates the movement of the hand.

Fig. 3. Electronic board.

3.3 Interpretation of the Message-Glove

The message is issued through the communication channels of the mobile application and enters the microcontroller, where the decoding algorithm unravels the message. The appropriate tactile stimulation is achieved with the block of haptic actuators of the glove formed by six micro-vibrators of 10 mm eccentric rotation mass, placed inside the back of the glove, Fig. 4 and they are arranged strategically between the distal phalanges, proximal and carpal of the index and annular fingers to simulate a haptic response of the arrival of each character in braille. Each character of the message generates a vibratory stimulus through a sequence of directions of the micro-vibrators and PWM signals that allow the deaf-blind user to perceive the messages.

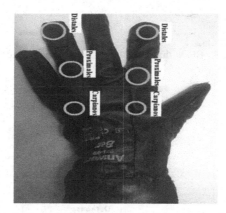

Fig. 4. Location of the micro-vibrators in the glove.

3.4 App Implementation

The interpreter of the information sent by the glove is a mobile application distributed into two interfaces. The first scenario of the application called chat shows the information sent and received, a button for sending messages and access to the main menus enabled. It works with a logic similar to the programming implanted in the microcontroller of the glove, Fig. 5.

The second interface of the mobile application acts as a guidance and learning system, which is implemented in order to teach both the deaf-blind user and the user with its five full senses the Braille alphabet through haptic stimulation. This interface acts according to the block diagram shown in Fig. 6.

The system is responsible for sending each of the letters that contain the braille alphabet to be received and interpreted by the haptic glove. Captured the sequence proceeds to generate that sequence on the braille keyboard, if the sequence entered is correct, a message of the correct case of incorrect will appear. The learning routine is done until to learn all the characters of the Braille alphabet.

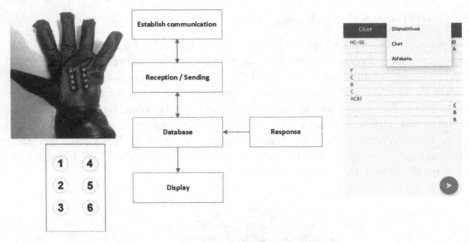

Fig. 5. Block diagram of the Chat mode interface.

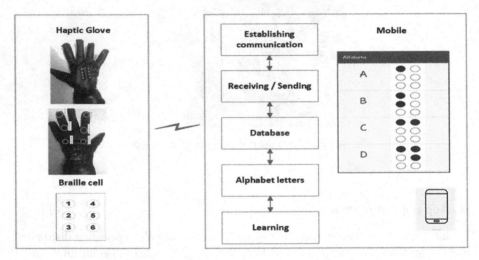

Fig. 6. Block diagram of the learning mode interface.

4   Experimental Results

Once implemented the braille haptic glove and the mobile application for the inter-communication of deaf-blind people, we proceed to testing with the collaboration of Association blind Cotopaxi; account with 16 people between children and adults. The population to perform the tests was the group of adults consisting of 3 people who use the bar and punch as a means of communication.

4.1 Writing Tests

The test of writing decide the time that a deaf - blind person can be late to order a message to a recipient by means of the glove haptic braille and the method of regleta and punch; a chronometer measures the times of writing of the chosen words random, the device of communication obtained major speed of fingering where the user receives a vibratory confirmation whenever it deposits a character, generating a determined reflection and a rapid reaction in the moment to express an idea. In the Table 1 is observed the times of writing of both methods.

Table 1. Times of writing Glove vs. Regleta.

	WORD	Cantante	Mónica	Hola	Viento	Colores	Figura	Mar	Esperanza
Time (S)	Application	13	11	12	12	13	14	4	18
	Regleta and punch	18	16	21	23	19	22	11	34

4.2 Test of Communication Presents Deaf - Blind and Presents without Disabilities

The test of communication was realized between a deaf - blind person and a person without disabilities, to the deaf - blind person uses the glove haptic, and another user uses the mobile application Fig. 7, To initiate the communication is necessary that the application links itself to the glove haptic route bluetooth, once linked the devices the user who uses the mobile application, must accede to the way chat, once there one proceeds to realize the tests of communication, the deaf - blind user writes the message using the tactile switches absorbed in the frontal part of the glove, once finished the word or phrase, it presses the switch of he sent of message, which is received in the mobile application, of equal form the user without disabilities, he sends the message using the keyboard of the cellular one, the message is unraveled and activates the motive micro vibrators located in the dorsal part of the glove haptic.

Fig. 7. Deaf-blind person using the Haptic glove.

To validate the efficiency of the usability of the glove haptic and of the mobile application there is in use the method of summarized evaluation HIS, in that there is in use a method that obtains a scale of style that generates an alone number represented by an average of compound by the usability of the global system in study. The selected questions are 10, Table 2, the selected points have a correlation of between 0,7 and 0,9. The ranges of weighting go from the 1 to 5, which means total disagreement and complete agreement, respectively.

Table 2. Result of the Questionnaire.

Questions	Punctuation application	Value	Punctuation glove	Value
I think I would like to use this app-glove frequently	4.3	3.3	4.5	3.5
I found this application-glove unnecessarily complex	1.8	3.2	1.8	3.2
I think the glove app is easy to use	4.3	3.3	4.6	3.6
I think I would need the support of a technical person to be able to use this application - glove	1.9	3.1	2.4	2.6
The functions of this glove application are well integrated	4	3	4.5	3.5
I thought there was too much inconsistency in this application - glove	2.4	2.6	2	.
I imagine that most people would learn to use this glove app very quickly	4.5	3.5	4.7	3.7
I found that the application - glove is very difficult to use	1.7	3.3	1.9	3.1
I felt very safe using the app - glove	4.3	3.3	4.2	3.2
I needed to learn many things before being able to use this application - glove	2	3		3
	VALUE	78,5		81

The usability indexes for the glove and the application are 81 and 78.5 respectively, the average scores of the usability scale as indicated by the standard are greater than 68, indicating that the glove-application system is well and could be improved. In addition, both the glove and the application are easy to use and do not have greater complexity when using them.

5 Conclusions

In the writing tests it was observed that the writing time with the haptic glove is faster than the regleta and punch method. The proposal in the present article is satisfactory since after realizing the different tests, the communication improves and is diminished the times of writing and reading message to come to the recipient by means of the implementation of a mobile application for the intercommunication of deaf - blind people. In the tests of conversation of a deaf - blind people and person who does not know the language Braille across the real time utilization of the glove and the mobile application, they delivered like proved an ideal communication, which implies a good time of response between the glove Braille and the mobile application, allowing to handle fluently the Braille alphabet between persons with the type of disabilities described and users who do not know and know the Braille language.

Acknowledgements. The authors thank the Association of the blind in the province of Cotopaxi for collaborating in the usability of this glove, so that future beneficiaries can easily handle this device, to improve their lifestyle.

References

1. Gomez Mora, M.: Aplicación de realidad virtual en la rehabilitación cognitiva. Rev. vínculos **10**(1), 130–135 (2013). https://doi.org/10.14483/2322939x.4682
2. Bayón, M., Martínez, J.: Rehabilitación del ictus mediante realidad virtual. Rehabilitación, **44**(3), 256–260. ISSN 0048-7120. https://doi.org/10.1016/j.rh.2009.11.005
3. Ozioko, O., Hersh, M.: Development of a portable two-way communication and information device for deafblind people. Researchgate, pp. 1–9 (2015)
4. Choudhary, T., Kulkarni, S., Reddy, P.: A Braille-based mobile communication and translation glove for deaf-blind people. In: 2015 International Conference on Pervasive Computing (ICPC), Pune, pp. 1–4 (2015). https://doi.org/10.1109/pervasive.2015.7087033
5. Shrivastava, P., Anand, P., Singh, A., Sagar, V.: Medico stick: An ease to blind & deaf. In: 2015 2nd International Conference on Electronics and Communication Systems (ICECS), Coimbatore, pp. 1448–1452 (2015). https://doi.org/10.1109/ecs.2015.7124825
6. Sarkar, R., Das, S., Rudrapal, S.: A low cost microelectromechanical Braille for blind people to communicate with blind or deaf-blind people through SMS subsystem. In: 2013 3rd IEEE International Advance Computing Conference (IACC), Ghaziabad, pp. 1529–1532 (2013). https://doi.org/10.1109/iadcc.2013.6514454
7. Khambadkar, V., Folmer, E.: A tactile-proprioceptive communication aid for users who are deafblind. In: 2014 IEEE Haptics Symposium (HAPTICS), Houston, TX, pp. 239–245 (2014). https://doi.org/10.1109/haptics.2014.6775461

8. Ozioko, O., Taube, W., Hersh, M., Dahiya, R.: SmartFingerBraille: A tactile sensing and actuation based communication glove for deafblind people. In: 2017 IEEE 26th International Symposium on Industrial Electronics (ISIE), Edinburgh, pp. 2014–2018 (2017). https://doi.org/10.1109/isie.2017.8001563

9. Ohtsuka, S., Hasegawa, S., Sasaki, N., Harakawa, T.: Communication system between deaf-blind people and non-disabled people using body-braille and infrared communication. In: 2010 7th IEEE Consumer Communications and Networking Conference, Las Vegas, NV, pp. 1–2 (2010). doi: https://doi.org/10.1109/CCNC.2010.5421647

10. Gollner, U., Bieling, T.: Mobile Lorm Glove–Introducing a communication device for deaf-blind people. The Association for Computing Machinery, Inc., pp. 1–4 (2013). https://doi.org/10.1145/2148131.2148159

11. Mohamed Kassim, A., Yasuno, T., Jaafar, H.I., Aras, M.S.M., Abas, N.: Performance analysis of wireless warning device for upper body level of deaf-blind person. In: 2015 54th Annual Conference of the Society of Instrument and Control Engineers of Japan (SICE), Hangzhou, pp. 252–257 (2015). https://doi.org/10.1109/sice.2015.7285379

12. Mirri, S., Prandi, C., Salomoni, P., Monti, L.: Fitting like a GlovePi: A wearable device for deaf-blind people. In: 2017 14th IEEE Annual Consumer Communications and Networking Conference (CCNC), Las Vegas, NV, pp. 1057–1062 (2017). https://doi.org/10.1109/ccnc.2017.7983285

13. Hersh, M.: Deafblind people, stigma and the use of communication and mobility assistive devices. Biomedical Engineering, University of Glasgow, Glasgow G12 8LT, Scotland, UK, pp. 1–18 (2013). https://doi.org/10.3233/tad-130394

14. Rajapandian, B., Harini, V., Raksha, D., Sangeetha, V.: A novel approach as an AID for blind, deaf and dumb people. In: 2017 Third International Conference on Sensing, Signal Processing and Security (ICSSS), Chennai, pp. 403–408 (2017). https://doi.org/10.1109/ssps.2017.8071628

15. Nasrany, C., Abdou, R.B., Kassem, A., Hamad, M.: S2LV—A sign to letter and voice converter. In: 2015 International Conference on Advances in Biomedical Engineering (ICABME), Beirut, pp. 185–188 (2015). https://doi.org/10.1109/icabme.2015.7323283

16. Ohtsuka, S., Chiba, H., Sasaki, N., Harakawa, T.: Alternative vibration presentation methods for the two-point body-braille system. In: 2016 IEEE 5th Global Conference on Consumer Electronics, Kyoto, pp. 1–3 (2016). https://doi.org/10.1109/gcce.2016.7800451

17. Islam, M.D., Mondol, A.S.: Braille Thermometer: Thermometer for deaf-blinds. In: 8th International Conference on Electrical and Computer Engineering, Dhaka, pp. 69–72 (2014). https://doi.org/10.1109/icece.2014.7026867

Author Index

Abascal-Mena, Rocío 42, 136
Agredo-Delgado, Vanessa 263, 275
AlSekait, Deema M. 275
Aponte, Alejandro 155
Arango-López, Jeferson 171
Aranguren, Ramón Valera 171
Argumanis, Daniela 52

Baranauskas, M. Cecília C. 126
Barba-González, Lorena 181
Becerra, Diego Iquira 146
Beltrán, F. Cristian 155
Bolaños, Manuel 203
Buitrago, Gabriel Ávila 233

Capdevila, Marc Gonzalez 285
Cardona-Reyes, Héctor 181
Carlos-Chullo, Juan Deyby 295
Castro, Bryan J. 305
Castro, Juan 1, 213
Castro-Gutierrez, Eveling 295
Ceballos, Nathalia 213
Celaya-Padilla, José M. 30
Cerón, Jorge Alberto Martínez 42
Chavez-Helaconde, Estefany 160
Cisneros-Chavez, Betsy 160
Collantes-Jarata, Luis 107
Collazos, César A. 30, 73, 203, 263
Condori, Klinge Villalba 10
Condori-Mamani, Cristian 160
Crespo, David 223
Cristóbal, Sony Solano 42

De la Cruz, Jefferson A. 305
de la Torre, Mario Iván Oliva 30
Domínguez, Carlos Andrés Casas 275
Domínguez, Kevin 223

Fardoun, Habib M. 263
Fernández Joya, Jovan F. 233
Fernández, Rocío 117
Ferreira, Cleiton Pons 243

Franco, Kevin 223
Fuentes, Melissa 223

Gallardo-Echenique, Eliana 85
Gamboa, Edwin 1, 193, 213, 223, 253
Gamboa-Rosales, Hamurabi 30
García, Axel Alonso 136
Gomes, Anabela 20
Gomez-Cruz, Oscar 85
González, Carina Soledad González 243
Gutiérrez, Francisco 203

Iraola-Real, Ivan 107

Laura-Ochoa, Leticia 94
Luna-García, Huizilopoztli 30, 233

Marqués-Molías, Luis 85
Martins, Valéria Farinazzo 285
Meléndez, Graciela Karina Galache 42
Mendoza, Yusseli Lizeth Méndez 126
Millares, Diana 213
Mina, David Oidor 275
Mon, Alicia 263
Monzón, Gianfranco 117
Moquillaza, Arturo 52
Moreyra-Cáceres, Lesly 107
Muñoz-Arteaga, Jaime 10, 181

Navarrete, Laura Vázquez 136

Ortiz, Diana Katherine Toro 253
Ortiz-Aguiñaga, Gerardo 181

Pancca-Mamani, Israel 160
Páris, César 20
Paz, Freddy 52

Quiroz, Alicia Lozano 10

Ramírez, Alondra Ayala 136
Redondo, Miguel A. 73
Reis, Pedro 20

Revelo-Sánchez, Oscar   73
Rodrigues, Karine Aparecida Pistili   285
Rodríguez, Aldemar   193
Rodriguez, Patricia Paderewski   171
Ruiz, Pablo H.   263, 275

Salcedo, Juan José Salazar   253
Samiento, Wilson J.   233
Santos Covarrubias, David E.   42
Sarmiento, Wilson J.   30, 155
Serrato, Andrés   1, 213
Silveira, Ismar Frango   285
Sotelo-Castro, Briseida   146
Subauste, Daniel   117

Tejada-Toledo, Franco   94
Toro, Diana   193
Torres-Berru, Yeferson   63
Torres-Carrión, Pablo   63
Trujillo, María   1, 193, 213, 223, 253

Vaca-Barahona, Byron   85
Valdez-Aguilar, Wilber   160
Vela, Francisco Luis Gutiérrez   171
Velasco, Miguel   193
Vera-Sancho, Julio   160
Vilca-Quispe, Marielena   295
Villarreal, Lenin R.   305

Printed in the United States
By Bookmasters